Civil War Sesquicentennial Edition

Virginia's Black Confederates

Essays and Rosters of Civil War Virginia's Black Confederates

Copyright © 2014 by Greg Eanes
2nd Edition (Revised)

Manufactured in the United States of America
Published by the Eanes Group, LLC, Crewe, Virginia

Virginia's Black Confederates

About the Author

Greg Eanes holds a B.S. in Occupational Education from Southern Illinois University-Carbondale and an M.A. in Military History from American Military University. A 34-year military veteran and retired Air Force Colonel, Eanes served combat tours in Saudi Arabia, Kuwait, Iraq and Afghanistan. He holds two Bronze Star Medals and two Defense Meritorious Service Medals for wartime contributions. A former journalist, he was general manager of The Crewe-Burkeville (Va) Journal, the family owned newspaper started in 1959 by his father Jim R. Eanes, from 1993 until it was sold in 1999 when he began a career in education that lasted until 9/11 and his return to active duty. He has served on various full-time and adjunct faculties to include the U.S. Air Force Intelligence School, the Joint Military Intelligence Training Center, Randolph-Henry High School, Southside Virginia Community College, Patrick Henry Community College and one semester as an adjunct lecturer at the Wilson Center for Leadership in the Public Interest at Hampden-Sydney College, Va. In public life, he served as an elected member of the Nottoway County (Va) School Board, an elected member of the Crewe (Va) Town Council and as an appointed member of the Nottoway County Planning Commission. He is a graduate of the U.S. Air Force Air War College and Air Command and Staff College. He is married to the former Rosanne Lukoskie of Shamokin, Pa.

About the Eanes Group, LLC

The Eanes Group, LLC is a consultant and services provider on American and Virginia History specializing in rural community development with an emphasis on historical research and analysis, rural heritage tourism development, recreational tourism and history publications. It is a Service Disabled Veteran Owned Small Business and SWAM Certified in the Commonwealth of Virginia (#709249).

Virginia's Black Confederates

Forward

The History Historians' Leave Out

When we consider the American past, certain stories have been hijacked. Mainstream historians will often give a failing grade to your children if your children argue against the "National Narrative" because we, as a society, no longer value the truth of history but only want to see and hear what we already believe. Without examining the facts in evidence dispassionately, the biases, prejudices, and preconceived notions of some historians skew the truth.

Our task as historians is to simply find the truth by bringing the primary sources of history to bear. Author and regional military historian Greg Eanes has done that with the *Civil War Sesquicentennial Edition* of Virginia's Black Confederates: Essays and Rosters. In this update to an earlier work, Eanes returns to original period source materials to discuss something that disturbs the modern sensibilities of some of our fellow-countrymen: free and enslaved African-Americans who served the Confederate military.

As a scholar of this topic, I cannot describe to you the opposition I myself faced at North Carolina Central University (NCCU), the nation's oldest, state-supported Historically Black College & University. To Dr. Freddie Parker's credit, he said to my critics that I was fully documented in the primary source materials from the war and subsequent state pensions, and, perhaps most importantly, followed the scholarship of the late Dr. James Howard Brewer, a professor at NCCU and one of Dr. Parker's mentors. It is Brewer's book, The Confederate Negro: Virginia's Craftsmen and Military Laborers, 1861-1865, which provides details about the men who should not have worn gray uniforms. Free, enslaved, and manumitted people of color, men (and some women) who fought, served, and died in the army and navy of the Confederate States of America. Some volunteered, some were volunteered, some appeared to have been conscripted, and some the passage of time has obscured. However, they served. I have often wondered about the Federal copyists, the ones who actually transcribed the records from the Muster Rolls, Hospital Records, and Prisoner of War Rolls, who wrote down "Negro" or "Colored" next to the name of a Confederate serviceman. What did they think? Did they see any rhetorical problems with African-Americans fighting against the "Army of Emancipation?" Or did they simply do their jobs without the information actually sinking in? Why have we forgotten their service particularly when there's a significant amount of primary source materials available to scholars?

An example is that of black Confederates serving as Army cooks. Diaries and letters are filled with comments about cooking multiple days' rations in preparation for a campaign. We think today of 20th Century Army cooks standing before enormous cauldrons of soup or porridge, cooking for hundreds or thousands at a time. However, an 1860's army on the move prepared rations beforehand. An exception to this general rule occurred during the Pennsylvania Campaign. Quoted in Kent Masterson Brown's Retreat from Gettysburg, a Union Private, Dyer B. Pettijohn of the 1st Minnesota, who became a POW at Gettysburg, wrote that as he was passing to the rear of Lee's Army at Gettysburg the morning of 3 July

Virginia's Black Confederates

1863, he came upon a "'long line of negro cooks baking corn pone (Yankee for corn bread) for rebel soldiers at the front' about two miles behind Lee's battle lines." (Brown, 50)

When one examines an actual letter, written by Private John Taylor Smith of the 13th Alabama Infantry, (which Brown cites from the Museum of the Confederacy collection), *in context*, it reads:

> *I am again without a servant; the master of the boy I had hired, asks now $40 per month which I refuse to pay. Tell Mr. Heath I will give him $25 per month for Boss. If he won't hire Boss I will give $20 for any ordinary field hand if he can procure me one. There is but little danger of losing a negro in the army. There are 25 or 30 in this regiment and only one has been lost. I think $300 very good hire for Boss, and if Mr. Heath can spare him I had rather have him than any other negro I know of **provided he wants to come.***

PROVIDED HE WANTS TO COME!! He had the right to REFUSE!! This hired-out enslaved man had the right to reject employment if he did want to work for this white man. In this instance, there was a reciprocal system where the power structure was bottom up, not top down because, in the end, this particular enslaved person determined who his boss was. When was the last time a historian told you about this one?

<u>Virginia's Black Confederates: Essays and Rosters</u> helps fill some of the historical gaps, provides stories behind names and helps us remember the service of these men and women through a collection of focused essays, primary source materials and rosters containing over 1,600 names of persons of color whose work supported of the Confederate army. The author's goal is not to address the complexities of the institution of slavery, but merely to provide historical snapshots of Virginia's black Confederate experience as well as help identify some of those who wore the gray. Through these personal stories, we gain a greater understanding of their presence, roles and contributions to the Confederate war effort.

Included are images of period primary source documents and an index listing individuals and units in which they served. It is an excellent source book for historians, teachers, journalists, genealogists and others generally interested in Virginia's black Confederates. Most importantly, it makes a positive contribution to the continued scholarship of this topic.

Eric Richardson, Author
<u>The History Historians Leave Out: Minorities in the Confederate Military</u>

Eric Richardson served as an Intern and Assistant Archivist of the Museum of the Confederacy. He holds a Master's of Arts in History and is a Master's of Arts Candidate in English from North Carolina Central University, the nation's oldest, state-supported Historically Black College & University (HBCU). He earned an A.B. in History from the College of William & Mary in Virginia.

Virginia's Black Confederates

Introduction

<u>Virginia's Black Confederates: Essays and Rosters</u> is a collection of materials on African-Americans who engaged in work that supported the Confederate war effort. It is not a defense of the pre-war institution of American slavery nor is it a study of slavery (a condition not unique to the American experience).[1] This work is very limited in scope in that it is designed as a handy reference to make publicly available in one location primary source documentation and essay vignettes of Virginia's black Confederates in their military role during the American Civil War in Virginia. With that in mind, it is not complete and will always be subject to continual updates.[2]

For purposes of this study, the term 'Black Confederate' is defined as *"persons of color, free or slave, who performed work or rendered services in support of the Confederate war effort; Work may have been performed as a volunteer, as a contractor or as an involuntary conscript (draftee, free or slave). Work may have been performed in or out of uniform but had to be performed at the direction of, under or in support of Confederate authority. The term includes men, women and children."*

The primary source documentation in this work can serve as a resource for teachers to identify black Confederates whose stories may be incorporated into school lesson plans. It will aid journalists looking for 'local' angles in the black Confederate experience as well as researchers. More importantly, it may help African-American genealogists get beyond the research 'brick wall' many encounter due to lack of pre-1870 family records.

Black Confederates fell into two categories; free persons and slaves. Records show that free persons of color served as conscripts (draftees), volunteers and contractors providing services to the Confederate war machine. Free men of color were paid for their labor even when conscripted. Many were integrated into combat units. Women often worked in hospitals or as company laundresses and were paid. Based on documentary record data, it can be inferred that there was economic benefit to working for the Confederate government.

Slaves were conscript labor provided for a local emergency or a Confederate levy for fortification or other labor. Pension record and post-war statements indicate some slaves 'volunteered' to serve in various roles. As a rule, slave labor wages went to the slave owner. There may have been exceptions though as some sources have suggested the slave received the pay for services in the unit, such as a cook. Memoir evidence suggests slaves that worked side jobs were able to keep their wages for personal use.

---

[1] **Involuntary servitude still exists. According to the Coalition to Abolish Slavery and Trafficking,** *"an estimated 12.3 million people are enslaved around the world today"* **(April 2013). See** http://www.castla.org/key-stats; **The National Human Rights Center in Berkeley reports there are about 10,000 forced laborers in the United States however the number may be higher. See '***Hidden Slaves: Forced Labor in the United States'***, p15. (**http://www.law.berkeley.edu/files/hiddenslaves_report.pdf

[2] **Individuals who wish to share publicly any post-war or wartime photographs of family members who were black Confederates may send a copy to the publisher or contact the publisher for a contact e-mail for the transfer of an electronic file.**

Virginia's Black Confederates

There are widespread public discussions on whether conscript slaves should be called 'soldiers'. After all, they were slaves, were directed to perform the work and did not necessarily have a choice in whether to go or not. This also is not unique to the American experience. History provides examples of slaves used as soldiers or to serve military purposes. Daniel Pipes has identified extensive Muslim use of slaves for military purposes from 661 to the 19th Century in places as geographically diverse as Central Africa, Central Asia, Spain and Bengal.[3] Ancient Rome likewise used slaves as soldiers and to support military operations. Ancient Latin texts give us the term "volones". It was used to describe slaves who were allowed, often by choice, to take up arms "in defence of their masters".[4]

One former American slave and U.S.C.T. veteran observed the early Confederate use of black labor on military fortifications saying, *"They didn't call them soldiers but they was doing soldier's work."* Primary source documents indicate that some black men (free and slave) were "enlisted" into the ranks to perform military duties as part of organized units. In regards to slaves, honest individuals will continue to differ on whether the term 'soldier' is an appropriate term. This work will not resolve that debate but it will provide food for thought. For purposes of this work, the individuals named in this collection rendered services that could have resulted in a post-war Confederate pension therefore they are recognized as Confederate veterans. Carrying a rifle was not a requirement for veteran or pensioner status. While an individual's status as a 'soldier' may continue to be argued, their status as a Confederate 'veteran' is confirmed by state pensions, fellow veteran and even general public acceptance and recognitions.

A special thanks to Dr. John Coski, Archivist Teresa Roane and Assistant Archivist Eric Richardson of the Museum of the Confederacy (MOC) for reviewing the initial drafts and making recommendations. Their contributions made it possible to include another 220 names of men who worked as teamsters at First Manassas and the Craney Island defenses in Norfolk and over 50 names of free men of color who helped construct the Gloucester Point battery on the York River. A special thanks also to Teresa for bringing to my attention a photo of Callie Hill Estes, one of Virginia's black Confederate pensioners of the 38th Virginia Infantry. This photo is the property of the Museum of the Confederacy and was used on the cover. Thanks also to Ann Drury Wellford, MOC Manager of Photographic Services for making it available. Recognitions must also be given to National Park Ranger Michael D. Gorman for his extensive publicly available Chimborazo Hospital research, Virginia State Park Historian Chris Calkins for his lifelong study of the Appomattox Campaign and former Sailor's Creek Battlefield Historic State Park Chief Ranger Interpreter Samuel V. Wilson, Jr. for providing feedback on the initial draft. Finally, thanks must also be given to my wife Rose for her understanding and support of my historical research work.

---

[3] **See Daniel Pipes, *Military Slaves: A Uniquely Muslim Phenomenon*, (http://www.danielpipes.org/448/military-slaves-a-uniquely-muslim-phenomenon) written for the conference on 'The Arming of Slaves from the Ancient World to the American Civil War' at Yale University, November 16-18, 2000. He is the author of Slave Soldiers and Islam, (New Haven: Yale University Press) 1981 (http://www.danielpipes.org/books/Slave-Soldiers-and-Islam.pdf)**

[4] **The Historia Augusta, *The Life of Marcus Aurelius*, Part 2, p. 185-187. The Loeb Classical Library edition at (http://penelope.uchicago.edu/Thayer/E/Roman/Texts/Historia_Augusta/home.html)**

Virginia's Black Confederates

This edition includes an index to aid researchers. Names are categorized under different index headings: 'Pensioners', 'Denied Pensions' and 'Misc Sources'. Other individuals found in narratives are also indexed by last name. The Chimborazo and Gloucester Point rosters are not indexed because names are displayed alphabetically.

Confederate units are indexed under the major headings of Artillery, Infantry or Cavalry, Engineers, etc. Readers will note some non-Virginians listed. Their names were obtained during research which indicated their service was performed in Virginia. They are listed as a matter of record.

Transcription errors are mine. This list is not complete. There are thousands of African-Americans from Virginia who worked under Confederate military authority yet their names, like many of their white counterparts, are lost to history or on muster rolls, pay rolls and documents not yet transcribed. Hopefully this work will serve to motivate others to dig deeper into unexplored primary source materials.

Greg Eanes
Crewe, Va

Virginia's Black Confederates

<u>Table of Contents</u>

1. The Black Confederate ~~Myth~~ Fact — 1
2. Mosby's Black Confederates — 33
3. 'A Faithful Soldier to the Rebellion' — 38
4. The Black Experience during the Wilson-Kautz Raid — 39
5. Black Confederates at Sailor's Creek — 49
6. Black Confederates at High Bridge — 57
7. Black Confederates on the Appomattox Campaign — 61
8. Black Confederates on the Appomattox Parole — 62
9. New Appomattox Data: Pension Rosters and Other Records — 63
10. Lee Servant Profiled: Joseph Preston Norris — 65
11. Lee Servant or Fake? Rev. William Mack Lee — 69
12. A Reported Lee Servant: Anthony Riley Profiled — 71
13. Captain Benjamin Scott — 73
14. Dick Slate and His Bowie Knife — 77
15. Black Confederates at Craney Island and Pay Roll — 79
16. Gloucester Point Battery and Pay Roll — 85
17. Confederate Teamsters and Manassas Teamster Roster — 91
18. Primary Source Materials — 100
19. Rosters
    a. Denied Pension Applications — 121
    b. Approved Virginia Pensions — 122
    c. Identified in Confederate Records & Other Sources — 147
    d. Black Confederate Employees at Chimborazo — 167
20. Index — 185

Virginia Standards of Learning

This work meets Virginia Standards of Learning for Virginia and U.S. History for the War Between the States era. This includes Virginia Studies VS.7 (c) describing the roles played by enslaved African Americans and free African Americans; U.S. History Skills USI.1 (a) identify and interpret primary and secondary source documents to increase understanding of events and life in U.S. history to 1865; USI (d), interpret ideas and events from different historical perspectives; USI.9 (f) describing the effects of war from the perspectives of Union and Confederate soldiers (including African American soldiers), women and enslaved African-Americans; VUS.7 (e) examining the social impact of the war on African-Americans, the common soldiers, and the home front, with emphasis on Virginia.

Virginia's Black Confederates

The Black Confederate ~~Myth~~ Fact

By
Greg Eanes

"My only object is to transmit, if possible, the truth to posterity, and do justice to our brave soldiers."
Robert E. Lee to Jubal Early, November 1865

Four years into the Civil War Sesquicentennial, the major events mentioning black Confederates generally have critics dismissing that service, explaining away black Confederate contributions as performed unwillingly or irrelevant to the Confederate war effort. The bottom line assessment of the critics is that the 'Black Confederate' is a 'myth' because there was no organized body of black Confederate infantry until 1865.[5]

Modern experiences, modern moral judgments and political viewpoints can skew objectivity. Objective historical analysis needs to consider Civil War era and post-war documentary evidence, period mores and the social complexities of the era when attempting to place black Confederate service in historical context.[6] Those most critical of the black

---

[5] Two landmark studies on the black Confederate exist. Dr. James Brewer's The Confederate Negro: Virginia's Craftsmen and Military Laborers, 1861-1865 (Durham: Duke University Press) 1969 and Professor Ervin L. Jordan's Black Confederates and Afro-Yankees in Civil War Virginia (Charlottesville, Va: UVA Press) 1995. These are 'must reads' for interested persons. See also Eanes' Virginia's Black Confederates (Burkeville, Va: E&H Publishing Co., Inc) 2005; also Black Confederates (Gretna, LA: Pelican Publishing Company) 2004 compiled and edited by Charles Kelly Barrow, J.H. Segars and R.B. Rosenburg, originally titled Forgotten Confederates, and Black Southerners in Confederate Armies: A Collection of Historical Accounts (Gretna, LA: Pelican Publishing Company) 2007, compiled and edited by J.H. Segars and Kelly Barrow; also Black Southerners in Gray: Essays on Afro-Americans in Confederate Armies (Redondo Beach, CA: Rank and File Publications) 1994, edited by Richard Rollins; see also Blacks in Blue and Gray: African American Service in the Civil War (Tuscaloosa: Portal) 1979 by H.C. Blackerby. Also noteworthy is E. Renee Ingram's In View of the Great Want of Labor: A Legislative History of African American Conscription in the Confederacy. Ingram's work is an excellent research source containing verbatim legislation concerning conscription and, more importantly for researchers and genealogists, a list of 1,800 free men of color conscripted by law to support the Confederate war effort between May 1864 and January 1865.

[6] An interesting observation of the social complexity between slave and slave owner is depicted by Booker T. Washington in Up from Slavery: An Autobiography (Garden City, NY: Doubleday & Co) 1901, pages 12-14. Washington describes the trying conditions of life as a slave but adds the following: "One may get the idea, from what I have said, that there was bitter feeling toward the white people on the part of my race, because of the fact that most of the white population was away fighting in a war which would result in keeping the Negro in slavery if the South was successful. In the case of the slaves on our place this was not true, and it was not true of any large portion of the slave population in the South where the Negro was treated with anything like decency. During the Civil War one of my young masters was killed, and two were severely wounded. I recall the feeling of sorrow which existed among the slaves when they heard of the death of "Mars' Billy." It was no sham sorrow, but real. Some of the slaves had nursed "Mars' Billy"; others had played with him when he was a child. "Mars' Billy" had begged for mercy in the case of others when the overseer or master was thrashing them. The sorrow in the slave quarter was only second to that in the "big house." When the two young masters were brought home wounded the sympathy of the slaves was shown in many ways. They were just as anxious to assist in the nursing as the family relatives of the wounded. Some of the slaves would even beg for the privilege

Virginia's Black Confederates

Confederate came of age during the modern Civil Rights era, suggesting this national experience influences their bias and interpretations of America's Civil War history and perhaps explains an inability to accept as fact that any black Southerner might have willingly served a Confederacy which kept the institution of slavery.[7]

What is a 'Black Confederate'?
A disconnect in the entire public discussion is the lack of a common definition or term of reference for a 'black Confederate'. Most observers have come to interpret 'black Confederate' as meaning 'black Confederate *soldier*'. The term *'soldier'* then leads to verbal wrestling matches because interpretations over the term *'soldier'* will differ based on individual perceptions. Individuals unschooled in military affairs have a limited perception of what a *'soldier'* actually does and generally interpret the term to mean 'one who carries a gun in the Army'. It is that limited perception of military duties that causes much misunderstanding.

For purposes of this study, the term 'Black Confederate' is defined as:

> *"Persons of color, free or slave, who performed work or rendered services in support of the Confederate war effort; Work may have been performed as a volunteer, as a contractor or as an involuntary conscript (draftee, free or slave). Work may have been performed in or out of uniform but had to be performed at the direction of, under or in support of Confederate authority. The term includes men, women and children."*

---

of sitting up at night to nurse their wounded masters. This tenderness and sympathy on the part of those held in bondage was a result of their kindly and generous nature. In order to defend and protect the women and children who were left on the plantations when the white males went to war, the slaves would have laid down their lives. The slave who was selected to sleep in the "big house" during the absence of the males was considered to have the place of honour. Any one attempting to harm "young Mistress" or "old Mistress" during the night would have had to cross the dead body of the slave to do so. I do not know how many have noticed it, but I think that it will be found to be true that there are few instances, either in slavery or freedom, in which a member of my race has been known to betray a specific trust. As a rule, not only did the members of my race entertain no feelings of bitterness against the whites before and during the war, but there are many instances of Negroes tenderly caring for their former masters and mistresses who for some reason have become poor and dependent since the war. I know of instances where the former masters of slaves have for years been supplied with money by their former slaves to keep them from suffering. I have known of still other cases in which the former slaves have assisted in the education of the descendants of their former owners. I know of a case on a large plantation in the South in which a young white man, the son of the former owner of the estate, has become so reduced in purse and self-control by reason of drink that he is a pitiable creature; and yet, notwithstanding the poverty of the coloured people themselves on this plantation, they have for years supplied this young white man with the necessities of life. One sends him a little coffee or sugar, another a little meat, and so on. Nothing that the coloured people possess is too good for the son of "old Mars' Tom," who will perhaps never be permitted to suffer while any remain on the place who knew directly or indirectly of 'old Mars' Tom'."

[7] Oddly, critics of the black Confederate have no problem accepting as fact that over 5,000 African-Americans served the Continental cause during the American Revolution even though the British side offered emancipation and recruited, said one National Park Service historian, over 18,000 black Americans. Many of these later resettled in Canada receiving land grants in recognition of their service to the British Army.

Virginia's Black Confederates

Using that term of reference, the position that there were no 'black Confederates' because there were no black Confederate infantry units is factually incorrect. While the weapons of war have changed, the fundamentals have not. Those persons performing support duties to the combat arms (i.e.; infantry, cavalry and artillery) were as important then as they are today. Documentary evidence suggests black Confederates performing work for the Confederate war machine were 'soldiers' in all but name. Even the former slaves, in post-war pension applications and public statements, suggest they were in the 'infantry' or 'cavalry' and considered themselves soldiers even though they may have been common laborers. A soldier does not have to physically "fight" to have "served" in support of a war effort. Many types of service support the "fight" and can be as critical to victory or defeat as a field maneuver.

The U.S. Army's segregated service in the Civil War, World War I and World War II shows those wars were filled with African-Americans serving in support roles. While much is made of U.S. Colored Troops as organized Union infantry, little is generally said of those African-Americans who served the Union in support roles, much like their Confederate counterparts.[8] In the First World War, approximately 80% of the 237,000 black U.S. Army troops deployed in World War I were support personnel in the Services of Supply.[9] In World War II, African-Americans also served primarily in support units, integrated into white combat units.[10] This patriotic service was performed at a time when the United States

---

[8] See **A Question of Manhood: A Reader in U.S. Black Men's History and Masculinity** edited by Darlene Clark Hine and Earnestine Jenkins (Bloomington, IN: Indiana University Press, 1999). In note 30, page 563 they cite slave testimony, *God Struck Me Dead*, p116 noting "[General George H.] Thomas's Union Army of the Cumberland used thousands of black laborers as part of his Quartermaster Corps, Engineering Corps, Pioneer Corps, Medical Department and Subsistence Department. For this reason, Thomas was able to place a huge number of soldiers in the battle itself."; see also George Washington Williams, **History of the Negro Race in America, 1619-1880** (New York: G.P. Putnam's Sons) 1883, Vol. 2, Chapter XVIII, *Employment of Negroes as Soldiers*. Williams wrote, "In September, 1862, an order from Washington directed the employment of fifty thousand Negro laborers in the Quartermaster's Department (p260)…They did fatigue duty in every department of the Union Army. Wherever a Negro appeared with a shovel in his hand, a white soldier took his gun and returned to the ranks. There were 200,000 Negroes in the camps and employ of the Union armies, as servants, teamsters, cooks and laborers. What a mighty host!" (p262)

[9] A good World War I source is **The American Negro in the World War: A Complete and Authentic Narration, from Official Sources of the Participation of American Soldiers of the Negro Race in the World War for Democracy** by Emmett J. Scott, AM, LLD, Special Adjutant to the Secretary of War. (1919). See http://www.gwpda.org/wwi-www/Scott/ScottTC.htm. Chapter XXII covers *'The Negro in the Service of Supply'* and Chapter XXIII covers specialized training. Scott wrote, "War is not all 'death and glory'. For every soldier who gets even a glimpse of the enemy or risks his life within range of shellfire, there must, in all modern warfare, be from twenty to thirty men working at such commonplace and routine tasks as loading and unloading ships, building piers, laying railroad tracks, making roads, in a thousand other ways making it possible for the fighting men to get to the front and for the necessary food, ammunition, and other supplies to reach them." He estimates 80% of the 237,000 Negro troops who served the U.S. Army in World War One were in the Services of Supply. These men served in support elements to include the Engineer Corps, Medical Corps, Hospital and Ambulance Corps and Veterinary Corps. They served in Stevedore Regiments, Butchery Companies, Engineers, Labor Companies and Labor Battalions. Many received specialized training as bench workers, carpenters, blacksmiths, wheelwrights, 'horseshoers', truck drivers (i.e. teamsters), mechanics, and woodworking.

[10] See *U.S. Army in World War II Special Studies*, **The Employment of Negro Troops** by Ulysses Lee (Washington, DC: GPO 1966). Table 10 (p414) indicates 922,965 African Americans served the U.S.

was still a much segregated society. African-Americans were treated as second-class citizens, denied the right to vote, to sit at public lunch counters or use public restrooms. Does being relegated to second-class citizen status in their own country mean they were less patriotic or performed military duties unwillingly? No, it does not. The military support jobs performed were similar and, in some cases, exactly like those jobs performed by black Confederates. The key difference in these comparisons is that most of the black Confederates were slaves and most of the basic laborers were sent to work in response to conscription. Their status as slaves however, should not demean the military work performed or their participation as many were proud of that service in the post-war period.

The same types of work are still performed. Modern infantry cannot operate without the expertise and contributions of a Sustainment Brigade whose troops hold non-combat arms military occupational specialties (MOS) in supply, logistics and transportation. In the Civil War, as now, a wide variety of skills were needed to support an army. Logically, one cannot dismiss the black Confederate's service as irrelevant or his presence as a 'myth'.

The 'Soldier' – Definition and Motive
Various dictionaries provide definitions of 'soldier'. These include: One who serves in an army; an enlisted person or a noncommissioned officer; an active, loyal, or militant follower of an organization; a person engaged in military service; a person who contends or serves in any cause.[11] A large number of black Confederates fit these definitions. Even early black historians made note of this fact.

"As a matter of fact," Booker T. Washington wrote, "it was in the Confederate armies that the first Negro soldiers were enlisted..."[12] Black Historian and Union Civil War veteran George Washington Williams, credited with writing the first history of African-Americans, noted in his landmark study, "The rebels took the first step in the direction of the military employment of Negroes as soldiers."[13] The father of Black History, Carter G. Woodson likewise noted Confederate military use stating, "the seceders had not only made use of the

---

Army in World War II representing about 9.2% of the Army's aggregate strength of 10,030,927. While there were black combat units, most African-American soldiers served in Engineer units, Port Companies, Quartermaster service companies, laundry, kitchen police, construction, bands, ammunition, truck companies, and other support units. A 1942 Army-wide shift from a fixed organization to a functional organization provided deployment opportunities for smaller units allowing all-Negro support companies to be integrated into all-white organizations. Chapter XX, *Service Units around the World* details port and truck company support of Saipan, Tinian, Iwo Jima and Okinawa and other overseas campaigns. Five Army support companies were assigned to the Marine V Amphibious Corps for the Iwo Jima landings. These included the 442nd and 592nd Port Companies and the 471st, 473rd and 476th Amphibian Truck Companies. The troops moved ammunition, supplies and wounded Marines.

[11] Professor Ervin Jordan estimates 180,000 Afro-Virginians were engaged in military service as non-combatant laborers He further estimates 15% of Virginia's slave population (73,500) and 25% of the free black population (59,025) for a total of 132,525 were supporters of the Confederacy. See Jordan's essay *Different Drummers: Black Virginians as Confederate Loyalists* in Black Southerners in Gray: Essays on Afro-Americans in Confederate Armies, edited by Richard Rollins (Murfreesboro, TN: Southern Heritage Press, 1994). It is part of the Journal of Confederate History Series (Vol XI).

[12] Booker T. Washington, The Story of the Negro, the Rise of the Race from Slavery, (New York: Doubleday, Page & Company) 1909. Vol. 1, p. 320.

[13] Ibid, Williams, History of the Negro Race, p277.

Virginia's Black Confederates

Negroes as laborers, but in Tennessee and Louisiana had actually organized free Negroes for military service in the Confederate Army."[14]

In his 1907 biography on Frederick Douglass, Booker T. Washington wrote:

"In the South, thousands of Negroes were at home, protecting the families of the men who fought in the field, and raising crops as subsistence of the Confederate soldiers and their wives and children; thousands more were employed in building fortifications, digging trenches, and doing work which otherwise would have had to be done by the men who were needed at the front; and, anomalous as it may seem, a few colored men, it is said, were actually enrolled and enlisted as soldiers in the Confederate army, fighting for their own continued enslavement."[15]

A member of the 10th Alabama Infantry recalled, "In our regiment we had judges from the bench, lawyers of high rank from their offices, merchants of wealth from stores, farmers of large plantations, and numerous negroes who served through the war as privates."[16] Persons not carrying a rifle were not normally called 'soldiers' but their work as laborers was recognized as contributing to the Confederate war effort.

What motivated black Southerners to serve the Confederacy? One school of thought is that "all" black Confederates were "forced" to serve due to racial oppression or slave status while another school of thought suggests most served willingly. The truth is likely somewhere in the middle with some black Confederates volunteering to serve due to the 'war fever' of the era, to better their own lot in life (financially or socially) or in the hopes of having a better life after the war similar to those black troops who served the Continental cause in the American Revolution. Others, free men and slaves, were indeed "conscripted". It should be noted that the white population – North and South - was also subject to conscription or 'the draft'

Two points need to be made in regards to conscription. First, it can be argued the slave had no choice and was exploited labor however; oftentimes free white men also had no choice in the Civil War conscription or even in U.S. 'drafts' in 20th Century conflicts. During the Civil War, a rich man in the North could pay commutation money or find a substitute. Those unable to pay or find a substitute had to report for duty. The New York City Draft Riot of July 1863 illustrates Northern resistance to conscription. By comparison, in World War I, bounties and exemptions were prohibited and three million men were conscripted. Some of those who refused went to jail with military courts imposing death sentences in some cases.

---

[14] **Dr. Carter G. Woodson, The Negro In Our History (Washington, DC: The Associated Publishers, Inc.), 2nd Edition, 1922; p232; see also Woodson and Lorenzo G. Greene, The Negro Wage Earner, (Washington, DC: The Association for the Study of Negro Life and History, Inc.) 1930; Chapter II,** *Labor In Transition,* **p19-25. Woodson cites services rendered as servants, "builders of fortifications, mechanics and miners" as well as railroad laborers (p21). In footnote 14, he says, "The Confederates outstripped the Unionists in thus using the Negroes."**

[15] **Booker T. Washington, Frederick Douglass, (Philadelphia: George W. Jacobs & Co., Publishers) 1907, p220-221**

[16] **W.W. Draper, Major of 10th Alabama Infantry, in Confederate Veteran Magazine (1915), p487,** *'How Forney Saved the Day at Manassas'.*

Over ten million were drafted in World War II and 6,000 went to prison for refusing to serve. While the Vietnam era draft had several legal exemptions, many of those who resisted went to jail. Over 9,000 were convicted or imprisoned. An estimated 100,000 left the country. With this in mind, could it not be argued that so called 'free men' involuntarily conscripted were also exploited labor?

Second, involuntary service through conscription does not automatically equate to unpatriotic service, substandard service or lack of fidelity to one's country or unit. Conscripts have served valiantly on the battlefield with some conscientious objectors earning the Medal of Honor, the nation's highest award for valor, the most notable being Sergeant Alvin C. York. Records suggest many black Confederates willingly and faithfully served 'the cause' – not the 'cause' of continued servitude but the 'cause' of home and family – the only home and family they knew.

The social complexities of the period cannot be fully appreciated or adequately explained by most contemporary commentators whose 21st Century mores, values and politics influence their bias. This bias taints public interpretations which may not be fair or accurate. Certain elements of history (the black Confederate is certainly one of them) are complicated and one cannot take a blanket approach or oversimplify when attempting to interpret known facts.[17] For example, Joe Mayo, the servant of Captain William Parker, after the war, would send a Christmas turkey every year to Parker and would constantly remind Parker's wife that in the war, the two men were "just like brothers".[18] At the same time, Royall W. Figg, the writer of the Parker Artillery unit history says Joe:

> *"was not a soldier, and he knew it. He was helping to fight, and he helped manfully; but shooting, or being shot at, was not his plan or purpose."[19]*

This comment is revealing. Joe is *'helping to fight, and he helped manfully'* so he is obviously considered part of the team and the 'war effort'. At the same time, he is not a regularly enlisted artilleryman and therefore in Figg's interpretation *"was not a soldier"*.

Another story involving Joe Mayo helps illustrate how wartime camaraderie overcame of the social complexities of the period. Figg recalled,

> *"One morning I strayed near Captain's tent, and the smell and sizzle of the bacon that 'Captain's Joe' was frying caused me to appreciate as never before the temptation of Esau; for I felt almost willing to barter the whole Confederacy, my birthright of liberty included, for a few morsels of that same fried bacon. Indeed, I did unbend most benignly, if not humbly; for the moment social inequalities and*

---

[17] **I encourage individuals seriously interested in the black Confederate should do their own research, delve into the original documents and primary source materials and draw their own conclusions.**
[18] **Figg, Royall W. Where Men Only Dare to Go! Or the Story of a Boy Company by an Ex-Boy (Richmond: Whittet & Shepperson) 1885, p.248-255. Joe Mayo later became the Sexton at Trinity Church in Richmond. He is quoted as saying, "Miss Ellen, me and Mars' William in de war, was jest like brothers."**
[19] **Ibid, p253**

difference of color were forgotten, and Joe and I became brethren at the frying-pan of King Hog. Perhaps we were symbolizing the march of coming events; and perhaps if all the "colored brethren" were as good as Joe Mayo, I would say to events, 'March on!'."[20]

Captain Wayland Fuller Dunaway, Company I, 40th Va Infantry also recalled his servant, Charles Wesley of Lancaster County, Va., in a similar light, reflecting on the social bond. Said Fuller:

There was one man that should have been mentioned before this time, -a negro of my own age, whose name was Charles Wesley. We had grown up on the farm together, and had played, and boxed, and wrestled without respect to color. Not as a slave but as my friend he followed me to the war, -- my launderer, my cook, and when I was sick, my nurse. Having orders to keep himself out of danger he very willingly remained far in the rear when a battle was in progress, but when the firing ceased he faithfully sought me and reported for duty. While writing about Charles, I may anticipate a little and say that when we were in Pennsylvania I told him that we were on Yankee soil, and that he had the opportunity of deserting me and remaining there as a free man. He replied that he already knew that, but that he was going to abide with me."[21]

'Soldiers' in All But Name
Regardless of their motives[22] for service, it can be argued from a technical perspective that the enlistment status, pay, integration into Confederate military organizations and loyal service under the Confederate War Department of many black Confederates defines them as 'soldiers' in all but name.

The Virginia Pension and Confederate Compiled Service rosters[23] are filled with black Confederates whose rank is cited as 'Private'. Wartime rosters indicate many (including slaves) were in fact, "enlisted" into service. One slave, G.W. Smith of the 32nd Virginia

---

[20] Ibid, Figg, Where Men Only Dare Go, p62-63
[21] Dunaway, Rev. Wayland Fuller. Reminiscences of a Rebel (New York: The Neales Publishing Company) 1913, p.61-62
[22] The intent of this essay is to address the black Confederate's existence and performance of 'soldier's work' and their recognition as 'veterans' however 'motive' needed to be mentioned. Those interested in the draft can access a large volume of data. Two works of interest will be Stephen M. Kohn, Jailed for Peace: The History of American Draft Law Violators, 1658-1985 (Westport CT: Greenwood Press), 1986 and John W. Chambers, To Raise an Army: the Draft Comes to Modern America (New York: The Free Press) 1987.
[23] Just over 500 black Confederates from Virginia applied for pensions. Mr. E.R. Combs, Virginia's Comptroller stated in a 7 October 1930 letter to the Assistant Superintendent of the Robert E. Lee Camp Home that *"there are of course no records of Confederate servants."* That information void presents a challenge for genealogists seeking family connections or historians wanting a 'body count'. But even with those limitations, there are company muster rolls that cite the presence of servants even though they were not enlisted like Cooks or Musicians. See Eanes, Virginia's Black Confederates for transcribed pensions and other source materials; One observation made while researching Black Confederates is that not all muster rolls for known black Confederates are annotated with the

Virginia's Black Confederates

Infantry has a certificate of discharge issued at the completion of his one year enlistment. This document can be found in the National Archives in Smith's Compiled Service Records. Some men were "regularly enlisted" while others were not. Confederate records even reflect the names of black Confederates on rolls *"of non-commissioned officers and privates"* employed in extra duty or detailed to hospitals. They also appear on various company and regimental returns. Their ranks are cited as Private, Cook, Musician, Bugler, Drummer, or Servant. They served fully integrated into combat infantry units at the company and regimental level.

Table 1	Pay Chart Comparison		
CSA Enlisted Rank	Pay	Pay	Black Confederate Positions
Private	$11	$11	General Defense Work
Corporal	$13		
		$15	Assistant Cook
Sergeant	$17		
First Sergeant	$20	$20	Chief or Head Cook
Quartermaster Sergeant	$21		
Sergeant Major	$21		

General Defense includes work upon fortifications, in government factories for the production or preparation of war materials, and in hospitals. All personnel were to receive the same rations, clothing and commutations as rank and file soldiers. Evidence suggests teamsters may have earned as much as $20 a month. Each infantry company had a Chief cook and three assistant cooks. Cooks could be white or black.

African-American musicians were allowed the same pay as white musicians.[24] The First (Gregg's) Regiment of South Carolina Infantry had at least six black musicians very early in the war. Four of these were enlisted in Suffolk, Va when the regiment was there though most only served a short period of time.[25] One member of the Surry Light Artillery noted in an August 1864 letter home:

> *"The Battalion has roll calls and drills at the same hour, and the Battalion bugler – a negro – sounds the calls for all the Companies."*[26]

---

identifying 'Negro' or 'Free Man of Color' suggesting there may be many more African-Americans listed on muster rolls than can be positively identified.

[24] *Acts of the Confederate Congress*, Chap XXIX, *an Act for the payment of musicians in the army not regularly enlisted*. Approved 15 April 1862 contained in Public Laws of the Confederate States of America Passed at the First Session of the First Congress 1862, edited by James M. Mathews, Attorney at Law, Clerk in the Department of Justice (Richmond: R.M. Smith, Printer to Congress, 1862) p.29. This document is publicly accessible via the web at http://books.google.com/. It is interesting to note the Chief Cook received the same pay as a Confederate First Sergeant. The Assistant Cook's $15 ranked between a Corporal's $13 and a Sergeant's $17 a month. Pay scales for Union and Confederate armies can be found on the Civil War Trust (CWT) website http://www.civilwar.org/education/history/warfare-and-logistics/logistics/pay.html.

[25] South Carolina Troops in Confederate Service, (Columbia, SC: The R.L. Bryan Company) 1913. Volume 1. Published for the South Carolina Historical Commission. See p257, William Rose, Co. C; and p 297, James Bright, James Williamson and John Graves, Co. F.

[26] Jones, Benjamin Washington. Under the Stars and Bars: A History of the Surry Light Artillery: Recollections of a Private Soldier in the War Between the States. (Richmond: Everett Waddy Compnay) 1909, p210, letter dated 15 August 1864.

Virginia's Black Confederates

Even though several claims for a bounty were paid to black musicians, by 1863 the Confederate Comptroller Lewis Cruger determined that Negro musicians were not to be allowed bounties, as authorized by an 11 December 1861 act of Congress, for the conclusion of one's first year of service and for all who "volunteer or enlist" for three years or the war. Per Cruger's interpretation, only white men could volunteer or enlist so the language *"surely cannot embrace, or refer to a negro, who cannot either volunteer or enlist, but is only hired or employed."*[27] Cruger further argued the 15 April 1862 act authorizing equal pay for "colored persons [who] are employed as musicians" as saying nothing about bounties which he said was limited to white persons "volunteering or enlisting" noting the"

> *"term 'employed', which is used here used in reference to colored persons, shows the distinction made between 'enlisting' and being hired or 'employed'. Besides this, the restriction imposed by this act, subjecting these persons to the consent of the Brigadier General, also shows the distinction between the employing (or hiring) of a negro and the volunteering or enlisting of a citizen or white person. This bounty cannot, therefore, be allowed to a negro."*[28]

The Comptroller, by interpreting the musicians as contractors, was able to forgo additional payments from the treasury. As a matter of practice, musicians continued to 'enlist' in companies and regiments and were carried on the rolls and treated as other soldiers. The Confederate Congress also authorized Captains of companies to *"enlist four Cooks for the use of his company"* and *"the Cooks so directed to be enlisted, may be white or black, free or slave persons: Provided, however, That no slave shall so [be] enlisted without the written consent of his owner."* Chief Cooks were paid $20 per month (the same pay as the First Sergeant) and each Assistant Cook was paid $15 per month. They were allowed the same clothing and commutation allowed the rank and file of the company.[29]

One soldier's February 1862 letter noted, "Nearly every mess of eight or ten men has a negro man for [a] cook."[30] Another man recollected as many as 25 servants in his company "who waited on their masters, cleaned their horses, cooked their meals, etc…as the service got harder and rations became scarcer, these negro servants were gradually sent back home, and the men did their own work, cooking, etc."[31]

Company memoirs contain numerous mentions of camp servants. The post-war history of the Laurel Brigade has unit rosters compiled from the memory of veterans. Among those

---

[27] ***Digest of the Comptroller's Decisions in some of the Leading Cases Presented to him for Settlement*** (Richmond, Va: Smith, Bailey & Co. Printers) 1863, p15-16, Section 34 ***Bounty not allowed to Negro Musicians***. "This claim for bounty was allowed…in the account of Captain Groce, A.Q. M., on the ground that the act of April 15th 1862, authorizes the employment of colored musicians for the same pay as musicians regularly enlisted…".

[28] **Ibid**

[29] Underline is author's for emphasis; Ibid, Chapter LXIV, ***an Act for the enlistment of Cooks in the Army***.

[30] Ibid, Jones, Benjamin Washington. **Under the Stars and Bars**, p25

[31] **Life in the Confederate Army and Some Experiences and Sketches of Southern Life** by Arthur Peronneau Ford and Marion Johnstone Ford (New York: The Neale Publishing Company) 1905, p11.

named are three individuals in Company H, 7th Virginia Cavalry listed as cooks and as "Colored". One other man listed as a cook does not have a compiled service record suggesting he was a man of color though the unit history does not state. The work also has a post-war photo of Colonel Turner Ashby's Headquarters cook, a man named John, also known as Black Hawk[32]

Table 2

Black Cooks - 32nd Virginia Infantry		
Name	Company	Status
Texas	2nd Company I	Slave
Chrisman, Oliver	2nd Company I	Slave
Smith, Charles	2nd Company I	Slave
West, Richard	A	Slave
Nelson, W.B.	C	Slave
Smith, G.W.	C	Slave
Adam	E	Slave
Taylor, James	E	Free
Page, Charles	E	Slave
Ezekiel (free)	F	Free
George	F	Slave
Gustin	F	Slave
Burwell, Carter (Chief Cook)	H	Slave
Jones, William	H	Slave

Captain George Baylor, Co. B, 12th Virginia Cavalry, identified four such men who went with him to war to serve as a wagon driver, a mess cook and two as hostlers. Three of the men were his age and referred to as "playmates in our boyhood". Said Baylor, "These boys were eager to accompany us, and their wish was duly gratified…They shared with us our hardships, and at times even our dangers, entered into our sports and jests, and never were more joyous than when taking part with us in our horse races." One of the four, Tom Langford, and another black cook named Overton armed themselves and, in the battle of Brandy Station, "joined in the company charges" capturing, in one event, a Union Army servant. Said Baylor, "Tom and Overton, not only good soldiers, but excellent foragers".[33]

Another memoir names 'Billy' as the servant to Colonel (later General) Thomas T. Munford. Billy is described as "a cook, hostler and man servant". He was sixteen years of age.[34] The Washington College company of the Rockbridge Artillery also had a black cook named Pete. The same memoir makes mention of a black cook with the Alleghany Rough Battery who was observed taunting some Federal prisoners being held in a churchyard. The writer also recalled, after the First Battle of Manassas, "hearing the colored cook of one of [the] messes asking in piteous tones, over and over again, 'Marse George, where's Marse

---

[32] McDonald, William N., Captain and Brigade Ordnance Officer. <u>A History of the Laurel Brigade, originally The Ashby Cavalry of the Army of Northern Virginia and Chew's Battery.</u> Edited by Bushrod C. Washington. Self-Published by Mrs. Kate S. McDonald, 1907. Among those listed are Billy Smith, Thomas Marshall and Noah Smith of Company H and William Bean of Company H. Bean's race is not identified however a check of unit Compiled Service Rosters does not reflect his name while other men listed as cooks and teamsters have CSR records showing them to be on detached service. See p41 for photo of Black Hawk, cook for General Turner Ashby.

[33] *Southern Historical Society Papers.* Vol. XXXI, Jan-Dec 1903, 'The Army Negro' by Captain George Baylor. The men were Carter Robinson, Phil Williams, Tom Langford and an older man named John Sorrell.

[34] Peck, R.H. <u>Reminiscences of a Confederate Soldier of Co. C, 2nd Virginia Cavalry.</u> Self-Published, Fincastle, Va., 1913, p68

Charles?' No answer was made, but the sorrowful face of the one interrogated was response enough."[35]

A February 1864 *'Act to Increase the efficiency of the Army by the employment of free negroes and slaves in certain capacities'* provided for the conscription of free men of color and slaves to work at the direction of the Secretary of War for National defense. Specifically cited were "duties with the army" or in support of defenses to include fortifications, production of war materials, and military hospitals. They were to be paid the same as the Confederate private: $11 a month, clothing and rations.[36] Contrast this to the pay of the U.S. Colored Troops at $10 a month when their white counterparts received $13 a month. Further, the USCT had $3 a month deducted from their pay to cover clothing until the practice was abolished in September 1864.[37]

Documentary evidence also indicates black Confederates earned in Confederate military service as much, if not more, than Confederate privates. Those working on breastworks were paid $11 a month, Teamsters were paid $20 a month; and Laundresses were paid $10 to $11 per month.[38]

As a rule, conscript slave labor wages were paid to the slave owners. Documentary evidence of unit rosters suggests there may have been some exceptions to this rule. Memoir evidence suggests many slaves had an opportunity to earn personal money by doing side jobs.

Military Jobs
Critics of the black Confederate have derisively called them 'ditch diggers'. Individuals ignorant of military affairs do not always understand the value of a good 'ditch' when artillery, rocket and mortar shells start impacting one's locale. (Modern lessons in the value of 'earth works' have been demonstrated extensively in the recent wars in Iraq and Afghanistan where every Allied outpost was surrounded by the now familiar HESCO barriers and Jersey Walls.)[39]

One former Virginia slave recalled how the Confederates started forming units of Negroes for military jobs shortly after the war started. He said:

---

[35] Moore, Edward Alexander. <u>The Story of a Cannoneer Under Stonewall Jackson</u>. (Lynchburg, Va: J.P. Bell Company, Inc.) 1910. See p68 for Pete, p55 for churchyard incident and p 33 for death incident.
[36] Ibid, p235-236.
[37] Ibid, CWT
[38] See *Virginia Confederate Pension Applications*, Andrew Beverly on breastworks; Jesse Brown and Alvah Vinton were Teamsters; see also *Confederate Citizens File; Confederate Papers Relating to Citizens or Business Firms, 1861-1865. Papers received by Confederate War and Treasury Departments*; NARA Publication M346 for Laundresses Jennie Bartlett and Martha Bartlett, paid $10 a month and Martha Bragg was paid $11 a month. One receipt shows Jordan Cousins, a free man, worked as a breastwork laborer at 50 cents a day earning $4.25 for eight and one-half days' work.
[39] HESCO barriers are large, collapsible wire mesh containers filled with earth. These are complemented by Jersey Walls or the larger 'Texas barriers', 12-foot high, steel-reinforced walls of concrete. Both protect against incoming fire, explosive shrapnel, rocket propelled grenades and suicide bombers. These modern, movable 'earthworks' replaced the need to fill sandbags or dig entrenchments and no soldier ever ridiculed the men and women (support personnel and contractors) who brought them in and set them up!

Virginia's Black Confederates

> *"De Confederates were already forming [Negro] companies fer de defence of Richmond and building fortifications. Dey didn't call 'em soldiers but dey was doin' soldier's wuk."*[40]

Black Historian Williams documented a 3 February 1862 item in the *Baltimore Traveller* which contained the following:

> *"ARMING OF NEGROES AT RICHMOND – Contrabands who have recently come within Federal lines at Williamsport, report that all the able-bodied colored men in that vicinity are being taken to Richmond formed into regiments and armed for the defence of that city."*[41]

The news item was likely referring to the formation of labor battalions.

Another role of the black Confederate was that of 'Body Servant' which, in postwar years was likened to the position of 'valet' or 'body guard'. In British military parlance, it is a 'batman'.[42] Short for 'Battalion Man', the individual was an officer's personal servant. Nowadays in the U.S. Armed Forces, similar duties are performed by an 'Enlisted Aide'.[43]

Body servants performed a variety of duties from cooking, caring for the horses, foraging, caring for the camp and camp equipage, rendering medical assistance and serving as couriers. Captain William Parker's servant Joe Mayo was described as "hostler, cook, washer and ironer, miler and caterer for the Captain's table." Joe had another job, that of watch keeper. A veteran recalled,

> *"Before going into battle, it was common for the men and other officers who had watches to hand them over to Joe, who was sure to keep well to the rear. The reader may not know that the first thing sought for on the dead soldier's body was*

---

[40] Cornelius Garner (b.11 Feb 1846), a former Norfolk slave and Private in the USCT 38th Infantry Regiment, Co. B. Quoted in Weevils in the Wheat (Charlottesville, Va: UVA Press, 1976) p99-102.

[41] Ibid, Williams, Negro Race in America, p278. Williams cited the Union's use of black men in the U.S. Quartermaster Department, used much as they were by the Confederates. Williams wrote, "Wherever a Negro appeared with a shovel in his hand, a white soldier took his gun and returned to the ranks. There were 200,000 Negroes in the camps and employ of the Union armies, as servants, teamsters, cooks and laborers. What a mighty host!" (p262)

[42] One famous 'batman' of the British Army was actor Peter Ustinov, then a Private, temporarily serving under the command of actor and Lieutenant Colonel David Niven. They reportedly became 'life long friends'. See BBC News, Obituary of Sir Peter Ustinov at http://news.bbc.co.uk/2/hi/entertainment/1260975.stm

[43] U.S. General or Flag officers are entitled to an enlisted aide. U.S. Code Title 10, Section 526 details the General and Flag Officer allocations for the Armed Forces. Currently they are as follows: Army, 302; Navy, 216; Air Force, 279 and Marine Corps, 80 for 877 active duties. An additional 22 may be appointed to Joint Duty and sub-unified Command assignments bringing the total to 899. These limitations may be suspended in time of war. An additional 422 (Section 12004 of Title 10) are found in the Reserves for a total of 1,321. This excludes State Adjutant Generals and certain Naval Medical Corps requirements. See http://codes.lp.findlaw.com/uscode/10/A/II/32/526.

Virginia's Black Confederates

his watch. Joe took great pride in guarding well his treasures, though no compensation was made him for his services."[44]

This post of trust may have been customary. Stewart Pringle, "a noted Confederate negro" of Morehouse Parish near New Orleans is recorded as having performed a similar duty. Pringle's obituary stated:

"At one time his Captain drew the money to pay off the company just as it was ordered into battle. The money was handed to old Pringle for safe keeping. The officers and privates gave him their money and watches to keep until the fight was over, and the faithful old man proved true to the confidence reposed in him."[45]

Many servants are mentioned in post-war memoirs. General E. Porter Alexander's servant Abram worked as a teamster.[46] A William Evans and a man named Albert were servants to Chaplain (Lt.) Richard McIlwaine of the 44th Virginia Infantry.[47] William Poole, a mulatto, was the servant of Captain William Chamberlaine of the Artillery staff of the 2nd Corps, Army of Northern Virginia and was captured during the Gettysburg Campaign.[48] The father of the great African-American educator Robert Russa Moton was a Confederate body servant. Moton wrote:

"When the Civil War broke out my father [Booker Moton] went with Mrs. Crowder's brother - Captain Womack of Cumberland County, Virginia, who was afterward Colonel Womack - into the fray as his "body servant." I think they would say "valet" today. He was with him during the first three years of that bitter struggle, suffering all the privations and hardships so familiar to those who know what the Southern Army endured.

"One experience he used often to relate was that near Petersburg he accidentally got within the Union lines and was told that he might remain with the Yankees if he so desired; but he told them that he could not do so at the time because he had given his definite promise that he would stand by Colonel Womack until the war was over. He could not break his promise. He had also sworn to see to it, so far as he could, that no harm came to his master and he felt that he would remain true to that pledge so long as Colonel Womack was equally true to his promises to him. I

---

[44] Ibid, Figg, <u>Where Men Only Dare</u>, p253. Joe was in Parker's Battery Virginia Light Artillery.
[45] *The Somerset Herald*, 10 March 1886; 'A Colored Rebel'. He served under Captain Henry D. Brigham, Co. G, 15th Louisiana Infantry Regiment, Army of Northern Virginia. Brigham was the Acting Commissary of Subsistence. Pringle was a janitor in the local public school and the town fiddler of Bastrop. Pringle's obituary states, "He was interred by the Confederate veterans whom he had served so faithfully and who held him in so high esteem." Pringle was also a Mexican War veteran.
[46] Ibid, Figg, <u>Where Men Only Dare</u>, p192
[47] McIlwaine, Richard. <u>Memories of Three Score Years and Ten</u>. (Washington: The Neale Publishing Company) 1908, p193 and 209.
[48] Chamberlain, William. <u>Memoirs of the Civil War Between the Northern and Southern Sections of the United States of America 1861-1865</u>. (Washington, DC: Press of Byron S. Adams) 1912, p52, 73-74 and 136. Chamberlain notes, "Officers were allowed two rations each day, one for himself and the other for his servant…".

am told that the friendship between the two men, one black, one white, was very strong; that nothing ever separated them save Colonel Womack's death which, as I recall my father's account of it, occurred in one of the famous charges near Petersburg."[49]

Body servants served enlisted and officer alike at all echelons of command. Because they were not 'regularly enlisted' like cooks and musicians, the only government documentation of their service are post-war pensions and the occasional muster roll listing body servants. Most documentation of names will be found in post-war memoirs, newspaper reports or period letters. It has been estimated each Confederate company in the Gettysburg campaign had 20 to 30 servants attached. British Lieutenant Colonel Arthur Fremantle recorded this impression of the Confederate Army's march to Gettysburg noting:

> *"In the rear of each regiment were from twenty to thirty negro slaves, and a certain number of unarmed men carrying stretchers and wearing in their hats the red badges of the ambulance corps."*[50]

A Confederate officer recorded, "It was the custom of officer's servants to accompany the wagons on the march."[51] An interesting story was recorded after the war that one day General Lee "asked a negro, whom he noticed doffing his hat to him, who he was. The black man answered, 'One of your soldiers, Gin'ral'. 'Have you been shot?' inquired Lee. 'No sah'. 'Well you can't be one of my soldiers, the; for all my men get shot'. 'The reason I haven't got shot is that I stay back where the generals stay."[52]

Many were interviewed after the war, generally in conjunction with United Confederate Reunions. Earl Jerdon was 101 years old when he was interviewed in the African-American newspaper, *The Tulsa Star* in September 1918. He was a servant of Dr. C.W. Jerdon of

---

[49] **Finding a Way Out: An Autobiography** by Robert Russa Moton (Garden City, NY: Doubleday, Page & Co), 1921, p12-13. Electronic edition available at: http://docsouth.unc.edu/fpn/moton/moton.html
[50] **Arthur Fremantle, Three Months in the Southern States, p234 (New York: Pub by John Bradburn) 1864. Based on Fremantle's estimate, using known units to calculate, it can be inferred the Army of Northern Virginia contained between 4,900 and 7,400 black Confederates marching behind the regiments. Likely body servants and cooks, they were exclusive of teamsters driving wagons.**
[51] **Ibid, Chamberlaine, Memoirs, p73.**
[52] **The Methodist Review, Vol. 86, p171. (Fifth Series, Vol. XX). (New York: Eaton and Mains) 1904. The grammar of the original story is cleaned up for reader comprehension.**

Huntsville, Mississippi. He recalled, "General Nathan Bedford Forrest sent out a call for 15,000 Negro soldiers. The doctor came to me and asked me if I wanted to go. I said sure, and enlisted that day…he didn't say that I had to go. He treated all of us fine."

The reporter asked Jerdon, "Were you a servant?"

Jerdon replied with a grin, *"Yeh. I served with a gun and two pistols."* He served throughout the war as an orderly and claimed to have attended every post-war reunion.

A similar reaction came from two former body servants of the 7th Georgia Infantry, Joe Bloke and Andy Bailey. Andy was asked, "Did you fight or hold horses?" He quickly responded, "We fit and held horses boaf [both] but we fit most of de time, sir."[53]

Exposed to Danger
Being a non-combatant did not mean one wasn't exposed to combat. One veteran recalled a September 1862 engagement near Leesburg, Va with the Union's Loudon Rangers under Capt. Samuel C. Means. He wrote,

> *"An interesting incident of this fight was that Edward, the servant of Private [W.O.] English, of Company K, followed his master in the charge and shot one of the Means party who had made himself especially obnoxious."*[54]

On another occasion J.E.B. Stuart's servant Bob was captured and made a prisoner.[55] In another incident, a Union cannon ball cut the head off one horse on a team driven by servant Joe Mayo of Parker's Battery of Light Artillery.[56]

The 9th Virginia Cavalry's Joseph Yerby was a cook in the mess of Captain R.H. Pratt and served throughout the war. A report says:

> *"This soldier slave…deserves a place of distinction in Confederate annals…At the battle of Gettysburg two of the troop, Cockrell and Sampson were wounded. Jo. Went into the city, stole a horse and harness, secured a buggy in like manner from a farm bear by and in it placed the wounded men and started them towards their home in Northumberland county, with the parting reminder that it was his team and he should*

---

[53] *The [Richmond] Times*, 25 July 1902, p6. This vignette is contained in 'Gathered From the Passing Throng' column. The two men were among 150 Georgia veterans in Virginia to visit the battlefields.
[54] McClellan, H.B. **The Life and Campaigns of Major-General J.E.B. Stuart, Commander of the Cavalry of the Army of Northern Virginia**. (Richmond, Va: J.W. Randolph and English) 1885, p109 McClellan was a Major and Assistant Adjutant General and Chief of Staff of the Cavalry Corps, ANV. Private English was later promoted to Lieutenant of Ordnance. See also *OR, Report of J.E.B. Stuart of Cavalry Operations of First Maryland Campaign, From August 30th to September 18th, 1862* as reported in the *Southern Historical Society Papers*, Vol. III, May and June 1877. As quoted, **"In this engagement, Edmund, a slave belonging to one of the men, charged with the regiment and shot Averhart, one of the most notorious ruffians of Means' party."**
[55] Ibid, p161
[56] Ibid, Figg, **Where Men Only Dare Go**, p253. An entire section is devoted to Joe Mayo, p248-255.

call for it when he returned home. When he got home the grateful 'rebels' delivered him his, and what some might say, ill-gotten gains."[57]

The 1911 report said Yerby's "love for the cause and the men he so faithfully served four years is still dear to his heart. When the day comes for unveiling the monument to the 'Confederate Negro' one of its foundation stones should bear the simple name of 'Jo. Yerby'." He went to Washington, D.C. after the war with $15 in his pocket and by the time of the report had become a wealthy contractor.

Another remarkable story was that of a slave who served as a Confederate spy. Peyton (no last name referenced) was a slave of 2nd Lt. W. Lynn Hemmingway of Co. K, 11th Mississippi Infantry (the Carroll Rifles). Peyton was a noted fiddler and "highly respected by black and white" and accompanied Hemmingway as a servant to Virginia where he was with the unit through several campaigns. He returned to Mississippi in early 1863 when he was recruited (in February or March) as a spy to visit the Federal gunboats then threatening Vicksburg. He was able to pose as a fugitive slave to the commanders of the various gunboats "and was well received". Peyton managed to identify and "secrete their official papers, maps, etc., and escaped with these documents to Fort Pemberton." He left Vicksburg before it fell and returned to Virginia with Hemmingway remaining until Lee surrendered at Appomattox. Peyton was sent home before surrender ceremonies and was identified to Federal authorities "as the spy who had deceived them above Fort Pemberton." He was taken prisoner, placed in irons and sent to New York.

According to the report, rather than a Federal prison, Peyton was diverted to a ship that took him to Cuba. He was:

> *"sold as a slave together with many others. The vessel on which he was taken was a Federal gunboat. In Cuba he worked as a slave in factories for nearly fifteen years, being entirely cut off from all communication with home and friends. He made seven attempts to escape from bondage, all but the last, of course, being unsuccessful. Finally he found an American vessel, commanded by a Southerner, to whom he related the history of his capture, enslavement and forced exile, and begged to be returned to his home and family. The captain secreted him in the hold of his vessel, carried him to Costa Rica, thence to New York. Peyton then worked his way to Virginia, where a number of ladies raised the means to return him to his home after an absence of seventeen years. He reached Winona, Miss[issippi], on the 15th of April 1880."*[58]

---

[57] *The [Fredericksburg] Free Lance*, 4 March 1911, p1; 'Co. K, 9th Virginia Cavalry'
[58] Originally published in the *Washington (Mississippi) Gazette* and picked up by the *Florence (Ala) Gazette*, 5 Nov 1892 as 'The Remarkable Adventures of a Noted Mississippi Fiddler, the *St. Paul Daily Globe*, 16 June 1880 as 'A Very Strange Story' and other newspapers. Peyton's wife had remarried but her second husband drowned in the interim so she and Peyton remarried. The story states, "He left his children as babes, and finds them married and with children of their own."

Once when their Confederate position was under bombardment, black Confederate Stewart Pringle remained to gather up important quartermaster papers and records, placed them in a bag and sought refuge in the woods to ensure they were saved.[59]

Some actively participated in battle. At First Manassas, Charles, the servant of 30th Va Cavalry Adjutant B.H. Burk, "unaided, captured a prisoner armed with gun and pistol, and turned him over to the commanding general of the First Brigade".[60] In the First Shenandoah Valley Campaign, two servants in J.E.B. Stuart's cavalry participated in combat and killed two Union soldiers of the 15th Pennsylvania Cavalry. It was reported "that one of the enemy was killed by Captain Carter's negro servant and one of the Captain Patrick's company."[61] Another man of note is Pompay Tucker, 16th Virginia Infantry who reportedly had entered service as a body servant and took the place of his master in the Seven Days campaign when the latter gave up his position to Tucker. The servant reportedly killed several Union soldiers in the battle.[62]

Two interesting wartime reports originate with *The Pacific Appeal* of San Francisco which advertised itself as "a weekly journal, devoted to the Interests of the People of Color".[63] In an article titled 'Colored Confederate Soldiers' the paper reports on an article in the *Nashville Daily Union*:

> *"The Confederate Attorney-General has decided that men with any portion of the blood of the white race are liable to conscription. This decision admits to the rebel army all the mualttoes and quadroons in the Confederacy, and they are numbered in the thousands...All these chaps according to the Attorney-General's decision, are to be made to fight side by side with the white concripts of Davidson, Williamson, Henry and Shelby counties...Colored sharpshooters have for months been destroying our [Union] soldiers in Virginia."*[64]

Another article on the same page was entitled 'The Negro to Fight on Both Sides'. The article reported:

> *"there is good evidence that the rebels themselves have been the first to use the negroes as soldiers, and if they dare trust them with arms they may yet have a larger black army than the [U.S.] Government. As yet they have only employed the negroes as artillerists. Negro slaves worked a portion of the batteries at Vicksburg, by which our assailing columns were so savagely mowed down, and negro slaves stand behind the batteries at Port Hudson...As to the use of negroes in*

---

[59] Ibid, *The Somerset Herald.* 10 March 1886.
[60] **Official Records of the War of Rebellion**, *Report of Col. R.C.W. Radford, Thirtieth Virginia Cavalry*, dated 1 August 1861 for The Bull Run, or Manassas Campaign, Virginia, July 16-22, 1861. (Series I, Vol. 2, p532-533)
[61] **Confederate Military History,** Vol. 3, Chapter VI, *'The First Shenandoah Campaign – April to July 1861'*, p79
[62] **The Long Lost Journal of Confederate General James Johnston Pettigrew**, p486, January 24, 1863 entry. Dan Bauer (Lincoln, Nebraska: Writers Club Press) 2001.
[63] *The Pacific Appeal*, Vol. I, No. 51, March 21, 1863, San Francisco, California.
[64] Ibid, p4, *The Nashville Daily Union* report was in the 7 February 1863 issue, p2.

the southern forts, a recent letter from an officer of the Bank's expedition at Baton Rouge, says: 'The fortifications of Fort Hudson are said to be very strong, the heavy artillery guns of monstrous size, and are worked entirely by negroes, who, it is now fully admitted, make the best soldiers in the world, for heavy artillery service, being very muscular men...they can endure fatigue much better than white men, and seem to be perfectly in their element while working the heavy guns within the fortifications. Our own [U.S.] government are beginning to realize this fact...". [65]

Black Confederates were wounded and killed. Ben Shropshire of the 5th Texas Cavalry (and later New Orleans) was wounded one time and entitled to a post-war Louisiana pension but declined as he "was supported by the Confederate veterans". When he died, he was buried wearing a Confederate uniform.[66] Jacob Ransell, "colored bodyguard" to J.E.B. Stuart was wounded twice; once in the ear and once in the thigh.[67] Moses Dallas, a river pilot of the crew of the *CSS Savannah*, was killed while helping capture the Union gunboat *Water Witch* on the Little Ogeechee (Ga) river.[68]

George McDonald of St. Clair County, Florida enlisted there and served in the west. He was seriously wounded during the battle of Wilson's Creek "when a Minie ball plough[ed] through his hip and buckshot struck him in the face." According to a news report, McDonald was "made the object of one of the finest displays of heroism witnessed anywhere in the war." The report said:

"George lay groaning upon the ground when he was found by Owen Snuffer, Lieutenant of his company...The white man stooped down, examined the black man's wounds and staunched the flow of blood from them. 'For God's sake' Cried the suffering negro, 'give me a drink of water.' Snuffer's canteen was empty, but midway between the firing lines was a well. To reach it...was to become the target of sharpshooters, and it meant almost certain death. But the groans of his black friend

---

[65] **Ibid**
[66] *The Daily Herald*, 23 Dec 1907, 'Confederate Negro Buried'.
[67] *The Washington Times*, 29 February 1912, p6; 'Old Uncle Jake Will Be Buried At Village of Vienna: Bodyguard of Gen. Stuart Never Ceased to Mourn War Time Master'; see also *Washington Times*, 25 September 1911, p12; 'Stuart's Slave is Dying In Tenement on Bed of Husks: Life of Confederate General's Bodyguard Slowly Is Flickering'.
[68] Confederate Military History, Vol. 6, Chapter XV, p287, *'The Campaigns of 1864-Battle of Olustee—Operations Near Savannah—The Wilderness to Cold Harbor—Georgia Troops Engaged—Early's Valley Campaign'*; see also OR of the Union and Confederate Navies,(afterwards OR Navy), p304, *Muster Rolls, Etc., Confederate Vessels, Vol. 1*; see also *OR Navy*, p704, *Report of Commander Webb, C.S. Navy, regarding the Pilots Fleetwood and Dallas*. Confederate Navy Squadron Commander advised Confederate Secretary of the Navy S.R. Mallory, "I have also been compelled to increase the pay of Moses Dallas from $80 to $100 per month, in order to retain him. He is a colored pilot, and is considered the best inland pilot on the coast."; see also OR Navy, p494, *Telegram*, 3 June 1864 to Flag Officer W.W. Hunter, C.S. Navy from LT Jos. Price, C.S. Navy on the capture of the *Water Witch*. "We have captured the U.S.S. Water Witch, carrying four guns...We lost in killed...six men, vis. Moses Dallas, pilot..."; see also p501, *Report of Lieutenant Price, C.S. Navy*, second in command of expedition, 8 June 1864. He says Dallas was in the lead boat and killed during the initial assault before the Federal vessel was reached.

were more powerful than the love of life, and with bullets falling around him like hailstones he pushed forward until the well was reached. And then he discovered that the bucket had been taken away and the windlass removed. The water was thirty feet down and the depth unknown. The well was an old-fashioned stone walled one and Owen determined to get water or know the reason why. He pulled off his long cavalry boots and taking one in his teeth he let himself down slowly, laboriously, hand over hand until the water was reached and the boot filled, and then he began climbing up the same way he went down, straddling the well and clutching with hands and feet at the rocky walls. Reaching the surface again, he picked up the other boot and safely made his way back to the Confederate lines. George drank copiously and the cooling water was poured upon his burning wound....he still insists that the only water fit to drink was that which he drained out of that boot." [69]

James Mosby, a free man of color of Pulaski (Va), "a colored Confederate veteran, who fought in the Southern army throughout the Civil War" was taken prisoner and managed to escape from a Federal prison in the North and made his way home to rejoin his unit, serving until the end of the war. He died at the age of 70. [70] At least two servants identified as Haywood and Walter of Company K, 23rd Texas Cavalry died of pneumonia at Camp Chase POW Camp. Their Captain, M.L. Sims sent money to have flowers placed on their graves after the war. [71] Captain James Dinkins recalled the winter of 1863-64 at the notorious Union prisoner of war camp at Johnson's Island. Said Dinkins:

> *"My recollection is that there were thirteen negroes who spent the dreadful winter of 1863-4 with us at Johnson's Island, and not one of them deserted or accepted freedom, though it was urged upon them time and again.*
>
> *"...the Federal authorities assured the negroes they were as free as their masters had been, and were not prisoners of war; that they would give them no rations and no rights as prisoners of war if they went in the prison, but they all elected to go in, and declared to the Yankees they would stick to their young masters to the end of time, if they starved to death by doing so.*
>
> *"Those Confederate officers, of course, shared their rations and everything else with their servants.*
>
> *"When we went in prison in August, 1863, there was a sutler's shanty in the grounds, where those who had money could purchase what they wanted to eat. Most of the Port Hudson men had money, and for a time they and their negroes fared well, until late in the fall, when the Yankees shut down on us. They had failed*

---

[69] *The Sun*, 21 August 1903 quoting the *Kansas City Journal* repeat of an article from *The Osceola Democrat*; 'A White Man's Love For A Negro: How Owen Snuffer Risked the Union Fire to Comfort George McDonald'. Snuffer was likely Owen M. Snuffer, Senior Second Lieutenant, Co. B, 16 Regiment, Missouri Infantry.

[70] *The [Richmond] Times Dispatch*, 12 October 1912, under 'Lynchburg Will Honor Founder'.

[71] Knauss, William H. <u>The Story of Camp Chase.</u> (Publishing House of the Methodist Episcopal Church, South: Tennessee and Texas) p81. See also the article, 'Uncommon Incident' in *The Colored American*, Washington, D.C., p15 (no issue number).

to influence the negroes, and decided to confine us strictly to prison rations, which were very scant.

"It was then that the devotion and fidelity of the negroes was put to a test, but without exception, master and servant clung together in heroic sacrifice, and no more wonderful magnetic tie ever existed than that between those Southern officers and their slaves.

"One of those gentlemen was my intimate friend and companion and roommate, Colonel I. G. W. Steadman, of Alabama. I do not recall his regiment. His brother, a lieutenant in the same regiment, was also a prisoner there. Colonel Steadman's negro was named 'George.' He waited on us and was untiring in his efforts to do anything in his power for our comfort.

"Frequently, to my knowledge, George was sent for to go before the commanding officer outside. We often said: 'We have seen the last of poor George,' but at night George would be escorted back by a guard. I asked George what they said to him. He told us that Mister Pearson (he was the Yankee Major in command of the prison) would tell him he was a free man; that he had but to say the word and he would be taken out and given work at $2 a day, and good clothes to wear, and go and live anywhere he wanted--told him he was a fool, that his master would never be exchanged or get out of prison--that if he stayed with the Rebel officer he would starve in prison. He said Pearson told him all this and more. I then asked George what he said in reply, and what George said was: 'Sir, what you want me to do is to desert. I ain't no deserter, and down South, sir, where we live, deserters always disgrace their families. I'se got a family down home, sir, and if I do what you tell me, I will be a deserter and disgrace my family, and I am never going to do that'."[72]

A mulatto slave named Abe Goodgame was captured in the Shenandoah Valley and imprisoned by Federal authorities at Fort McHenry. While there he refused to take the oath of allegiance to the United States. He managed to get a letter to a Confederate officer he knew and asked that the officer report his POW status to his owner Lt. Colonel J.C. Goodgame of the 12th Alabama Infantry Regiment.[73] Jacob Biscoe was captured on 19 October 1862 at Herring Creek, Maryland for trying to smuggle goods in a canoe to Virginia.[74] William Lucas, also running the blockade, was captured on 24 October at Nanjemoy Creek and Lewis Davis was captured on 30 October.[75] The Schooner *Hampton* was captured by the Union Navy on 13 January 1863 running the blockade at Dividing

---

[72] *Southern Historical Society Papers*, Vol. XXXV, Jan-Dec 1907, 'The Negro as Slaves', Capt. James Dinkins.

[73] *Southern Historical Society Papers*, Vol. III, March 1877, No. 3, 'Diary of Captain Robert E. Park, Twelfth Alabama Regiment', March 19th entry.

[74] OR Navy, Vol. 5, p. 131, *Report of Commodore Harwood, U.S. Navy, commanding the Potomac Flotilla, transmitting duplicate certificates of capture*, 22 October 1862

[75] Ibid, p135, *Report of Commodore Harwood, U.S. Navy, commanding the Potomac Flotilla, transmitting certificates of capture made by USS EUREKA, 27 Oct 1862. See also p144, Potomac Flotilla –Certificate of Capture.*

Creek, Va. Of the eight captured crew members, three were men of color: Wesley Milburn of Deal's Island, Frank Evans and Daniel Rice of Baltimore.[76] One blockade runner had an entirely black crew, captured on 26 January 1863 near St. Clement's Bay. The crew included Albert Ball, George Thompson, William Thompson and A. Lincoln. Their boat was destroyed and the contraband of five barrels of whisky, two bags of coffee, one bag of pepper and five bags of shot, were confiscated.[77]

An 1864 diary entry of a Confederate clerk contains 'A Yankee Account of the Treatment of Confederate Prisoners' from the *Chicago Times*. Describing activities at Camp Douglas the news report stated:

"It is said also that a mulatto boy, a servant of one of the Confederate captains, and, of course, a prisoner of war, who was well known to have a pass to go anywhere within the lines, was walking inside the guard limits...when the guard commanded him to halt. He did not stop, and was instantly killed."[78]

The same clerk reported, "By the last flag of truce boat a negro slave returned. His master took the oath, the slave *refused*. He says, '*Massa had no principles*'."[79] He also recorded a newspaper account of "two negroes captured by General Hunter in the Valley last summer, and forced into the Yankee army, deserted yesterday and came into General Pickett's lines, and were brought over to this city."[80]

SENSIBLE COLORED FOLKs.
The Petersburg Express is informed by Lieut. Daniels, who has just arrived at Petersburg from Fort Norfolk, that some 35 or 40 Southern negroes, captured at Gettysburg, are confined at Fort McHenry. He says that they profess an undying attachment to the South. Several times Gen. Schenck has offered to release them from the Fort, if they would take the oath of allegiance to the Federal Government and join the Lincoln army. They had peremptorily refused in every instance, and claim that they should be restored to their masters and homes in the South. They say they would prefer death to liberty on the terms proposed by Schenck.

Civil War Newspaper Report

An estimated 35 to 40 black Confederates were captured at Gettysburg and were held at Ft. McHenry in Baltimore. They reportedly "profess an undying attachment to the South" and refused to take the oath of allegiance noting "they would prefer death to liberty on the terms" proposed by the Federal officer in charge.[81] Servants and teamsters were all subject to capture and many ended up in Union POW camps. Body servant William Tabb and black

---

[76] OR Navy, Vol. 5, p210, Potomac *Flotilla-Certificate of Capture*.
[77] Ibid, p225, Potomac *Flotilla-Certificate of Capture*.
[78] J.B Jones, A Rebel War Clerk's Diary at the Confederate States Capital, (Philadelphia: J.B. Lippincott & Co), 1866, Vol. 2, p129, diary entry for 14 January, p128-129.
[79] Ibid, p424, 16 February 1865 entry.
[80] Ibid, p342, 29 November 1864 entry.
[81] *The Staunton Spectator*, 13 October 1863, p2; 'Sensible Colored Folks', quoting *The Petersburg Express*.

Virginia's Black Confederates

Confederate sailor C.P. Terry were captured at the battle of Sailor's Creek and sent to Point Lookout POW Camp.[82]

Confederate and post-war records show the black Confederate was more than just a 'ditch digger'. He had his share of heroism and danger. Whether conscript or volunteer, they were a vital element of the Confederate war machine attached to combat units and support elements (Hospitals, Engineers, Quartermasters, etc.).[83] They were in War Department service performing national defense jobs. The jobs they held are similar and, in some cases, nearly identical with military occupational specialties still in use by the United States Army. While there are occupational differences imposed by the evolution of modern technology, the occupational fundamentals are the same as illustrated in next Table.

Table 3

Comparison of Confederate Jobs with US Army Military Occupational Specialties (MOS)		
Confederate Position	**Comparable Army Position (MOS)**	**Brief Duty Descriptions**
Body Servant (likened by post-war Confederates to a 'valet')	Enlisted Aide on personal staff to General Officers (aka in the British Army as a battalion man or 'batman')	Perform tasks and details that, if performed by the officers, would be at the expense of their primary military and official duties; Assist with care, cleanliness, and order of assigned quarters, uniforms, and military personal equipment; Help to purchase, prepare, and serve food and beverages in the General Officer's quarters.
Cook	Food Service Specialist (MOS 92G)	Preparation and service of food in field or garrison food service operations.
Teamster	Motor Transport Operator (88M); Cargo Specialist (88H)	**Motor Transport Operators** (88Ms) are the backbone of the Army's support and sustainment structure, providing advanced mobility on and off the battlefield; **Cargo Specialists** load and unload supplies and materials …are primarily responsible for transferring or supervising the transfer of passengers, cargo and equipment
Laborer-Breastworks	Combat Engineer (12B); Carpentry/Masonry Specialist (12W)	Duties as a **Combat Engineer** may include: Construct fighting positions, for individuals and weapons; Construction of fixed and floating bridges; Construction of obstacles and defensive positions; **Carpentry and Masonry Specialist** individuals perform general heavy carpentry, structural steel and masonry duties.
Laborer-Railroad	Railway Section Repairer (88T); Railway Operation Crewmember (88J) and Railway Equipment Repair	**Railway Equipment Repairers** are primarily responsible for supervising or performing maintenance on …locomotives and rolling stock; **Railway Section Repairers** are primarily responsible for performing maintenance on railway tracks, roadbeds, switches, fences and other railway facilities;

---

[82] See Eanes, <u>Virginia's Black Confederates</u>, 'Battle of Hillsman's Farm'.
[83] **National Archives and Records Administration communications with the author reveal the Confederate 'slave rolls' have been identified for reproduction so they can be made available to genealogists and researchers through such sites as Ancestry.com and Fold3.com. These muster rolls will provide the names of those slaves working at the more permanent military establishments (hospitals, armories, etc.) as well as on Confederate defenses under Confederate Engineers. There is no estimated time of release.**

Virginia's Black Confederates

		Railway Operations Crewmembers are primarily responsible for supervising and operating diesel-electric locomotives and related equipment. They also serve as a crewmember or brakeman in the makeup and movement of railway cars/trains.
Laborer-Burial Details	Mortuary Affairs Specialist (92M)	Perform duties relating to deceased personnel to include recovery, collection, evacuation, establishment of tentative identification. They also inventory, safeguard and evacuate personal effects of deceased personnel.
Hostler	Animal Care Specialist (68T)	Provide the care, management, treatment, and sanitary conditions for animals …comprehensive care for government owned animals.
Hospital Steward/Nurse	Health Care Specialist (68W)	Responsible for providing emergency medical treatment, limited primary care and health protection and evacuation from a point of injury or illness; Assist with outpatient and inpatient care and treatment; Prepare patients, operating rooms, equipment and supplies for surgery
Musician	Bandperson (42R)	Perform as a professional musician within an Army band. Duties include: Perform on a musical instrument in a variety of ensembles, ranging from solo performance to full concert band; Tune an instrument to a given pitch; Discriminates and matches pitch; Perform operator maintenance on a musical instrument
Blacksmith	Allied Trade Specialist (91E)	Perform fabrication, repair and modification of metallic and nonmetallic parts; operate lathes, drill presses, grinders & machine shop equipment.
Mechanic	MOS 91 series; Ammunition Specialist (89B)	Perform maintenance and repairs on artillery, small arms; handle and store ammunition. (91 Series include Armament Repairer, 91K, Artillery Mechanic, 91P and Small Arms/Artillery Repairer, 91F
Carpenter	Carpentry and Masonry Specialist (12W)	Perform general heavy carpentry, structural steel and masonry duties.
Boatman	Watercraft Operator (88K)	Responsible for navigation, cargo operations and supervising other Soldiers on Army watercraft.
Laundress	Shower/Laundry & Clothing Repair Specialist (92S)	Responsible for supervising and performing laundry, shower, personnel, and clothing decontamination functions.
Preacher	Chaplain Assistant (56M)	Support Unit Ministry Team programs and worship services.
Scouts/Spies	Cavalry Scout (19D)	Responsible for reconnaissance; track and report enemy movement and activities; Gather and report information.

The importance of the black Confederate's wartime contribution was not lost upon their contemporaries as attested to in many Confederate memoirs and recollections. These statements were not made just for public consumption but were also privately held. In 1930, black Confederate Buena Vista (Va) resident John A. McManaway, 83, was attempting to get into the Robert E. Lee Camp Confederate Soldier's Home in Richmond. His attorney, Mr. Charles S. Glasgow of Lexington, remarked in his letter to the Virginia's Comptroller:

> *"Mr. MacMana [way] is now receiving a small pension, having served in the capacity as a teamster in the Confederate Army…as*

Virginia's Black Confederates

well all know, in the late war <u>that Department was as much a part of the Army as the man in the front line.</u>"[84]

This vignette is important in that the statement was not made for public consumption. It was a simple observation of fact; one generally known, understood and accepted by those who served. It is only in this modern era where political correctness attempts to re-interpret (misinterpret?) history that we see efforts to dismiss the service of this element of the Confederate Army.

Recognition as Veterans
Another common indicator of one 'having served' is one's public recognition as a 'veteran'. Black Confederates were officially recognized as 'veterans' by individual State government actions and, more importantly, by their white Confederate peers.

JERRY MAY - Servant, Co. D, 7th Georgia Infantry
(*Confederate Veteran*, V13, p423)

In Virginia, before the black servant pensions were specifically authorized, some African-Americans applied and were accepted on the form for 'Disabled Confederate Soldier'. All pensions had to be attested to by living Confederate veterans or a respected member of the local community.

Pensioners would often identify company and unit of assignment citing they were in the infantry,[85] cavalry, artillery, etc. When the final servant law in Virginia was updated, it was more specific for persons *"who served the Confederate States in the war between the States as body servant, cook, hostler, or teamster or who worked on the Confederate breastworks."*[86] It was amplified to include performance of guard duty, burying

---

[84] Underline is author's emphasis. Letter, October 6, 1930, Charles S. Glasgow to E.R. Combs, State Comptroller, Richmond, Va. Contained in *Robert E. Lee Camp Confederate Soldiers' Home Applications for Admission* for John A. McManaway, p5. This is accessible in the Library of Virginia digital holdings.
[85] Even if the company and regiment are not readily identified it can often be ascertained through additional research by identifying the unit of the white person listed as the supervisor or master.
[86] There were several Confederate Pension Acts in Virginia between 1888 and 1934. The March 14, 1924 Act was specifically for servants. The 1928 Act broadened recognized duties to include performance of guard duty, burying Confederate dead, work in railroad shops, blacksmith shops or hospitals. See Ervin Jordan, <u>Black Confederates and Afro-Yankees in Civil War Virginia</u>, (Charlottesville, Va: UVA Press) p198-199.

Confederate dead, work in the railroad shops, blacksmith shops and hospitals. Nevertheless, the pensions were in recognition of *wartime* service to the Confederacy.[87]

As important was the black Confederate's post-war recognition by white counterparts. A large number of period photographs (many now generally available on the internet) made at various United Confederate Veteran (UCV) reunions show black Confederates. Many were often reported on in the local press. The point being these black Confederates were considered wartime comrades whose company and presence at UCV reunions were desired and likely encouraged.

The Minutes of the 18th National Reunion of the United Confederate Veterans reported,

> *"A good many of the negro veterans have arrived, and a special place has been set aside for them. Most [of] these served as bodyguards during the war but a few of them were enlisted soldiers who bore their muskets beside their masters. They are being well cared for and treated as their faithfulness deserves."*[88]

This little paragraph, written by a Confederate veteran in 1908 calls them *veterans* and recognizes some as *enlisted soldiers.* A subsequent paragraph describes the reunion's grand parade in which 8,000 veterans participated and was viewed by 200,000 people:
"From the dear old commander-in-chief, Clement A. Evans, who led his army forth, sitting upon a black steed and spreading all around him the influence of his radiant face, to the black old negro who carried the chicken in his arms, every veteran realized the warm place which he occupies in the heart of the young South...They were given an ovation that kings never knew; not the honor of fear, but the outburst of love."[89]

Elsewhere it was noted, *"Conspicuous in the throng was a number of former slaves... [they] were cheered throughout the march."* One black Confederate *"received an ovation as he passed down the lines carrying a tremendous banner on which was inscribed: 'Aged 78. Served four years for the Confederacy. Governor Comer aint'gin me no pension yet.'"* The paragraph continued, *"Another venerable colored man walked arm in arm with a white comrade who [on] frequent intervals fanned him with one of the old-style 'turkey tails'...The number of colored heroes marching in the procession elicited much comment."*[90]

---

[87] Even the NAACP made note of some of the Confederate pensions in 1921. It was reported in *The Crisis* (Vol. 22, No. 4, p183 and Vol. 22, No. 6, p274) that Tennessee Governor Alfred Taylor of Tennessee signed into law "a bill to pension Negroes who served in the Confederate Army". It was later reported at least 47 such veterans were receiving $10 a month.

[88] *Minutes of the Eighteenth Reunion*, United Confederate Veterans, Birmingham, AL, June 9-11, 1908, p14-16

[89] Ibid, Minutes, p18-19

[90] Ibid, Minutes, p27-28.

Because of their Confederate wartime service, these men of color, in the 1908 Jim Crow South, are described as *veterans* and *heroes* by white Confederate veterans.

These men were also noted at regional reunions as well. *The Houston Daily Post* reported on a Nick Blaine, "a colored Confederate soldier" who made "quite a speech" at the John Johnston Camp UCV reunion in Mexia, Texas on 2 August 1901.[91] The *Times Dispatch* of Richmond reported on "George Washington Cole, colored, of King George, a Confederate veteran, who served and fought the entire four years" who attended a Fredericksburg reunion in 1910. He was 80 years of age.[92]

A white-haired man named Smith Woods, of Dyersburg, Tennessee, was in attendance at the 1912 Macon, Georgia UCV reunion and reportedly had attended many such reunions. According to the report, "Smith had his breast decorated with medals and badges presented by his white friends and received as much attention as any of the high officers in their gold braid and fixings. And it is a cinch he was the proudest man on the grounds." Smith said he served under Nathan Bedford Forrest who called him 'Cap'n' [Captain] . The report said, "Smith has been attending Reunions for years and is known to a great many of the veterans, lots of whom gravely salute him and give him his title of 'Captain' when they meet him."[93]

There is evidence to suggest that black Confederate veterans also held their own reunions. One 1889 news report stated:

> "At Jacksonville, Ala., Saturday last there was a unique reunion. The colored men who served in the confederate army in various capacities, as teamsters, servants, cooks, &c., had a 'confederate reunion'. The day was celebrated with a barbecue, speeches, and base ball. (sic) At a meeting a debate was held on the

COLORED CONFEDERATE REUNION.

The announcement sent out from Jacksonville, Ala., last Saturday of a reunion of colored Confederates at that place was a matter of considerable surprise to many persons, inasmuch as it is not generally known that colored men were enlisted in the military service of the Confederacy. For active service as soldiers of the line they were not, though a large number in the aggregate were carried into the army by officers and many wealthy privates as body servants, cooks, etc., and during the last year of the war many were enlisted as teamsters, artisans, and in other capacities as laborers, thus relieving a like number of whites who were sent to the ranks. During the last months of the conflict the question of arming the negroes capable of performing active service was seriously discussed and virtually determined upon by the authorities at Richmond, but it met with such a remonstrance from the army, the officers and men in many instances openly declaring that they would lay down their arms and quit the service before they would serve in line with or command the negro troops, that it was abandoned, and with the exception of cases mentioned negroes were not regularly enlisted in the armies of the Confederacy. Nevertheless the negroes of the south performed a more important service for the Confederacy by remaining at home and faithfully laboring to support not only the white women and children while the men were in the army, but to maintain the armies in the field, and herein lies the secret, no less than in any of the boasted characteristics of the southrons, of their ability to hold out on the field so long. So that, in point of fact the negroes of the south during the war were just as much Confederates as the most loyal and enthusiastic whites, and re-unions among them commemorative of the part they played in the great drama are equally as fitting and appropriate, if they choose to do so, as among the whites.

---

[91] *The Houston Daily Post,* 3 August 1901, p5, 'Joe Johnston Camp U.C.V."
[92] *The [Richmond] Times Dispatch,* 20 Nov 1910, image 3 of Color Section, Sunday edition, 'A Colored Confederate Veteran'
[93] <u>Confederate Veterans of the State of Oklahoma</u>, (McAlester, OK: Oklahoma Division of the United Confederate Veterans) 1913. 'Faithful Old Negro in Evidence', p73

question of whether the democratic or the republican party was the best friend to the negro. Good humor prevailed throughout."[94]

Another report added to the story, *"The negroes who were in the war and heard the bullets whistle are very proud of it."*[95]

A 1917 news item from the *Washington Herald* reported on a special church service "in honor of the Colored United Confederate Veterans".[96]

Black Confederate veterans participated at memorial services as well. The NAACP's *The Crisis* noted in 1911 "a Confederate veteran participating in the unveiling of a statue to Jefferson Davis is partly of Negro blood and partly white".[97] At the unveiling of the Lee Monument in Richmond, it was reported:

> *" 'Col' Tarleton Alexander, over eighty years old, a colored confederate who served from alpha to omega of the rebellion and surrendered at Appomattox, was on the streets in the morning wearing numerous badges and souvenirs presented by the veteran confederates as decorations of honor."*[98]

The unveiling and dedication of the Confederate statue in Charlottesville involved a parade and included "colored Confederate cooks and body servants" who marched in line just before the R.T.W. Duke Camp, Sons of [Confederate] Veterans.[99]

Booker T. Washington suggested wartime service helped change white attitudes. He noted:

> *"The Southern soldiers also altered their attitude when they discovered in black skin courage and character worthy of honor and respect...On both sides of the firing line, the colored men proved themselves to be friends of the white race. They shrank from no danger, however great; they refused no task, however difficult; but worked, and fought, and died without complaint....The armies on both sides of the conflict were indebted to the black man as friend and as fighter."*[100]

---

[94] This event was widely reported. See *The [Washington] Evening Star*, 3 September 1889, p7; 'A Colored Confederate Reunion'; see also *Rock Island (IL) Daily Argus*, 3 Sept 1889, p2; 'Colored Confederate Reunion'; *Wichita Daily Eagle*, 5 Sept 1889, p4; 'Colored Confederate Reunion'.
[95] *The Anderson (SC) Intelligencer,* 5 Sept 1889, p2, 'Colored Confederates'
[96] *The Washington Herald*, 9 June 1917, p4. Last paragraph under 'Churches Continue Patriotic Services'.
[97] *The Crisis*, Vol 1, No. 6, 1911, p26, a paragraph in 'Color Hysteria' by Oswald Garrison Villard. The statue was unveiled in New Orleans on 22 February.
[98] *The [Washington] Evening Star*, 31 May 1890, p5, 'Richmond Aftermath: Some Features of the Lee Statue Unveiling Not Covered by the Press Reports'.
[99] *The Washington Herald*, 6 May 1909, p10, 'Shaft is Unveiled: Confederate Statue Erected at Charlottesville'
[100] Ibid, Washington, Douglas, p234-2325

A news item in the Norfolk *Virginian Pilot* on the 1900 Confederate Reunion there noted:

> "Several old negroes will be at the Reunion of Confederate Veterans in this city May 30-31, June 1-2-3. There is no stranger sight in history than these faithful colored servants accompanying the master to the field, waiting on him, fighting with him, bearing home his letters and personal trinkets when dead."[101]

The ladies of the United Daughters of the Confederacy (UDC) even presented honors. In 1904, Preston (Pete) Roberts of Collierville, Tennessee was presented a Southern Cross of Honor by the UDC. According to the news report, "This is the first time in the history of the southern camps that this honor has been accorded a negro, and the fact that there are a hundred or so white men ready to endorse his application is proof sufficient of his worthiness."[102] Roberts was a camp servant and cook in the command of Nathan Bedford Forrest. In his veteran capacity, he was in Company A, First Tennessee Regiment. He served four years in the war.

According to the news report, when Roberts observed a ceremony where 19 of his comrades received the UDC Southern Cross of Honor, he asked permission to apply for one. The report states:

> "Permission was not only readily given by the women, but the men present who knew "Uncle Pete" – and there are few who do not know him – immediately volunteered to furnish the indorsement which is necessary before any veteran is qualified to receive one. The application has been forwarded and when the next presentation of crosses is made the rebel negro will stand in line with the men by whose side he served...".

PRESTON ROBERTS.
(Colored Veteran Who Is to Receive Southern Cross of Honor.)

Artist Drawing of Preston Roberts (1904)

The report states Roberts was:

> "not a regularly enlisted soldier, but, to use his own expression, was 'one of the most importantest men in the army'. He supervised 75 negro cooks "with money and

---

[101] *Virginian-Pilot*, 3 March 1900, p11
[102] *The Richmond Planet*, 12 March 1904, p2, 'Cross for a Negro: Confederates to Honor Veteran Who Was a Slave'. The *Planet* was an African-American newspaper circulating from 1882 to 1938.

authority to buy whatever was needed for his mess, and also to 'raise' the rations anyway, whether they could be bought or not."[103]

The bond between black and white veterans appears to have been strong in many regions. A 15 June 1900 news item in the *New York Times* was headlined *'Negro Confederate Veteran Shot'* and reported on the shooting deaths of two black men, Henson Williams and his son William. The report said the men were:

"shot dead from ambush in Brazos County, while they were plowing in a field. Officers are searching for a white man who is believed to have shot them. The elder Williams fought through the civil war as a Confederate soldier and made such a good record that he was a full member of the Confederate Veterans' camp at Milliken. The old white Confederate soldiers are enraged at the assassination and threaten vengeance on the assassin, when captured."[104]

Virginia's 1902 Constitution

Another interesting observation is the sometime recognition of black Confederate service as justification for voting following passage of the 1902 Virginia Constitution. The new Constitution was orchestrated by Democrats to "legally" disfranchise black voters and working class whites who could not pay a poll tax, did not pay a property tax, or were too illiterate to explain the Constitution to registrars. All Civil War veterans and their sons were exempt from these requirements by law but in practice there were attempts to lock out white ex-Confederates who were paupers or hospital inmates as well as some black ex-Confederates.[105]

The Democrat machine appointed registrars at local examining boards to discriminate and reduce the voter rolls thus ensuring political power. Local registration boards, which usually included one Confederate veteran, wielded great authority but rulings appear inconsistent across the state. For example, African-Americans Samuel Davis of Norfolk and Richard Cook of Gloucester had regularly enlisted and served in the Confederate Navy and this service was recognized by

THE (Richmond) *TIMES*
17 October 1902

---

[103] Ibid, *Richmond Planet.*
[104] *New York Times*, June 15, 1900.
[105] **Encyclopedia Virginia**, *Virginia Constitutional Convention* (1901-1902)

the registrar. At least 21 "colored" voters registered under the "soldiers' clause".[106]

Addison Armstead of Luray, a laborer on breastworks, was disqualified and contested the registrar decision in court. His appeal was rejected.[107] In Wytheville however, Circuit Judge Robert C. Jackson approved the appeals of a white ex-Confederate pauper and a black ex-Confederate. According to the press report, "Another applicant who was allowed to register was a colored man who drove an ordnance wagon for the Confederate government".

Once established, the Democrat machine used its political muscle to prevent black Confederate veterans from receiving Confederate pensions from the state. Virginia Attorney General Samuel W. Williams had ruled against a black pension application and Pension Clerk E.L.C. Scott likewise turned down many such applications. Williams issued an official opinion that "a negro cannot be a pensioner because he could not be a Confederate soldier." This happened after the last black Confederate pensioner, identified as a "colored Hospital Guard", died in Hanover County.[108] The Attorney General ruled the pensions could only be paid "to men who served in the army or navy as regular members of the forces".[109]

The news report states the Attorney General, the Auditor "and everybody else connected with the matter, wishes that pensions might be paid to some colored people. Their services on the field with their masters, and at home with the women and children, are well remembered, and today many of them live in poverty. But there seems no warrant in law for allowing a pension claim from a member of that race."

A COLORED CONFEDERATE?

NORFOLK, VA., October 2—(Special). The only colored Confederate soldier or seaman admitted to registration here as such was Samuel Davis, who served in the Confederate navy.

Richmond Dispatch, 4 Oct 1902

One of the side effects of the ruling is that it appears to have removed the black Confederate's eligibility – as a former Confederate 'soldier' -- to be a voter. It would take several years – 1924 -- before the pension portion of this ruling was remedied with pensions established for black Confederates who served in support roles.[110]

---

[106] *Richmond Dispatch*, 3 October 1902, p1, "A Colored Confederate?"; Ibid, 4 October 1902, p1, 'That Confederate Negro'; see also *The Times* (Richmond), 4 October 1902, 'The Registration and Its Effects: A Colored Giant Registers as a Sailor in the Confederate Navy'
[107] *Richmond Dispatch*, 4 October 1902. p1, 'Turned Old Negro Down'. The report does not identify the outcome of Armstead's protest; see also *The Times* (Richmond), 4 October 1904, 'Employed on Breastworks'; see also *The Times* (Richmond) 11 October 1902, 'Must Fight As Well As Dig: Addison Armistread Cannot Vote Under Old Soldier Clause'
[108] The report states, "The Hanover pensioner helped to guard Confederate hospitals in Richmond and was a member of a sort of negro home guard, which drilled in the Capitol Square." The individuals name is not given.
[109] See http://www.ag.virginia.gov/Opinions%20and%20Legal%20Resources/OPINIONS/index.html; According to the current Attorney General website, "Official opinions represent the attorney general's analysis of current law…They are not rulings and do not create new law nor do they change existing law."
[110] There is no 'record copy' of the Attorney General's opinion in the holdings of the Library of Virginia and State Archives (LVA). According to LVA, the Annual Report of the Attorney General to the

Virginia's Black Confederates

Contractors

Critics of the black Confederate may also argue many of the 'free men of color' working for the Confederacy were contractors providing services therefore not 'soldiers' and not wartime veterans. This criticism can be easily dismissed by the very practice of the United States government. Public Law 95-202, Section 401, authorized 'veteran' status of civilian persons or contractual organizations providing critical wartime services during major conflicts.[111]

While centered on the World Wars and Korea, those civilians covered were recognized as having performed "active military service". The services were deemed valuable to their respective war efforts establishing recognition as war veterans.[112] Using U.S. Government criteria, the same case can be made for the black Confederate – their military services were valuable to their war effort and therefore it is appropriate they be recognized as having performed "active military service" and called 'veterans'.

There is still extensive work to do in identifying and transcribing wartime rosters containing the names of black Confederates performing duties for the Quartermaster, Medical and Engineer Departments. With that in mind, those wartime and post-war primary source records that are readily available today make it plain that the black Confederate is fact, not fiction. While primarily support personnel, existing records show many men of color were enlisted and mustered into combat units at the company and regimental level and suffered the same fates of many combatants: hunger, disease, life in prisoner of war camps and violent death in battle. Many more served in rear area military organizations.

The public record is clear that these men and women, and in some cases children, worked for the Confederate war effort. Some of that work was voluntary and some involuntary. Free men and women of color were paid for such services. Many former slaves and free men of color received post-war pensions in recognition of military services performed in support of

---

Governor of Virginia for the Year 1912 (p10) indicates "a great many" Attorney General opinions "were given in writing and many more orally, to the Auditor of Public Accounts, and other officers at the seat of government…". An Archives search did not turn up any unpublished opinions or ruling from the state attorney general to the Auditor for Public Accounts. This information was provided to the author by Sarah Huggins, Library Reference Services at the Library of Virginia in October 2013.

[111] See P.L. 95-202, approved November 23, 1977 (91 Stat 1433) at http://www.ssa.gov/OP_Home/comp2/F095-202.html for basic law.; see also http://edocket.access.gpo.gov/2006/06-4671.htm, the Federal Register, 19 May 2006 (Vol 71, Number 97) for updated organizations listed under 38 CFR Part 3, Department of Veterans Affairs, *Individuals and Groups Considered to Have Performed Active Military, Naval or Air Service*; see also http://edocket.access.gpo.gov/cfr_2011/julqtr/pdf/38cfr3.7.pdf, Department of Veterans Affairs, 38 CFR, para. 7 for full list. Organizations recognized include the Quartermaster Corps Female Clerical Employees serving with the American Expeditionary Forces and civilian American Field Service ambulance drivers and stretcher bearers in World War I. Those from World War II included merchant seamen and employees of various civilian airlines to include pursers, ground crew and flight crew, Women Air Service Pilots (WASPs) and all members of the American Volunteer Group (AVG), better known as 'the Flying Tigers'. Excluding the handful of Flying Tiger pilots, the rest were 'support personnel'.

[112] The major civilian airlines supported operations overseas. These included Pan American, TWA, American Airlines and others. Some personnel were presented military decorations such as the Bronze Star Medal.

the Confederate Army. They were a critical part of the Confederate war machine. They performed duties in wartime and in government employ making their contributions akin to "active military service".

They may not have been infantry but, using primary source documents it can be argued that they were "soldiers" in all but name, for they were doing "soldier's work". They were without a doubt 'veterans', recognized and referred to as such by white contemporaries and state governments in the post-war period.

'Black Confederates' were not myth. They existed. They are fact.

Levi Miller

Levi Miller

Levi Miller was profiled in the Library of American History[113] article on the 'Great Reunion' of blue and gray at Gettysburg in 1913.

Born a slave in Rockbridge County, Va on 9 January 1836, Miller became a preacher with reported gifts of oratory and "held in high respect by all who knew him, as a man whose life and practice were in accord with his profession."

Miller was hired as a servant for Captain J.J. McBridge of Co. C, 5th Texas Infantry. Miller was "in all the fighting around Richmond in 1862". McBride was wounded at 2nd Manassas and Miller nursed him back to health. Both were at Fredericksburg and the Suffolk Campaign.

During the Gettysburg Campaign Miller was encouraged to desert "but he sturdily refused and remained an ardent Confederate to the end." Miller went with his unit to the west participating in Chickamauga, Chattanooga and Knoxville returning to Virginia in early 1864. At Spotsylvania Miller demonstrated extraordinary bravery crossing, under enemy fire, 200 yards of open field to take rations to his company. According to Capt. J.E. Anderson, Co. C, 5th Texas Infantry, as Union forces were preparing an attack, Miller "asked for a gun and ammunition, which were given to him…a furious charge was made. Levi Miller stood by my side, and man never fought harder and better than he did when the enemy tried to cross our little breastworks…no one used his bayonet with more skill and effect than he." Miller was enrolled as a full member of the company afterwards.

---

[113] **Ellis, Edward Sylvester. Library of American History (Cincinnati, Ohio: The Jones Brothers Publishing Company) 1900. Volume 7, 'Reunion of the Blue and the Gray', p201-218. The article focused on the 50th Anniversary Gettysburg encampment in July 1913.**

Mosby's Black Confederates

By Greg Eanes

At least four African-Americans supporting the Confederate war effort with Colonel John S. Mosby received pensions and one other, Aaron Burton, is featured in several post-war memoirs from Mosby and members of his command. Two others are identified in post-war memoirs by first name only. Additionally, the several memoirs written by members of this command suggest they were routinely assisted by African-Americans, both free and slave.

Aaron Burton
When John S. Mosby went to war, he was accompanied by Aaron Burton, a servant and coachman to A.D. Mosby, father of the soon-to-be famed guerilla leader. Burton reportedly remained with Mosby throughout the entire war. He is mentioned prominently in Mosby's published Memoirs and as well as letters. There's also a photo of him in later life published in the Memoirs. He is also written about in the post-war memoirs of one of Mosby's men.

In a comment in a December 9, 1862 letter to his sister Pauline Mosby suggests Aaron might have participated in his earliest raid as a partisan. In late November Mosby took nine men on a reconnoitre around Manassas. The small squad surprised and charged at an equal number of Federals who ran and ended up stampeding the entire regiment "thinking all of Stuart's cavalry were on them". In commenting on this activity in general terms, Mosby wrote, "Aaron thinks himself quite a hero, though he does not want to come again in such disagreeable proximity to a bombshell."[114]

AARON BURTON (COLORED), AGED 84 YEARS
An old servant and coachman of A. D. Mosby, who went through the entire Civil War as body-servant to his son, Colonel John S. Mosby. Taken in 1898

Apparently Aaron was keen on ensuring the famed Confederate partisan always had a good horse, ready to ride. Recalled John W. Munson, "When we started on a scout or a raid, [Mosby's] old colored groom, Aaron, would take up from pasture one or two of his horses and begin to get them into shape for him by the time he returned. Thus he always had a fresh horse to depend on."[115]

---

[114] John Singleton Mosby, The Memoirs of Colonel John S. Mosby (Boston: Little, Brown and Company) 1917, p146-147. Letter to his sister Pauline dated 9 December 1862.
[115] John W. Munson, Reminiscences of a Mosby Guerilla (New York: Moffatt, Yard and Company), 1906, p31.

Virginia's Black Confederates

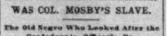

Richmond Planet profile of Aaron Burton. The *Planet* was an African-American newspaper circulating from 1883-1938

Munson wrote, *"Aaron accompanied Mosby in the regular service before the Command was organized. There was a fight near Barbee's cross-roads in Fauquier [C]ounty in which Mosby was engaged, and old Aaron accompanied him at an entirely safe distance, leading one of his extra horses. He sat down on the porch of an old house to listen to the noise of the firing, 'sniffing the battle from afar', and waiting for his master to come back and give him orders. Suddenly, and without warning, a misdirected shell swept high over the old building and burst in the air, a part of it striking the roof and scattering splinters all over Aaron. He jumped upon his horse, leading the extra and much needed animal, galloped away and did not stop, or make any perceptible slackening of his speed, until he reached the old Mosby plantation, about one hundred and fifty miles away. It was three months before he could be persuaded to return to the army."*[116]

Munson's recollections suggest Aaron was treated as a regular member of their little band and Aaron, as the servant of the commander, felt he was himself of some importance. At one place that hid Mosby and some of his men was an Irishman named Lat Ryan who worked the farm. Munson recalled Lat and Aaron spent most of their time "fussing". Munson said Aaron "was always the boss wherever he was living, and who ordered Lat around all day and every day."[117] In a letter to his sister early in the war when Mosby was still a junior officer, he wrote his sister, "Aaron considers himself next in command to Captain Jones..."[118]

Aaron was also on the receiving end of practical jokes by Munson who recalled one occasion. Munson said, *"Once, as a joke, Johnny Edmonds and I galloped into the barnyard where Aaron was currying one of the Colonel's horses and closed the big gate behind us. We fired our pistols and yelled to him to look out for the Yankees. Without waiting an instant he mounted his horse bare back, jumped the gate and flew for the hills. At each jump we fired a pistol and yelled to him to stop, but he kept on and we did not see him again till next morning. He never quite forgave us when he found out the facts."*[119]

---

[116] Ibid, p33.
[117] Ibid, p244
[118] Ibid, Mosby, Memoirs, p89. Letter to his sister Liz dated 17 September 1861 from "Camp near Fairfax Court House".
[119] Ibid, 32-33

Aaron apparently helped nurse the wounded during the 1862 battle of Manassas. Mosby said he was "doctoring the sick men during the battle. He is a good deal thought of in the company". The "sick" men were covered with blankets and shivered during the artillery bombardments. When they weren't shivering they would "raise up and ask Aaron, 'Haven't you got a few more of those corn cakes?'" suggesting Aaron also worked as a cook.[120]

Aaron became something of a celebrity in old age and was remembered his death. The 23 December 1902 issue of the *Richmond Times Dispatch* contained the following obituary:

AARON BURTON DEAD
New York, December 22—(Special)-From the residence of his daughter, Rosa Hamilton, there was held to-day the funeral of Aaron Burton, who during the "civil" war was the body servant of Colonel John S. Mosby, the great Confederate cavalry raider. "Father Burton," as he was known, was with the great guerrilla chieftain in many raids, and although nearly a hundred years of age, his mind was fresh with memories of those stirring events. Richard T. Smith, of Brooklyn, will publish Burton's memoirs, they having been dictated to him.

The funeral services were conducted by Re. William T. Dixon, pastor of the Concord Baptist Church of Christ, of which the deceased was a member.

Burton was born in Charlottesville, Va., and was the slave of Colonel Mosby's father. When the Colonel determined to organize his cavalry command, he selected Aaron as his body servant.

The colonel had the greatest confidence in his body servant, and he was frequently left in charge of all booty that was captured from the Union soldiers, while the cavalry raiders went out on other expeditions.

The high estimate in which he was held by Mosby was the same as those of recent times who knew Burton. He was a familiar character in the vicinity of Princeton and Willoughby streets, and was to be found on all sunshiny days seated upon the stoop of the house in which he lived. He was the perfection of politeness, and if even a child said "Good morning, Father Burton," this old fellow would lift his hat.

Mosby did not forget Aaron in his old days, and frequently sent him checks for substantial sums of money to keep him housed.

Burton came to Brooklyn about seven years ago to live with his daughters. He had three of them living in Brooklyn, and he lived at the home of each of them, dividing the time about equally among them. He is survived by four daughters and two sons. The interment will be at Evergreen Cemetery.

---

[120] Ibid, Mosby, p91-92 and Note 1 on page 92.

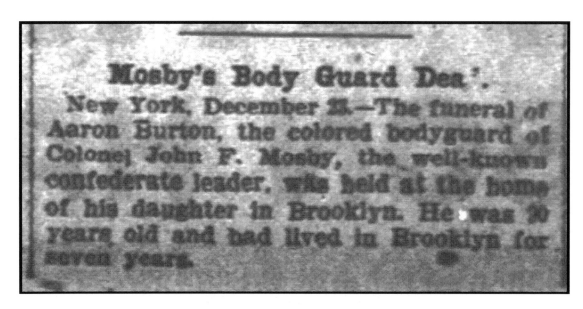

DEATH NOTICE FROM *ATLANTA JOURNAL CONSTITUION*

Other Servants and Assistance

Other African-American servants were mentioned in the memoirs of Mosby's men. One John Scott makes mention of Juniper, servant of the Reverend Adolphus Adam Gog, the battalion chaplain. On at least one occasion, Juniper carried a message through enemy lines.[121] Whether or not this was a routine mission was not stated. Mosby's surgeon wrote of his servant named Henry, relating the first time Henry saw Union prisoners of war. Henry is said to have remarked, ""If [they] dress like [the rest] of us you couldn't [tell] [them from] our [soldiers]."

There are also unnamed slaves and servants who helped Mosby and his men during localized combat actions. In one incident, a Confederate describes how he and another soldier and a negro rode towards a fight in an ox cart. On December 21, 1863, Mosby is wounded and left for dead by some Union cavalrymen. Two young slaves put him in an ox cart and helped move him to safety.[122]

In another incident in November 1863, Mosby's Surgeon Dr. Aristides Monteiro, Colonel Welby Carter, formerly of the 1st Va Cavalry, Colonel Joseph Blackwell, Mosby's Chief of Staff, Adjutant Willie Mosby (the Commander's little brother), a wounded officer named Grogan and a 20-year-old named Waller, also a relative of Jeff Davis, chose to remain overnight at Glen Welby near Upperville. While sleeping, the house was raided by Union cavalry and the men inside tried reacted by running with their clothes in their hands in an effort to escape. Willie Mosby and Dr. Monteiro were led by "a young negro girl" to a safe place on the roof while another servant helped the wounded Waller get to the top of "an old

---

[121] **Partisan Life with Colonel John S. Mosby** by John Scott of Fauquier (London: Sampson Low, Son and Marston) 1867, p. 167
[122] **Mosby's Rangers** by James Joseph Williamson, Co. A (New York: Ralph B. Kenyon, Publisher) 1896, p62; 328-331.

Virginia's Black Confederates

fashioned wardrobe" to hide. Colonel Blackwell managed to get out of the house running naked through a field, pursued for some distance by Federals before they gave up the chase. He was later aided by a free man of color.[123]

Virginia Confederate Pensions
Virginia Confederate Pension applications identify four men who served with Mosby's command. Two were servants, one was a hostler and one was a cook. In at least several cases, the children of Confederate soldiers served as witnesses on the applications.

Willie Mosby, Adjutant

John B. Withers of Culpeper, Virginia was only eight years old when he began service in 1861 or 1862. His master was William Bussey, a close friend of Colonel Mosby. Bussey's daughter wrote a letter support Withers claim stating, "I recall that Colonel John S. Mosby and my father were great friends and the Colonel used to come to our house very often and he asked my father to let John go in the Army and assist the cook and he consented and John went and helped the cook under Colonel Mosby." Based on this statement, it appears that Withers may have been an assistant to Aaron Burton. Withers said, "I assisted the cook by washing dishes, preparing vegetables, carrying water and wood, and doing other small jobs, for Col. Mosby's company. I believe this should be considered serving the Army." He served three years before he returned home.[124]

George F. Harrison of Fairfax County was also about nine years old when he supported Mosby primarily in helping to man relay stations. Harrison said he was a helper and hostler taking "care of horses for Col. John Mosby and his officers." Enlisting in 1863, Harrison left at the end of the war. In written statements, it is determined that Harrison's job was to care for horses at various points in the Bull Run mountains "where they would be safe from raids of the Federal army". The horses were reserves "kept at the request and direction of Colonel Mosby" and used by Mosby and his scouts. This was a military duty that facilitated the rapid movement of Mosby's rangers.[125] Among the individuals instrumental in helping facilitate Harrison's pension application was Fairfax County Commissioner of Revenue James U. Kincheloe whose father was Sgt. W.S. Kincheloe (1836-1905) of Company H, 43rd Battalion of Partisan Rangers and whose uncle was Captain James Cornelius Kincheloe (1833-1889). The Kincheloe family plantation was More Hill in Fairfax County near Bull Run.

---

[123] Ibid, Partisan Life by John Scott of Fauquier (London: Sampson Low, Son and Marston) 1867, p155-156; Mosby's Rangers by James Joseph Williamson, Co. A (New York: Ralph B. Kenyon, Publisher) 1896, p107-110 and War Reminiscences by the Surgeon of Mosby's Command by Aristides Monteiro (Richmond: C.N. Williams, Printer) 1890 2nd Edition, p71-81 and 89-90.
[124] Virginia Confederate Pension Application of John B. Withers, Library of Virginia Digital files. The pension was filed in 1932.
[125] Virginia Confederate Pension Application of George F. Harrison, Library of Virginia Digital files. The pension was filed in 1935.

Carter Ford was about 23 or 24 years of age when he served with Mosby's command as the body servant to Captain William Smith. When Smith was killed in combat, Ford became the servant of Lt. Colonel William H. Chapman. Ford filed for and was granted a pension in 1927 at the age of 89.[126]

Morris Wright was 84 when he filed for a pension in 1932 which would place him at the age of 14 when he began service in 1862. He received a pension for service as a body servant and laborer. Initially serving under Mosby's younger brother and Adjutant William Mosby, he identified his owner as the family patriarch Alfred D. Mosby. At some point, Wright was transferred to serve at the salt works near Wytheville. Wright says he left service "after the surrender [and] Col. [John N.] Clarkston[127] disbanded the men employed under him at Wytheville, Va and order them home.[128] The Oath of Resident Witnesses testifying to Wright's service was signed by John S. Mosby's oldest son, Beverly C. Mosby (1860-1946) and Beverly Mosby Coleman (1899-1993), also of Washington, D.C. where Wright was living. Coleman was the son of Mosby's daughter Victoria and her husband Eugene W. Coleman.

'A Faithful Soldier to the Rebellion'

The following is an excerpt from a St. Louis *Republican* (pro-Union) editorial of 4 November 1864 republished in the 28 December 1864 issue of Richmond's *Daily Dispatch*.

"So far, we have only viewed the different interests which prevail on the respective sides. But there is another influence at work upon the Southern slave tending to make him play the part of a faithful soldier to the rebellion. It is that relation, affection and sympathy between himself and his master. Its existence was once generally discredited in the North, in spite of manifold proofs; but the war has furnished too many notorious incidents of the devotion of a majority of the slaves to allow it longer to be doubted. Thousands of slaves follow their masters, be they in the ranks or at the head of armies, through the dangers of the battlefield, and many have laid down their lives as the price of the temerity dictated by their love. During Early's last invasion of Maryland, General McCausland owed his life to the valor of his faithful body servant, who came to the rescue of his master when hard pressed by Averill's troops, and relieved him by seriously wounding the Federal captain at the head of the attacking party. General McCausland is represented as the roughest of Virginia's cavaliers, yet he binds the heart of his lowly slave by the ties of affection that cannot be stifled by the dangers of battle. There are many such masters and slaves in the South."

---

[126] Virginia Confederate Pension Application of Carter Ford, Library of Virginia Digital files.
[127] Clarkston was the commander of the Confederate States salt works at Wytheville. He had earlier served as an aid to General Henry Wise and Colonel of the 3rd Regiment of the Virginia State Line. He became Superintendent of the Salt Works by mid-1863 and on 8 March 1864 was elected by the Senate of Virginia to serve as the Superintendent for another year starting 30 March 1865. See Compiled Service Record for Colonel John N. Clarkson, 3rd Regiment, Virginia State Line; see also the Journal of the Virginia State Senate.
[128] Virginia Confederate Pension Application of Morris Wright, Library of Virginia Digital files.

The Black Experience In the Wilson-Kautz Raid

By Greg Eanes

Was the role of the African-American in the American Civil War that of loyal servant or runaway slave? Was he a detached victim, bystander or active participant? Federal or Confederate? The reality is that it was all of these. No single event provides a better 'snapshot' of that participation than a study of black experience during the June 1864 Wilson-Kautz Raid.

A footnote to Union General U.S. Grant's Petersburg Campaign, the Wilson-Kautz Raid (June 22-July 1, 1864) was launched in an attempt to cut the South Side Railroad running from Lynchburg to Petersburg and the Richmond and Danville Railroad operating between those two cities. The two railroads formed a junction at Burkeville. Both were vital supply lines to Confederate General Robert E. Lee's Army of Northern Virginia then manning defenses around Richmond and Petersburg.

In order to avoid a siege, Grant sought to destroy the vital rail links to the city and other rail lines that serviced Lee's Army. Union General 'Black Dave' Hunter's raid on Lynchburg, Phillip H. Sheridan's Trevilian Station Raid and the Wilson-Kautz Raid targeting the railroads in Virginia's heartland were a significant part of that effort.

Federal General James H. Wilson commanded a 5,500-man expedition consisting of his cavalry division and the cavalry division of General August V. Kautz along with three batteries of regular U.S. artillery. They traveled through 12 Southside Virginia counties destroying railroads, depots, military supplies and support infrastructure. They were pursued from the beginning by elements of James Dearing and Rufus Barringer's Confederate cavalry brigades. They did battle June 23 at Nottoway Court House and skirmished daily but it wasn't until June 25 that the Federals were stopped by 'old men and young boys' at the Staunton River Bridge. At that point the Union raiders began a cross-country retreat resulting in the pillage and plunder of the citizens in their path until finally stopped at the battles of Sappony Church and Ream's Station on June 29-30.

While a great number of Southside Virginia slaves saw the raiders as liberators and attempted to flee to freedom, analysis reveals an even greater number remained at their Southside Virginia homes. Some are even documented as having defended those homes.

-Soldiers in the Field-

African-Americans were involved in the Confederate effort to defend the railroads and the Staunton River Bridge. The 5th North Carolina Cavalry of Barringer's Brigade played a critical role in the pursuit of the Wilson-Kautz raiders practically from the beginning, engaging them at Nottoway Court House, at the Staunton River Bridge and continuing the chase through southern Virginia to be in on the kill at Ream's Station.

Among the ranks of the 5th North Carolina were black Confederates. Joe Farrington of Company E later received a pension for his services, which did not end until Lee surrendered. Farrington was a body servant or orderly to a man in the company. Also listed in the regimental roster are William H. Dove, Willis Dove, William Lynch and William Rudd. William Dove was listed with the "rank of cook". The others were also listed as cooks. Lynch was later reported missing as of 28 June suggesting he was either killed, captured or ran off with the raiders.[129]

While not regularly enlisted soldiers, there are at least two African-Americans documented at the defense of the Staunton River Bridge. One is known only as Ned. He was a servant to Thomas Watkins Leigh, a 17-year-old among the students of the John Powell Academy that responded to defend the bridge. Another servant is known only as Murry. An older man, Murry worked for the Logan family at Oakville Plantation, about 25 miles from the Staunton River Bridge. Col. Eaton Coleman was at the home recovering from wounds and insisted on going to help defend the bridge. Murry was the man who drove the Colonel to the battlefield and undoubtedly remained for the battle. Their actual duties in the defense of the bridge can only are speculated on however it is fair to assess they played some role during the battle, either manning the defenses or providing some kind of support.[130]

Even more important to the Confederate effort were the unnamed slaves used by Captain Benjamin Farinholt to strengthen the incomplete fortifications at the Staunton River Bridge. When Farinholt, the bridge detachment commander, received word of the raid, he impressed into service area slaves to help complete construction of the defenses. Farinholt also had a body servant and cook named Oscar present at the works.[131]

African-Americans laborers, probably a combination of free and slave, helped repair the rail lines when the raid was over. Many of these men began the work of repair on June 26, the day after the Federal repulse at the Staunton River Bridge. The Richmond and Danville line was reopened for business on July 16, though portions of both railroads were in use before that date. While not carrying combat arms, these laborers served under the supervision of the Confederate Corps of Engineers effectively doing the job of modern day combat engineers and quartermasters. The military value of this work cannot be underestimated, particularly in regards to maintaining supply lines.[132]

---

[129] *Pension Application of Joe Farrington*, Tennessee State Archives; Manarin, Louis H., ed., North Carolina Troops, Vol. II, Cavalry, 1861-1865, A Roster (Raleigh, NC: State Dept of Archives and History), 408-411.

[130] W. Carroll Headspeath, The Battle of the Staunton River Bridge (s.p) 30; Ibid, 27.

[131] Letter, Benjamin Farinholt to wife Lelia, dtd 28 July 2th 1864, from his Headquarters, Staunton Bridge. Copy of letter on file at Staunton River Battlefield State Park. Farinholt returned Oscar to a cousin and notes in the letter the existence but not the names of two other men employed as body servant and cook, respectively.

[132] Farinholt's Report, SHSP, V19, p203; see also *Seventeenth Annual Report of the Richmond and Danville Railroad Company*, 14 Dec. 1864.; see also O.R., correspondence between Lee and Seddon, June 26- 28, 1864.

There were no organized regular black combat troops in either Wilson or Kautz's cavalry divisions. Primary source information reveals there were body servants to Federal officers and at least two unit cooks. The muster rolls 2nd Ohio Cavalry reveal names of Abram Farnsworth, 21, and Samuel Laurey, 24. Both are identified as "colored cooks" with Company D.[133] The body servants of three senior officers were in the raid and later captured. These included an unnamed body servant to Col. John B. McIntosh, First Brigade Commander of Wilson's Division and Henry Washington, age 15, body servant to Col. Samuel J. Crooks of the 22nd New York Cavalry. According to a news report Washington claimed, "To be from Washington City. Henry gives a poor account of his Colonel's valor, and says he ran at the first fire of the Southerners." Also captured was George Washington Lee, body servant to General August V. Kautz, the raid's co-commander.[134]

One former Nottoway slave named Alfred Royal escaped in May 1864 when Kautz led an earlier raid to destroy some railroad bridges in upper Southside Virginia. He apparently attached himself to Kautz's cavalry for some kind of service and returned on the second raid to retrieve his wife.[135]

-Bystanders-

By choosing not to flee or fight, the remainder of the African-American community (like many of their white counterparts) would have to be classified as bystanders though not necessarily disinterested parties.

During the battle of Nottoway Court House 14-year-old Stith Ingram of Edge Hill Plantation "stood in the yard of his home and listened to the roar of the guns and saw the smoke rise from the battle site…Nearby a neighbor was calling his hogs and an old slave who was with the young Ingram was heard to say 'How can he call hogs in these stressful times?'" Another slave in the area named Red Randall was also present but chose to remain rather than ride off with the raiders.[136]

In Charlotte County one of the slave families cooked meals for some of the Federal raiders though they were not inclined to join them. Corporal Wilbur Lunt of the First Maine

---

[133] **Ohio AGO Report**, Unit Roster. The 2nd Ohio Cavalry was in McIntosh's Brigade, Wilson's Division, at Nottoway Court House.

[134] OR, John C. Babcock to Major General Humphreys, July 8, 1864; *New York Times*, July 7, 1864, reprint of a July 4, *Richmond Enquirer* report; August V. Kautz, *Reminiscences of the Civil War.* (Washington, D.C.: Mrs. Austin Kautz, 1936), p81 (manuscript, U.S. Army Center for Military History Collections, Carlisle, Pa.). "Stragglers from my Division followed [Wilson] in his wild flight, my colored servant, George Washington Lee, among the number with my extra horse."

[135] R. Walton Sydnor, *Notes on History of Nottoway County*, (undated manuscript, Nottoway County Library Collections), p10. "Many of the slaves were carried off, some unwillingly. One of my father's slaves, Alfred Royal, went off with [Kautz's May 1864 raid] and came back with the second (Wilson's) in June and took his wife with him"

[136] A.B. Cummins, <u>The Battle of the Grove</u>, (Blackstone, Va: Nottoway Publishing Company, 1961) p19; Randall's recollections were written down in 1927 by Mrs. R.F. Dillard of the Association for the Preservation of Virginia Antiquities under the title, *'An Old Colored Man's Account of the Battle of the Grove'*, (manuscript, Nottoway County Library).

Cavalry recalled, "About midnight [June 24] a family of Negro slaves prepared a turkey supper for us, which was a very welcome change from hardtack and pork."[137]

-Runaways and Faithfuls-

Slaves flocked to the Federal raiders almost as soon as they entered Confederate lines at Prince George Court House. One report says, "All citizens in the vicinity were robbed of their bacon and horses, and such negroes as manifested a willingness to accompany them were gladly welcomed."[138]

The population increased the farther west the Federals traveled. When Kautz's Division arrived in Burkeville in Nottoway County on June 23 one group treated them as liberators. The First Maine Cavalry's Corporal Wilber Lunt recalled, "calling at some Negro quarters adjoining a fine old mansion which had been deserted by its proprietor, and there informing the Negroes that we were Yankees coming to set them free. Some of these colored people were almost white, and I shall never forget their eagerness, coupled with a doubt, which their countenances expressed. They could not believe that a day so long hoped for, and delayed, had at last arrived."[139]

Other slaves from Nottoway also made their way with the raiders. Some went willingly and others reportedly at the point of a gun. At one Nottoway County plantation the overseer gave his slaves permission to leave. The report said, "His Negroes behaved in a most commendable manner. When the enemy was known to be approaching, the overseer told the Negroes they could go with them if they wished, but if they desired to remain they must hide in the woods. They all declared they would stay, and were the first to propose that all the stock, provisions, clothing, valuables &c, on the place should be taken to the woods and hid. This was agreed to, and they went to work with a will, and soon had everything in a safe place, the Negroes remaining with the property night and day until the Yankees left the county…everything was hauled back to the house, and not the smallest article was found missing. It is proper to add that the Yankees took only such Negroes as were willing to go."[140]

---

[137] Edward P. Tobie, <u>History of the First Maine Cavalry, 1861-1865</u>. (Boston: Emery and Henry Press, 1887) p339.

[138] *Richmond Examiner*, June 25, 1864.

[139] Tobie, <u>First Maine Cavalry</u>, p339

[140] *Richmond Examiner*, July 1, 1864; Sydnor, p10; *Richmond Dispatch*, June 30, 1864; see also *Richmond Dispatch*, July 6, 1864. "Many negroes have been captured with these Yankees, who say they were forced from their masters…"; *Petersburg Express* as quoted in the *Galveston Weekly News*, August 17, 1864. "The yankee prisoners said the negroes would follow them…[one slave] once safe in the Confederate lines, flatly denied the assertion, telling his blued robed brethren face to face, 'you made us go, and said you'd kill us if we didn't'."; There are numerous news reports that many of the slaves were "forced" or "kidnapped" from their homes with many of the recaptured slaves being quoted as saying they were forced to accompany the Federals. While the quotes from recaptured slaves are probably accurate, it is likely they were given in an effort to spare themselves harsh treatment upon return to their plantations. According to statements made by Federal officials there was no plan to try to free the slaves though they acknowledged later the disruption of the labor force would probably hinder the harvesting of the wheat crop. This labor disruption however appears only to have been considered as collateral damage.

Virginia's Black Confederates

At another Nottoway location a Federal cavalryman entered a home and began scaring the women when an older black servant "stood it as long as she could then turned upon the intruder and 'gave him a piece of her mind', so that he soon retreated, in some confusion, no doubt."[141]

One slave in the Campbell household in Nottoway aided the Federals during the raid and paid for it with his life. W.R. Turner recorded the story in 1932:

"Tom Campbell's playmate was Mammy Sallie's son, Bob. The boys grew up together and when Tom went to William and Mary College, Bob accompanied him as his body servant. When Tom married and went to live at The Oaks, which his father had built for him, Bob was given him also, and became a trusted servant.

"On account of weak lungs, Mr. Campbell did not serve in the army, but was appointed by the Confederate government to look after the confiscation of Federal property within the bounds of the Confederacy.

"When the news came that Kautz and Wilson's raid was coming through Nottoway, Mr. Campbell had Bob and Griffin, his servants, pack several trunks of valuables and hide them in 'The Horse Trough' woods nearby. When the raiders came, Bob in a moment of weakness was persuaded by the Yankees to tell where the valuables were hidden, and also where his master was. He took them to the trunks, but fortunately Mr. Campbell was not found. Soon the Confederates came and the raiders were driven back.

"Bob was found hiding in the woods and was arrested, tried for his treachery and sentenced to be hanged. Greatly distressed, Mr. Campbell at once went to Richmond to see the Governor seeking a full pardon for Bob.

This the Governor refused to grant.

"At the trial Mr. Campbell himself conducted the defense, and in his closing speech he said, 'Robert, I have tried to save you. I have done my best, Robert. I love you, Robert, Robert, goodbye.' The day Bob was executed, so great was Mr. Campbell's distress that he left home." [142]

In Brunswick, the slave of one man apparently assisted in rounding up Union raiders and sending them off to Libby prison. The Rev. George W. White and his slave Ned helped capture some stragglers from Wilson's column during the latter part of the raid. White wrote, "Dr. E.B. Jones came riding in great haste to my house and called me out.

'Do you know', said he, 'that the Yankees are passing by your big gate?' This gate was 300 yards distant out of view and I had not heard of their passing.

---

[141] **Cummins, Grove**, p18. This incident occurred at Battleview Plantation on June 23 during the battle of Nottoway Court House.
[142] **Old Homes and Families in Nottoway** by W.R. Turner (Blacktone, Va: Nottoway Publishing Company, Inc., 1932) Related to Turner by Fannie Campbell Wilson, a daughter of Thomas Harris Campbell.

'Well, get your horse and arms. Capt. White and I are down here in the field and we ['ll] capture some of them.'

White said, "I called my boy Ned to get my horse and my house servant Judy to get my gun and belt of pistols—never thinking for a moment how completely I was putting my life in the hands of these Negro servants. But I had learned to trust them as I would my children."

White wrote that he and Ned "were soon ready and dashed off to the public road…". White, Ned and several other citizens captured eight cavalrymen in the First D.C. Cavalry. The prisoners were marched off to White's house where they were fed under the guard of White and the watchful eyes of several servants before being sent to Richmond.[143]

Those slaves choosing to escape followed the example of the Federal raiders and took horses and mules (and quite a bit of plunder) from the plantations when they escaped. Further south the slave entourage increased in size and composition including men of all ages, women and children (including babies). This caused problems for the Federal raiders. Some escaped slaves were walking while others rode horses, mules or in carriages. General Kautz noted in his journal, "A large flock of Negroes have joined our column; that encumbers it very much.[144]

Unidentified former Confederate Servant
(*Confederate Veteran*, Vol. 5, p22)

Col. Edmund M. Pope, 8th New York Cavalry recalled, "contrabands to the number of several thousands, crowded the roads and hindered the column…This exodus of Negroes

---

[143] Ervin L. Jordan, Jr., Black Confederates and Afro-Yankees (Charlottesville, Va: University Press of Virginia, 1995), p228; *Memoirs of Rev. George W. White*, manuscript, U.Va. Special Collections, 34-35.
[144] *Journal of August V. Kautz*, June 27, 1864; Ibid, June 24, 1864; see also History of the Eleventh Pennsylvania Cavalry (Philadelphia, Pa: Franklin Printing Company) 1902, 131. "Here and there, frenzied Negroes from the woods and thickets would join the columns and insisted on going with us…".; see also Edmund M. Pope, *Personal Experience: A Side Light of the Wilson Raid*, MOLLUS, MN Vol. 4, p587;. Raleigh (N.C.) *Daily Confederate*, July 11, 1864. "Negroes to the number of three or four hundred were also mounted on the horses and mules stolen from the wealthy section through which they passed.". Note: By the third day, the Union troopers were losing their horses to the heat and hard travel. They would shoot their horses rather than let them be nursed back to health and used by the Confederate cavalry. Horses from the nearby plantation were stolen to replace the ones they lost.

was not desired or encouraged, but it could not be prevented by us without the use of more severe measures than the commander would authorize."[145]

While most of those fleeing with the Federals appear to have gone willingly, there are reports that some were removed forcibly perhaps as a way to disrupt the labor force needed to harvest the early wheat crop or, in some cases, to be the victim of sexual assaults. Federal records indicate several rapes may have occurred on the raid. In one documented incident a party of Federal cavalrymen attempted to kidnap and apparently ravage a black servant woman. According to the report, "They insisted on carrying off a favorite servant woman, but she became so much alarmed that she ran off and hid herself, nor were they able to find her. Upon this they became furious, and threatened to shoot the lady of the house, and the lady visitor before alluded to, if she [the servant woman] were not produced, and it was through the mercy of Providence that they were not shot…"[146]

Other slaves were also victimized by some of the Federal cavalrymen. In Prince George County at the home of a Mrs. Armstrong it was reported, "a large body of the enemy visited their house on Thursday, stole every dust of meal, every pound of bacon, and every fowl on the plantation. They even took a pipe out of the mouth of an aged Negro woman, and seemed to enjoy to smoke from it with high satisfaction." Some of the Federal troopers also reportedly plundered the possessions of slaves.[147] Some of the slaves escaping aided the

---

[145] Pope, *Personal Experience*, p587; see Louis N. Boudrye, Historic Records of the 5th New York Cavalry, First Ira Harris Guard (Albany, NY: S.R. Gray) 1865, p147. "Our column had been reinforced by hundreds of contrabands, who flocked to our banners from the country far and near"; Ibid, 148. "contrabands flocked to us in unusual numbers."; OR, James H. Wilson, *Report to Gen. S. Williams*, July 3, 1864. "The negroes who had joined our columns in large numbers in all parts of the route added greatly to the embarrassment…".; G.G. Benedict, Vermont in the Civil War (Burlington, Vt.: Free Press Association) 1889, 654. "Some 1,200 colored fugitives from slavery had accompanied the column."
[146] *Richmond Examiner*, July 1, 1864. "From Mr. Edward Scott and brother they stole some forty or fifty Negroes…From Mr. Freeman Eppes, of Nottoway, they stole twenty-seven likely Negroes. From Thomas H. Campbell, Esq., they stole all his Negro men but two…They also took all of Mr. [Edward] Stokes' Negro men…"; see also *Richmond Dispatch*, July 9, 1864. "…[a fifth party of raiders] carried off seven young athletic, valuable Negro men, much against their inclination, as is proved by the fact that five of them escaped and returned to their master."; see OR, July 1, 1864 report of Assistant Secretary of War C.A. Dana and diary entry of Union Provost Marshal Brigadier General M.R. Patrick, Army of the Potomac. Patrick said, "It is said that Wilson's raid has been one continuous scene of plunder and burning, and I am afraid, too, that Sheridan's is no better"; These stories continue to be repeated in oral tradition in Southside Virginia. In 2001 in Brunswick County an 80-year-old man is related as often telling of his father's recounting the day the father, a young child during the Wilson raid, watched two Federal soldiers kidnap and ride off with his mother in order to sexually assault her. According to his testimony they pulled her up in the air by her hair, threw her over the neck of one horse and rode off. The man says his father's eyes always filled with tears and his voice cracked with emotion whenever he recounted this story.; Jordan, Black Confederates, p131. Professor Jordan states "Rape is the war's least reported crime."; Ibid, p133. Jordan states, "Black women were the victims of the majority of the war's rapes." Jordan cites several instances Union soldiers attacking African-American women.
[147] *Richmond Examiner*, June 28, 1864; *Richmond Examiner*, July 12, 1864. see the letter to the editor. "Sir: It has been discovered that in the indiscriminate plunder by the Yankee raiders of everything they could lay their hands on including the wearing apparel of both sexes, they have not confined themselves to our white citizens, but have taken clothing from the persons of negroes, allowing neither the fraternity they court, nor, as one would think, other more potent considerations to deter them. You will please give notice, that four uniform coats, two belonging to General Wilson, one to General Custer and

Federals in various ways. Confederate Captain James J. Waggoner, the Burkeville Depot Quartermaster attempted to hide in the woods when the raiders came by his home "but a Negro guided them to his place of concealment, when they not only captured him but broke open and rifled his trunks." In Charlotte County a slave led a detachment of Federals to several wagons of provisions and valuables hidden in the woods by a Confederate family.[148]

The vast majority of the slaves were recaptured following the collapse of Wilson's force at Ream's Station on June 29 when they found their return route completely blocked by a superior Confederate force. While Wilson and Kautz were organizing their force for a breakout, a combined Confederate cavalry-infantry assault from three sides broke Federal resistance leading to a complete Federal route. While many of the escaping slaves chose to hide in the woods until the battle was over, a large number attempted to flee and mixed in with the retreating Federals.

One Union cavalryman recalled, "We had scarcely commenced to move when it was apparent that the retreat was a route. The road, the fields on each side and the woods were a mass of men and horses. Each man intent on making his own way with all speed. A large number of contrabands had followed us and they too were making the best time they could. I saw a colored woman on a horse with a small child in her arms and another sitting behind her on the horse clinging to her."[149]

After retreating for several miles, Wilson attempted to organize a rearguard at Stony Creek Bridge. The river was swollen and unfordable leaving the bridge as the only avenue of escape. Wilson ordered the bridge blocked with only mounted men allowed to pass. As a result, escaped slaves and dismounted Federal troopers crowded around the mouth of the bridge in an effort to get across.[150]

Pursuing Confederate cavalry arrived on the scene and began firing artillery on the bridge. The bombardment created more panic and confusion. The Confederates initiated a mounted and dismounted charge in an effort to seal off the escape route, capture retreating artillery, and capture the raiders and the escaped slaves. As the Confederates attempted to seal off the bridge several of the escaped slaves were killed along with the dismounted Federal troopers.

---

one to Colonel McIntosh, acting Brigadier General, all of Yankee cavalry, have been deposited by Major-General Fitz Lee with Dr. F.W. Hancock, corner of Third and Main Streets, Richmond, subject to the order of any citizen whose faithful Negro or Negroes have been robbed of their clothing by the thieving scoundrels of Wilson, Kautz & Co., as a partial compensation for their losses. Very Respectfully, Your obedient servant, J.D. Ferguson, Major and Assistant Adjutant General."

[148] *Richmond Dispatch*, July 2, 1864. Waggoner remained a prisoner until able to escape at Ream's Station.; Tobie, First Maine, p339.

[149] George L. Cruickshank, Back In the Sixties: Reminiscences of the Service of Company A, 11th Pennsylvania Regiment (Ft. Lodge, Iowa: Times Job Printing House, 1893) p72-73.

[150] Boudrye, 5th New York, p149-150. "The road was literally packed and for rods in the woods on either side, wherever a man could ride, was a mass of human beings with anxious, throbbing hearts."; see also Wilson's Report, July 3, 1864; Benedict, Vermont In the Civil War, p654.

Trooper G.G. Benedict recalled, "Some 1,200 colored fugitives from slavery had accompanied the column. With these were hundreds of dismounted troopers. General Wilson placed a guard at the bridge and allowed no men on foot to pass till the mounted men had crossed. These had not all filed over the bridge, when the enemy rode up and opened fire on the helpless mass of unarmed men. The bridge at once became filled with a mass of footmen, black and white, mingled among the horsemen. Many were pushed over its sides, and fell upon the rocks or into the stream below. The enemy shot and sabred the Negroes without mercy. Most of them that were not killed were surrounded and retaken, some 200 only succeeding in crossing the river and keeping up with the cavalry column."[151]

While there are several second hand references to runaway slaves getting killed in the heat of battle at Stony Creek Bridge, the exact number of killed is undetermined. What is clear is the Confederate cavalry was in 'hot pursuit' of the Federals and swarmed upon them at the Stony Creek Bridge where five guns, many prisoners of war and many of the escaped slaves were recaptured.

Civil War sources say between 500 and 800 runaway slaves were recaptured. About 400 are reported to have entered Federal lines with Wilson's survivors. This gives a total with the column of about 900 to 1,300. Another 120 that broke off to go home on their own were not counted for a total of about 1,020 to 1,420. These included men, women and children of all ages including newborn infants. At least two births occurred on the battlefield following the Federal debacle at Ream's Station.[152]

An analysis of the slave and free black census for the Southside counties visited by the raid reveal the escaped slaves represented only between two to three percent of the total slave population for the primary counties affected by the raid. This low number attempting to flee bondage suggests many of the slaves were not necessarily eager to leave familiar surroundings or blindly join the Federal troopers. Their motivations for not leaving are subject to speculation but probably included loyalty to their known community (both black and white), no desire to leave the familiarity and relative safety of their homes, or a desire to

---

[151] Wilson, Ibid; Benedict, Ibid; Peter Batte Epes, ltr dtd 05 March 1914 *Epes Family Papers*, Sec. 12; see also *Report of W.C. Wickham*, July 2, 1864, SHSP, Vol. II (March 1881); Kautz, *Reminiscences*; Wilson's Official Report, July 3, 1864.

[152] Roger Hannaford, *'The Wilson Raid, June 1864: A Trooper's Reminiscences'*, ed. By Stephen Starr, Civil War History, (Sept 1975), p229. Hannaford cites 1,200; *Richmond Dispatch*, July 1, 1864; *Richmond Dispatch*, July 2, 1864; and *Richmond Examiner*, July 2, 1864. Contemporary news reports estimate 500-700 recaptured; Gen. Fitzhugh Lee's *Report of Operations of the Cavalry Division from May 4, 1864 to Sept. 19, 1864*. Recalls 18 months after the event about 400 recaptured.; Major Robert Hunter, SHSP, Vol. 35, *An Address Delivered on Fitzhugh Lee*, estimates 800 Negroes recaptured; O.R., C.A. Dana to E.M. Stanton, July 3, 1864. "Wilson brought in about 400 negroes…".' Ibid, July 4, 1864; *New York Times*, July 4, 1864; Benedict, Vermont, p654. "Some 1,200 colored fugitives from slavery had accompanied the column"; Kautz, *Reminiscences*, p80. Kautz estimates 1,000 to 1,500 runaway slaves with the column; *Richmond Examiner*, July 5, 1864. "A drove of one hundred and twenty took fright during the fight Wednesday and fled back in the direction of their homes…this defeat of Wilson's band has reclaimed at least one thousand slaves." For report of births, see *Richmond Dispatch*, July 1, 1864; *Richmond Examiner*, July 2, 1864; *Richmond Dispatch*, July 6, 1864; McCabe, SHSP, Vol. 2, Dec. 1876, p275-276.

'sit the war out' and await the final results rather than take a chance on escaping to Federal lines and an unknown future or if recaptured, possible retribution.[153]

An examination of the Wilson-Kautz raid clearly illustrates the black experience was varied. African-Americans served in multiple capacities in both the Union and Confederate armies. Some chose to defend their homes while others sought to escape from bondage in an effort to find better homes. Others still, chose not to get involved at all and remain detached from events. In short, the African-American experience in the Wilson-Kautz Raid reflects the full spectrum of white experiences in the Civil War and serves as an excellent snapshot in understanding those events.

Primary Source Document

Extract of List of Bodies Returned from Gettysburg for Burial at Hollywood Cemetery[154]

James Godman, Negro Teamster

---

[153] *1860 Slave/Free Black Census*, Report of the Auditor of Public Accounts, 21 November 1861. Based on the pre-hostility estimates, the total slave count for the affected counties was 54,573. Two percent of that amount is 1,091 and three percent is 1,635. By county the slave count is broken down as follows: Prince George, 4,996; Dinwiddie, 7,071; Nottoway, 6,468; Lunenburg, 7,305; Charlotte, 9,236; Mecklenburg, 12, 419 and Brunswick, 9,148. The border counties of Prince Edward, Amelia and Sussex had another 21, 392 but these are not factored into the total.

[154] Library of Virginia Collection; obtained from MOC which identified Godman as a teamster.

Black Confederates at Sailor's Creek

By Greg Eanes

The April 6, 1865 battle of Sailor's Creek was the last major engagement of the General Robert E. Lee's Army of Northern Virginia during the Appomattox Campaign. Hotly pursued by Sheridan's cavalry and VI Corps infantry, a portion of General Lee's column under the command of Gen. Richard Anderson was intercepted at Marshall's Crossroads by Federal cavalry. Behind him was the Corps of Gen. Richard Ewell. Behind Ewell was the Corps of Gen. John B. Gordon, acting as the rearguard. When Gordon follows the wrong road, he becomes separated from Ewell. The pursuing Federal infantry splits its force with one element confronting Ewell at the Hillsman Farm and another element confronting Gordon at Lockett's Farm. The three fronts set the stage for three distinct battles at Sailor's Creek.

After a full day of fighting, Anderson and Ewell are surrounded and captured. Gordon manages to fight his way to safety but at significant loss of troops and wagons. Observing this devastation, Lee said to himself, "My God, has the Army dissolved?" The events lead Union General Ulysses S. Grant to open communications inviting Lee to discuss surrender. Lee fights onto Appomattox, surrendering on April 9th, 1865 effectively ending the War Between the States.

It was the Appomattox Campaign that saw the employment of a regularly mustered black Confederate military unit during the battle of Painesville where about 300 of these men were made prisoner after a gallant defense of a wagon train. Not all the black Confederates in the Appomattox Campaign were in this unit and a great number are documented at the battles of Sailor's Creek.[155]

There were no U.S. Colored Troop units involved at Sailor's Creek. The only known African-Americans were those integrated with Confederate units. Extensive research of primary and secondary source materials allows the name identification of some men directly or because their units were known to be involved in the actions at Sailor's Creek. Many of these units are known to have had free and slave African-Americans on the muster rolls as teamsters, cooks and hostlers. Others were servants of unit members though it is believed most of these had been sent home before the spring campaign. This overview of black participation at Sailor's Creek will address each particular battle.

---

[155] See **Black Day of the Army, April 6, 1865: The Battles of Sailor's Creek** by Greg Eanes (Burkeville, Va: E&H Publishing Company, Inc) 2002 for a detailed account the events of April 6, 1865.

Battle of Marshall's Crossroads
(Also known as Harper's Farm)

<u>Anderson's Brigade-Teamsters</u>
Field's Division Commissary train was under guidance of Capt. A.L.C. Tennille and contained a large number of black teamsters. Walter Nelson Jones recalled the teamsters on this train "were mostly negroes". When attacked by Union cavalry at Marshall's Crossroads Jones recalled, "the Federals suddenly fell upon the Confederate trains, including the wagons I had in my charge. Seeing the uselessness of resistance, I told the negro teamsters to save themselves and to follow me. We, and a good many others of the wagon train, found shelter in a neighboring wood..." He relates to two others after leaving Farmville.[156]

<u>Charley Crowley</u>: Servant of E.P. Alexander on Longstreet's staff.
While setting up a line of battle in Rice, Alexander said, "As we expected to be there all day, I dispatched my servant Charley to hunt up our wagon, on one of the roads to the right, and see if he could scare up something to eat and bring to us. I had him riding my extra horse, Meg, and keeping [him] near me all the while, and someone had given him to carry a haversack containing our headquarters flag. In the afternoon Charley came back, but without rations and without the flag. He had just found the train, when it was charged by a brigade of Federal cavalry, Custer's, I believe. Charley, on Meg, fled across a field, and declared that he was pursued and, being afraid they would hang him if they caught him carrying one of our flags, he threw the haversack off as he fled!"[157]

<u>Morgan:</u> Servant of General Eppa Hunton, Pickett's Division
Hunton was one of George Pickett's Brigade commanders. In an April 13, 1865 letter to his wife, written as a prisoner of war, Hunton indicates his body servant was on the field of battle and was told to escape.[158]

<u>Joshua and Smith</u>: Two-body servants of General Henry Wise.[159]
Gen. Wise made reference to the servants during a postwar speech without naming the men however the names are derived from his son's account of the war. John S. Wise was riding as a courier to General Lee and met his father in Farmville following the battle. Young

---

[156] Walter Nelson Jones, <u>A Virginia Boy's Experiences in 1865, While On The Retreat With General Lee From Petersburg To Appomattox</u>, Virginia Historical Society Collection.

[157] Edward Porter Alexander, <u>Fighting for the Confederacy</u>, p522. Alexander was Longstreet's Chief of Artillery and on the retreat.

[158] *Papers of Eppa Hunton*, Va Historical Society Collection, (VHS Mss1H9267a, items 38-65, Sec. 12); see also Colonel Jack 'Black Jack' Travis's article in <u>Confederate Veteran</u> magazine, *'General Edward Porter Alexander: Soldier, Author, Scholar and Captain of Industry'*. Travis was Chief of Artillery for Longstreet's Corps. Charley was 15 when hired. Travis writes, *"Alexander acts as a father figure and comments that he had to give Charley a little licking twice---once for stealing pears from a tree without asking the owner and the other for stealing apple brandy and getting tight on it at Gettysburg. Charley is an admirable body servant and stays with Alexander throughout the War. A strong bond of friendship and respect evolves between the two men."*

[159] Henry Wise, SHSP, Vol. 25, p16-18, *'The Career of Wise's Brigade'*; see also Barton Haxall Wise, <u>The Life of Henry A. Wise of Virginia</u> (New York: MacMillan and Co, Ltd., 1899) p364; see also John Sergeant Wise, <u>The End of an Era</u> (New York: T. Yoselof, 1965) p318 and 433

Wise (then 19 years old) recorded a part of the conversation, quoting General Wise as stating, "Yes, the Yanks got the bay horse, and my servants Joshua and Smith, and all my baggage…". Joshua and Smith were described as young slaves who "performed all the offices of groom, butlers and dining room servants for the staff."

Battle of Lockett's Farm
(aka Double Bridges)

Tom Peters-Teamster: Wagon driver for Capt. Frederick M. Colston and was at the battle of Double Bridges.[160]

Aleck Kean: Aleck Kean was the body servant to Private James M. Vest of Louisa, in the Second Company of the Richmond Howitzers. Kean became the cook for the squadron mess. Vest was killed in the fall of 1863 but Kean stayed on with the 2nd and 3rd Companies of the Howitzers and surrendered with them at Appomattox. The Howitzers were engaged at Lockett's Farm.[161]

Louisiana Brigade: Many in the Louisiana Brigade were Creoles and of mixed French, Spanish and African blood. The brigade participated as part of Gordon's rearguard and is given battle honors for Sailor's Creek. John O'Donnell-Rosales has compiled a list of such persons. Using his work as a starting point, more intensive research might reveal persons of color.[162]

Ordnance Train, Third Corps: Sixteen unnamed servants surrendered at Appomattox and are credited to the Ordnance Train of Artillery of the Third Corps, Army of Northern Virginia. The trains of the Second and Third Corps were the ones diverted on the Jamestown Road across the Double Bridges. It is possible these men were present for the fight as the trains became bogged down in the bottomland, slowing the retreat and resulting in the capture of many wagons.[163]

1st Regt of Engineers, CSA: It is known that elements of the 1st Regiment of Engineers, C.S.A. were at this location. They undoubtedly had members of the labor battalions with them as well as many of the teamsters.[164]

Reserve Ordnance Train: Over 300 Confederate wagons and ambulances were captured or destroyed at Double Bridges. Evidence reflects many of the teamsters were African-Americans. A 22-year-old artillery Lieutenant in the Reserve Ordnance Train recorded the

---

[160] *Southern Historical Society Papers*, Vol. 38, p9.
[161] Barrow, p133, citing Judge George L. Christian in *Confederate Veteran Magazine*, 20 [1912]
[162] **Hispanic Confederates Of the South Central Gulf States**
[163] **Appomattox Paroles**
[164] Chris Calkins, **The Appomattox Campaign; March 29-April 9, 1865.** Calkins has a sidebar article entitled *'Black Troops of the Union and Confederate Armies in the Last Campaign'*, p183-84, in which he quotes a source citing the use by Engineer Officer's of Major Thomas P. Turner's black troops after the battle of Sailor's Creek along the road to Farmville.

train consisted of 44 wagons of artillery ammunition, one wagon for mining stores and miscellaneous equipment, 12 wagons with artificer equipment, four wagons for forage and two or three wagons with cavalry ammunition for a total of 60 wagons. The length of the train was about one-half mile. He described the train before leaving Richmond. He said, "I may say that we had no soldiers with us at all. We simply had the train with its teamsters—half of them detailed men from the Army and many of these were disabled in some way or other, and the other half were colored men." About 20 of the wagons survived the Amelia Springs burning and were at the Lockett Farm.[165]

Lockett House: Two black civilians were also present during the battle. According to one source, "The [Lockett} house was used as a hospital for the wounded of both armies. Lockett, his daughter, Miss Lelia Lockett, and two colored boys, Branch and Henry Booker, helped nurse the soldiers."[166]

Mahone's Brigade at Rice: Francis (Frank) Smith Robertson, an officer of the 48th Va Infantry, Mahone's Brigade reports the presence of Bob, a free African-American, who performed duties as a "camp boy" or officers orderly. Robertson wrote, "Bob was my third camp boy. Sam, Ben and Bob—all were sincerely attached to me, I'm sure. Sam belonged to me—my only slave. I offered him his freedom several times—explained all necessary was to wave my handkerchief—ride up and deliver him to a Yank picket and the thing was done. He showed no disposition to adopt my plan however and seemed quite as adverse to capture as I was myself."[167]

53rd North Carolina: The 53rd NC was in Grimes Brigade; Grime's Division of Gordon's Crops engaged in the retreat and Battle of Double Bridges. At least two body servants were with the unit when it surrendered at Appomattox.[168]

George Wallace: Body servant of Capt. Howard Tinsley, Co. G, 12th Georgia Infantry, Doles-Cook Brigade, Grime's Division, Gordon's Corps. Wallace surrendered at Appomattox. Wallace became a politician, was elected to the State Senate and later became a postal employee in Macon Georgia.[169]

Ab Lee: Body servant of Capt. A.S. Reid, 12th Georgia Infantry, Doles-Cook Brigade, Grime's Division, Gordon's Corps. Remained until the surrender and later became a member of the Confederate Veterans Association of Putnam Co. (Ga) and Doles Cook Brigade Survivor's Association.[170]

---

[165] *The Retreat From Petersburg To Appomattox: Recollections by J.P. Packard*, p10, VHS.
[166] Bradshaw, *History of Prince Edward County*, p403
[167] *Reminiscences*, p48 VHS
[168] Barrow, p27, citing the *Georgia Hicks Papers*, North Carolina Department of Archives and History, Raleigh
[169] Barrow, p145, citing Confederate Veteran Henry W. Thomas p612, *History of the Doles-Cook Brigade, Army of Northern Virginia* (Atlanta, Ga: The Franklin Printing & Publishing Company) 1903.
[170] Barrow, p146, citing Thomas p163 in *Doles-Cook Brigade*, 1903.

Morris (Thomas): Body servant of H.W. Thomas, Co. G, 12th Georgia Inf., Doles-Cook Bde, Grime's Division, Gordon's Corps. At surrender.[171]

Veterans of the 6th South Carolina Infantry, Bratton's Brigade, Field's Division, Longstreet's First Corps. During the battles of Sailor's Creek these men were at Rice. E.B. Mobley enlisted as a private rising to the rank of Sergeant. He was paroled at Appomattox. Could Hampton Stratford have been there with him?

---

[171] **Barrow, p. 146, citing Thomas, p614, <u>Doles-Cook Brigade</u>, 1903.**

Battle of Hillsman's Farm

18th Georgia Infantry Battalion
(Dubose's Bde, Kershaw's Division)[172]

The 18th Georgia was on the right flank at Hillsman's Farm. The following African-Americans were among 16 members of the 18th Georgia "enlisted for the War" who escaped from Sailor's Creek and surrendered at Appomattox. They include

Joe Parkman	Co. A	Musician
Henry Williams	Co. B	Musician
George Waddell	Co. A	Musician
Louis Gardeen	Co. C	Musician
James Polk	Co. B	Cook
Scipio Africanus	Co. B	Cook
William Read	Co. C	Cook
John Leroy	Co. A	Cook

It appears one musician did not escape and was captured at Sailor's Creek:

Henry McCleskey-(Colored) Musician: Enlisted 10 August 1861 for six months. Roll for Feb 1862 shows him present. Appointed Musician of Co. B, 18th Battalion Georgia Infantry. Paroled near Sailor's Creek, Va April 7, 1865.[173]

Confederate Naval personnel included:

Charles Cleapor-Sailor: Cleapor was a Confederate States sailor in Commodore Tucker's Brigade, Lee's Division at the Battle of Hillsman's Farm. He survived Sailor's Creek and surrendered at Appomattox.[174]

Joseph Johnston-Sailor: Johnston was a Confederate States sailor in Commodore Tucker's Brigade, Lee's Division at the Battle of Hillsman's Farm. He survived Sailor's Creek and surrendered at Appomattox.[175]

---

[172] **Appomattox Surrender Rolls**
[173] **Roster of the Confederate Soldiers of Georgia, Vol. 1 (Hapeville, Ga: Longina & Porter, 1959-1964) Georgia State Division of Confederate Pensions and Records, p116-117; six volumes.**
[174] **Appomattox Surrender Rolls; Va State Archives service roster.**
[175] **Ibid**

J. Heck-Sailor: Heck was a Confederate States sailor in Commodore Tucker's Brigade, Lee's Division at the Battle of Hillsman's Farm. He survived Sailor's Creek and surrendered at Appomattox.[176]

C.P. Terry-Sailor: Black Confederate States sailor in Commodore Tucker's Brigade captured at the Hillsman Farm. His name is reflected on the POW rolls of Point Lookout where many of the Appomattox Campaign POWs were taken. His entry is annotated 'Col'd Prisoner'.[177]

Battlefield Locations Undetermined

William Tabb: The body servant of August Crenshaw, a citizen of Richmond. Tabb's name is reflected on the POW rolls of Point Lookout where many of the Appomattox Campaign POWs were taken. His entry is annotated "body servant" captured at High Bridge on April 6 (likely Sailor's Creek). Many of the POWs listed their points of capture on the nearest identifiable site (for some that was Burkeville over ten miles away).[178]

Donaldsonville Artillery: Among those surrendered at Appomattox were four African-Americans in the Donaldsonville Artillery. This particular battery was on duty at the High Bridge fortifications at the time of the retreat and moved retreated with Lee's Army. Those African-Americans documented with the unit include:[179]

H. Blum	Cook
L. Leport	Cook
Jonathan Memply	Servant
Jonathan Semple	Servant

The participation of others can be ascertained through a detailed examination of muster rolls of units involved in the action. For example, the Goochland (Va) Light Artillery, C.S.A. was involved in the action at the Hillsman Farm as part of Crutchfield's Brigade, GWC Lee's Division. The unit lists about six African-Americans on its muster rolls. The Confederate States Navy and the Chaffin's Bluff artillery batteries are said to have employed African-Americans as gunners. These units were also at the Hillsman Farm.

Lee's Division consisted of the various battalions of Richmond local defense troops who worked full time in the various war arsenals, hospitals and factories. Many of these men were free blacks and slaves and may have served at the Hillsman Farm. For the record, at least one company of black hospital troops saw action in the trenches during the siege. These men were the Jackson Hospital Battalion under Major Henry C. Scott. They were later transferred to Major Jackson Chambliss' Negro Battalion (two companies) which

---

[176] **Ibid**
[177] **National Archives, Record Group 109, Confederate States Records,** *POW Rolls for Pt. Lookout, Md.* **Boxes 283-285, Roll 8, Volume II. Paper copies of microfilm on file at Appomattox National Historic Park.**
[178] **POW Rolls for Pt. Lookout**
[179] **Appomattox National Historical Park**

served as part of the Negro Brigade raised by Majors James W. Pegram and Thomas P. Turner. It is this brigade that participated in and repulsed a Federal cavalry attack at Deatonsville on April 5, 1865 before being overwhelmed and forced to surrender. A Union officer reported about 320 of these men were captured and made prisoners of war. There is eyewitness evidence that some escaped and continued on the retreat. One squad of 12 was observed on April 6 constructing hasty fortifications however the site is believed to be west of Sailor's Creek.[180]

Over 300 Confederate wagons and ambulances were captured or destroyed at Double Bridges and others were destroyed at Marshall's Crossroads. As was a common practice, a large number of the teamsters were probably African-American. At least one Federal account refers to black Confederate prisoners of war marching to Petersburg but it has long been assessed to refer to the regular black Confederate infantry unit captured on April 5 at Deatonsville.

An extremely large number of those men surrendered at Appomattox were listed as teamsters, hospital stewards, musicians and "hired men". A detailed search of these names may reveal that some are African-American.

APPROPRIATION FOR ENGINEER SERVICE: This document reflects Confederate government payment to "Jordan Cousins (f[ree] negro Nottoway Co)". Cousins was paid $52.50 on July 11, 1864 for a variety of services. The document reads, *"For my services as labourer on public defenses at Richmond in Feb 1862. 8 ½ days at 50 c[ents] per day---$4.25. For my services as Carpenter in public defenses at Fort Boykin in March 1862 – 25 ¾ c[ents] per day $25.75. For my services as above [carpenter] in April 1862. 22 ½ days at $1 per day -- $22.50"* reflecting a total of $52.50. He was paid by Captain J. B. Stanard, Engineers, PACS [Provisional Army of the Confederate States].

---

[180] Jordan, Black Confederates and Afro-Yankees; Calkins, Appomattox Campaign; OR, Davies Report of combat action.

Black Confederates at High Bridge

Documentary evidence indicates black Confederates performed military duties at the High Bridge defenses near Farmville, Va between June 1864 and February 1865. The records further suggest that the hiring of Negro substitutes to perform guard duties at the bridge was an accepted and officially condoned practice.

The 1st Virginia Reserves under Colonel Benjamin Farinholt were placed on active status in August 1864 to provide security to the Richmond and Danville Railroad. Bridges were previously threatened by a May 1864 raid by Union General August V. Kautz and a June raid by Union General James H. Wilson accompanied by Kautz. Farinholt's mission was to guard the High Bridge, the Staunton River, Chula and Mattoax bridges.

While not all unit records have been examined, a cursory investigation shows at least two unit members found African-American substitutes to perform their duties. Substituting was not an uncommon practice. It resulted when a man of some means was conscripted (drafted) and wanted to avoid military service. He merely found a substitute to go in his stead, usually with some financial bounty in exchange for the service. It appears that at least four unnamed African-Americans served as substitutes under Farinholt's command.

Private J.R. Adams of Company H of Amelia County was listed as "absent" on the 31 December muster roll. Remarks indicated he was "absent having put in a negro substitute for 30 days." The following month, Private J.W. Borum of Company F of Burkeville (neighboring Nottoway County) as listed as "absent" on the 28 February 1865 muster roll. The remarks indicated he was "absent on sixty days furlough from Jan. 13, he having furnished [a] negro substitute." Their companies were at the High Bridge during this period.

Using African-Americans as substitutes appears to have been an accepted and officially condoned practice. A service record entry for Private A. J. Angel, also of Co. H, Amelia County, shows he was "absent on negro furlough for 30 days" on the roll dated 28 February 1865. Private J.H. Goodman, Company I, of Powhatan, was also listed on the 28 February roster as "Absent on Negro furlough for 60 days from 13 January [to] 13 March 1865."

Engineer Department Activities
Probably more important than the men used as guards were the men supporting the Confederate Engineer Department in constructing the High Bridge Defenses. The Confederate Congress authorized the draft for free men of color to support military activities

and a significant number were called up to help build the bridge defenses. Free men were paid $11 a month and provided the same rations, allowances and clothing as other soldiers.

Free African-American Men Helping Construct the High Bridge Defenses				
Name	Age	County of Birth	Civilian Occupation	When Enlisted
Bacchus, Frank[181]	19	Richmond City	Laborer	15 June 1864
Burks, Hubbert	32	Albemarle	Jobber	10 June 1864
Davis, R.	40	Prince Edward	Laborer	15 June 1864
Desmul, S.	23	Buckingham	Groom	10 June 1864
Goins, Ben	18	Rockingham	Laborer	28 June 1864
Gray, Elas	40	Spotsylvania	Laborer	30 June 1864
Homes, E.	33	Prince Edward	Laborer	15 June 1864
Hill, Booker	40	Prince Edward	Laborer	1 July 1864
Johnson, Joseph	40	Prince Edward	Unknown	1 July 1864
Jones Albert	18	Amherst	Jobber	10 June 1864
John, W.	25	Rockingham	Farmer	10 June 1864
John W.V.	30	Rockingham	Farmer	10 June 1864
Logan, S.	23	Buckingham	Blacksmith	10 June 1864
Logan, William	34	Buckingham	Jobber	10 June 1864
Perkins, George	40	Prince Edward	Laborer	1 July 1864
Stauntton, J.T.	32	Buckingham	Farmer	10 June 1864
Stauntton, John	26	Buckingham	Farmer	10 June 1864
Thomhill, W.	36	Appomattox	Laborer	1 July 1864
Thomas, William	33	Prince Edward	Farmer	1 July 1864
Thomas W.H.	30	Mecklenburg	Shoemaker	14 June 1864

As of 14 September 1864, there were about 30 free men of color supporting the Confederate Engineer Department at the High Bridge defenses. Confederate Chief Engineer J.F. Gilmer complained to Secretary of War Seddon that, with that small force, it would take at least four months to complete the planned fortifications. Gilmer wanted the Bureau of Conscription to be directed to institute another levy with free African-Americans from Appomattox, Prince Edward, Amelia, Buckingham and Cumberland ordered to the High Bridge to report to Captain William G. Bender, the engineer in charge of construction. Seddon concurred in the request.[182]

---

[181] **Confederate Bureau of Conscription *Register of Free Negroes Enrolled and Detailed* (May 1864-Jan 1865) Chapter 1, Vol. 241, as transcribed and published by E. Renee Ingram's In View of the Great Want of Labor: A Legislative History of African American Conscription in the Confederacy.**
[182] **Letter, 14 September 1864, Major General J.F. Gilmer, Chief of the Engineer Bureau to Secretary of War James Seddon. See Ingram, p38-39.**

By December of 1864 there were at least 50 free men of color engaged in work as indicated by Capt. Bender who made an urgent request for blankets and uniforms due to the cold weather.[183]

SPECIAL REQUISITION for clothing for free men of color working on the High Bridge defenses. Capt. W.G. Bender's request for blankets and uniforms is annotated, "That the negroes have no so little clothing, that they cannot work in very cold weather." Chief Engineer Gilmore endorsed the request to Secretary of War Seddon stating , "It is important that this clothing should be supplied to these free negroes working on the Defences at High Bridge, as they are represented being [in] great want. I would ask that the [QM] General be directed to issue this clothing to Capt. W.G. Bender, Engrs through the proper officers at High Bridge." His need of 50 blankets suggests the black workforce was then about 50 people. The request was made on 17 December 1864.

Virginia Pension Data
Of the six pensioned personnel who worked on the High Bridge defenses, only George Brogden, a free man of Charlotte County appears to have been working for the Confederate Engineers. The remainder were individual or officer servants.

Charles Slaughter, whose pension application was denied, claims he worked as a servant to "transport soldiers" to Pamplin and High Bridge.

John W. Harris was a body servant to Captain R.M. (Dick) Scott of Co. H, Amelia Reserves, 1st Virginia Reserves. Harris said he was employed in "cooking and working on breastworks at High Bridge and Chula" serving from 1863 through the end of the war. At some point, Capt. Scott went into the Confederate hospital in Farmville and Harris helped him there as well.

---

[183] Receipt in CSR of Captain W.G. Bender, Confederate Service Records, Officers.

Virginia's Black Confederates

Tom Lee was the servant to a Captain Joseph H. Godsey, Commanding Co. I, 3rd Virginia Reserves. Company I was the Appomattox County company. Lee says he "waited on Captain Godsey" and helped put up breastworks noting his service began in 1863 and ended in 1864 when his "time was out".[184]

Another free man who performed duty as a servant was Alexander B. Davenport of Gloucestor. He worked for Colonel Benjamin Farinholt, Commander of the 1st Virginia Reserves which was responsible for the security of the High Bridge and Staunton River Bridge. Davenport served from 1862 to 1865 in Richmond and at High Bridge. He says he was "digging trenches, cooking and washing" under Farinholt. Oddly, he made no mention of being at the Staunton River Bridge, which he undoubtedly was if he was under Farinholt the entire time he was in service. In fact, this would have placed him at the Staunton River Bridge during the historic battle there on 25 June 1864.

Individuals Performing Duty at High Bridge Defenses
from Virginia Pension Applications

Pension	Age	County of Pension	Status	Source
Brogden, George	19	Charlotte County	Free Man	Approved Pension
Coles, Peyton	19-20	Prince Edward	Slave	Approved Pension
Davenport, Alexander B.	22-23	Gloucestor	Free Man	Approved Pension
Harris, John W.	22-25	Amelia	Slave	Approved Pension
Lee, Tom	18-19	Appomattox	Slave	Approved Pension
Slaughter, Charles	19-20	Charlotte County	Slave	Denied Pension

Peyton Coles was also a servant to a Confederate soldier stating he "carried my master's baggage" where he served at High Bridge from January 1864 "until Lee surrendered at Appomattox". Coles' statement suggests he evacuated the High Bridge defenses during the Confederate retreat in the Appomattox Campaign and traveled with the Army until Lee surrendered.

---

[184] **Godsey was in command at High Bridge on 30 September 1864 when his company held an election for two Lieutenant vacancies. By 1 January 1865, the company was on duty at the Staunton River Bridge.**

Black Confederates on the Appomattox Campaign

By Chris Calkins, Chief Historian
Sailor's Creek Battlefield State Park

(Editor's Note: The following essay is part of a larger public informational brochure written by former Petersburg Battlefield National Park Chief Historian Chris Calkins and produced by the National Park Service to tell the story of *Black Soldiers on Lee's Retreat* during the Appomattox Campaign. While the NPS brochure also addressed the black experience in the Federal Army, only that part concerning the Confederate Army is included here.)

With General Robert E. Lee's manpower reserves quickly draining, on March 23, 1865, General Orders #14 was issued which allowed for the enlistment of slaves into the Confederate service. Shortly thereafter, a notice was posted in Petersburg's The Daily Express, "The commanding General deems the prompt organization of as large a force of negroes as can be spared, a measure of the utmost importance, and the support and co-operation of the citizens of Petersburg and the surrounding counties is requested by him for the prosecution to success of a scheme which he believes promises so great benefit to our cause...To the slaves is offered freedom and undisturbed residence at their old homes in the Confederacy after the war. Not the freedom of sufferance, but honorable and self won by the gallantry and devotion which grateful countrymen will never cease to reward."

The recruitment effort did bear fruit in Richmond where Majors James W. Pegram and Thomas P. Turner put together a "Negro Brigade" of Confederate States Colored Troops. The Richmond Daily Examiner noted of the unit "*the knowledge of the military art they already exhibit was something remarkable. They moved with evident pride and satisfaction to themselves.*"

As the Confederate army abandoned Richmond on April 3rd, apparently these Black Confederate soldiers went along with General Custis Lee's wagon train on its journey. They would move unmolested until they reached the area of Painesville on April 5. Here they were attacked by General Henry Davies' cavalry troopers.

A Confederate officer, who rode upon this situation as it was transpiring, recalled: "*Several engineer officers were superintending the construction of a line of rude breastworks...Ten or twelve negroes were engaged in the task of pulling down a rail fence; as many more occupied in carrying the rails, one at a time, and several were busy throwing up the dirt...The [Blacks] thus employed all wore good gray uniforms and I was informed that they belonged to the only company of colored troops in the Confederate service, having been enlisted by Major Turner in Richmond. Their muskets were stacked, and it was evident that they regarded their present employment in no very favorable light.*"

On April 10th, as Confederate prisoners were being marched from Sailor's Creek and elsewhere to City Point (present day Hopewell) and eventually off to Northern prison camps, a Union chaplain observed the column. This incident along the retreat to Painesville, seems to be the only documented episode of "official" Black troops serving the Confederacy in Virginia as a unit under fire.

African-Americans also accompanied the Confederate army on the retreat with the First Regiment Engineer Troops and provided yeoman service. One member of this unit remembered that they mounded roads, repaired bridges and cut new parallel roads to old ones when they became impassable. When this was not possible, an engineer officer would post a group near the trouble spot to extricate wagons and artillery pieces.

When Lee surrendered his army at Appomattox, thirty-six African-Americans were listed on the Confederate paroles. Most were either servants, free blacks, musicians, cooks, teamsters or blacksmiths.

A Black woman was to become the only civilian casualty in the final fighting at Appomattox. Hannah stayed behind with her husband in the home of Doctor Coleman located on the battlefield and was mortally wounded by an artillery round. A Union chaplain remembered: *"she was sick with fever and unable to be moved. As she lay upon her bed, a solid shot had passed through one wall of the house at just the right height to strike her arm, and then passed out through the opposite wall."*

Black Confederates on the Appomattox Parole[185]

Quartermaster Department
3rd Corps (Ordnance Train)   16 slaves (names unknown)

18th Georgia Battalion

Musicians		Cooks	
Louis Gardeen	Company A	Scipio Africanus	Company B
Joe Parkman	Company A	John Lery	Company A
George Waddell	Company A	James Polk	Company B
Henry Williams	Company B	William Read	Company C

Gary's Cavalry Brigade		**Donaldsonville Artillery**	
Quartermaster Department		Company B	
James Barabsha	Guard	H. Blum	Cook
Thomas Bowen	Teamster	L. Leport	Servant
Burress Bowen	Teamster	Jno. Mamply	Servant
John Bowen	Teamster	Jno. Semple	Servant
Jack Caldwell	Teamster	Bob	Servant[186]
		Jim	Slave[187]
		Solomon Wright	Blacksmith

---

[185] **Appomattox Court House National Park Service website (http://www.nps.gov/apco/black-soldiers.htm)**
[186] **Servant of David Bridges.**
[187] **Slave of T.M. Dittrick.**

New Appomattox Data
Pension Rosters and Other Records

By Greg Eanes

A review of the Virginia pension roster and other sources makes it clear many more black Confederates were at Appomattox than previously identified. At least 48 individuals specifically state they served until Appomattox while many more state they left service at the "end of the war" or "after Appomattox" without naming the specific place of service termination. A more detailed study of their units and unit locations may reveal their presence at Appomattox Court House at the surrender.

Of those that specifically mention Appomattox, many make clear they were present on the morning of April 9, 1865. The roster includes teamsters, body servants, cooks and hostlers. Two General officer servants are identified. These were Henry Jackson, a body servant of Gen. A.P. Hill who attached himself to Gen. James Walker's staff when Hill was killed at Petersburg and William Jones who identified himself as a messenger/courier for Gen. Robert E. Lee.

Names Assessed as at or near Appomattox at the time of the surrender include:

Name	Unit/Role	Source[188]
Bell, Benjamin	Teamster	P
Bolden, Clem Read	Poage's Bn Artillery, Teamster	P
Boyd, William Henry	2nd Engineer Regt, Cook	P
Cain, Charles	Cook	P
Clark, John	Co. A, 4th Va Cavalry, Body Servant	P
Coles, Peyton	18th Va Infantry, Servant[189]	P
Cook, Richard	C.S. Navy	Richmond Dispatch[190]
Davis, John	Hospital Steward	SHSP V28 p21
Edmonds, Frank	Laborer	P
Eggleston, John	Teamster[191]	P
Epps, George	Teamster	P
Estes, Callie Hill	38th Va Infantry, Cook	P
Evans, William T.	Servant on Lee's Staff	Misc
Ford, Fred	Teamster	P

---

[188] P reflects the source is a Virginia State Pension; SHSP is *Southern Historical Society Papers*; Barrow is Kelly Barrow's research.
[189] Coles was the slave of Samuel Crute of the 18th Va Infantry, Prince Edward County.
[190] *Richmond Dispatch*, 4 October 1902, p1
[191] Appears to be a good match for the 60th Va Infantry, Wise's Legion.

Virginia's Black Confederates

Glascoe, George T.	Teamster	P
Goodwyn, Thomas	Hostler	P
Hackley, Joseph	Infantry, Teamster	P
Hawthorne, Rufus	Laborer	P
Henderson, Jesse	Engineers, Cook	P
Jackson, Henry	Infantry, Servant, Gen Walker's staff	P
Jones, Moses	Laborer	P
Jones, William	Messenger/Courier Lee's Staff	P
Johnson, Whit	Artillery, Laborer	G. Robinson Pension
Kean, Aleck	2nd Co, Richmond Howitzers	Barrow, p133
Lansdown, Charles	Hostler/Teamster	P
Lee, William Mack	Cook to Robert E. Lee	P
Majors, Tillman	6th Va Cavalry, Cook	P
Moore, John	Co. A, 20th Battalion Va Heavy Artillery	P
Moorman, Tom	Artillery, Laborer	G. Robinson Pension
Norris, Joseph Preston	Servant on Lee's Staff	Misc.
Pollard, Emanuel	9th Va Cavalry, Hostler	P
Porterfield, Jacob	16th Mississippi Infantry	P
Robinson, George W.	Co. C, 11th Va Infantry/Longstreet's Arty	P
Shields, Tom	Cook & Servant to Thomas Cook, Cavalry	P
Skipwith, Ben Fuller	Teamster	P
Smith, John	Co I, 44th Va Infantry	P
Stewart, Richard	Artillery, Cook (free man)	P
Tucker, Pompey	Infantry, Cook	P
Turpin, Henry	Laborer	P
Tweedy, Sam	Teamster	P
Turner, Phil	Blacksmith	P
Walker, Fielding	Servant on Lee's Staff	see Misc Sources
Walker, Richard	Cavalry, Hostler	P
Wallace, George	Co. G, 12th Ga Infantry	Barrow, p145
Williams, Flemming	Cavalry, Cook	P
Williams, John	Cook	P
Willis, Charles	Teamster	P
-----, Howard	Hospital Steward	SHSP V28 p21

Lee Servant Profiled: Joseph Preston Norris

Joseph Preston Norris of Lexington was reported to be a servant to General Robert E. Lee. Born in slavery, Norris "grew up on the plantation until my people were freed. Then I went into the Southern army just like all of the folks of the South did." A 1913 *New York Sun* profile quoted Norris' story:

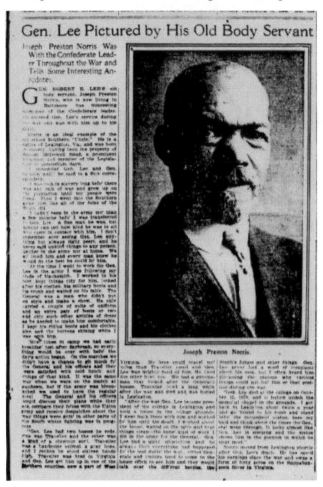

New York Sun, 29 June 1913

"I hadn't been in the army mo' than a few months befo' I was transferred to Gen. Lee. A fine man he was to all who came in contact with him. I don't remember ever seeing Gen. Lee anything but always right peert, and he never said unkind things to any person, neither in the army nor at home. We all loved him and every man knew he would do the best he could fo' him.

"At the time I went to work for Gen. Lee in the army I was following my trade of blacksmith. I worked in his tent, kept things tidy for him, looked after his clothes, his military boots and his truck and waited on his table. The General was a man who didn't put on style and make a show. He only carried a couple of suits of uniform and an extra pair of boots or two and only such other articles of dress as he needed to make him comfortable. I kept his riding boots and his clothes nice and the buttons shining while I was with him.

"Most times in camp we had early breakfast just after daybreak, so everything would be over with befo' the day's action began. On the marches we didn't have a chance to git much fo' the General and his officers and they were satisfied with cold lunch and things of that kind. It was the same way when were on the march at sundown, but if the army was bivouacked we used to have the regular meal. The General and his officers would discuss their plans while they ate, compare their forces with the Union army and receive despatches about the way things were goin' in other parts of the South where fighting was in progress.

Virginia's Black Confederates

"Gen. Lee had two hosses he rode. One was Traveller and the other was a kind of chestnut sor'l. Traveller was a handsome animal, a gray hoss, and I reckon he stood sixteen hands high. Traveller was bred in Virginia and Gen. Lee got him up in one of the Northern counties, now a part of West Virginia. No hoss could travel mo' miles than Traveller could and Gen. Lee was mighty fond of him. He liked the hoss too. We had a groomsman that looked after the General's hosses. Traveller lived a long while after the war and died and was buried in Lexington.

"After the war Gen. Lee became president of the college in Lexington and took a house in the college grounds. I went back there with him and worked fo' him until his death. I worked about the house, waited on the table and kept things clean --- the same kind of work I did in the army for the General. Gen. Lee had a quiet disposition and he always tho't everything had happened fo' the best during the war. Other Generals and visitors used to come to the house often to see him and they would talk over the diff'rent battles, the South's future and other things. Gen. Lee never had a word of complaint about his men but I often heard him discussing the reasons why various troops could not hol' this or that position during the war.

"Gen. Lee died at the college on October 12, 1870, and is buried undah the memorial chapel in the grounds. I get back to Lexington about twice a year and go 'round to his tomb and stand befo' the recumbent statue, bare my [head] and think about the times the General went through. ;It looks almost like Gen. Lee is sleeping and the statue shows him in the position in which he slept most.'

Norris moved from Lexington [to Baltimore] shortly after Gen. Lee's death. He has saved his earnings since the war and owns a farm of forty acres on the Rappahannock River in Virginia."

Norris said he served Lee at Lexington and, after Lee's death, took a position at the B&O Railroad as a messenger eventually becoming the personal messenger for B&O President Daniel Willard in Baltimore. Norris was profiled in the *B&O Employees Magazine*[192] in August 1913 where the writer attempted to capture in writing his distinguished Southern accent as he described various aspects of army life. Norris described being born into slavery in Lexington, Va and some of plantation life. His father was a blacksmith and Norris learned that trade. When the war started Norris was initially engaged in repairing army vehicles and shoeing horses.

Norris said General Jackson: *"had a deep voice that carried far and no one had trouble in hearing him...I joined the Sunday School conducted by General Jackson. We slaves always knew him as 'Marster Tom' Jackson, fo' then he hadn't gone to wah and was a colonel at the Virginia Military Institute. All of the membahs of the class like General Jackson tho, and he was nice to us. The Sunday School was held in the lecture room of the church in the aftahnoon, and it was opened by a hymn that all of the slaves sang, with General Jackson leading. Then after singing, the General would pray."*

---

[192] *B&O Employees Magazine*, Vol. 1, No. 11, p15-19.

Of the war Norris said;

"When the call fo' men came from Richmond, all of the slaves that were old enough went into the ahmy. Lots of us went in as cooks and servants and others as 'hands' on the breast-works and in the ranks. Lexington sent a good many cooks to the ahmy, among them Jeff Shields, who goes to all the Confederate reunions now.

"I hadn't been in the ahmy mo' than a few months befo' I was transferred to General Lee. A fine man he was, but nobody can tell how kind he was to all who came in contact with him. I don't remember evah seeing General Lee anything but always right 'peert' and he never said unkind things to any person neither in the ahmy nor at home. We all loved him and every man knew he would do the best he could fo' him."

"It was after Bull Run, some call it the battle of Manassas, when I went with General Lee. He had some terrible fighting while I was with him…When General Lee mad hi no'thn trip on the Gettysburg campaign, I was sent off to Richmond to attend to otha' matters and was left behind. I returned to the General afta' he retreated across the Potomac and back into Virginia and served until the surrender at Appomattox."

"In the Southern ahmy ev'rybody felt like it was all over afta' the no'thn invasion and that afta' the defeat at Gettysburg, it was only a question of time until we would have to surrender. What made it so hard was that our men had nothing to eat and often the entire ahmy went without food, including the Generals and othah officers. In the ahmy in those days we were all alike, and when food was short, all felt it and were cut down acco'dingly. We were short of food when the General signed the papers of surrendah at Appomattox. When it was all ovah all of us were glad—I known General Lee was and often heard him say so.

"I was in Lexington when General Jackson was buried, and there were sad times when word came that he had been killed. Every person loved him in Lexington and all through the South, for he was a pow'ful fighting man. The day of his funeral the cadets at the Institute had charge and they fired guns ev'ry half hour until the fune'al had been held.

General Lee was mighty grieved when General Jackson was taken off, not only because of their personal friendship, but because General Lee had such faith in him as a leader.

"At the time I went to work for General Lee in the ahmy, I was following my trade [blacksmith]. I worked in his tent, kept things tidy fo' him, looked after his clothes, his military boots and his trunk and waited on his table. The General was a man who didn't put on style and make a show. He only carried a couple of suits of unifo'm and an extra pair of boots or two and only such other articles of dress as needed to make him comf'table. I kept his ridin' boots and his clothes nice and the buttons shining while I was with him.

"Most times in camp we had early breakfas' just after daybreak, so everything would be over with befo' the day's action began. On the marches we didn't chance to fix much fo' the General and his offisahs, and they were satisfied with cold lunch and things of that kind. The General and his offisahs would discuss their plans while they ate, compare their fo'ces with the Union ahmy and receive dispatches about the way things were goin' in other parts of the South where fighting was in progress.

"General Lee had two hosses in the service. One was Traveler and the other was a kind of chestnut sor'el. Traveler was a handsome animal, a gray hoss; and I reckon he stood sixteen hands high. He was bred in Virginia and General Lee got him upo in one of the no'thn counties, now a part of West Virginia. No hoss could travel mo' miles than Traveler could and General Lee was mighty fond of him. He liked the other hoss too. We had a groom that looked after the General's hosses. Traveler lived a long while after the wah and died and was buried in Lexington.

"After the wah General Lee became president of the college in Lexington and took a house in the college grounds. I went back there with him and worked fo' him until his death. I worked about the house, waited on the table and kept things clean—the same kind of work I did for him in the ahmy. General Lee had a quiet disposition and he always tho't ev'rything had happened fo' the best. Other generals and visitahs used to come to the house often to see him and they would talk over the diff'rent battles, the South's future and other things. General Lee nevah had a word of complaint about his men, but I often head'd him discussing the reasons why various troops could not hol' this or that position during the wah.

"He died at the college on October 12, 1870, and is buried under the memo'ial chapel in the grounds. I get back to Lexing'ton about twice a yeah and go 'round to his tomb and stand befo' his statue, bare my haid and think about the times the General went through. It looks almost like General Lee is sleeping, and the statue shows him in the position in which he slept most."[193]

---

[193] **Ibid, p15-19**

Lee Servant or Fake?
Reverend William Mack Lee

The Reverend William Mack Lee, one of the more publicly identified men who claimed to be a servant of General Robert E. Lee may very well have been an imposter who used his knowledge of Lee to help fund his church work after the war. The Commonwealth of Virginia did however recognize his service as a cook in the 27th Virginia Infantry of the famous Stonewall Brigade.

In his 1918 autobiography, the Reverend William Mack Lee said he was born June 12, 1835 in Westmorland County, Va and raised at Arlington Heights, a servant in the house of the Lee family. He said he was freed like all the Lee family servants, ten years before the war and all the servants "remained on the plantation until after the surrender." He married in 1854 and the union produced eight daughters. His wife died in 1910. By 1918, Rev. Lee had 21 grandchildren and eight great-grandchildren. He began preaching around 1859 and, when the war started, entered Confederate service. After the war, he remained with General Lee. At the latter's death, Rev. Lee returned to preaching and used his connection with Robert E. Lee to help raise funds to support his Christian work. In 1881 he became an ordained Missionary Baptist Preacher organizing churches in Washington, DC., Baltimore

REV. WM. MACK LEE

Rev. Lee claims he served as a cook and servant for General Lee during the entire Civil War from First Manassas through Appomattox. Rev. Lee said he was "there at the fire of the last gun for the salute of the surrender on Sunday, April 9" at Appomattox. The Rev. Lee was in action on July 12, 1863 when fragments from a shell burst hit him in the head and in the hip. The latter wound caused him to limp the rest of his life.

Rev. Lee said he had just provided breakfast to General Lee and left the tent to get his horse, Traveler. He said, "I went out an' curried and saddled Traveler. I heard dem jack battery guns begin to pop an bust an' roah." He saddled Traveler and took him to General Lee's tent. The old man recalled, "Jes' as Marse Robert cum out'n his tent a shell hit 35 yards away. It busted, and hit me, an' I fell over." General Lee attended to him to check his wounds and called for an ambulance which took the Rev. Lee to the hospital.

Rev. Lee said the only time General Lee ever scolded him was when he sacrificed their egg-laying hen (named Nellie) for a chicken dinner. He explained the chicken had been with them for two years of war and laid eggs almost daily. The hen was kept in the General's ambulance where she had a nest. General Lee was preparing for a staff meeting at Headquarters that would involve Generals Stonewall Jackson, A.P. Hill, D.H. Hill, Wade Hampton, Longstreet, Pickett and others.

As cook he prepared what he had available to include flannel cakes, tea and lemonade but he knew that would not be enough to feed so many visitors. As nothing else was available, he decided to kill the chicken, pluck it, and stuffed with bread stuffing mix with butter. When General Lee found out he was upset because the hen had been giving them eggs daily and they didn't have another. Rev. Lee said General Lee would get "awful sad" when thinking of anything being killed, whether it was one of his soldiers "or his little black hen".[194]

Confederate Veteran Magazine Editor E.D. Pope alleged in a September 1927 issue that Mack Lee "was sailing under false colors in claiming any association whatever with General Lee as camp servant or otherwise." Pope said, "There is no mention of his name in any of General Lee's letters, though some other negro servants are referred to, and if he [Mack Lee] had the close association which he claims, his name would doubtless appeared in some of General Lee's letters to his family." Pope charged, "[Rev. Lee] is not the first who has profited by claims too absurd to be given credence."[195]

With that in mind, the Rev. Lee did receive a Virginia pension based on his claims that he was a cook in the 27th Virginia Infantry entering service on January 12, 1861 and "stayed through entire war". In question seven, 'Who were your immediate superior officers", he notes only "Robert E. Lee". The 86-year old man claimed in 1925 that he was born in Westmorland County, Va and was normally a fisherman and that his current disability included "old age and rheumatism"   His 'Affidavit of Comrades' was signed by two veterans in the Soldier's Home in Richmond, S[amuel].H.Humphries and J[ames].E[dward].Dooley, who were in Guy's Battery, Floyd's Brigade and Co. B, 10th Battalion of Artillery, respectively.[196]

---

[194] **This article is a summary of information contained in the History of the Life of Rev. Wm. Mack Lee, Body Servant of General Robert E. Lee Through the Civil War – Cook from 1861 to 1865 (S.P.: 1918) by Rev. Wm. Mack Lee.**
[195] Confederate Veteran Magazine, Vo. 35, (September 1927), p324, *'More Historical Bunk'*.
[196] *Pension Application for a Disabled Confederate Soldier*, Act 1918 for William Mack Lee, 1132 Church Street, Norfolk, Virginia; see also *Robert E. Lee Camp Confederate Soldiers' Home Applications for Admission*, Library of Virginia.

A Reported Lee Servant
Anthony Riley Profiled: Deserted to Union Army

One of the slaves of the Custis estate that reportedly ended up in the care of Robert E. Lee was man named Anthony "Andy" Riley. He was born on the Custis Plantation about 1834 to Atrolins Riley, a slave belonging to the Custis family of Arlington Heights. Atrolins' father was also a slave of the Custis family.

Riley explained in an 1886 interview that he was about 15-years-old when Robert E. Lee married Martha Custis. He remembered a part of the courtship stating then U.S. Army Captain Lee would ride up on his horse named 'Rob Roy' and "linger near Miss Custis for hours". After the marriage, Andy was made a house servant and recalled Lee was very fond of partridge hunting "especially as he was a crack shot with the sporting gun".

Andy was eventually made a hostler of horses. He accompanied Lee to Harper's Ferry during John Brown's Raid. The news report states Andy remained a body servant to Robert E. Lee from this time forward and attended to Lee's horses "Robert" and "Dick", Kentucky thoroughbreds. He said Lee was extremely fond of both horses, would ride them very hard and was "particular" in giving instructions on their care. Andy said he was with Lee in the early campaigns and said "it was his duty to keep very near Lee, even in engagements, in order to take care of his horse at a moment's notice."

Riley described Lee's manner as "always kind to his servants". According to the report, "When everything was running smoothly, [Lee] would sometimes speak to Andy and show evidence of his feelings. Andy says he was decidedly tickled after Bull Run. [Lee] very often gave his men a $5 bill, suits of clothes and other presents. He loved his own people [his servants], and was a domestic man, according to Andy's statement. At home, he used his slaves very kindly, and all were happy and contented." He said Lee had great affection for his horses, his family and his men in general.

Andy ran away during the Antietam Campaign when Lee's Army was on its way to South Mountain. According to the report, "Instead of leading the General's horse around to him, as was his custom every morning, he turned him over" to another groom and left the camp. He reached Union lines at Fairfax Court House three days later and reportedly became the servant of General Joshua Reynolds, performing the same duties he performed for Lee.

Afte the war Andy worked in New York before settling in Boston in 1872 eventually landing a position at the Horticultural Hall.[197]

---

[197] *The Fairfield News and Herald* (Winnsboro, SC), 16 June 1886, p4, 'General Lee's Body Servant' (from the Boston Post).

Virginia's Black Confederates

Primary Source Document
A Black Confederate's Parole

PAROLE OF ARMSTEAD PAUL – Private Paul was the Chief Cook for Co. H, 22nd Virginia Infantry. Enlisting in May 1861, he served all four years of the war. His unit surrendered after Appomattox the last week of April 1865 in the vicinity of Lewisburg, (now West Virginia). He collected his official parole (above) in Charleston on 11 May 1865. One of his service records is on the left.

Captain Benjamin Scott
Was this Black Confederate A Civil Rights Leader?

One black Confederate from Richmond served as a cook, carried a rifle, served in the first black Confederate infantry company in Richmond and became a local Republican political leader.

Most of what is known of Captain Benjamin Scott of Richmond is contained in postwar newspaper reports of activities in public life. The greatest detail however comes from a letter he wrote and was later published in the *Richmond Dispatch* during the planning for the 1896 United Confederate Veterans reunion that was to be held in Richmond that year. Following a report of the reunion planning where it was noted the United Confederate Veterans were going to reserve a place in line for black veterans, Scott sent a letter to one of the organizers who shared it with the newspaper. Though Scott's spelling and grammar is rough, he was literate enough to get his story across.

Published in the 21 June 1896 issue under the headline *"An Old Army Cook: "Capt" Ben Scott Tells His Experiences in the Late War"*. The article stated:

> *"Captain" Ben Scott was a colored cook in the Confederate army, and he is proud of it. He was present at the very first battle fought in Virginia, and he is going to be in the big parade on July 2nd, or know the reason why. He could, no doubt, tell many amusing experiences he passed through while following the soldier boys with his kettle and frying-pan..."*.[198]

Scott was born free and was apprenticed to a Mr. Patrick Russell learning the plastering trade when the war broke out. He recalled hearing the gun fired at the armory when it was announced that Virginia would secede. Caught up in the patriotic fervor of the time, Scott enlisted as a cook in Company H, 15th Virginia Infantry, also known as the Young Guard. He said he was a mess cook for the company commander and other officers in that company.

---

[198] *Richmond Dispatch*, 21 June 1896

Scott recalled his Captain [Charters] gave him a gun, equipment and an ammunition (cartridge) box when they left Richmond. He wrote the regiment marched from the Fairground (present location of the Science Museum of Virginia) to Rocketts Landing, boarded a boat and sailed to Grove Wharf where they disembarked and marched to Williamsburg. After remaining in camp for several days they marched to Yorktown where they were directed to Little Bethel with the Lafayette Artillery before becoming involved in the battle. Scott claimed to have fired three shots "at the yankee" during that battle.

Shortly after the battle, he was called home because his mother had died. He soon "enlisted" in another regiment, believed to be the Special Louisiana Battalion or "Louisiana Tigers" commanded by Major C.R. Wheat which were headed for Manassas. Scott said he arrived by train at Centerville just after 6 a.m. on a Sunday morning [July 21] and heard the artillery. Scott said he was on the battlefield all day up to the time General Johnston arrived by train around 4 p.m. He remained with the unit until Major Wheat was mortally wounded at Gaines' Mill.[199] In between he recalled watching the execution of two men condemned by court martial.[200] Scott also recalled seeing Confederate President Jefferson Davis visit Manassas.

Scott said he had many more stories to tell. While he did not address what he did in the latter part of the war, at least one post-war newspaper article made mention of him when addressing the topic of "Negro Confederates". The article said:

> *"Negro soldiers—a few of them—were enlisted when the Confederacy was on the ragged edge of desperation and dissolution. One such company we remember to have seen drilling in the Capitol Square here. Our impression is that it was made up largely of servants employed in or about the Confederate military hospitals and departmental bureaus here.* **Ben Scott, who afterwards figured in the colored militia here, was one of its officers.**"[201]

Post-War Activities
A post-war record of Scott shows up in Union army records. A 23 June 1865 letter from the War Department, Bureau of Refugees, Freedmen and Abandoned Lands requested the Richmond Provost Marshal to "give the Bearer Benj Scott on duty in this Bureau an order to purchase an pair of dark blue pants and a linen coat." What he did in the employ of the Freedman's Bureau was not determined.

During the military occupation of Richmond, the Union authorities, the defeated Confederates and the newly freed black population co-existed in fully undefined boundaries. One of the local arrangements called for four of the six streetcars in Richmond to be reserved for general public use while two were reserved strictly for white women and other white men if space was available. News reports indicate Scott tested this regulation in May 1867 when he attempted on two occasions to ride the 'white only' street cars. He was ejected from the first car and peacefully departed rather than risk arrest. He rode the second

---

[199] **The unit served in the Shenandoah Valley Campaign before the Seven Days battles.**
[200] **Two enlisted members of the Louisiana Tigers were executed after having been found guilty of drunkenness and insubordination when Brigadier General Richard Taylor commanded the brigade.**
[201] *Richmond Dispatch*, **4 October 1902.**

car until the driver intentionally drove it off the tracks at which point Scott left the scene without disturbance. While other details are sketchy, it appears that Scott made one of the first documented attempts to ensure "equal access" to public conveyances making him, in a sense, an early civil rights crusader.[202]

Public news reports show he was active in Republican Party politics as early as 1871 when he got into trouble for passing a counterfeit $10 note a Republican operative had paid him to help get out the vote. Scott was bailed out of jail and appears to have been cleared. He is documented in the news as having given rousing political speeches throughout the 1880s and 1890s at local Republican meetings.[203]

When the Virginia militia was reformed, Scott was elected Captain of the Virginia Grays, a 59-man company.[204] He was referred to as "Captain" in an 1871 news item and was reported in 1880 as being elected again suggesting he held this position for many years. It further suggests his Confederate military experience coupled with his natural leadership traits got him elected and re-elected to the position. He apparently felt very strong about his military service and continued to visit the armory well into age. The 15 January 1898 *Richmond Planet*, an African-American newspaper, had a headline stating 'Capt. Scott Injured'. According to the article:

> "While attending a drill at the armory of the First Battalion, Virginia Volunteers on Wednesday night, 12th inst., in moving out of the way Capt. Ben Scott, a visitor, stepped backward into a four-foot cellar opening. He was immediately lifted out and beside a shaking up, and a bad sprain in the left knee he was not seriously injured. Surgeon S.H. Dismond ministered to his suffering and while suffering much pain, he is not seriously injured."

This article over a minor incident speaks to his status in the black community of Richmond at that time.

Ending his 1896 letter Captain Scott said:

> "I have often wondered by you people forget the negro who followed you through the war as Cooks and Washers and Waiters and stood by you through the thick of battle and have been so far forgotten. Sir, I hope you will excuse bad writing and accept the same from a friend to the colored and a Virginian negro that have laid on the field of battle with the old veterans of the South."[205]

---

[202] *Staunton Spectator and General Advertiser*, 14 May 1867 quoting a *Richmond Times* article, 'Another Street Car Difficulty'.
[203] *The Daily Journal*, 8 December 1871, 'Captain Ben Scott' for the arrest. He is reported on many times regarding Republican party political activities.
[204] *Richmond Dispatch*, 1 January 1880.
[205] The grammar and spelling was corrected for clarification from the published copy of the letter. See the *Richmond Dispatch*, 21 June 1896 issue, 'An Old Army Cook' for the full original.

Virginia's Black Confederates

LEE SERVANT AT APPOMATTOX – Fielding Walker and his wife on their small farm in Loudon County, Virginia in 1918. Walker was also reported to be one of General Robert E. Lee's body servants in 1861 and "was present at the surrender at Appomattox Court House. He thought he was 87 years old in 1918. Photo on p19 of *The Evening Herald*, Albuquerque, New Mexico, 13 April 1918. There is no record of Walker applying for or receiving a Virginia pension.

DISPATCH RIDER - Eli Jackson was a slave of Capt. Forbes, a member of Longstreet's staff. He reportedly served as a dispatch rider carrying "satchels containing valuable military documents from one Southern Army to another." He was 83 when this photo was taken.

Dick Slate and His Bowie Knife

Dick Slate of Pittsylvania County was one of three black Confederates musicians on the 18th Virginia Infantry's headquarters staff. Slate went home to visit when he ran into difficulties that were reported in the January 2, 1862 issue of the *Richmond Dispatch* under a headline reading 'Old Dick, the Drummer'. The report read:

"A few days ago there appeared in the local department of this paper the following paragraph: 'Dick, a venerable darkey in uniform, was arrested for carrying a huge bowie-knife. He was on his return home to Danville from a campaign against the Yankees, and the Mayor discharged him after confiscating the knife.'

"This has elicited from 'A.B.V.' a 'vindication' of old Dick, including a sketch of his career, which we publish entire, not only as an act of justice to 'the subject of this notice', but because it fully repays perusal:

"The person above referred to has occupied the position of chief drummer for the 18th Virginia regiment for the last eight months and is highly esteemed by the regiment, not only as a musician, but as a brace and gallant old man. He is a hero of two wars, and in several instances has rendered good service to the country. When the war with Mexico broke out, he enlisted as musician for a South Carolina regiment and followed it through the war, and was present when the glorious Gen. Butler fell.[206] The war being successfully terminated, he returned home to his usual avocations. Upon the breaking out of our present war, though old and gray, he was among the first to respond to Virginia's call for volunteers, and was regularly mustered into service with the 18th Regiment. Since that time, he has not only carried his drum, but also the bowie-knife referred to above, and a musket. In the memorable battle of the twenty-first July[207], he deserted his drum, and with musket in hand followed the regiment throughout the battle. Several days after the battle, while strolling through the woods, he discovered the hiding place of what he thought a Yankee, and, or reporting it, went down with several of the regiment and captured three of the creatures – one of them Colonel Wood, of the Fourteenth Brooklyn.[208] In every scene of danger or of difficulty, old Dick has accompanied the regiment with bowie-knife by his side and musket in hand. When on picket duty at Mason's hill, in sight of the enemy, he would go beyond the picket lines to get a fair crack at the Yankee pickets. In fin, old Dick, we believe, is a gentleman and true patriot, and we feel sorry that his knife, around which clung so many proud associations to him, should have been taken from him. He valued it above all things except his musket. It is true the law may have required its confiscation, as setting a bad example to darkeys in civil life; but, under the circumstances, it does seem hard to have subjected the old man not only to the loss of his bowie-knife, but the mortification attendant, or a suspicion of evil designs. We hope old Dick may live to prove his character still further by bagging his Yankee."

---

[206] Colonel Pierce Butler, former South Carolina Governor, commanded South Carolina's Palmetto Volunteers. He was killed at the Battle of Churubusco. The Volunteers served from December 1846 to July 1848 with Winfield Scott and were reportedly the first regiment to storm the gates of Mexico City.
[207] Battle of First Manassas
[208] 14th Regiment of New York State Militia also called the 14th Brooklyn under Colonel Alfred M. Wood. He was wounded in the battle and later exchanged for a Confederate Colonel. Wood's wounds caused him to be discharged for disability in October 1861.

Virginia's Black Confederates

Primary Source Document

News Photograph

LYNCHBURG PARADE – From the *blackconfederates.blogspot.com*, this photo was contributed to that site by Calvin Johnson. The cutline on the image says, *"Black Confederates Ludwell Brown, Silas [G]reen, and Gabe Hunt in parade in Lynchburg, Va. in early 1900s. Ludwell is buried in Charlotte Co., Va [at] the Patrick Henry Plantation. Gabe is buried in Campbell Co., Va and Silas is buried in the Old City Cemetery in Lynchburg".* The original source of photo is not stated but it appears to be a newspaper photograph of a Confederate veteran parade.

IYNCHBU

Black Confederates at Craney Island

Craney Island is located at the mouth of the Elizabeth River. It served as a defensive point in the War of 1812 (repelling a British attack on Norfolk) and was used by both Confederate and Union forces to defend Norfolk, Portsmouth and the Gosport Navy Yard. The *CSS Virginia* was scuttled just off Craney Island when the Norfolk defenses were abandoned in 1862. It continues in use today as a U.S. Navy refueling point a site for dumping dredge materials.

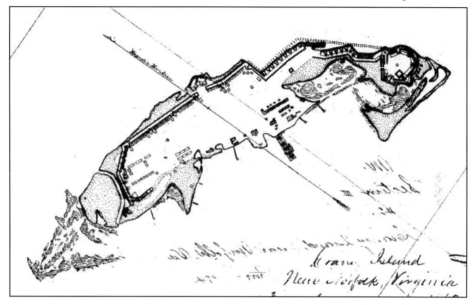

Critical Chokepoint
Craney Island was a critical chokepoint at the mouth of the Elizabeth River. Guns from its position could command the primary sea lanes in Hampton Roads. Its military importance was well recognized by Confederate military authorities who took early actions to improve its defenses. When the Provisional Army of Virginia occupied Norfolk on 18 April, the critical defensive points were assessed and actions were taken to place batteries at key points. On 20 April Engineer Colonel T.M.R. Talcott was directed to take a force of local militia "and with all the negroes" that could be pressed into service to erect earthworks at various locations. He was also, "under cover of night", to proceed to Craney Island "and repair the old works there, and gave orders for the immediate mounting of as many pieces as would be necessary to supply the several works."[209]

Talcott identified troop, material and tool requirements to be collected for repairs before he made an inspection of the island. With an assistant, Talcott traveled to Craney Island in a small boat where they inspected the site "by moonlight". The troops, laborers and tools

---

[209] **Navy OR, Series I, Vol. 4,** *Report of Major-General [William B.] Taliaferro, of Virginia's Provisional Army, to the governor of Virginia, of the occupation of the Norfolk Navy Yard and regarding affairs in Norfolk,* **23 April 1861.**

arrived around 8 a.m. and by 10:20 there were about 120 laborers from area plantations.[210] This suggests the 120 were local slaves.

Free men of color were also employed to improve defenses as well as white labor. As early as 2 May Union observers on the USS Monticello "saw a number of soldiers in tents and upwards of 500 men busy throwing up earthworks."[211]

General Lee was concerned about Craney Island, writing on 25 May 1861 to General Benjamin Huger who was, by this time, commanding Virginia Forces in Norfolk. Lee wrote:

> *"I wish to call your attention to the condition of Craney Island. It is the first point that will arrest the passage of a vessel to Norfolk; it is the most exposed and the least prepared for defense. I cannot urge upon you too strongly the necessity of putting it in good condition. More troops should be ordered there, and laborers, if practicable. If laborers cannot be obtained, the troops must work at the trenches at that point and all others within your lines of defense."*[212]

The defensive improvements made to the site included 18 artillery batteries.[213] Confederate Navy records indicate 21 guns were initially emplaced, including one 10-inch pivot gun, six 8-inch guns of 55 cwt; ten 8-inch guns of 63 cwt and four 32-pounder guns of 51 cwt with the intent of mounting a total of 30 guns at the location.[214] By October 1861, there were 42 guns emplaced consisting of a 10-inch pivot gun, 18 8-inch guns, seven 9-inch guns, three 8-inch solid shot guns, 12 32-pounders and one rifled 32-pounder.[215] The works hosted roughly 35 officers and 455 to 525 enlisted men.[216] The nature of the works constructed by the laborers can be seen in an early 1862 map of the island in addition to a Union Engineer map, for the U.S. Coast Survey, made after the location was captured.[217]

Union Naval Captain John Marston reported to U.S. Secretary of the Navy Gideon Wells on 21 February 1862, "The whole of Craney Island is a fortified camp, mounting at least 30 guns, perhaps more, bearing directly down the river."

---

[210] OR, Series I, Vol. 2, Confederate Correspondence, *Report of Andrew Talcott, Engineer, to General Robert E. Lee, Commanding Virginia Forces*, 26 April 1861.
[211] Navy OR, Series I, Vol. 4, *Letter from Lieutenant D.L. Braine, U.S. Navy, Commanding U.S.S. Monticello, to W.H. Aspinwall, esq, giving an account of reconnaissance by that vessel*, 2 May 1861.
[212] OR, Series I, Vol 2, Lee to Huger, 25 May 1861; see also Lee to Huger, 11 June 1861 where he again expresses concern for the Craney Island works.
[213] Testimony of CSN CAPTAIN Robert B. Pegram, 29 January 1863 to C.S. Navy Department investigation, Navy O.R., Series II, Vo. 1, p632.
[214] Navy OR, Series I, Vol. 5, *Report of Captain Barron*, Virginia Navy, to the governor of Virginia, regarding naval defenses of the rivers of Virginia, Enclosure A, *Naval Defenses of Virginia.*, p802-805, dated 10 June 1861.
[215] Navy OR, Series I, Vol. 6, *Report of the Armament of Batteries around Norfolk*, October 29, 1861, p741.
[216] OR, Series I, Vol 4, Chapt XII, *Abstract from Return of the Department of Norfolk*, Major General Benjamin Huger, C.S. Army, commanding, for November 30, 1861; Ibid, January 1862.
[217] Both maps are accessible at NOAA website: (http://www.nauticalcharts.noaa.gov/history/CivilWar/index.html).

Virginia's Black Confederates

The Civil War Battles and Leaders series also has an image of the defenses depicting Confederates in the Craney Island defenses observing the *CSS Virginia* on its way to do battle. The *Virginia* anchored under the protection of the Craney Island defenses for much of its life defending Norfolk. When the city was abandoned, so were the defenses at Craney Island. About 39 guns were spiked and abandoned with 5,000 pounds of powder and a large number of shells.[218] The *Virginia* was run aground at Craney Island so its crew could escape overland through Suffolk. It was then set on fire and blew up at 4:58 a.m. on 11 May 1862.

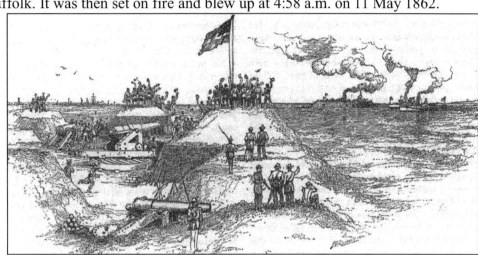

Watching the Merrimac (Battles and Leaders Vol 1, p713)

Federal forces occupied the site the next day, took down two Confederate flags and ran up the U.S. flag. President Lincoln regarded the Confederate "evacuation of strong batteries erected by the rebels on Sewell's Point and Craney Island and the destruction of the rebel iron-clad steamer Merrimac [Virginia]…as among the most important successes of the present war."[219] The Federals continued to use the strong fortifications and the site for a coal fueling depot and powder depot. There was also a Union military hospital at the site. On April 5, 1865, it was to be prepared to house Confederate prisoners of war but, with Lee's surrender on April 9, it is unlikely POWs were held within the earthworks.

The Museum of the Confederacy Archives Section has several pay rolls from Craney Island providing the names of free men of color and slaves who worked there. The May 1861 payroll is partially transcribed to provide names. The payrolls also include the names of slave owners and additional data that might be of interest to genealogists or persons doing study on the Craney Island defenses.

---

[218] OR, Series I, Vol 11, *Report of Major General John E. Wool, U.S. Army to Secretary of War Stanton, 12 May 1862*

[219] OR, Series I, Vol 11, Secretary of War Stanton *Order Thanking General [John E.] Wool for the capture of Norfolk*, 11 May 1862.

Pay Roll of African-Americans (free and slave) Defenses of Craney Island, Va May 1861

Museum of the Confederacy Collection *African-American Enslaved and Free Men of Color Pay Roll-Defenses of Craney Island, Va May 1861(4-13)*; Payroll of Sundry Persons employed by the Commonwealth of Virginia for Coast Harbor and River defenses in the defense works at Craney Island in the month of May 1861 (J.A. Johnson AQM)

Names	Status
Clayton, Edward	Free
Deans, [Shaifir or Shafer]	Free
Elliott, Alex	Free
Garrison, Caleb	Free
Holland, Caleb	Free
Jones, Arnise	Free
Langley, William	Free
Owens, William	Free
Perkins, John	Free
Smith, John	Free
Capps, Moses	Slave
Capps, William	Slave
Carney, John	Slave
Carney, Willis	Slave
Chulle, William	Slave
Coleman, Dw T	Slave
Cooper, John	Slave
Crocker, William	Slave
Deans, Henry	Slave
Deans, Jesse	Slave
Deans, John	Slave
Deans, Moses	Slave
Deans, Phillip	Slave
Dennis, Jas	Slave
Duke, William	Slave
Elliott, Zacky	Slave
Fuller, William	Slave
Gordon, Jim	Slave
Graves, Lewis	Slave
Grimes, Godfrey	Slave
Grimes, John	Slave
Ham, Lewis	Slave

Virginia's Black Confederates

Ham, Luke	Slave
Hillary, John	Slave
Holliday, Theodore W.	Slave
James, George	Slave
Johnson, Lewis	Slave
Johnson, Theo	Slave
Kingman, Chris	Slave
Kingman, Daniel	Slave
Kingman, Phillip	Slave
Leigh, Jack	Slave
Lewis, Willis	Slave
Mackey, William	Slave
McCall, Joseph	Slave
Migar, Harry	Slave
Morris, John	Slave
Oden, John	Slave
Riddicke, Jas	Slave
Riddicke, Joe	Slave
Rix, Corneilus	Slave
Rix, Gus	Slave
Robertson, Jonathan	Slave
Shephard, Miles	Slave
Simmons, Allen	Slave
Stephens, John	Slave
Tart, Abraham	Slave
Tart, George	Slave
Tart, Simon	Slave
Taylor, Alex	Slave
Taylor, Beverly	Slave
Taylor, George	Slave
Taylor, Moses	Slave
Thomas, Plate	Slave
Thoroughgood, Peter	Slave
Ustace, George	Slave
Wilson, Robert	Slave
Wise, Frank	Slave
Wise, Westly	Slave

Gloucester Point Battery

One of the main sea lanes of communication in Virginia was the York River which had a critical chokepoint in the half-mile strait between Yorktown and Gloucester Point. These locations were fortified with artillery batteries to close off any Federal attempt to move troops up the river and Virginia's interior. It played an important part in the 1862 Peninsula Campaign and Union Siege of Yorktown.

Among those constructing earthworks at Gloucester Point were free men of color from Gloucester County who were contracted to perform the labor.[220] Work under the authority of the State of Virginia was already underway when the Federal ship *USS CUMBERLAND* made a reconnaissance of the location. According to U.S. Navy Lieutenant Thomas O. Selfridge:

GLOUCESTER POINT WATER BATTERY – constructed by free men of color working as contractor labor to the Confederate Engineer Department.

> *"At Gloucester Point there is in the course of erection a breastwork, or water battery, which, when completed, will effectually command the approach of the river. These preparations thus far consist only in a heavy rampart and the collection of a large amount of turf. In its present condition it is useless for defense, as it has not attained a height sufficient to protect its occupants, and there are no means at present to mount its guns…I would respectfully call the attention of the flag-officer to the importance of a command of York River, which, from its depth and ease of access, leading into the heart of Virginia, would be invaluable in the case of offensive measures being decided upon by the United States. For the present it is my humble opinion that a small steamer could prevent the further progress of the work at Gloucester Point, as I firmly believe there are no heavy*

---

[220] **Collections of the Library of Virginia,** *Pay Rolls of Free Negroes, Coast Works, May and July 1861.*

guns in the neighborhood, and it could effectually retard for some time the transportation of such from Richmond."[221]

The first shots were exchanged the next day when the steamer *USS YANKEE* approached to within 2,000 yard of the Gloucester Point battery. A Confederate battery of six-pound guns of the Richmond Howitzers was manning the Point. The Second Company under the command of Lieutenant John Thompson Brown -- fired two shots across the bow of the ship. The Federals answered with four round shots and two shells but these dropped harmlessly in the water. Another ten shots were fired by the Confederates but all reportedly missed their mark.[222] This was the 'Battle of Gloucester Point' and the first reported combat action in Virginia.

GLOUCESTER POINT BATTERY

Confederate Colonel W.B. Taliaferro assumed command of Gloucester Point the night of 7 May. He learned of the exchange of gunfire and ordered the 250-man Gloucester militia to duty at the battery to help repel any Union landing. As early as April 28, at least ten 9-inch guns and two 11-inch guns had been ordered for Gloucester Point.[223] Taliaferro's orders from Lee were clear in that once a Federal ship was in range, the battery was to fire a shot across the bow to deter further travel. Should the Federal boat continue a second warning shot over the ship was to be fired and, if the ship still continued, fire was to be directed into the ship and it was to be captured, if possible.[224]

Captain H.C. Cabell, commanding a battery, reported:

---

[221] **Navy OR,** *Report of Flag-Officer Pendergrast, U.S. Navy, commanding Home Squadron, transmitting report of Lieutenant Selfridge, U.S. Navy, of a reconnaissance in York River, Va. 6 May 1861.*
[222] **Navy OR,** *Report of Flag-Officer Pendergrast, U.S. Navy, commanding Home Squadron, transmitting report of Lieutenant Selfridge, U.S. Navy, 7 May 1861.*
[223] **Navy, OR,** *Report of Colonel Taliaferro, C.S. Army, commanding at Gloucester Point, 8 May 1861; Order of the Commandant Navy yard, Norfolk to Captain Fairfax, Virginia Navy to Furnish Ordnance for batteries, 28 April 1861*
[224] **Navy OR,** *Instructions from major General Lee, commanding Virginia forces, to Colonel Taliaferro, commanding at Gloucester Point, Va, relative to defense of that place, 8 May 1861.*

'If you could see the place you would be satisfied of its great importance. To allow it to be lost would be a fatal error. The force here, consisting entirely of volunteers, is prepared to defend it to the last extremity. They are perfectly aware of the strangeness and peril of their situation, but though "there is plenty of danger, there is no fear."[225]

Reinforcements and more guns arrived over time. By 14 May at least three 9-inch guns had been mounted and the gun crews were constantly drilling. By 10 June, there were eight 9-inch guns of 9,000 pounds and four 32-pounders of various weights with five more en route. The site had been fortified and consisted of both Army and Navy personnel with the Navy under the command of Commander Thomas Jefferson Page, an Annapolis graduate and former U.S. Navy officer. Eventually at least 14 large Columbiad guns would be on the water battery. By 1 December the battery consisted of nine 9-inch guns; seven 32-pounders of various weights and two 42-pound cannonade.[226]

McClellan's Peninsula Campagin was initiated on 17 March 1862. By April the Federal Navy were focused on the destruction of the Yorktown and Gloucester Point batteries in support of General George B. McClellan's Peninsula Campaign. Commodore L.M. Goldsborough stated to lead naval officer Captain J.S. Missroon, "The first object in view, as you are aware, is the reduction of Yorktown and Gloucester Point, and thus to open the navigation of York River and its

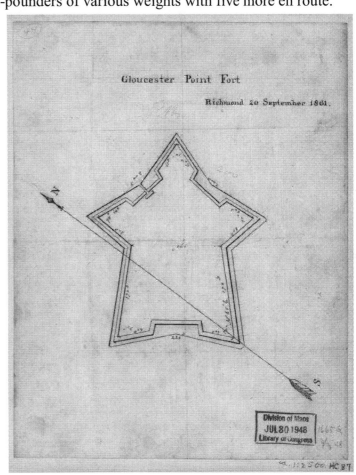

GLOUCESTER POINT FORTIFICATION (LOC Geography and Map Division 2005625005)

---

[225] **Navy OR,** *Report of Captain Cabell, Virginia forces, of the movements of the United States vessels near Gloucester Point, Va and calling attention to the importance of defending that place, 10 May 1861.*
[226] **Navy OR,** *Report of Colonel Taliaferro, Virginia forces, commanding at Gloucester Point, Va., of the movements of United States vessels near that place, 14 May 186;* see also *status of batteries, 10 June 1861; Letter from Brigadier-General Mansfield, U. S. Army, commanding at Camp Butler, to the Secretary of the Navy, transmitting diagram and information regarding the York River batteries, 25 Feb 1862; Monthly report of Commander Whittle, C. S. Navy, commanding York River defenses, 6 Sept 1861; Batteries of York River, as reported by commanding officer, December 1, 1861. Gloucester Point Battery.--Commander Page, commanding*

Virginia's Black Confederates

tributaries to our army transports and navy vessels."[227] Two days later Missroon advised McClellan:

> *"The forts at Gloucester are very formidable indeed, and the water batteries of Yorktown have evidently been increased in dimensions within a few days, as indicated by the new earth... The enemy are still on Gloucester Point; how strong I can not say. So long as he holds that formidable work (or, indeed, upper and lower work) we surely can not command the York River. All the gunboats of the Navy would fail to take it, but would be destroyed in the attempt".*[228]

By 14 April Commander Missroon has an African-American man, an information source, pulled from a canoe. Missroon reports to McClellan:

> *"...that the battery at Gloucester Point is commanded by Jeff Page, late of U. S. Navy, a good officer; Richard L. Page, also formerly of Navy, in command of one of the upper works at Gloucester; that they are very sanguine of sinking vessels, and have practiced their firing, which is very accurate; says Page (Jeff) can kill a dog at a mile."*[229]

From 14 April to the end of the month, the U.S. ships shelled Gloucester Point and Yorktown almost daily. The Confederates abandoned the both Gloucester Point and Yorktown the night of May 3-4, 1862 to retreat up the peninsula. On 4 May McClellan marched into Yorktown. When news was received on the USS WACHUSETT, Commander W. Smith dispatched an officer to enter Gloucester Point Battery and raise the U.S. flag. The Confederate guns had been spiked before abandonment. The site was occupied by Federal forces until 1865.

Pay Roll of Free Negroes from Gloucester County employed by the Commonwealth of Virginia for Coast, Harbor and River Defences on the defensive works at Gloucestor Point in May and July 1861 from 1st Lt. James Maurice, Acting Pay Master for the Engineer Department of Virginia

Name	Occupation	Days	Rate of Pay	Net Amount	Pay Roll Month
Adie, Andrew	Laborer	11	42 cents a day	$4.62	July 1861
Alman, Samuel	Laborer	3	50 cents a day	$1.50	May 1861
Banks, Henry	Laborer	10 3/4	50 cents a day	$5.39	May 1861
Berry, William	Laborer	4 3/4	50 cents a day	$2.37	May 1861
Booker, John	Laborer	5 1/4	50 cents a day	$2.62	May 1861

---

[227] **Navy OR,** *Instructions of Flag-Officer Goldsborough, U. S. Navy, to Commander Missroon, U. S. Navy, regarding cooperation with the army for the reduction of Yorktown and Gloucester Point.*
[228] **Navy OR,** *Letter from Commander Missroon, U. S. Navy, to Major. General McClellan, U. S. Army, giving additional information regarding the fortifications in York River, Virginia.*
[229] **Navy OR,** *Letter from Commander Missroon, U. S. Navy, to Major-General McClellan, U. S. Army, regarding the battery on Gloucester Point, 14 April 1862.*

Virginia's Black Confederates

Bristow, William	Laborer	10	42 cents a day	$4.20	July 1861
Casey, John	Laborer	4 1/2	50 cents a day	$2.25	May 1861
Casey, William	Laborer	13 1/2	42 cents a day	$5.67	July 1861
Casey, William	Laborer	4 3/4	50 cents a day	$2.37	May 1861
Chapman, Alexander	Laborer	3	50 cents a day	$1.50	May 1861
Davenport, Thomas	Laborer	5 1/4	50 cents a day	$2.62	May 1861
Dennis, Charles	Laborer	15	42 cents a day	$6.30	July 1861
Dennis, Thomas	Laborer	4 3/4	50 cents a day	$2.37	May 1861
Dennis, Thomas (Tom)	Laborer	4	42 cents a day	$1.68	July 1861
Digges, Henry	Laborer	10	42 cents a day	$4.20	July 1861
Driver, Addision	Laborer	4	42 cents a day	$1.68	July 1861
Driver, Addision	Laborer	3	50 cents a day	$1.50	May 1861
Driver, Gus	Laborer	4	42 cents a day	$1.68	July 1861
Driver, Lem	Laborer	4	42 cents a day	$1.68	July 1861
Driver, Thomas	Laborer	3	50 cents a day	$1.50	May 1861
Dungey, Robert	Laborer	4 1/2	50 cents a day	$2.25	May 1861
Gregory, Robert	Laborer	11	42 cents a day	$4.62	July 1861
Harmon, James	Laborer	3	50 cents a day	$1.50	May 1861
Harris, Ceasar	Laborer	5 1/2	50 cents a day	$2.75	May 1861
Hayes, Alexander (Alex)	Laborer	5 1/4	50 cents a day	$2.62	May 1861
Hayes, Alexander (Alex)	Laborer	7	42 cents a day	$2.94	July 1861
Hayes, Frank	Laborer	5 1/2	50 cents a day	$2.75	May 1861
Hayes, Thomas	Laborer	4 1/2	50 cents a day	$2.25	May 1861
Hayes, Thomas (Tom)	Laborer	4	42 cents a day	$1.68	July 1861
Hill, John	Laborer	26	42 cents a day	$10.92	July 1861
Jackman, Edward	Laborer	4 3/4	50 cents a day	$2.37	May 1861
Jackman, James	Laborer	9 1/4	50 cents a day	$4.62	May 1861
Jordan, Henry	Laborer	4 1/4	50 cents a day	$2.12	May 1861
Kelly, Henry	Laborer	6	42 cents a day	$2.52	July 1861
Kelly, Henry	Laborer	4.5	50 cents a day	$2.25	May 1861
Kelly, John	Laborer	10	42 cents a day	$4.20	July 1861
Kelly, Thomas	Laborer	4 3/4	50 cents a day	$2.37	May 1861
Lackland, Albert	Laborer	4 3/5	50 cents a day	$2.37	May 1861
Lemon, James	Laborer	4 3/4	50 cents a day	$2.37	May 1861
Lemon, Lewis	Laborer	10 1/2	42 cents a day	$4.41	July 1861
Lemon, Lewis	Laborer	5	50 cents a day	$2.50	May 1861
Lemon, Theodore	Laborer	3	50 cents a day	$1.50	May 1861
Lemon, Thomas	Laborer	3	50 cents a day	$1.50	May 1861

Virginia's Black Confederates

Lester, James	Laborer	12 1/2	42 cents a day	$5.25	July 1861
Lockley, James	Laborer	12	42 cents a day	$5.04	July 1861
Meigs, Peter	Laborer	10	42 cents a day	$4.20	July 1861
Miles, Davis	Laborer	5	42 cents a day	$2.10	July 1861
Miller, John	Laborer	4 1/4	50 cents a day	$2.12	May 1861
Olives, Cary	Laborer	10	42 cents a day	$4.20	July 1861
Olman, Sam	Laborer	4	42 cents a day	$1.68	July 1861
Pate, Andrew	Laborer	5 1/2	50 cents a day	$2.75	May 1861
Robinson, Lewis	Laborer	4 1/2	50 cents a day	$2.25	May 1861
Robinson, Lewis	Laborer	4	50 cents a day	$2.00	May 1861
Sampson, Major	Laborer	3	50 cents a day	$1.50	May 1861
Samson, James	Laborer	10 1/2	42 cents a day	$4.41	July 1861
Saunders, William	Laborer	5	50 cents a day	$2.50	May 1861
Slaughter, John	Laborer	3	50 cents a day	$1.50	May 1861
Wallace, George	Laborer	4 3/4	50 cents a day	$2.37	May 1861
Washington, George	Laborer	12	42 cents a day	$5.04	July 1861
Washington, George	Laborer	4 1/4	50 cents a day	$2.12	May 1861
Webb, James	Laborer	7 3/4	50 cents a day	$3.87	May 1861
Wilson, Frank	Laborer	13	42 cents a day	$5.46	July 1861
Wilson, Robert	Laborer	13	42 cents a day	$5.46	July 1861
Wilson, William	Laborer	5 1/4	50 cents a day	$2.62	May 1861

Confederate Teamsters

An old Air Force axiom says 'bullets win battles but logistics win wars'. Things were no different in the American Civil War when wagons were the primary source of transport support for Armies in the field. Wagons required teamsters and many African-Americans served in this capacity. Slaves were conscripted but many of the free men of color were hired (much like defense contractors today) to drive wagons and care for teams of horses and mules. Confederates in the ranks were also detailed to serve as teamsters.

The Confederate Quartermaster Department was responsible for providing transportation for the movement of equipment, supplies and ambulances. Confederate regulations stipulated allowances for baggage based on rank. The Quartermaster's Department also had oversight for hiring mechanics, laborers, teamsters, extra-duty men, wagon and forage masters and other persons and services. Teamsters received extra daily pay per regulation.[230]

On the march the Quartermaster of each division made arrangements for the transportation of the wounded, identifying ambulance depots and providing directions for servicing the ambulances and removing the wounded. The ambulances would follow the troops to the point of engagement to be near enough to provide for the rapid evacuation of wounded.

The baggage trains of general officer headquarters and divisions were also in the charge of the Quartermaster. Assistant Quartermasters had charge of wagons, horses, equipment and other transport employed in the services of individual regiments. On the march the regimental wagons were under the direction of the Quartermaster of the division. The senior Assistant Quartermaster would serve as Brigade Quartermaster when regiments marched by brigade. Wagon-masters were employed with each train of wagons. The regimental trains were loaded, unloaded and guarded, generally, by convalescents and "men not effective in the ranks". Wagon-masters, under orders from the QM Department, were responsible for exercising restraints over teamsters and servants who left their teams, did not properly conduct them, who ill-treated their horses or attempted to pillage or run away in case of an attack.

---

[230] *Regulations of the Confederate States Army for the Quartermaster's Department including the Pay Branch Thereof with an Index and Appendix* (Richmond, Va: J.W. Randolph, 1864) details the duties of the Quartermaster's Department, identifies pay and allowances; see also *Digest of the Comptroller's Decisions in some of the Leading Cases Presented to him for Settlement* (Richmond, Va: Smith, Bailey & Co. Printers) 1863, p11 Section 25, 'Extra Duty Pay'. Per Comptroller decisions, "twenty-five cents per day is intended for the lower grade of employees, '*laborers and teamsters,*' and the higher rate of forty cents per day is intended for the higher grades of 'mechanics' and other *skilled persons*, under which designation Druggists and Clerks, must come. They are to be paid by the Medical (or Purveyor's) Disbursing Clerk. 'Cooks and nurses,' may, by the Regulations, be paid by a Quartermaster in *absence* of such disbursing officer."

Among the responsibilities of the Quartermaster Department was keeping muster rolls providing the names of men serving in various capacities. These rolls provide the names and numbers of African-Americans providing services to the Confederate war effort.[231]

Duties of Teamsters

One of the best sources for detailing the duties of teamsters is the 1914 U.S. Army *Manual for Farriers, Horseshoers, Saddlers and Wagoners or Teamsters*.[232] Per Army instructions, the Wagoner or Teamster was responsible for his team, the harness, the wagon, repair tools and repair parts. Their primary duty was to keep the animals in good health and wagons in good repair so they were able to move their wagons and loads.

Teamsters were to water their teams before themselves, check the feet of the animals, clean the hooves and ensure shoes were not loose. Teamsters were cautioned to check swollen streams before making crossings and to releasing animals from harnesses if the animals should get into water over their heads. Draft animals (mules, ox, horses that pulled teams) were never to be driven out of a walk to protect the animal's strength and endurance for the long haul. They were to ensure harnesses appropriately emplaced to keep from causing sores on the animals.

Trains also contained escort wagons which carried spare wagon parts, spare wheels, bolts, rivets, horseshoes, mule shoes, horseshoe nails and tools. Also included were spare harness and repair parts for the harness. Grease was also required as wagon wheels were to be greased about every 30 miles but only after the old grease was cleaned out of the wheel. Teamsters had to check all the nuts on the wagon and examine the axles for wear and tear. Teams generally consisted of four or six animals. These also required extra equipment such as nose bags for feeding, brushes, curry combs, halters and straps.

The Army regulations identify the routine duties of teamsters as follows:

> *"Certain duties should be attended to daily and some weekly. The following is suggested daily: Immediately after rising, water your animals; when taking to water note carefully if they walk lame; then feed grain to animals, wash yourself, and get breakfast; give animals a very hasty cleaning, clean and inspect feet and shoes carefully, clean the ground where animals have stood during the night; hitch up and report where ordered; water at every opportunity either from running stream or from bucket—never from public trough unless pronounced healthy by proper authority. When work is finished in evening, park the wagon in place designated, remove harness and hang up, rub off collars, belly bands, and cruppers; water; tie animals to picket line; clean out and examine the feet carefully, make a note of loose or lost shoes; fed grain and hay; report animals*

---

[231] The muster rolls reside in various locations and have yet to be fully transcribed. Efforts are underway in the Archives branch of the Museum of the Confederacy to focus on the Quartermaster Department records.

[232] War Department, Office of the Chief of Staff, *Manual for Farriers, Horsehoers, Saddlers and Wagoners or Teamsters* (Washington, DC: Government Printing Office) 1915. While written nearly 50 years after the Civil War, it is inferred the fundamental duties were the same.

requiring shoeing or veterinary attention, especially examine carefully for any abrasion or enlargement; wash and get dinner; glance over harness and the nuts on wagon, making any minor repairs and reporting those which require attention of a specialist; grease the wagon, if required; groom, wash animals' shoulders, and fix the harness so as to remove the pressure the next day from any swollen parts."[233]

These regulations make it clear the Teamster did much more than drive a wagon. They were personally responsible for the care of the wagon and its team, the failure of either one could cost the Army a wagon load of supplies or equipment needed to support combat operations.

Gettysburg Combat

The combat service support role of teamsters did not prevent them from being in battle. On 2 May 1863 near Yanceyville, Virginia, a Confederate wagon train that had bivouacked for the night was captured by Co. C of the 5th U.S. Cavalry. Captured were 15 black Confederate teamsters, 15 wagons, 60 mules.[234]

The Army of Northern Virginia's retreat from Gettysburg was led by a wagon train about 17 miles in length under the protection of the cavalry brigade of John D. Imboden and one 6-gun battery of artillery. In addition to remaining supplies, the wagons carried the Confederate wounded. The train departed Gettysburg in a pouring rain that would last 12 hours. They reached Williamsport on the afternoon of 5 July, stopping long enough to eat, harassed along the way by probing Federal cavalry and civilians. It was also at Williamsport that two regiments of Confederate infantry coming from Virginia were met.

According to E. Porter Alexander:

> *"Imboden required every family in town to cook provisions for the wounded, under pain of having its kitchen occupied. The river was in flood and impassable except by two small ferry-boats. Next morning [Imboden] learned of the approach of five Federal brigades of cavalry – about 7000 men, with 18 guns. The flanks of the city fortunately rested upon creeks, leaving only the north front to be defended. He armed about 800 teamsters and convalescents, and with the two regiments of infantry and his dismounted cavalry he marched about so as to create the impression of a large force. He put in the line all of his guns and brought over some ammunition in the ferry-boats. A sharp fight ensued, the teamster acquitting themselves handsomely. The enemy was driven back and held off until the approach of Stuart's cavalry in the afternoon caused the Federal cavalry to withdraw."*[235]

The Museum of the Confederacy has a list of some teamsters who were made prisoners of war during Gettysburg Campaign but these have not yet been transcribed.

---

[233] **Ibid, p74**
[234] **OR, Series I, Vol. XXV, (39-1093)** *Report of Captain James E. Harrison, Fifth U.S. Cavalry.*
[235] **Edward Porter Alexander, <u>Military Memoirs of a Confederate: A Critical Narrative</u>, (New York: Charles Scribner's Sons) 1907; p437-439**

Black Confederate Teamsters at Manassas

Major William L. Cabell was General P.G.T. Beauregard's Chief Quartermaster, Confederate Army of the Potomac, for the Manassas Campaign. Camp Pickens was the post that served as Beauregard's headquarters.[236]

Major Cabell was a native of Bridgewater (near Danville) in Pittsylvania County, Va. He entered West Point in 1846 and was appointed brevet 2nd Lieutenant, 7th U.S. Infantry in 1850. By 1858 he was a Captain and assistant quartermaster. Appointed as Major of the Quarter Master Department on 16 March 1861, he resigned his commission on 20 April which is the same day he entered Confederate service. He served as the Chief Quartermaster and Commissary for the State of Virginia until 25 May 1861 when he was appointed Chief Quartermaster of Beauregard's Army.[237]

Parts of his duties were to ensure provisions were available for troops arriving from other areas to join the main army.[238] Provisions had to be transported by wagon or rail. Wagon travel required dispatching wagons, teams and teamsters to various commands. He kept track of teams, teamsters and wagons with a log book that provided the assessed value of the wagons, the horses. and teamsters in the Confederate Army of the Potomac. He coordinated supply deliveries and would note to which Assistant Quartermaster and Unit the teams were to report. His list of teamsters include white men, free men of color and slaves. In one of his record books, at least 151 African-Americans working as teamsters can be fully or partially identified.

Beauregard reported after the battle that, "Valuable assistance was given to me by Major Cabell, chief officer of the quartermaster's department, in the sphere of his duties – duties environed by far more than the ordinary difficulties and embarrassments attending the operations of a long organized regular establishment."[239]

On 14 January 1862 Cabell transferred to the Army of the West. He was appointed Brigadier General in command of troops at White River, Arkansas on 21 March 1861. He became QM General of the Trans-Mississippi Division of the Army. He was captured on 25 October 1864 near Fort Scott, Missouri, sent to Johnson's Island and then Fort Warren in Boston where he was released on oath on 24 July 1865.

Major Cabell's Roster

Most of the identifiable units in the roster below are from Beauregard's Confederate Army of the Potomac while others are from Joseph E. Johnston's Army of the Shenandoah. This list of 151 names was compiled from Major Cabell's original notebook now housed in the

---

[236] OR, Series 1, Vol. 2, July 16-22, 1861, The Bull Run, or Manassas Campaign, Virginia. No. 64, *Reports of General G.T. Beauregard, commanding Confederate Army of the Potomac, of Operations from July 17-20.*
[237] Compiled Service Records, William L. Cabell, Officers, Confederate Records.
[238] Ibid, *Letter of R.S. Garnett, Adjutant General, HQs Virginia Forces, Richmond, Va to Lieutenant Colonel E.K. Smith, Commanding Confederate States Troops, Lynchburg, Va, 14 May 1861.*
[239] Ibid, No. 84, *Reports of Gen. G.T. Beauregard, C.S. Army*, and resulting correspondence.

Virginia's Black Confederates

archives of the Museum of the Confederacy in Richmond, Va. Major Cabell's list also contained the names of many white teamsters whose names are not included in this extract.

This list is by command rather than by name. Names are listed in index. Terms of reference: A/AQM is Assistant Quartermaster; QM is Quartermaster; Regt is Regiment; Bde is Brigade; Vols is Volunteers; Reg is Regulars; Bn is Battalion.

Major W.L. Cabell, Quartermaster
Camp Pickens, Manassas Junction, Va, 1861
Roster of hired wagons and teams transferred [listed by command]

Name of Driver	Status	To Whom Delivered
Richard	Slave	Lt. L.Q. Washington, AAQM, [First Brigade, Confederate Army of the Potomac]
Michael (of Wm Stout)	Slave	Lt. L.Q. Washington, AAQM, [First Brigade, Confederate Army of the Potomac]
Daniel	Slave	Lt. L.Q. Washington, AAQM, [First Brigade, Confederate Army of the Potomac]
Charles	Slave	Lt. L.Q. Washington, AAQM, [First Brigade, Confederate Army of the Potomac]
Sam	Slave	Lt. L.Q. Washington, AAQM, [First Brigade, Confederate Army of the Potomac]
Bob	Slave	Lt. L.Q. Washington, AAQM, [First Brigade, Confederate Army of the Potomac]
Jesse	Slave	Lt. L.Q. Washington, AAQM, [First Brigade, Confederate Army of the Potomac]
Reuben	Slave	Lt. L.Q. Washington, AAQM, [First Brigade, Confederate Army of the Potomac]
Jim	Slave	Lt. L.Q. Washington, AAQM, [First Brigade, Confederate Army of the Potomac]
Edward (of Jas Notman)	Slave	
Jim	Slave	W.D. Webb, QM 5th Alabama Regt
Major	Slave	W.D. Webb, QM 5th Alabama Regt
Nace	Slave	W.D. Webb, QM 5th Alabama Regt
Edward	Slave	W.D. Webb, QM 5th Alabama Regt
William	Slave	Capt B.F. Lovelace AQM 7th Regt SC Vols
Bob	Slave	Capt B.F. Lovelace AQM 7th Regt SC Vols
Ben (of S. Hutchinson)	Slave	Capt B.F. Lovelace AQM 7th Regt SC Vols
Harrison	Free	Capt B.F. Lovelace AQM 7th Regt SC Vols
Ned	Slave	Capt A. Anderson, QM, 18th [Va] Reg Withers
Lewis	Slave	Capt A. Anderson, QM, 18th [Va] Reg Withers

Virginia's Black Confederates

Thornton	Slave	Capt A. Anderson, QM, 18th [Va] Reg Withers
McKagen	Slave	Capt EH Harris, AQM, 6th Ala Regt
Jim	Slave	Capt EH Harris, AQM, 6th Ala Regt
Harry	Slave	Capt Heard, 2nd NC Reg
Jerry	Slave	Capt Goodwin, 17th Regt Miss Vols
Oliver	Slave	Capt Goodwin, 17th Regt Miss Vols
Tyler, Jack	Free	R.C. Woods, AQM [24th Virginia Infantry]
Rains, Burwell	Free	
Solomon	Slave	
Jones, Daniel	Slave	Jones' Bde Capt DW Wright
Payne, David	Slave	Jones' Bde Capt DW Wright
Watson, Robert	Slave	Jones' Bde Capt DW Wright
Parrott, Bill	Slave	Jones' Bde Capt DW Wright
Henderson, Forest	Slave	Jones' Bde Capt DW Wright
Swann, Jas	Slave	Jones' Bde Capt DW Wright
Cole, Jim	Slave	Jones' Bde Capt DW Wright
Carter, Walker	Slave	Jones' Bde Capt DW Wright
Johnson, Manuel	Slave	Jones' Bde Capt DW Wright
Allen, Wilson	Slave	Jones' Bde Capt DW Wright
Monroe, Nathan	Slave	
Powell, Adolphus	Slave	Hampton's Legion, Capt Goodwin
Kian, Hillory	Slave	Hampton's Legion, Capt Goodwin
Norris, Isaac	Slave	Hampton's Legion, Capt Goodwin
Lee, Ford	Slave	Hampton's Legion, Capt Goodwin
Payne, Presley	Slave	Hampton's Legion, Capt Goodwin
Simm, Lee	Slave	Hampton's Legion, Capt Goodwin
Rains, Wm	Slave	Hampton's Legion, Capt Goodwin
Harrison, James	Slave	Ewell's Brigade
Hill, Lewis	Slave	Early's Brigade
Green, Charles	Slave	Early's Brigade
Simm, Lewis	Slave	Early's Brigade
Jackson, Madison	Slave	Early's Brigade
Parker, Anthony	Slave	Early's Brigade
Peyton, George	Slave	5th North Carolina
Carter, Wash	Slave	5th North Carolina
Butler, Harrison	Slave	5th North Carolina
Lucus, Flaveus	Slave	5th North Carolina
Aldridge, Bill	Slave	5th North Carolina

Virginia's Black Confederates

Monroe, George	Slave	5th North Carolina
Waters, Henry	Slave	5th North Carolina
Ward, Charles	Free	5th North Carolina
Mastrom, John	Slave	5th North Carolina
Nailer, Ben	Slave	5th North Carolina
Hoi, Ed	Slave	5th North Carolina
Ward, Eli	Slave	Ewell's Bde Capt Rhodes AQM
Wilkinson, Austin	Slave	Ewell's Bde Capt Rhodes AQM
Puckett, Simon	Slave	Simm's Bde
Barney, Addison	Slave	Simm's Bde
[?], Jack	Slave	Simm's Bde
Colson, Jacob	Slave	Simm's Bde
Brook, Henry	Slave	Simm's Bde
Lewis, Alfred	Slave	Simm's Bde
Jackson, Wm	Slave	Simm's Bde
Romax, Henry	Slave	Simm's Bde
Alec, George	Slave	Seymour's Bde
Oates, Reuben	Slave	Longstreet's Bde
Brown, Joe	Slave	Longstreet's Bde
Johnson, Sandy	Slave	Longstreet's Bde
Turner, Perry	Slave	Longstreet's Bde
Majors, Howard	Slave	Longstreet's Bde
Thornton, Dangerfield	Slave	1st and 2nd NC Regt
Nichols, Hubbard	Slave	1st and 2nd NC Regt
Arnett, Charles	Slave	1st Regt GA Regulars
Newman, Henry	Slave	Capt [Louis] Delaigle, 1st Georgia Regulars
Newman Frank	Slave	Capt [Louis] Delaigle, 1st Georgia Regulars
Brent, Richard	Slave	Capt [Louis] Delaigle, 1st Georgia Regulars
Smith, Beverley	Slave	Capt [Louis] Delaigle, 1st Georgia Regulars
Gray, John	Slave	Capt [Louis] Delaigle, 1st Georgia Regulars
Jones, Henry	Slave	Capt [Louis] Delaigle, 1st Georgia Regulars
Jones, Anthony	Slave	Capt [Louis] Delaigle, 1st Georgia Regulars
Ashby, George	Slave	Capt [Louis] Delaigle, 1st Georgia Regulars
Lucas, Charles	Slave	12th Mississippi Bde
Stuart, John	Slave	Capt Blount, AQM, 4th NC Regt
Hinton, Izreal	Slave	Capt Blount, AQM, 4th NC Regt
Richards, Daniel	Slave	Capt Blount, AQM, 4th NC Regt
Tait, William	Slave	Capt Blount, AQM, 4th NC Regt
Neal, Levi	Slave	15th Georgia Regt (Capt Thomas AQM)

Virginia's Black Confederates

Johnson, Henry	Slave	15th Georgia Regt (Capt Thomas AQM)
Jackson, Sam	Slave	15th Georgia Regt (Capt Thomas AQM)
Champ, Alfred	Slave	15th Georgia Regt (Capt Thomas AQM)
Cleaveland, Adam	Slave	15th Georgia Regt (Capt Thomas AQM)
Carter, Thomas	Slave	15th Georgia Regt (Capt Thomas AQM)
Peters, Joe	Slave	15th Georgia Regt (Capt Thomas AQM)
Howard, Jake	Slave	15th Georgia Regt (Capt Thomas AQM)
Averall, Henry	Slave	15th Georgia Regt (Capt Thomas AQM)
Pearson, Newton	Slave	3rd Georgia Bn
Parker, Tom	Slave	Capt I.F. Morgan, AQM
Gibson, George	Slave	Capt I.F. Morgan, AQM
Webster, Gustry	Slave	Capt I.F. Morgan, AQM
Field, Charles	Slave	Capt I.F. Morgan, AQM
Thomas, Beverly	Slave	Capt I.F. Morgan, AQM
Thomas, Wyat	Slave	Capt I.F. Morgan, AQM
Carter, French	Slave	Capt I.F. Morgan, AQM
Beverly, Rubin	Slave	Capt I.F. Morgan, AQM
Carter, Welan	Slave	Capt I.F. Morgan, AQM
Jackson, Lewis	Slave	Capt I.F. Morgan, AQM
Wouser, Aaron	Slave	Capt I.F. Morgan, AQM
Vessy, Tilman	Slave	Capt I.F. Morgan, AQM
[Gowin] Thomas	Slave	Capt I.F. Morgan, AQM
Jonhson, Gary	Slave	Capt I.F. Morgan, AQM
Sweeny, Peter	Slave	Capt I.F. Morgan, AQM
Smith, Alfred	Slave	Capt I.F. Morgan, AQM
Champ, Alfred	Slave	Longstreet's Bde (Lt Manning, AQM)
Butler, Wm	Slave	Longstreet's Bde (Lt Manning, AQM)
Parker, Dav	Slave	Longstreet's Bde (Lt Manning, AQM)
Johnson, Sam	Slave	Longstreet's Bde (Lt Manning, AQM)
Smith, Charles	Slave	Longstreet's Bde (Lt Manning, AQM)

Sanford, Dav	Slave	Longstreet's Bde (Lt Manning, AQM)
Roberson, John	Slave	Longstreet's Bde (Lt Manning, AQM)
Brooks, Ned	Slave	Longstreet's Bde (Lt Manning, AQM)
Champ, Burchase	Slave	Longstreet's Bde (Lt Manning, AQM)
Butler, Billy	Slave	Longstreet's Bde (Lt Manning, AQM)
Puckett, Henry	Slave	Longstreet's Bde (Lt Manning, AQM)
Denny, Wash	Slave	Longstreet's Bde (Lt Manning, AQM)
Redman, Lewis	Slave	Texas Battalion
Royster, Reubin	Slave	Texas Battalion
Marcus, George	Slave	Texas Battalion
[Woylus]	Slave	Texas Battalion
Taylor, Elie	Slave	Texas Battalion
Redman, Saul	Slave	Texas Battalion
Williams, George	Free	13th NC Regt
Eli		1st Georgia Regt
Negro John		1st Georgia Regt
John		1st Georgia Regt
Frank	Slave	1st Mississippi Regt
Joe	Slave	1st Mississippi Regt
[Polk]	Slave	1st Mississippi Regt
Washington		1st Mississippi Regt
Ben	Slave	1st Mississippi Regt
John	Slave	1st Mississippi Regt
Wilson, William	Slave	24th [Virginia] Regt

Primary Source Materials

LABORERS – Black Confederates, free and slave, supported the Confederate war effort in a variety of ways to include services that would today be termed as engineers, transportation and logistics. This painting is entitled 'Negroes mounting cannon in the works for the attack on Ft. Sumter'. (Waud Collection, 1861, Library of Congress Collection, LC-USZC4-690).

DIGGING TRENCHES - This wartime drawing shows black Confederates in the lower right corner, digging trenches. Both slaves and free men of color labored on fortifications. Periodic levies would be issued to each county to provide slave laborers for periods of up to three months. Records show the free men of color were paid for their services.

Virginia's Black Confederates

POWER OF ATTORNEY OF FREE NEGROES OF POWHATAN COUNTY: The document reads, *"We the undersigned free negroes of Powhatan County Va do hereby appoint John L. Brackett of Powhatan County, Va, our true and lawful agent to sign receipts for and receive payment of all monies due to us by the Engineer Department of the Confederate States of America for Services as Labourers on the defensive works at Richmond, Va. Witness our hands and seals at Powhatan Station this fifth day of February 1862 (signed in duplicate)."*

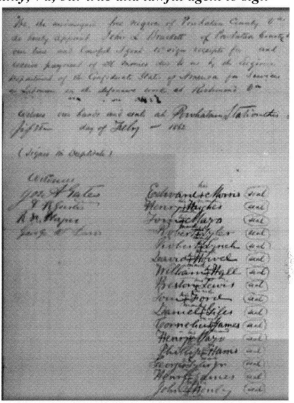

The witness signatures were Joseph A. Gates, L.K. Gunter, R.F. Wayne and George W. Davis. The Free Negroes are as follows: Edward Morris, Henry Hughes, Tom Mayo, Robert Tyler, Robert Lynch, David Howel, William Hall, Preston Lewis, Tom Ford, Daniel Giles, Cornelius James, Henry Mayo, Phillip Harris, George Tyler, Jr., Henry James and John Henley." All signed with an 'x' annotated 'his mark' in the middle of each name.

Jackson's Cook Jim Lewis in the John Buttre painting of PRAYER IN STONEWALL JACKSON'S CAMP (1866). This close up segment of the left side of the painting shows Lewis immediately behind Jackson.

REBEL NEGRO PICKETS.

So much has been said about the wickedness of using the negroes on our side in the present war, that we have thought it worth while to reproduce on this page a sketch sent us from Fredericksburg by our artist, Mr. Theodore R. Davis, which is a faithful representation of what was seen by one of our officers through his field-glass, while on outpost duty at that place. As the picture shows, it represents two full-blooded negroes, fully armed, and serving as pickets in the rebel army. It has long been known to military men that the insurgents affect no scruples about the employment of their slaves in any capacity in which they may be found useful. Yet there are people here at the North who affect to be horrified at the enrollment of negroes into regiments. Let us hope that the President will not be deterred by any squeamish scruples of the kind from garrisoning the Southern forts with fighting men of any color that can be obtained.

HARPER'S WEEKLY - Vol VII, No. 315 (10 January 1863)

REBEL NEGRO PICKETS AS SEEN THROUGH A FIELD GLASS

Virginia's Black Confederates

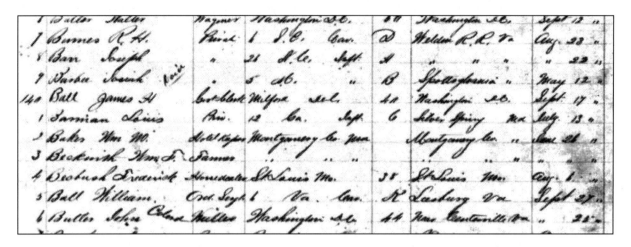

POINT LOOKOUT - Line 9 shows Josiah Barber of Company B, 5th N.C. Infantry, captured at Spotsylvania C.H. on May 12, 1864. His rank is listed as 'Private'. Line 146 shows John Butler, a Miller from Washington, DC captured near Centreville, Va on Sept 25, 1864.

MOSBY'S SERVANT – Confederate Partisan John S. Mosby, the 'Gray Ghost' of the Confederacy thought so highly of body servant Aaron Burton that Burton's photo was included in Mosby's Memoirs. Mosby said Burton helped tend to the wounded and wrote, "He is a good deal thought of in the company."

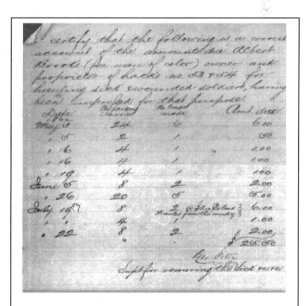

RECEIPT FOR CONTRACTOR SERVICES – Albert Brooks, "Free man of color", was paid $25.50 for renting out two wagons "for hauling sick and wounded soldiers" between 2 May and 22 July 1862. He was paid 25 cents for every man moved making up to 6 trips in one day. These activities coincide with the Peninsula Campaign.

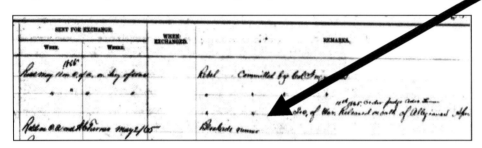

BLOCKADE RUNNER – This POW roster (line 5) lists "Wm [William] Berryman, Colored, a farmer of Westmorland County, Va, age 59, captured near Cuff Neck, Maryland on April 8, 1865. In the remarks section (below), he was listed as a "Blockade runner" and released on 2 May 1865 nearly a month after the April 9, 1865 surrender of Lee's Army.

CONFEDERATE REUNION - This unknown black Confederate bugler was photographed while attending a Confederate reunion in Richmond. (LVA Collection, Va State Chamber of Commerce Collection, Image 003115-010)

Virginia's Black Confederates

**Confederate Reunion
Richmond, Virginia**

Unidentified Black Confederate veterans were photographed attending a reunion years after the war.

(Library of Virginia, Virginia State Chamber of Commerce photograph collection, Images 003115-001 on left and image 003115-008 above).

REUNION PHOTO – Same group from previous page with additional black Confederate veterans present. (LVA Va State Chamber of Commerce photograph collection. Image 003115-013)

SUPPLEMENTAL STATEMENT FOR PENSION - Former Slave Whit Johnson submitted a statement in support of George Robinson's pension application. Johnson notes he and Robinson went from Petersburg *"to Appomattox where we worked on the roads in front of the big guns – at the surrender in [?] under Capt Moody."* Captain Moody was Capt George Moody, Longstreet's Corps Artillery. This document reveals Johnson and Robinson supported Longstreet's artillery and were at the surrender at Appomattox though they did not receive official paroles. We can also infer they supported the positioning of Longstreet's artillery guarding the road at Rice prior to the actions there on 6 April, 1865.

Virginia's Black Confederates

JEFF SHIELDS – A cook in Stonewall Jackson's Brigade

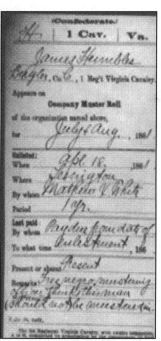

"FREE COLORED" – In the service record on the left, William Chavers appears on a "roll of non-commissioned officers and privates employed on extra duty at Petersburg, Va" in March 1864. In the service record on the right, Bugler James Humble, Co. C, 1st Virginia Cavalry, is reflected as having enlisted April 18, 1861 in Lexington, Va. The note at the bottom says, "Free Negro. Mustering officer thinks this man should not be mustered in."

Compiled Service Records Sample

SERVICE RECORDS - This National Archives record was transcribed from Confederate muster rolls. About 14 separate documents record Samuel Tatem's service as a cook. Only the September/October 1864 muster roll noted him as an "Enlisted Negro". His total record indicates he enlisted in September 1862 and appears to have served through the end of the war as a Cook in Company D, 61st Virginia Infantry. A Tidewater based unit, it was attached to Mahone's and Weisinger's Brigades in the Army of Northern Virginia serving at Antietam, Fredericksburg, Chancellorsville, Gettysburg, the Overland Campaign, Siege of Petersburg and Appomattox Campaign. The record on the right indicates Tatem held the rank of 'Private'.

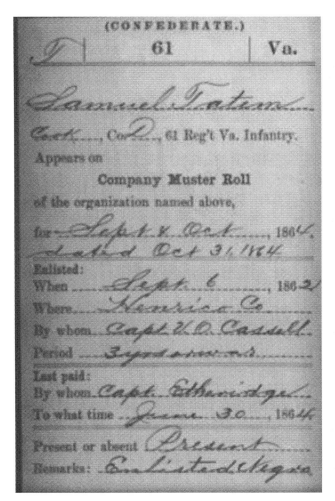

Compiled Service Records Sample

EZEKIEL - served as a Cook in Company F, 32nd Virginia Infantry. He enlisted June 4, 1864 and was present at least through 31 December 1864. He was listed as a "Free negro with the Wagons". Confederate muster rolls were not kept after 1864. It can be inferred Ezekiel served until the end of the war.

GEORGE GRIMES - Grimes was a Private in Capt E.A. Marye's Company, Pegram's Light Arty; "Tried for desertion and court decided he was a negro".

Virginia's Black Confederates

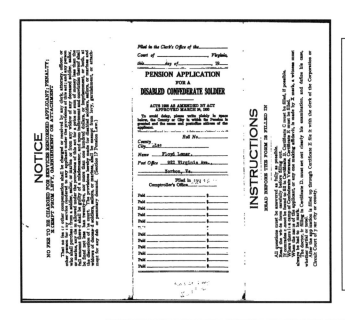

Pension Application of Floyd Lamar

The image on the left is the outside application. The bottom below is the questionnaire providing details of services. Lamar was living in Norton, Va when he applied for a pension on January 5, 1934. He lists his age as 91 making his birth year 1843. He served in the 6th Alabama Infantry and says he was "offered my freedom but would not leave." He injured himself trying to save his master who was wounded.

AT APPOMATTOX – Top half of Va Pension Application for Isaac Edmondson of Halifax County, Va indicating he was at Lee's Surrender at Appomattox.

MUSTER ROLL - Snapshot of 18th Va Infantry Muster Roll showing black Confederates in the Regimental band; Dick Slate, Drummer; Austin Dix, Drummer and George Price, Fifer. Price, of Culpeper, was 58 when he enlisted and was reportedly a Mexican War veteran. His discharge papers are part of his file in the Compiled Service Records for the 18th Va Infantry.

> State of Virginia,
> County of Dinwiddie, to-wit:
>
> George Wyatt whose pension application was certified to the Auditor of Public Accounts by the Circuit Court of Dinwiddie County on June 15, 1925, this day appeared before me and being first duly sworn says that he is the same person mentioned in the said application, that at the time of the commencement of the war between the states he was a slave, owned by Horace W. Mitchell of said County of Dinwiddie; that about the first of the said war, by order of said Mitchell he went into the service of the Confederate Government, as a servant and from that time to the close of the war he rendered service as a cook and servant.
>
> George Wyatt (his mark)
>
> Witness, Musa Hargrave
>
> Sworn to and subscribed before me by the said George Wyatt this 18th day of September, 1925.
>
> A.H. Organ, Clerk

**Supplemental Statement,
Pension Application of George Wyatt, Dinwiddie County**

VIRGINIA STATE LIBRARY
RICHMOND, VIRGINIA

April 23, 1925.

This certifies that on page 339 of volume 5 of the Confederate Records (manuscript volumes in the Virginia State Library) appears the name of Archie Sinclair. The entry shows that he was a cook in Company C – 49th Regt. Va. Inf. This Co. was known as "Fauquier Guards". of which company Edward Murray was captain. It is stated that he enlisted and served

Remarks: "Archie Sinclair, colored, Capt. B.W. Randolph's cook, as such he served throughout the war, was captured in 1864 near Fishers Hill Va. by the enemy, made his escape and returned to the Regt."

H. R. McILWAINE,
State Librarian.

Pension File of Archie Sinclair

Confederate Certificates of Service

Confederate Army regulations provide for the honorable discharge of military personnel. Records indicate that free men of color and some slaves who served in the ranks of Infantry regiments received Certificates of Service when discharged from that service.

The 1861 Army Regulations for the Confederates States[240] covers 'Discharges' in Article XIX. The regulation states, "When an enlisted man is to be discharged, his company commander shall furnish him certificates of his account, according to Form 4, Pay Department."

155

Form No. 4.

Certificate to be given a soldier at the time of his discharge.

I CERTIFY that the within named ———— ———, a ——— of Captain ——— ——— company (—) of the ——— regiment of ———, born in ———, in the State of ———, aged ——— years, ——— feet ——— inches high, ——— complexion, ———eyes, ——— hair, and by profession a ———, was enlisted by ——— ———, at ———, on the ——— day of ———, eighteen hundred and ——— to serve for ——— years, and is now entitled to a discharge by reason of———

The said ——— ——— was last paid by Paymaster ——— ———, to include the ——— day of ———, eighteen hundred and ———, and has pay due from that time to the present date.

There is due to him ——— dollars retained pay.

There is due to him ——— dollars on account of clothing not drawn in kind.

He is indebted to the Confederate States ——— dollars, on account of extra clothing, &c.

He is indebted to——— ———,laundress, at———, ——— dollars.

The contract price of the ration at ——— is ——— cents.

Given in duplicate at ———, this ——— day of———, 18—.

——— ———,
Commanding Company.

NOTE. When a soldier transfers his certificates, the transfer must be made on them, witnessed by a commissioned officer, when practicable, or by some other reputable person known to the Paymaster.

CSA Regulations (1861), Form 4 Confederate *"Certificate to be give a soldier at the time of his discharge"*

---

[240] <u>Army Regulations Adopted for the use of the Army of the Confederate States in accordance with the Acts of Congress, (Revised from the Army Regulations of the Old U.S. Army, 1857: Retaining all that is essential for officers of the line)</u> (New Orleans: Bloomfield & Steel, Publishing) 60 Camp Street, 1861. See p14-15 and p155.

The Form 4 is similar to the current DD214 *Certificate of Release or Discharge from Active Duty* in use by the U.S. Armed Forces in that it provided proof of honorable service and includes certain details on the individual.[241] Unlike the DD214, the Form 4 provides a pay and accounting mechanism to ensure all pay due to the recipient was noted for later accounting or, in some cases, to ensure the exiting soldier paid any debts he may have incurred while on duty.

The 1862 Regulations still cited the Certificate of Account as a Form 4 but the sample forms had been changed by time of publication: Form 4 was now Form 58 [242] and still noted as the *"Certificate to be given a soldier at the time of his discharge."* This was accompanied by Form No. 59, the Account to be made by the Quartermaster to ensure all debts were paid.

By 1863, the Form 58 *Certificate to be given a soldier at the time of his discharge* was to be accompanied by the *Soldier's Discharge*. The best way to describe these in modern terms is to recognize the Form 58 Certificate as akin to the DD214 that contains the details of the individual and that person's service. The Soldier's Discharge is like the modern DD Form 256 *Honorable Discharge Certificate* often referred to as a 'wall hanger' because that is

---

[241] Modern U.S. government forms are still identified by alpha-numeric figures. SF is a 'Standard Form' and 'DD' means 'Department of Defense'. The DD215 is the form which allows a correction or amendment to issued DD214s. See Army Regulation 635-5, *Personnel Separations: Separation Documents* for details on the modern forms. The DD Form 256A is the Army version, the 256N is the Navy version.

[242] <u>Regulations for the Army of the Confederate States, 1862</u>. Article XIX Discharges on p14-15; Form 58 and Form 59, *Account to be Made by Quartermaster*, on p134.

the document veterans hang on the wall.[243] By 1864, the forms are renamed Form 59 and 60 and are contained in the *Regulations of the Confederate States Army for the Quartermaster's Department including the Pay Branch Thereof* (Richmond, Va: J.W. Randolph) 1864 and on page 186 of the *Regulations for the Army of the Confederate States, 1864, Revised and Enlarged with a New and Copious Index* (Richmond, Va: J.W. Randolph) 1864.

Discharge of White Man

Private Charles Gilliam, Company D, 18th Virginia Infantry

---

[243] <u>Regulations for the Army of the Confederate States, 1863</u>; Article XIX, Discharges, p17-18; Form 58 and Form 59 are on p186.

Virginia's Black Confederates

Discharge of Free Black Man

Fifer George Price, Field & Staff, 18th Virginia Infantry.

Discharge of Slave

G.W. Smith, Cook, Company C, 32nd Virginia Infantry

Acts of the Confederates Congress Impacting African-Americans in the Confederates Army

Chap XXIX – An Act for the payment of musicians in the army not regularly enlisted

The Congress of the Confederate States of America do enact, **That whenever colored persons are employed as musicians in any Regiment or Company, they shall be entitled to the same pay now allowed by law to musicians regularly enlisted:** *Provided,* That no such persons shall be so employed except by the consent of the commanding officer of the Brigade to which said Regiments or Companies may belong.

Approved April 15, 1862[244]

Chapter LXIV - An Act for the enlistment of Cooks in the Army

The Congress of the Confederate States of America do enact, That hereafter it shall be the duty of the Captain or Commanding Officer of his company to enlist four Cooks for the use of his company, whose duty it shall be to cook for such company – taking charge of the supplies, utensils and other things furnished therefore, and safely keep the same, subject to such rules and regulations as may be prescribed by the War Department or the colonel of the Regiment to which such company may be attached:

[Sec 2] *Be it further enacted,* **That the Cooks so directed to be enlisted, may be white or black, free or slave persons:** *Provided, however,* **That no slave shall be so enlisted without the written consent of his owner.** And such Cooks shall be enlisted as such only, and put on the muster-roll and paid at the time and place the company may or shall be paid off, twenty dollars per month to the Chief or Head Cook, and fifteen dollars per month for each of the Assistant Cooks, together with the same allowance for clothing, or the same commutation therefor that may be allowed to the rank and file of the company.

Approved April 21, 1862[245]

---

[244] *Public Laws of the Confederate States of America Passed at the First Session of the First Congress 1862*, edited by James M. Mathews, Attorney at Law, Clerk in the Department of Justice (Richmond: R.M. Smith, Printer to Congress, 1862) p29. This document is publicly accessible via the web at http://books.google.com/
[245] Ibid, p48

Chapter LXXIX – An Act to increase the efficiency of the Army by the employment of free negroes and slaves in certain capacities

Whereas, the efficiency of the army is greatly diminished by the withdrawal from the ranks of able-bodied soldiers to act as teamsters, and in various other capacities in which free negroes and slaves might be advantageously employed: Therefore-

The Congress of the Confederate States of America do enact, That all male free negroes and other free persons of color, not including those who are free under the treaty of Paris of eighteen hundred and three, or under the treaty with Spain of eighteen hundred and nineteen, resident in the Confederate States, between the ages of eighteen and fifty years, shall be held liable to perform such duties with the army, or in connection with the military defences of the country, in the way of work upon fortifications or in Government works for the production or preparation of material of war, or in military hospitals, as the Secretary of War or the commanding general of the trans-Mississippi department may, from time to time, prescribe; and while engaged in the performance of such duties shall receive rations and clothing and compensation at the rate of eleven dollars a month, under such rules and regulations as the said Secretary may establish: *Provided,* That the Secretary of War or the commanding general of the trans-Mississippi department, with the approval of the President, may exempt from the operations of this act such free negroes as the interests of the country may require should be exempted, or such as he may think proper to exempt, on grounds of justice, equity or necessity.

Sec. 2. That the Secretary of War is hereby authorized to employ for duties similar to those indicated in the preceding section of this act, as many male negro slaves, not to exceed twenty thousand, as in his judgment, the wants of the service may require, furnishing them, while so employed, with proper rations and clothing, under rules and regulations to be established by him, paying to the owners of said slaves such wages as may be agreed upon with said owners for their use and service, and in the event of the loss of any slaves while so employed, by the act of the enemy, or by escape to the enemy, or by death inflicted by the enemy, or by disease contracted while in any service required of said slaves, then the owners of the same shall be entitled to receive the full value of such slaves, to be ascertained by agreement or by appraisement, under the law regulating impressments, to be paid under such rules and regulations as the Secretary of War may establish.

Sec. 3. That when the Secretary of War shall be unable to procure the service of slaves in any military department in sufficient numbers for the necessities of the department, upon the terms and conditions set forth in the preceding section, then he is hereby authorized to impress the services of as many male slaves, not to exceed twenty thousand, as may be required, from time to time, to discharge the duties indicated in the first section of this act, according to laws regulating impressments of slaves in other cases: *Provided,* That slaves so impressed shall while employed, receive the same rations and clothing, in kind and quantity, as slaves regularly hired from their owners; and, in the event of their loss, shall be paid for in the same manner and under the same rules established by the said impressments laws: *Provided,* That if the owner have but one male slave within the age of eighteen and fifty, he shall not be impressed against the will of said owner: *Provided further,* That free negroes shall be first impressed, and if there should be a deficiency, it shall be supplied by the impressments of slaves according to the foregoing provisions: *Provided further,* That in making the impressments, not more than one of every five male slaves between the ages of eighteen and forty-five shall be taken from any owner, care being taken to allow in each case a credit for all slaves who may have been already impressed under this act, and who are still in service, or have died or been lost while in service. And all impressments under this act shall be taken in equal ration from all owners in the same locality, city, county or district.

Approved February 17, 1864[246]

---

[246] Ibid, p235-236

Confederate Report on Use of Slaves for War Effort

From Southern Historical Society Papers.
Vol. II. Richmond, Virginia, July, 1876. No. 1.
Resources of the Confederacy in February, 1865.

C.S.A. War Department,
Ordnance Bureau,
Richmond, February 2d, 1866.

REPORT OF OPERATIONS (WHITE AND SLAVE) MADE

(copy)

To: Honorable J. A. Seddon, Secretary of War:

Sir -- In answer to the following extract of a resolution of the Senate of the 24th May, * * * "First: With information as to the number of white men between the ages of 18 and 45, and of the number of negroes who in addition to their own officers may be required for the necessary employment and the proper discharge of the functions of the department of * * the Ordnance Bureau * * ," I have the honor to submit that there were borne on the rolls of this department on the 1st October, 1864, 3,433 white men, between the ages of 18 and 45, including contractors and their employees. General Order No. 82 reduced this number to 2,691, turning over to the enrolling officers 742. Of this number thus turned over, full one half were mechanics of the classes now needed to push our work. There must be returned say 400. This will leave the working force at the arsenals less by about 342 men than on the 1st of October, but will suffice. In addition, in order to raise the product of our armories in time to 55,000 arms per annum, 800 good mechanics must be added -- say that three fourths of them will be white men, between the ages of 18 and 45, and the total required thus will be --

Number in workshops December 31.	2,691
Number of them taken by General Order to be returned	400
Number to be added for additional product of arms	600
	3,961

This would give us a total of 258 more workmen than we had October 1, 1864, but would raise the product of arms from 20,000 to 55,000 (in time). The number of negroes on the rolls of the department during the past year is 830; add to them, say 1,000 in the employ of contractors, of which there are no returns in the office, making 1,830 negroes. An addition of fifty per cent should be made to that part of the force employed at the arsenals, &c., in order that as much as possible may be done with labor of this description, making 1,245 as the number needed at these establishments. This estimate is reduced to the smallest figures with which the operations of the Bureau can be successfully carried on.

Recapitulation.

White men, between the ages of 18 and 45 (excepting officers)   3,691
Slaves   2,246

Very respectfully,

(Signed) J. Gorgas, Brigadier General, Chief of Ordnance.

Denied Pension Applications

The following pension applications were denied by the Commonwealth of Virginia due to insufficient evidence or documentation providing proof of service. This lack of approval does not necessarily mean the applicants were not in service, only that such service could not be proven beyond a reasonable doubt. With that in mind, denied applications are included in the roster.

Bundie (Bundy), Rybune L.-85/1931; Essex Co; Teamster and looking after cattle. Servant in Commissary Department and Quartermaster Department. "Assisted in assembling and driving cattle, sheep, and hogs collected for the Confederate Army's QM department." "I was a free man". Served under Major Robinson and Samuel Gresham. Applicant also known as Ryburn L. Bundy, 87/1934.

Canaday, Wilmore-89/1934; James City Co; Body servant to Capt Faust, 1861-1865.

Cubbage, David F.-88/1931; Elkton, Va; "No master"; "about 18 months in Infantry"; "Private in Capt Rippoto's Company"; 10th [Va} Regt, Culpeper Co., Va.

Davis, George W.-86/1934, Madison Co; body servant for Capt. H. Davis Tuyrion from 1863 to 1864 "when called home."

Goff, James-83/1929; Bedford; woodchopper, Jordan's Furnace. "I cut wood for the furnace to burn to melt iron."

Gordon, Jack-88/1930; Amelia; Body servant; bailed hay and took feed to the Army; worked for Nat Wilson and traveled back and forth as a body guard.

Hackney, Joseph-74/1924; Albemarle; Infantry; body servant to Mr. John Chewning, CSA; Master-Robert Chewning. Service from 1864 to 1865.

Jenkins, J.E.-79/1932; Burkeville (Prince Edward Co); began service in 1861 until end of war. Began service at Camp Lee. "Servant and went with company during four years. Brought water and waited on soldiers—father was a member of this company, Co. C [Old Dominion Riflemen], 53rd Va Regt, Pickett's Division. Service rendered to J.D. Jenkins, father of applicant who was born in 1852. State auditor writes, "This would make him about nine years old when he went with his father in the Army. We have no record of any Confederate servant serving the Confederacy so young."

Madesis, Charles H.-Charlotte Co., No image (Probably Charles H. Madison).

Madison, Charles H.-83/1933; Servant to Major R.V. Gaines from 1862 to "close of war"; served as "water boy, carried mail, attended horses"; "had leg broken in service"; born at Drakes Branch; Reference by Charles Slaughter ("colored"); pension denied because service was rendered on farm which Major Gaines was on furlough. Mr. Madison became a Baptist preacher.

Marshall, James Leonard- 87/1936; Sylvatus (Carroll Co.) Teamster; "Transferred soldiers to and from Camp" under Capt. George Turman and later transferred to Capt. Jerry Spence; In service of parent, Daniel Marshall; "I was not [a] regular teamster but was detailed by the said Captain (Spence) to transfer the soldiers which come home on furlough" to and from the Camps at Dublin, Va [and] also to Dublin Depot." [Note: CSR identifies a Capt George H. Turman, Co. G, 54th Va Infantry, enlisted Dugspur, Carroll Co, Va. And resigned in February 1862; Jeremiah Spence, Co. G, 54th Va Inf enlisted as a Sergeant before promotion to Captain.]

Marshall, Levi-Carroll Co. 84/1932. Servant/Nurse. Nursed Thomas N. Marshall at Hillsville, Va from the Fall of 1863 for about 12 months in an Army hospital. Pension denied because he was at home and not in the field.

Pullen, Thomas-83/1930; Moneta (Bedford Co); slave of Samuel Updike, Jr.; 1864-EOW; Teamster/harnessing.

Slaughter, Charles- 88/1933; Phenix (Charlotte Co); under supervision of Ben Sublett; slave of Charles H. Slaughter; worked as "servant to transport soldiers" to Pamplin and High Bridge.

Talbert, W.H.-Carroll Co. 85/1936. Requested pension for "aiding soldiers" from 1864 to EOW. Provided rides.

Washington, Richard-86/1931; Rockbridge Co.; body servant for Col. Baker, Infantry from 1861 or 1862; Master was Archer Alexander.

Webster, Robert-77/1925; Roanoke; Infantry; from April 1861 to 1863; service around Richmond under Co. A, Capt. DeWitt Booth [Co. D, 58th Va Inf]; Master-Anthony Simmons; born in Franklin County.

Approved Pension Applications Of the Commonwealth of Virginia

The Pension list names at least 45 free men of color from Virginia who served the Confederate States Army. Other sources identify free born African-Americans who served. At least one white man received a pension for service as a body servant. Scott County's S.M. Quillen was eleven years old when his father put him to work for Co. G, 64th Va Infantry collecting saltpeter for munitions manufacture. He was 82 when he applied for a pension in 1933.

Abbreviations
EOW-End of War
KIA-Killed in Action
WIA-Wounded in Action
FNU-First Name Unknown
Co.-Company
Bn-Battalion
Regt-Regiment

Div-Division
Arty-Artillery
Inf-Infantry
Cav-Cavalry
QM-Quartermaster
CH-Court House

Albemarle County
Brooks, William-65/1907; Afton, Va; 7th Va Infantry, Pickett's Division; WIA 1863 in "fist or face"; served under Capt John J. Winn, his master until end of war. Cooking and serving".
Henderson, Archie-90/1925; Teamster under Mr. Sinclair from "early in the war" to EOW.
Marks, Robert-81/1925; cleaned guns and worked on breastworks "all during the war".
Moore, Richard-unk/1926; Blacksmith Shop under Major Roche; enlisted in Gordonsville and served to EOW.
Tyree, Sr., Henry D.-94/1924; provided service as a "soldier" from 1861 to 1865; at Manassas; Co. K, 3rd Va Cavalry Prince Edward Dragoons]; Cook for W.C. Shackleford; also helped build breastworks.

Amelia County
Anderson, Peter W.-79/1924; Jetersville; "I was a free man"; served from 1862 to "just before the surrender"; I waited on General Joseph E. Johnston"; worked for Aaron Haskins, the Sheriff of the County; total of three years service.
Anderson, Robert-80/1924; Jetersville; in Army "building breastworks at Yorktown and other places" under General Magruder; Master was Truly Vaughan; served from 1862 to undetermined date. "I left on account of sickness and returned to service afterwards."

Booker, Henry-88/1930; born Prince Edward County; Laborer on breastworks.
Booker, J. Churchill-75/1925; Jetersville; "orderly servant" performing "general servant duties"; Master-Henry Wood; began service in 1864 to EOW; "war ended and was set free-1865"; "I was body servant for Mr. E.P. Davis and actually accompanied him during the war."
Epps, Milton M.-75/1924; Jetersville; Laborer making breastworks from 1862 until the surrender. Slave of Mrs. Lucy Bradshaw of Prince Edward.
Harris, John W.-80/1924; Amelia Court House; Infantry "cooking and working on breastworks at High Bridge and battery near Chula"; under Capt. Dick Scott, his master from 1863 to EOW; "in Farmville waiting on Capt Scott at Hospital." Note: Probably Capt R.M. Scott, Co. H, Amelia Reserves, 1st Regt, Va Reserves.
Haskins, Miles-87/1924; Amelia CH; Army; work on breastworks under Thomas Dearing; served 1862-1864 when "discharged"; Started service at Yorktown; Master-William Worsham.
Hundley, William-79/1924; Amelia; Laborer on breastworks; 1862 to EOW in Henrico County; Master-Thompson Herrick.
Jasper, Carry-90/1929; Mattoax; "Laborer on breastworks and trenches" under George Thranes; Master-William R. Barksdale; entered service 1863 at Chickahominy Swamp until the

EOW; Last worked at bridge at Mattoax on Appomattox River.

Johnson, Melvin-Over 80/1924; Morven; "I worked on the breastworks between Chula and Mattoax, Va" under Mr. Singleton; Master-William Ware; began service in 1865 and "left it at the surrender".

Jones, George R.-80/1925; Amelia CH; body servant to Capt W.E. Hinton "who was my master" from 1862 to EOW. Note: Capt Hinton was a member of second Co. E, 10th Va Cavalry with service as Dearing's Provost Guard from 4/29 to 12/1464.

Jones, Henry-78/1924; Mannboro; Laborer on breastworks; Master-Daniel W. Burton; worked on Mulberry Island in 1864. Under Major Robert Cousins.

Pegram, Arthur-89/1930; Laborer on Breastworks and Railroad under Capt Hinton, his master; service from 1862 at Drewry's Bluff until EOW.

Price, Jordan-77/1924; Jetersville; "putting up breastworks at Mattoax and batteries for (Lt) Southall"; Mrs. P.T. Southall was mistress; began service 1862 at Mattoax for a period of 12-14 months.

Scruggs, William T.-76/1924; Jetersville; "I was a free man" and cook in the Confederate Cavalry at headquarters. "I went with my brother who was also a cook---both of us under Capt Smith"; served in Luray Valley from March 1864 to January 1865.

Scruggs, (FNU)-brother of William T. and mentioned in pension application.

Waddell, Thomas-87/1932; Jetersville; servant in hospital; "I served in the hospital near Sailor's Creek"; Capt Jim Hillsman; Master-J.E. or J.A. Hillsman; "in the last year of the war in the said hospital."; "I left the hospital after the war was over and after the same had broken up."

Webster, Daniel-92/1936; Jetersville; body servant of Capt Fernando R. Farrar of Infantry (Farmville); Four years under Capt Farrar 1862-65; "On the retreat to Appomattox I became separated from Captain Farrar and was heading to Appomattox but I was turned back by Union solders and was forced to return to home of Capt Farrar. This was only several days before the surrender."

Winfree, Alpheus-78/1924; Amelia CH; Cook in Co. G, 1st Va Cavalry under Capt C.R. Irving; Master-R.H. Marshall; service from 1862 to later 1864 with his master who was a member of the troop.

Amherst County

Anderson, John Thomas-80/1924; Teamster and Hostler; Took care of horses for Capt Rook from 1861-1865.

Berry, John-79/1925; Teamster; 1863-1865; under Richard Knight. Master-Richard Shelton.

Broady, William H-78/1925; Hostler and carried dispatches from Greensboro to Columbia, S.C.; service under Maj Paxton at Lynchburg; Major Kirker, and Capt Hopkins; Master was C.B. Claiborne; Enlisted 02 August 1864 and was at Columbia, S.C. at the time of the surrender.

Carter, Sr., Anderson-84/1925; Laborer at breastworks from 1864; "Fortifying Richmond, Petersburg and Lynchburg."; released when "finished the work".

Carter, Henry-83/1926; Teamster; QM Department; teamster for one year and hostler for three years; under Major Patton; Master-W.H. Rose; began service in 1861 in West Virginia; left service "at the surrender".

Ellis, Charles-86/1924; "helped to build the breastworks on Williamsburg Road and Mechanicsville"; served from 1862-65, EOW.

Hollins, Archie-85/1925; Laborer on breastworks from 1863 to 1865; Master-George Ambler.

Johns, Preston-80/1925; Teamster; 1863.

Jones, Louis-83/1924; Teamster; 1863-1865; also helped to build breastworks; "I was at the surrender…".

Jordan, Charles-80/1924; "First as a body servant and then as a woodchopper…went with young master in Army for six months and then was hired to Confederate government as wood chopper."; Master was Col. Charles Green; service from 1862 to EOW.

Lee, George-82/1924; "helped build breastworks and toted water"; breastworks and water carrier; went into service with James Jennings who organized about 100 in his company; Master was Thomas Lee; service from 1862; worked about three months in Richmond then returned to Master.

Martin, Silas-89/1924; building breastworks; Free Man; "never belonged to any Master"; began service in 1862 near Manassas serving until the EOW.

Peters, Paul-81/1926; Wagoner and worked at Saltworks; "I was free born"; Hostler, wagoner and Laborer; at Saltworks in Washington and Smyth Counties from spring of 1862 until 1865 when he was "discharged".

Richeson, James D.-90/1931; servant; "blockading and guard in road on Blue Ridge mountain and caring for broken down horses sent from army"; Master-James Richeson; service at Long Mountain from Amherst to Jordan's Furnace. (see letter).
Rose, Given-88/1924; Laborer on breastworks with pick and shovel for Confederate government; near Richmond from 1861-1863.
Warner, William-78/1925; body servant and caring for horses for Capt Cowen; Master-Col Charles Given of Rappahannock; service from April 1862 to April 1865.
Patillo, Jack-79/1934; Madison Heights, Va; mail carrier in Georgia; "I carried mail from West Point, Georgia to Whitesville, Georgia and offices in between. I helped deliver soldiers to West Point, Ga Railroad Station."; "I also served as a teamster and hauled hides from West Point to James Patillo's tanyard which was operated by government." Service from 1863 to 1865.

Appomattox County
Abbitt, Archer-87/1924; Evergreen, Va; Infantry; "Aiding in throwing up the preparing breastworks for battle"; slave of George Abbitt; service from Fall of 1864 at Dinwiddie CH until December 1864; "Officers directed me to come home."
Green, Frank-80/1926; Infantry; Teamster; Master-W.D. Hix; began service at Hixburg at beginning of war until after the surrender.
Lee, Tom-78/1924; Infantry; putting up breastworks and waiting on Capt Godsey; service began at High Bridge in 1863 and ended in 1864; "time was out". [Probably Co. I, 3rd Va Reserves].
McKinney, Pink-79/yr; Infantry; "cooked all the war for Capt Sam Overton"; served from Spring of 1862 in Richmond until "after surrender. Came home with Captain [Samuel H.] Overton"; Master-Overton. [Co A, 44th Va Infantry which was reorganized as Co. A, 20th Battalion Va Heavy Artillery].
Page, Samuel-88/1924; Spout Spring, Va; Co. A, 20th Bn, Va Heavy Artillery; also body servant and put up breastworks at Manassas and then service as a cook; service under Lt. McKinney and Capt Alex (___); "I was free born. My mother was free but my father was a slave."; Service from Manassas to the surrender; Certification of Confederate veteran E.F. Collins, "I hereby certify that Samuel Page (a colored man) served in Co. A, 20th Battalion Va Heavy Artillery for two years as a cook. And I believe he would have taken his place in the ranks with his gun if told to do so. With great pleasure. E.F. Collins."
Whitaker, R.D.-80/1928; of Spout Spring, Va; "detailed to bury the Confederate dead during the war. Made coffin cases and hauled and buried Confederate soldiers."; "My father Daniel Whitaker and I were detailed by Confederate authorities to make coffins and bury soldiers, some who came home and died here and others shipped in, mostly without compensation." Master-"My father Daniel Whitaker was the principal."; served from 1861 to EOW; "did not leave".

Augusta County
Johnson, Jacob-80/1924; 6th Va Cavalry; "tend to horses, cook, wash and do anything that came to hand."; service under "Capt Bill Meade and Sgt Charlie Ball; Master-Joe Meade, father of Capt Meade; service from 1861 at Bull Run/Manassas until EOW; "I never left the war until the war was over." Note: Company K, 6th Va Cavalry.
Porterfield, Jacob-82/1924; Infantry; Cook under William Jefferson, a Lieutenant in 16th Mississippi Regt; from 1861 to EOW; "at surrender at Appomattox"; Master-Evans Jefferson.

Bedford County
Austin, Edward-80/1924; stableman and laborer; service included one year as a stableman and six months as a laborer; :Fed and cared for horses and mules. Dug cannon pits and ___ [for] ammunition." Under Jesse and ___ Burton; Master-Abraham Austin; served from October 1863 until April 1865 when "Lee surrendered."; started service in Bedford.
Goode, Patrick-85/1924; "Putting up breastworks...drove team width of lines but did general work."; Supervisor and Master-Samuel Hobson; began work at Petersburg and continued to EOW "at Lee's surrender".
Hall, Austin-72/1924; "Laborer. Worked on Confederate breastworks" under Madison; Master-W.P. Farrell; service started in September 1863 near Richmond; "stayed until my Master's time was out, then I was brought home."
Hardy, Jim-83/1924; Army; "throwing up breastworks" with pick and shovel; service under Capt David Newsom; Master-Capt Him Hardy; started service "about middle of war below Richmond" until "about the close of

war. Capt Newsom brought us home."
(Newsom was Captain of the Emaus Home Guard of Bedford County.]
Henderson, Thomas-75/'925; Servant from 1862 to EOW; at Drewry's Bluff; Master-Capt J. B. Jones.
Henderson, William-77/1924; Laborer on breastworks in Richmond, 1864-65; Master-Frank Henderson.
Holley, Austin-85/1924; Artillery service; laborer on breastworks from 1862-63; Discharged by Capt. Abe Lewis' staff.
Holmes, John-87/1925; Cook for Captain Charles Otey; fed mules at Dublin serving in Dublin, Lynchburg and Staunton from 1861 to EOW.
Johnson, Edmund-80.1924; Army; Free man; "serving teams and throwing up breastworks. I was with Col. Munford's regiment, 2nd Va Cavalry."; "My father belonged to Mr. Rufus Thomas. My mother was free."; served from mid-war to EOW; "at the surrender"; began service at Lynchburg.
Johnson, Henry-85/1924; Slave employed at Chaffin's Bluff and other places. Master-William Johnson of Bedford. Employed 60 days in November and December 1862 and January 1863; employed by artillery; "worked on breastworks and placed cannon on them" under the supervision of Capt Abe Lewis Stiff [Co. G, 1st Va Reserves].
Martin, John Wesley-86/1924; Army; "driving teams and working at furnace" under Capt Tom Peters; working boss was named Ben Shay; Master/Mistress-Mrs. Sophia Martin; service from second year of war at Cloverdale Furnace; "Was cut off by Hunter's Raid and did not get back. Was with them [Confederates] when we were trying to keep Hunter back."; J.O. Lackes and John Arrington of Thaxton (white men) testify he served as a wagoner.
Spinner, Henry-92/1928; in the "supply service"; "hauled supplies from the [Bedford] County and to Lynchburg and Bedford City" under Capt John Turpin (his master) from beginning of war to EOW.

Bland County
Green, Claiborne-80/1930; Teamster in Quartermaster Branch; "drove teams and gathered provisions hauling them to QM Depot" under James Bane; Master-Robert Morton; Service from August 1864 at Poplar Hill; "sent home about January 1, 1865".

Botetourt County
Brugh, R.M.-76/1925; Teamster; "drove teams for Commissary Department"; service from 1864-1865 in Buchanon and Salem; "Teams was discharged".
Kelly, John W.-79/1930; "veteran"; Teamster and distributor of supplies; "as a helper in distributing rations. Delivering government provisions to families of Confederate soldiers in service. Voluntary service. Volunteered to haul supplies as directed from stations at Amsterdam, Buchanon, Fincastle Barracks, etc.; age 11 to 15 years from 1862 to 1865 "at close of war"; service under Lt. Edward Brugh at the store, commissary and mill during the war; Co. C, 2nd Va Regt.
Wooden, Lewis-79/1926; Teamster of government wagon; "drove a supply wagon for Confederate government in Capt Donkin's company."; Immediate superior was Quartermaster James Mundy; Master-Wm. H. Garrett; served from 1862 "until war closed 1865"; in Buchanon, Va.

Brunswick County
Butts, Irwin-83/1925; Alberta, Va; Cook with Brunswick Guards (Infantry) [Co. A, 5th Bn Va Inf] under Tom Heartwell (master) a member of the Brunswick Guards. Served from May 1861 until 1864; "My master was discharged on account of sickness and I left when he did."
Davis, Davie-82/1925; Laborer; breastworks; from 1862 to EOW; served at Drewry's Bluff, Chesterfield County and mountains. Fed teams and cleared out for Army.
Meade, John-84/1926; worked on [artillery] battery; in service to Confederate Engineers; under the command of John Robertson; helped to build battery, ammunition magazines and breastworks under the supervision of Robert Turnbull and Robert Edward Haskins; "My mother had been set free, and I was born free". Service began in Richmond in 1862 and continued until 1865.
Moore, Henderson D.-80/1927; "Private and servant"; Laborer; Engineer Department under Dinkun and Capt Chambers; Master-S.T. Moore; began service in 1863 at Drewry's Bluff. Captured by Union Troops on 17 March 1865; also drove ammunition wagon in 1864.
Rivers, Freeman-87/1926; Free man; Laborer on breastworks and ammunition magazines under supervision of Sheriff Charles Turnbull of Brunswick Co; Master-William Samford; "Former master was dead and he had set me free at his death." Served from January 27,

1862 to March 1862 near Richmond; "Hands got frostbitten and doctor sent me home. Long time before hands got well."

Buchanan County
Boyd, Isaac-76/1930; driving a team; hauling supplies in Buchanan, Russell and Tazewell Counties.

Buckingham County
Banks, Jasper-105/1935; Infantry; Cook under General Charles Jones from 1861 in Richmond until EOW. Stayed until surrender.
Booker, Cornelius-99/1924; Laborer; breastworks; Infantry; "digging trenches, building breastworks" under Capt John Fisher; Master Joshua Davis; from 1861 in Hanover Junction to 1865 when "war ended." [Capt John Fisher, Co. B, Richmond City Bn, Va Local Defense Troops].
Cabell, William-107/1924; teamster for two years; hauled supplies from Richmond to Drewry's Bluff under Major Giske and others; Master-Mrs. Nancy Scruggs; service from 1863 to April 1, 1865; "My mistress sent a man in my place."
Cary, Tom-83/1927; Laborer; Breastworks; served three weeks; "I served with the Confederate forces as builder of breast-works, during the year 1863, and was sent home on account of my age."
Edmonds, Frank-78/1924; Laborer; breastworks; four years service from 1861 ending service at "Appomattox, April 9, 1865"; began at Drewry's Bluff under Robert Hubard, his master.
Ellis, Wilson D.-75/'926; Hospital Service; "as water servant at Camp Winder, Va"; Master-Lawrence G. Taylor; from 1864; left "at surrender April 1865".
Jones, Albert-86/1933; Laborer; "worked for the government at the saw mill."; made lumber for breastworks; Master-Tom Robertson; service from 1863 to 1865; "I went to a place called Belmont where I worked in the service of the Confederate Government, getting out lumber to be sent to Chickahominy Swamp and Manassas Gap to be used in breastworks."
Jones, Isaac-97/1925; Hostler and Teamster; "served wherever they sent me."; "stable boss, drive wagon and when where I was [in service]"; Under command of master-Col. W.A. Forbes; started in 1862 near Richmond; "Did not leave until surrender".
Jones, Moses-80/1924; Laborer; breastworks and wagon driver; Master-Edward Glover; Began service in 1862 near Chickahominy Swamp; ended service "at Appomattox 1865".
Jones, Simon-82/1930; Body servant to Capt Garland B. Hanes from 1861 to 1865; service near Richmond in 1864 to EOW; ended service "at surrender of Genl Lee 1865". [Garland B. Hanes was Captain, Co. F, 20th Va Inf which was reassigned as Co. A, 57th Va Inf.]
Lee, Thomas-83/1924-Laborer; breastworks; Master-Jno. J. Snoddy; service from September 1863 to November 1863 at Chaffin's Bluff; worked on Brook Turnpike trenches; During the war was known as Tom Snoddy. After the war, took his original name.
Miller, Andrew-83/1927; Teamster; under Master-Washington Snoddy; service from 1863; left service at "surrender of Lee".
Moseley, Cambridge-85/1928; Laborer; breastworks; artillery; Mater-Col. Thomas Bondurant; 18 months total service "to Lee's surrender".
Sadler, Henry-80/1926; Cook and body servant for Capt. Fairfax; served 18 months from September 1862 until Capt Fairfax's company was captured.
Sears, Tom-85/1924; Laborer; Army; "worked on breastworks and built roads" for John Dunkum and others; Master-Dr. Pratt; at Drewry's Bluff; from Fall 1864 to Lee's surrender.
Shields, Tom-80/1925. Cavalry. Cook and body servant under Thomas Cook. From 1863 to Appomattox 1865.

Campbell County
Brown, Sam-77/1925; Laborer; Breastworks; "dug trenches and worked on breastworks"; under supervision of master Dick Browne; Started service in Lynchburg in 1864 continuing until the surrender. Affidavit signed by James Brown, Co. I, 2nd Va Cavalry.
Burks, Pharoah-80.1924. Cook. Breastworks; in Lynchburg Home Guard; Master-George A. Burks of Lynchburg; service from 1861 until "master was killed"; in "burial squad under Geo A. Burks "to close of war".
Clark, Adam-91/1925; Servant building breastworks; under Master Bowling Clark and Mr. Duncan, boss; from September 1, 1864 to 24 December 1864 under Mr. Duncan, below Richmond.
Creasy, Wyatt-89/1924; Infantry; Laborer; Breastworks; under supervision of Sheridan Lagade, Mr. Duncan and Mr. Vaughan; Master-George Creasey; "my father. He was a free Negro and I was drafted."; June of 1863 to

Spring of 1864; "Left on furlough and war ended."; total of nine months service; served at Drewry's Bluff and ended service "at surrender in 1865."; Under Capt. Rice Booth; (see also Davidson file). [possibly Sgt Right Booth, Co. H, 54th Va Inf]

Hunt, Gabe-75/1924; Hostler; "cared for cavalry and artillery horses"; Served under Capt Richards and Lt. Jones; from 1865 to EOW; at Lynchburg, Salisbury, NC; Master-Sam Pannill;

Johnson, Burroughs Whitfield-78/1924; Laborer; Breastworks under Capt Moody; Mater-Capt Silas Banner; service from January 1864; service ended "at the surrender".

Linthicum, Carter-94/1931; Wagoner; "Driving wagons, hauling supplies for Army. Hauled supplies during last three years of war" under supervision of Capt Watson; Mater-William Lithicum; Entered service in 1862 from Henry County and left service upon hearing of Gen Lee's surrender.

Martin, Scott-81/1924; Laborer; breastworks; "I helped build rifle pits…and helped place cannons." Under supervision of Mr. Bacon; Master-Dabney Martens.

Moore, John-71/1902; Army; Co. A, 20th Va Bn Hvy Artillery; Under Capt. Sam Overton; Enlisted April 1861 to Appomattox; Served Four years, body servant to Tharp Nause, his master. "Left at the surrender at Appomattox."

Morgan, Walker-77/1925; Engineers; Laborer; Breastworks; Master-Dick Morgan; from 1864 to surrender.

Oulds, Henry-86/1925; Teamster and Laborer; Driving team and throwing up breastworks under supervision of William Bowlin; Master-Thomas Oulds; from Spring 1863 at Chickahominy Swamp to EOW when discharged.

Reed, John-83/1926; Laborer; Breastworks; Co. D, 12th Bn Va Infantry; Captured 04 April 1865 at Chester Station; in prison at Hart's Island; released June 20, 1865; born in Charlotte and sent to service by Master-Capt Thos S. Spencer. Served at Drewry's Bluff from to fall of 1864. Reed formerly known as John Spencer.

Robinson, George Washington-80/1923; Laborer; Co. C, 11th Va Infantry (Clifton Grays) and Longstreet's Artillery; under Col Samuel Garland & J.R. Hutter; Enlisted 16 May 1861 to EOW, April 1865; Captains Adam Clement, William Henry Morgan and Moody; Master-Major Robert Saunders; "at the surrender 1865"; built breastworks and did repair work on roads. With Whit Johnson from Petersburg to Appomattox; "at the surrender - under Capt Moody."

Terry, James-90/1924; Infantry "under Beauregard; served as cook and bodyguard for Master, John Terry; from 1861 to EOW; "discharged after CW was over". [Possibly John W. Terry, Co. F, 42nd Va Infantry].

Tweedy, Sam-87/1925; Laborer on breastworks; Teamster by order of Alex Cardwell; Master-Capt Ben Tweedy; "at Appomattox at Lee's surrender".

Caroline County
Bundy, Nat-87-1930; Cook; 9th Va Cavalry; entered service April 1861 and "left at close of war 1865".; under Captain Coffin; Master-Ham Kay. [Note: Probably in Co. B, Caroline Light Dragoons.]

Clark, John-79/1925; Body servant to Major William W. Thornton; Master/Mistress- Miss Betsy Buckner; Served January 1863 to April 1865 "at Appomattox C.H."; [Probably Co. A, 4th Va Cavalry, Prince William Cavalry.]

Hall, Leroy-80/1923; Teamster in Commissary Department; served from 1861 to Gettysburg under Major William S. ____; Master-Buckner;

Charles City County
Bradley, Edmund-87/1925; Laborer on breastworks' from 1861 to (illegible).

Brown, S.T.-84/1924; Free man; Cook and Hostler in Charles City Southern Guards [Co. K, 53rd Va Infantry]; general body servant to Capt. George Waddell; "no master, free born"; From May 1861 near Jamestown to 1863; Capt Waddell was crippled at Mt. [Cedar?] Hill battle—we were ordered to Louisa CH. He went to Lynchburg, Va and resigned."

Webb, William-80/1924; Southern Guards [Co. K, 53rd Va Infantry]; "on breastworks on Mulberry Island. Waited on officers and cooked. Gen. MacGruder, Phil Buffin, John Ragland"; Master-Ned Phillips; Entered service in May 1861 and "left when captured in 1864 by Gen. Sheridan's army."

Charlotte County
Brogden, George-79/1924; "worked on Fortifications on Staunton River near Randolph in Halifax County"; "I had no master"; served in 1864, also at High Bridge near Farmville. HOR: Randolph

Brown, Gabriel-87/1924; Laborer on breastworks; at Drewry's Bluff "for several

months".; sent by mother; master, Isaac Carrington. HOR: Drake's Branch
Carrington, Henry-105/1924; born in Charlotte but pensioned from Halifax; a Teamster in Captain William H. Easley's Company C, 3rd Virginia Cavalry from 1862 "near Gaithersburg" (MD) to March 1865." Master: William Howerton
Crawley, Silas-81/1924; Mail Carrier. "1861 until the end of the war" in Charlotte County. Master-Tom Garrett; HOR: Barnesville.
Evans, Aaron-85/1925; born in Charlotte but pensioned from Halifax; master was Capt. Charles Bruce of Staunton Hill; "working on fortifications and burying the dead"; worked from the outbreak of the war until late war; worked at a rock quarry on a canal between Lynchburg and Richmond; worked at a cemetery near Richmond to help bury the dead; "I was sent to work on the Breastworks between Richmond and Petersburg. Right in the midst of battle I worked on those entrenchments with my life in constant danger". Also worked at fortifications at Staunton River Bridge. U.S. Senator William Cabell Bruce sent a letter of support for Evans' pension stating, ""He was a man of Herculean strength; indeed, the strongest man undoubtedly, I imagine, that ever lived in Southside Virginia except, perhaps, the famous Peter Francisco of the Revolutionary Period. For a long time he was a bateau-man on the Staunton River and, I think, was in the employment of my father when the latter operated a steamboat on that River."
Howell, Richard-80/1925; Cook in Infantry; Free Born; Served from 1861 to EOW; "Never left. In service during the four years." Began service at Harding's Bluff.
Lacy, Horace-87/1935; Body Servant. Attended to horses and cooked for owner. Served Three years 1862-1865 "to end of war". HOR: Keysville
Miles, Mitchell-85/19r24; Laborer on breastworks; at Drewry's Bluff.; master, D.L. Morrow. HOR: Cullen
Robinson, Parker-87/1924; Ditcher; "digging ditches and building batteries"; 1863 for three months at the James River near Rockett's Landing in Richmond and Bragg's Mill; master, Garland Berkley. HOR: Saxe
Rogers, James-83/1925; Body Servant and Teamster; Known as James Price during the war; Infantry and Cavalry; "waited on soldiers and my young master, William Price, Jr. and drove wagon." Served under Capt. William Price, Sr.; joined in 1863 on the "muster ground in Charlotte, Captain Price's Place" serving till "close of war". HOR: Brookneal
Skipwith, Ben Fuller-82/1924; Teamster; "drove provision wagon"; served from "November 1863" to "April 9, 1865 from Appomattox C.H."; master is Fuller Skipwith. HOR: Red Oak
Smith, John-86/1934; Cook; enl. January 1862 and "stayed to the end"; "I served during the war at Ft. Monroe and Manassas Gap under Cap[t] Gilliam of Charlotte County and cooked for my young master Ed Roberts."; master, Frank Roberts. HOR: Saxe [Capt. William A. Gilliam or Richard H. Gilliam of the Mossingford Rifles, Co. I, 44th Va Infantry.]
Thornhill, William-85/1930; Body Servant and laborer on breastworks; "I waited on my master James Henry Harding. My master carried me."; served from 1863-1865 at Drewry's Bluff. "Sent home by my master"; "Digging trenches and carrying food to soldiers"; "This duty was performed around Drewry's Bluff and Petersburg and Richmond and Gettysburg…I entered service at 17 years of age and left service at age of 19 years old." HOR: Drake's Branch
Watkins, William-77/1924; Cook; served from 1864 to April 1865 "on account of Lee's surrender". Period of service was 14 months under Capt. Andrew B. Price of Staunton Hill Artillery, Johnson's (------). HOR: Drake's Branch

Chesterfield County
Bell, Wyatt-79/1924; body servant and cook; Master-Benjamin Morris; Service from 1862 to September 1864; "Master taken prisoner, I sent home."
Brown, Kit-90/1924; body servant and cook to Captain Walker Robertson; Master-Dr. D.W. Robertson; service from 1861 to "shortly after the battle of Gettysburg where Mr. Robertson was wounded. I brought him home. After he recovered he went back to the army but I was left at home."
Cypress, Eldridge-79/1925; Laborer on breastworks; "worked as laborer in building breastworks in Chesterfield County in the defenses of Richmond from Falling Creek to Broad Roach Road; Drafted man; Master-S.V. Burgess; service began in 1864 near Watkins Mill and Richmond/Petersburg Turnpike; left service "a few days before evacuation of Richmond."

Randall, William-78/1925; Cook; Began service in April 1861 in Arkansas serving until 1865; "Company captured by Union forces at Exeter Mills, Va." Served under Gen. Price and Sgt. Henry Wilkinson; Master P.H. Wilkinson.

Culpeper County
Banks, John L., Sr.-88/1935; Laborer at Iron Furnace in Louisa; General labor at the furnace making supplies for the Confederate Army; Master-William Stout, Jr.; Service began in 1863 to EOW.

Chivis, Jabe-87-1931; Teamster in QM Dept under Capt Poindexter and Major Richards; Master-Johnston Roberts; service from Fall 1862 to furlough in 1864; Started service in Gordonsville where the Army was located. "I made one trip from Gordonsville to Salem with a drove of government horses but continued with team on my return to Gordonsville."

Clore, Champ-84/1924; Laborer on breastworks; QM Dept under Master, Aaron Clore from 1863 to 1864 when ordered home. Service was around Richmond.

Evans, Marshall-80/1924; Hostler and Cook in Cavalry; Volunteer with Capt. William A. Hill, Co. D, 4th Va Cavalry, Little Fork Rangers; Began service in Spring 1862 and appears to have left service with Capt. Hill.

George, Duke-77/1924; Hospital service; under ____ Driver; "waiting on Master helping in Dining Room and Kitchen"; Master-Edward Tyson; service from 1863 to EOW; "In the spring of 1863 I went from Fauquier County, Va with the Williamson family to Lynchburg. I belonged to the Williamson family, who refugeed to Lynchburg. Soon after our arrival at Lynchburg, I was sold at the Market House, to Judge Edmund L. Taylor, of Culpeper, who at once sent me to the Confederate hospital in Lynchburg, where I worked in various capacities until April 1865. During all my service at the hospital in Lynchburg, I never received any pay for my work."

Glascoe, George T.-89/1931; Teamster; Master-William Lewis; service from 1863 to Appomattox "close of war"; sent to service by master "on call of Jefferson Davis for team[sters]."

Green, Louis-80/1924; Nurse, Orderly, Waiter; "waited on sick soldiers in hospital at Lynchburg" under Dr. Spencer; Master-Dr. Reuben Long; service from 1862 to EOW; "for more than a year a hostler at the Fair grounds just outside of Lynchburg at a camp under the direction of one Major Praxton, which was in the nature of a depot for the collection of supplies and horses for the Confederate Army; that he was at this camp and performed the duties of a hostler and laborer during two seasons, and he distinctly recollects being there in the fall of two years when the wagons would come in with corn and other supplies for the use of the army; that while there he was also at times cook for the men engaged in this business; that at this late date he does not recall all of his duties, but he was in the service of the Confederacy from before the first battle of Manassas until after the close of the Civil War, and as above stated a great part of this time he was nurse or orderly in the hospital; that his duties were so varied that at this time he cannot recollect any in particular except the two seasons he was with Major Paxton outside of Lynchburg at the depot established there for the collection of supplies."

Jackson, Henry-82/1924; Infantry; Servant of Gen. A.P. Hill then Gen. James Walker. Served from 1861 at First Manassas to surrender at Appomattox.

Jackson, Taylor-77/1925; Attendant and Nurse at hospital from 1863 to EOW. Served in Culpeper. Master-Dr. T.H. Carrington.

Johnson, Nathan-82/1930; Cavalry as cook and teamster; "cooked and drove teams and also did blacksmithing" under Lt. D. Corbin; Master-Joseph Armstrong; service from 1862 to EOW; "I was a teamster for Mr. Joseph Armstrong, who gathered meat, wood, etc., for the Confederate Army from Loudon, Fauquier and Culpeper Counties and hauled the same to Culpeper Court House. My first service in the war was as a body servant for my master, Lt. Oz Corbin of Centreville, Va., and was later sent back home to take charge of the team for Mr. Armstrong, who was the husband of a sister of Lt. Corbin. I am unable to say whether I would be considered in the employment of the government or of Lt. Corbin, but I have tried to the best of my recollection to tell you the facts."

Lightfoot, Addison-79/1930; Hospital Worker in Charlottesville "helping to care for the sick and wounded by dressing wounds, etc."; Master-Oliver Pinkard; service from 1863 to 1865.

Lightfoot, Henry Clay-79/1924; Body servant; waited on Capt. William Holcomb; Commissary Service; Master-Thomas R. Rixe.

Moore, Jesse-82/1929; Body servant to A.P. Kelly, Infantry; Cooked; Master-William Moore; Period of service 1861-1865.
Simms, Lewis-78/.1926; Teamster/Laborer on breastworks; Master-Capt. S.M. Payne; service from 1862 to 1865.
Slaughter, William H.-79/1924; Body servant; Cavalry; "all services of camp servant and offer[ed] to go in battle…I asked to go."; from May 1861 to April 1865; at Manassas.
Stuart, Mary-90/1930; Hospital Servant, Cook and Nurse.
Wallace, Henry-79/1925; Cook in Infantry for John Hull from 1863 to 1865; Master-Harles Smith.
Williams, Isham-81/1925; Teamster; "Drove commissary wagon under Capt John Lightfoot (master) from 1862 to EOW.; "war ended is why I left." [Possibly Assistant Commissary John Lightfoot, 7th Va Inf]
Winslow, Edmund-92/1930; Teamster; Commissary Dept; "hauling lumber for camp" under Capt. John Lewis (master); "Capt Lewis sent me home to care for his family."
Withers, John B.-79/1932; Cook; Master-William Bussey; in "Black Horse Company, Col. Mosby" in Fauquier Co. in 1861; "served three years and had to go home to my mistress." Was eight years old when he began service; "I assisted the cook by washing dishes, preparing vegetables, carrying water and wood, and doing other small jobs, for Col. Mosby's company. I believe this should be considered serving the Army."; Said Master was "too old for service" "but it was at his command that I served as a cook's helper in Fauquier and Loudon Counties. He and Colonel Mosby were great friends." In attached letter, Mollie E. Bussey states, "My father William Bussey was John's master and I recall that Colonel John S. Mosby and my father were great friends and the Colonel used to come to our house very often and he asked my father to let John go in the Army and assist the cook and he consented and John went and helped the cook under Col. Mosby. I am now 84 years of age and I recollect the incident very well." (dated 29 August 1932).
Yowell, John L [Y].-79/1928; Co. L, 10th Va Infantry, under Col. Lowry and Capt Newton Finks; served from November 1862 to Lee's surrender. "Succeeded his father (Stuart Yowell) as teamster when [he] was 14 years old. Father was promoted to a more important position." Transferred in January 1863; "helped his father drive a team and gather provisions for Co. L. John Y. Yowell and John Nethers shared same quarters. Capt. Finks writes, "At the time of the surrender I was in Madison County gathering supplies, when the team was taken over by Federals."

Cumberland County
Armstead, Moses-80/1924; Laborer on breastworks; Master-William Clarke; service from 1862 to 1865.
Brown, Randol-87/1924; Laborer on breastworks "around Richmond"; Master-James Shell; Service from 1861 to 1865; "I went South and was on duty when Lee surrendered."
Crump, George-81/1925; Free Man; Laborer and cook; waited on officers Meredith, Dickenson and Haskins; "I was born free. No master."; service from August 1862 to EOW.
Delaney, McDowel-80/1924; Born Free. Cook in 1862 for Captain A.M. Chappell and others.
Hill, Steven E.-72/1924; Cook and hostler. Attended horses from 1862 to EOW; in Lynchburg. Master-James D. Hill.
Hobson, Isaac-78/1924; Laborer on breastworks from 1864 to EOW in Richmond; Master-David Bradley.
Johnson, Stillman-79-1924; Infantry; worked for Dr. Thos Shield and R. P. Walton from 1861 to 1865.
Johnson, Watt-79-1924; Laborer on breastworks from 1861 to 1865; Master-Spencer Osborne.
Lipscomb, William E.-87/1924; Free Man; Laborer on breastworks and cook; "built breastworks also made salt peter and cook"; "I had no master"; "I never left the war until the end 1865."; service 1861-1865.
Randolph, Alfred Thompson-82/1924; Laborer on breastworks for three months in 1864; Master-James (illegible).
Randolph, Samuel-84/1927; Teamster from 1862-65; hauled supplies from Cartersville to Richmond; Master-S. Booker.
Robinson, James Henry-86/1924; Hostler and Miner; "I mined salt"; service 1863-65; Master-John Robinson.
Saunderson, Carter-82/1928; Teamster; wagon driver at Petersburg until discharged. Master-Willis Saunderson.
Scott, Morris-91/1924; Laborer on breastworks and cook at "Brown's Church" from 1863 to April 1865; "was wounded"; Master-Lee Scott.

Virginia's Black Confederates

Winfree, Augustus-92/1925; Cavalry; Master-Capt Miller and Dr. ___ Miller; 1861-1865.
Wood, Charles H.-75/1924; Cook; "I was cook in Quartermaster Dept" under Capt Freeman; Master-Miss Lucy Blair; 1863 to "Amelia in 1865---field at the time of end of war."
Woodson, George-81/1925; Laborer on breastworks; Master-James Woodson of Buckingham Co.; service from 1864-65.
Wooldridge, William-75/1924; Laborer on breastworks and cook; Master-B. Brooks; service from 1863-65.

Danville
Boyd, William Henry-70/1924; Cook; Army; Master-Richard Boyd; worked for Robert A. Boyd from 1861 to EOW; "Lee surrendered and I was at Appomattox at the time."; born in Mecklenburg and later resided in Farmville; Note: Appomattox surrender roles show R.A. Boyd, 2nd Engineer Regt, Engineer Dept.
Lawson, Abner-80/1931; Servant and Cook; Cavalry under Capt. Easley; Master-David Lawson; 12 months service from 1864-65; [Possible Co. H, 3d Va Cavalry].

Dinwiddie County
Cole, John-90/1925; Teamster; Infantry; driver of government wagon; from 1863 to EOW; "at time of surrender, discharged". Served under Capt Goodwyn; Master-John Dodson. [Capt Arthur M. Goodwyn, Co. I, 12th Va; later Co. H, 9th Va]
Cross, Richard-79/1925; Servant and Orderly; "wait on Capt Griffin"; Captain of the Dinwiddie Artillery; from 1861 to 1865 at surrender; born in Lunenburg County;.
Johnson, Andrew-95/1924; Laborer on breastworks; also served as cook; Master-Major Fitzgerald; service began illegible to 1865.
Jones, Sidney-78/1925; Supply branch. Driver of ammunition wagon from 1864 to 1865; under Major Crockram; Master-Newton Harper; b. in Nottoway County.
Lanier, Heartwell-85/ 1925; Body servant in cavalry; Master-Leroy Bowden; served from 1862-65.
Mitchell, George-88-1932;Teamster; QM Dept; Master-Green Mitchell; service from 1862-65; Worked on breastworks at Blandford for two weeks before being relieved by his brother.
Morgan, Sam-87/1925; Cook in Cavalry; served as "soldier"; from 1861 at Amelia CH to EOW; "I did not leave until the end of the war."; Master-Thomas Jackson. Born in Nottoway County.
Pegram, Paul-86/1925; Teamster "hauling rations from places to soldiers." Master-Madison Gill; "All he knows is the he was put in the Army by his Master Madison Gill". He went "from Dinwiddie County to Blackstone, Va" and served from 1862 and got out "at close of war 1865". Born in Brunswick and lived near McKenny.
Stewart, Richard-76/1925; Cook and Servant; Artillery; "Born free—entered service by order of father Levi Abraham Stewart" serving from 1861 to EOW "near Appomattox CH, Va". Born in Lunenburg County.
Taylor, John-82/1925; Nurse at Chimborazo Hospital; "nurse wounded soldiers"; Master-Dr. E.H. Smith, Chief Surgeon, from 1861-1865; Note: Dr. Edward Harrie Smith was Chief Surgeon for Third Division, CSA.
Tucker, Pompey-83/1936; Cook; Infantry; under Capt Nash and Everett Dreary; Master-Dr. Jonathan Tucker; "Left [at] Appomattox, war ended." [Capt Benj H. Nash, Co. B, 41st Va Inf]
Tucker, William-82/1921; Cook and Teamster; Co. I, 3rd Va Cavalry; took orders from Col. William Davis; Master-Col Hart Tucker; Served from 1862 to April 1865 "war over".
Tucker, William-80/1928; Free Man; Teamster for commissary collecting provisions and hauling supplies for the army from 1863 to 1865.
Walker, William-84/1924; Cook; 3rd Va Regt, Fitzhugh Lee's Cavalry under Col. William Davis; Master-Robert Neblett; served from July 1861 to 1865 "at surrender".
Winfield, Isham-85/1924; Cook; Cavalry, Stuart's Brigade; Cook and help throw up breastworks and general servant." Master & Supervisor-Berryman Hill; from 1861 in New Kent County; "Master killed third year of war." [Berryman Hill, Sgt to 1st Lt, Co. I, 3rd Va Cav]
Wyatt, George-74/1928; Infantry; Cook and Servant; Drewry's Bluff and Yorktown; Supervisor: Daniel ___; Master-Horace Mitchell; Left service in "1865, lines of surrender."

Elizabeth City
Russell, William-85/1927; Servant; "I carried messages and other duties; Master-John Jones of Pembroke; served from 1863-1865.

Essex County

Bundy, Ryburn L. 87/1934; Teamster; Supplying Commissary; sent around for cattle; Master/Supervisor-Major Robinson; served from 1862 to EOW.
Hays, William-86/1924; Cook; Cavalry; "cook, care of horses and general work"; Boss-Robert L. Warr; served from 1861 to EOW.
Lee, Frank-79/1925; Servant; 9th Va Cavalry; under Lt. Waring Lewis, his master; served from 1861 to EOW and "surrender of Lee's Army".; also served at Chickahominy.[Lewis was in Co. F]
Pitts, Robert-80/1925; Servant; 55th Va Infantry; under Lt. P.C. Waring from 1862 until sent home by Lt. Waring. [Capt Patrick C. Waring, Co. F & D, 55th Va Inf]
Taylor, Thornton-85/1924; Teamster and wagon repair in QM Dept; from February 1862 to 15 December 1864; Master-Hunter.
Washington, Lewis-77/1926; Servant to Capt Rice; "cooking and washing and helping him about his tent."; "My young master was killed and they sent me home."; Master-Preacher Rice.
Williams, John-89/1925; Servant and Cook; from 1861 to EOW "at Appomattox".; Master-Humphrey-.

Fairfax County

Chives, Edmund-83/1931; Hostler and Servant; Division QM for Major Charles Waite; attending to horse from 1861 to 1865; disbanded in NC; born in Spotsylvania.
Godfrey, J.W.-81/1933; Servant; Free man; Infantry, possibly Co. A, 49th Va Infantry; charged with removing and burying dead Confederate soldiers and nursing wounded; occasionally built breast works; ."No master"; "My father and five of my uncles were in this regiment and I followed them. I was too young to enlist." Served from 1861 to EOW; was in Culpeper when the news [of surrender] came.
Grayson, William-81/1928; Cook; 30th Va Infantry; Master-Mary Covington; served from 1861 to 1865.
Harrison, George F.-81/1935; Helper/Hostler; "Took care of horses for Col. John Mosby and his officers."; Enlisted 1863 and left at close of war; on duty in Fauquier County; kept horses hidden for Mosby's use (scouts); "he actually stayed away from home, in the mountains of Virginia and cared for the horses at points in the mountains, where they would be safe from the raids of the Federal Army."; "in the Bull Run Mountains", reserve horse kept at the request and direction of Col. Mosby.
Ball, Penny-82/1929; Teamster and body servant; Driver; Under Lt. Col. Barlow and Col Boyd; Master-Miss Alive Farris; served from 1862 to EOW.
Ford, Carter-89/1928; body servant; served with Col John S. Mosby; "with Smith who was killed then as servant to Colonel------." Master-James R. Jones; At EOW was servant for Col. Chapman.
Fry, Albert-83/1926; Cook; Co. A, 7th Va Infantry; service just after Gettysburg to after Lee's surrender (1863-EOW); Master----Long.
Hackley, Joseph-85/1925; Teamster; Infantry under Major Scruggs; served from 1862 to surrender at Appomattox. [Major/LtCol Daniel Emmett Scruggs, 2nd Quartermaster Bn, Va Inf, Local Defense Troops].
Jennings, Joseph-92/1930; body servant; 38th Va Infantry; cooked for several officers; served from 1861 to after battle of Fredericksburg; Master-John Fox.
Williams, Simon-87/1933; Nurse in hospital in Richmond and Lynchburg; Under Mr. Ferguson and Mr. Campbell from 1861-1865; Master-William Morgan.

Floyd County

Palmer, Thaddeus-87/1927; body servant; Infantry, Col Brubaker's Regiment; Cook for Capt R.T. Mitchell; from 1862; "young master was wounded and told me to stay away…he was taken by the Yankees".; Master-Robert T. Mitchell.
Turner, Charles-85/1924; Laborer on breastworks around Richmond for 60 days in 1862..

Fluvanna County

Anderson, John G.-69/1907; Co. H, 22d Va Bn Infantry; Capt Jno Carter, Hills Division, Jackson's Corps; from 1861 to EOW; left "at surrender of Gen. R.E. Lee."
Anderson, John-80/1924; Teamster; Cavalry and breastworks; Master-Wm P. Snead; Supervisor-Capt Rogers; left service "at Lee's surrender".
Holman, Harrison-81/1924; In August 1863; Laborer on breastworks at Richmond and Manchester until completed. Master-John W. Walker.
Hughes, Richard-78/1924;Laborer on breastworks and fortifications from Spring 1864 to Autumn 1864; Master-Robert H. Vest.

Mathews, Brice-78/1924; Cook; Artillery from 1864-65; Master-William Jennings.
Seay, William-80/1925; Servant/Cook; Infantry; servant to Capt William Allen, QM Dept; helped in kitchen as cook and helped to attend to the horses; from winter of 1861 to EOW.

Franklin County
Chandler, George-85/1925; Cook; from 1861-63; left because he was "sick with fever"; Master-Billie Mansfield.
Fralin, Jim-83/1925; Teamster; Drove team and hauled iron from 1862 to 1864; Master-Bob Fralin.
Holland, Claiborne-85/1925; Laborer on breastworks from 1862 to 1865 "when Lee surrendered"; Master-Johnson Holland.
Holland, Cornelius-84/1925; Teamster and Cook under Jubal Early; Master-Tommy J. Holland.
Holland, Creed-79/1925; Teamster for Infantry; "Looking after and driving teams hauling supplies for Confederate soldiers"; Under Capt Chandle; Master- Bill Holland.
James, Charles-77/1925; Cook/hostler; Master-Bruce Jones. Born in Pittsylvania County.
Kasey, Steven (Stephen)—79/1924; Laborer on breastworks; Master-Gen. Tom Kasey; served 1862 for about three months in Richmond area.
Law, Jack-78/1924; Teamster and laborer on breastworks; Master-Thomas Law; January to March 1862 at Chickahominy Swamp; 1863 in Richmond; 1864 from September to December in Charles City and Nine Mile Road area.
Lemons, John-85/1924; Servant and Laborer; 1861, near Richmond, five months on breastworks; then with master in cavalry, cooking and foraging; Master-George Lemons; with him in Kentucky and Georgia until EOW; Master was wounded.
Lumpkins, Ned-78/1924; Teamster under Abner Anthony (master); from 1862 until discharged; born in Bedford County.
Menefee, J.H.-81/1924; Laborer on breastworks from 1864 to April 1865 in Prince Edward County; Master-William Menefee.
Price, George-85/1925; Carpenter building stables and throwing up breastworks at Petersburg; Master-Piler Saunders; Served from June 1864 to March 1865 when he was called home.
Prichard, John-85/1924; Laborer building breastworks under Capt Mason at Drewry's Bluff; Master-Tom Prichard; served from 1862 to April 1865; sent home "about a week before the surrender".
Reeves, Armstead-86/1931; Cook "infantry"; "Cooked and tended horses"; started in 1862 in Dismal Swamp and "came home to serve master" at an undetermined date; served under Jake Dent [possibly J. Jacob Dent, Co. A, 37th Va Infantry]; Master-Josiah Reeves.
Robertson, Richard-77/1924; Teamster; "drove a team and hauled for the army" for his master James Robertson; began service in 1862 near Petersburg and served until April 1865; "discharged at surrender".
Smith, Daniel-83/1925; Laborer building breastworks near Richmond; under Capt Featherstone from 1862 to undetermined time. [Note: Possibly Walker Featherstone of Walker's Battery of Artillery.]
Smith, William-85/1924; Laborer on breastworks; from 1863 to 1865; Master-Theo Webb.
Turner, Arthur-85/1924; Laborer on breastworks in Richmond; served 12 months under Giles Clingenpeel; Master-George C. Turner.
Walker, Samuel-82/1924; Teamster and breastworks from Fall of 1863 to EOW; served under Gen. McGowan; Master-Nat Walker.
White, Henry-78/1925; Body Servant for Col Patrick Henry; Began service in Danville in 1861 and terminated "at surrender".
Woody, Peters-90/1924; Laborer on breastworks; slave; sent home in March 1863 after 60 days service; "I was honorably discharged".

Frederick County
Miller, Levi – 71/1907; Applied for pension in April 1907; 5th Texas Infantry, Co. C, Hood's Brigade; There is a two-page typewritten letter from Capt. J.E. Anderson, Co. C, 5th Texas but the microfilm version is unreadable. The local clerk notes he was "regularly enrolled" in the company.

Fredericksburg
Lucas, Cornelius-75/1920; Servant; Co. A, 47th Va Infantry; "waited on Capt Willie Pullock as body servant"; Master-William Pollock, father of Willie; began service in 1862 until April 1865; "Left home with young master—came home in 1865 with Capt Pollack who died about time of surrender".[Capt William G. Pollack, Co. A]

Willis, James-80/1923; Servant; Co. G, 40th Va Infantry under Capt Walter Bourne [Boure] from 1862 to 1865 and left service on "account of surrender"; Master-Walter Bourne; born in Caroline county.

Gloucestor County
Byrd, James Henry-83/1930; Servant/Cook; 26th Va Infantry under Sgt. William Dulton (master); from 1862 to "just before close of the war, master wounded."[Sgt William C. Dutton, Co. B(2), 26th Va]

Carter, Gabrel-87/1927; Cook; Richmond Howitzers under Capt Brown and Capt Segar; Master- Col Hayes; served from 1861-1862 in Tidewater region.

Davenport, Alexander D.-82/1924; Free man; Laborer: "digging trenches, cooking and washing under Col. Benjamin Farinholt; served from 1862 to 1865, EOW at Richmond and High Bridge.; "Born Free".

Moody, Peter-89/1930; Teamster, Co. A, 5th Va Cavalry; from May 1861 to April 1865 when "war closed"; worked form Col. Crump; Master-1st Lt John W. Leavitt.

Moody, Phillip-93/1930; Body Guard and Cook; Co. A, 5th Va Cavalry; under 1st Lt. J.W. Leavitt (master); from May 1861 to May 1862.

Pollard, Emanuel-81/1924; Servant/Hostler; "waited on officers and carried horses to rear when men dismounted to go in battle"; under Col. W.T. Robinson, 9th Va Cavalry, 1862-1865; "at surrender at Appomattox"; born in King and Queen County.

Goochland County
Adams, Powhatan-90/1928; Teamster; "hauled provisions for the army supplying the soldiers needs—hauled food and other provisions" under Capt John Gary; served from 1863 to 1865 "when Gen. Lee surrendered"; Master-D. Henry Holloman.

Ferguson, Walker-82/1925; Servant; Co. H, 4th Va Cavalry; to Thomas Harris, son of his master, Henry Harris; served from "Bull Run battle" to death of Master H. Harris.

Parrish, Edmond-77/1924; Teamster; "drove a provision wagon" under S. Hillary; Master-Thomas James; served from 1863 to EOW; constructed breastworks at Mulberry Island in then transferred to a provision wagon…until the close of war."

Willis, Charles-81/1925; Teamster, 1861-1865; "Was teamster in wagon train for Gen. Robert E. Lee from battle of Manassas to close of war." Terminated "at Appomattox".

Greene County
Archer, George W.-79/1926;Blacksmith; at government shop at Gordonsville; Capt Jim Smith was head of shop in last part of war; "did not leave til after surrender"; "I had started to go to the Army to enlist, but was stopped at Gordonsville and put to work in the shops."

Halifax County
Beard, Yancey-90/1933; Servant to Lt. William Beard; North Carolina soldier; served from about 16 to "when my master came home from the war."

Carrington, Henry-105/1924; Teamster in Capt. William H. Easley's Company, [Co. C] 3d Va Cavalry; served from 1862 near Gaithersburg to March 1865; Master-William J. Howerton; born in Charlotte County.

Edmondson, Isaac-85/1924; Servant for Major H. Edmondson, Infantry, from first part of war near Yorktown to EOW; "at the end of war (Lee's surrender)". [Capt Henry A. Edmondson, Co. A, 53rd Va, Halifax Light Inf]

Evans, Aaron-85/1925; born and served from Charlotte County; Master-Capt Charles Bruce of Staunton Hill, Charlotte County; "working fortifications and burying the dead"; served from outbreak of war 'til later part; worked in rock quarry on a canal between Lynchburg and Richmond then to cemetery near Richmond to help bury the dead; "I was sent to work on the breastworks between Richmond and Petersburg. Right in the midst of battle I worked on those entrenchments with my life in constant danger."; Four months service; Also served at Staunton River Bridge.

Haskins, Sib-88/1924; Cook for the Captain of the Company; Co. H, 3d Va Cavalry; Capt Clement Carrington; Master-Dr. W.H. Carrington; from June 1861; "staid" until surrender 1865.

Leigh, Samuel-86/1931; Teamster; Artillery; worked for Holly Anderson; Master-Judge William Leigh; served from April 1864 and "left after Lee's surrender".

Majors, Tillman-86/1930; Cook for S. G. Majors (Master) in 6th Va Cavalry; served from 1862 to EOW; "I left the service after the surrender at Appomattox".

Oliver, Kitt-82/1926; Laborer on breastworks; from 1862 to 1864, Drewry's Bluff; Master-Harrison Oliver.

Virginia's Black Confederates

Petty, B.S.-85/1932; Laborer on breastworks; began service in 1864 on Chapin Farm to EOW; Master-Doris Petty

White, Richard-85/1930; Laborer on breastworks; worked for Capt William White (master); "building breastworks and digging rifle pits."; served from 1862 until dismissed in 1865.

Wilkerson, James-87/1924; Laborer on breastworks; Supervisor-Mark A. Wilkerson; served from January 1864 to March/April 1865 when he was sent home.

Wimbush, Henry-84/1924; Laborer on breastworks; from 1864 to EOW; Master-Dock Anderson.; born in Pittsylvania County.

Hanover County

Allen, Samuel-75/1924; Servant to Capt William H. Burton, Co. F, 1st Va Reserves (master) from May 1864 to July 1864 when "My master was discharged from the army."; Allen was born and served from Nottoway County.

Anderson, David Lewis-82/1931; Hostler under C.H. Day from 1861 to 1865; Master-William O. Day. [Note: Charles H. Day is reflected as a private, Co. G, 4th Va Cavalry.]

Brown, Robert Lewis-80/1926; Servant and Cook for Lt. Merriwether Christian or Christenson from 1862-1864.

Coleman, Jordan-74/1924; Teamster from 1863 to EOW "after the surrender".; Master-Nathaniel Crenshaw; employed for 18 months prior to EOW as wagoner and aiding in construction of breastworks under Capt. C.W. Dabney of Patrick Henry Rifles [Co. C, 15th Va Infantry].; Mr. Joseph Leadbetter was overseer in charge of Jordan Coleman's ___ while working on the Mechanicsville Turnpike breastworks; Mr. John Brice was the overseer at Drewry's Bluff.

Cores, John-80/'925; Laborer on breastworks from 1864 to EOW; Master-Walter C. Shelton.

Fleming, Isaac-80/1927; Hostler and servant to "young master" Phillip Campbell; cooked, washed, cleaned guns; Master-James Campbell; "enlisted" in the winter before the surrender and left ten days before the surrender "by order of my young master".; born in Louisa.

Graham, John-82/1926; Servant to John Lewis Berkley who was badly wounded at Cold Harbor on June 3, 1864; in the Hanover Artillery under Capt William Wilson; Master-Landon C. Berkeley.

Jackson, Thomas-78/1925; Cavalry; Body servant to Allan and Norvelle Nuckols son of his master, Hardin Nuckols; Served from Spring 1862 to April 1865 "after the surrender of Gen. Lee."

Price Alexander-76/1924; Hostler and Servant to Major Benjamin W. Richardson of the Home Guard; from 1864-65 when "sent home".

Roane, General-80/1924; Servant and Hostler; Cavalry; looked after government horses for Capt Lateniey (master) [Note: probably Capt William Latane, Co F, 9th Va]; began service at start of war in "company in Essex County" and ended service "when Lee surrendered"; born and served from Essex County.

Robertson [Robinson], Warner-80/1924; Cook under Gallie Thompson, cavalry, from 1861 to 1863 when released from service; born at Beaverdam, Va; [Note: G.N. Thompson, 3d Corporal, Co. G, 4th Va Cavalry, Wickham's Bde].

Smith, Abram-82/1927; Cook for J.R.B. Winston, Rockbridge Artillery and Hanover Artillery; started served at Raccoon Ford; Master-William C. Winston.

Thomas, George Lee-83/1925; Laborer on breastworks; "construction of Confederate breastworks. There was a regular force of colored men of whom I was one."; built rifle pits; worked for Mr. Saunders "or whoever was foreman" from the period from 1862 to 1865 around Richmond; Master-Mrs. May Gardiner.

Henrico County

Epps, George-78-1925; Teamster; "drove headquarters wagon for Major Allen, of Tennessee, and for Gen. McCaub (?) of Maryland."; Master-Col William C. Knight of Wilton, Henrico Co; began service "about seven months before the surrender" near Petersburg and left "after surrender at Appomattox, I was at Appomattox at time of surrender."; born in Nottoway County.

Henry County

Burnett, Joe-86/1925; Teamster; "driver of rations wagons" of infantry for Ed Towns; Master-Mrs. R. Redd; from 1863-65 and left service "at the surrender".

Hairston, D.W.-83/1925; Railroad Construction Carpenter; Master-Marshall Hairston; aided in building stables to care for horses and mules; served in Danville from 1864 until worked completed and sent home.

Manns, George-81/1927; Cook for Lt. D.W. Spencer from September 1864 to April 1865 in Danville; Master-Mr. J. Wilson.
Mitchell, Jackson-90/1924; Laborer on breastworks in summer of 1864 until 1865; also known as Tap Mitchell.
Sheffield, George W.-76/1925; Teamster; Master/Supervisor-William A. Sheffield; entered service in November 1864 and left in April 1865 "at the surrender"; drove a "three-mule team hauling rations from the commissary department to the soldiers in the field."; under Company A, Captain Massey.

James City County
Brown, Dick-77/1924; Servant in cavalry under Major Coloaco Vaiden (master) from 1861 to 1865 "at end of war".

King George County
Conway, Harry-85/1930; Servant to Major E.S. Ruggles; looked after his horse and cooked from 1861 to EOW; Master-L.V. Wing.

King William County
Stewart, Osborne-79/1928; Hostler and servant; "horse boy with Mr. Willis Eastwood in 5th Va Cavalry, Capt Fox for six months during the last part of the war."; Master-Eastwood; Sent home on furlough 01 July 1864 and war closed. [Andrew Willis Eastwood, Co E, King and Queen Cavalry].
Wynne, Ben-97/1934; Servant and attendant; worked hospital in Richmond; "waited on soldiers in the hospital at Richmond, Va"; under Dr. Scott, Dr. Jenkins and Dr. Heath; Master-Thomas Starke; served from 1862 to EOW; "left Camp Jackson after war".

Lancaster County
Conaway, Hyram-92/1932; Cook and Servant; "bodyguard" to Major Cyrus Harding, 40th Va Regt; from 1861 until made prisoner; "was captured in the year 1864 and held prisoner near Winchester, Va 'till end of war then went home."
Fauntleroy, Lewis W.-81/1929; Teamster and Servant to Capt Bob J____, 9th Va Cavalry from 1863 to EOW.
Fauntleroy, Thomas-80-1924; Cook for Capt Lorton, Carr and others; Infantry; waited on Col. Robert Mayo, 47th Va Infantry; with Regiment at Gettysburg; served from 1862 to Christmas of 1864; Master-Henry Hathaway.
Gaskins, Beverly-86/1924; Cook, Servant and Hostler; for Major Andrews, 1861 to 1865.

Jackson, Lewis-84/1930; Teamster and body servant to Private Sam Williams, 9th Va Cavalry, under Capt. James K. Ball and Col. Merriwether Lewis; Served seven months in 1862 until sent home.[Pvt Samuel G. Williams was in Co. D, Lancaster Cavalry].
Williams, Steptoe-85/1924; Cook for Major Lawson (master); Master-George Cox; served from 1861 to EOW; "I never left until war closed."; "Major Charles Lawson carried me into the Confederate Army."

Lee County
Skaggs, Henry-92/1926; Hostler/Servant; served as "guard to keep the bush raiders off of women and children while their husbands were at war."; Master-John Skaggs; served from 1863 to EOW and ended service "at surrender".

Louisa County
Harris, Edward-87/1927; Free Negro; Teamster (wagoner); "driving wagons and waiting on wounded soldiers"; under Col. Jonathan Crawford from Fall of 1861 to 1865.
Johnson, Jacob-83/1925; Laborer on breastworks around Richmond for Confederate government under supervision of W.S. Cook; Master-Ket Valentine; served 1862 for three to four months when "work completed".
Mansfield, George-85/1924; Cook for Capt Cemcuis (? Illegible) from 1862 to EOW. Ended service "at surrender".
Michens, Roderick-86/1925; Teamster (wagoner) from 1861 to "surrender"; Master-Garland Waddy.
Mosby, Wash-80/1921; Ambulance driver and cook under Capt Clayton Cokemer; Master-Jonathan Hancock; from 1862 to EOW; "left when Army surrendered"; also worked with Captains Dick (Buckner) Trice and Capt Robert M. Trice; [May be Louisa (Va) Blues, Co. D, 13th Va Infantry.]
Thompson, Jerry-90/1928; Servant and waiter for Dr. William Pendleton (master) from 1862 to close of war in Isle County, NC.
Thornton, Joe May-illegible

Lunenburg County
Cheatham, Albert-82/1924; Laborer on breastworks; from 1862 near Richmond to EOW; Master-Tom Cheatham.
Hawthorne, Rufus-81/1925; Laborer on breastworks and cook; began service May 1864 on Appomattox River and ended service "on

Virginia's Black Confederates

April 9, 1865 at surrender".
Master/Supervisor-H.C. Hawthorne.
Ingram, Anderson-80/1925; Servant and cook from 1861 to EOW; 3rd Va Cavalry; Master-Dr. Tom Ingram.
Overby, Ned-86/1924; Laborer on breastworks; Master-H.G. Bagley.

Lynchburg
Coleman, James-87/1926; Laborer on breastworks under Master, Capt. Lindsy Coleman; began service near New London in 1862 serving to April 1865 "when Lee surrendered".
Green, Silas-85/1929; Capt Avlikes' Company under master, Mark ____; began service in Franklin County in 1861 to EOW; "at the end at Roanoke, Va".
Hunter, Phillip-85/1924; Laborer on breastworks from March 1862 for 19 months; served first at Manassas Gap then transferred to Chickahominy Swamp; Master-Mrs. Eliza Evans.
Preston, Isaac Lewis-85/1927; Servant to Master, Thomas Preston; served in field hospital sunder Dr. Jones; began service in May 1862 in Lynchburg and served to EOW; "at the end 1865, left from Malvern Hill."
Scott, Wise-81/1930; Private, Infantry; from 1863 to march 1865; Master-Isaac Stansfield.
Turpin, Henry-80/1925; Laborer on breastworks around Richmond and Petersburg; served from 1863 to EOW; ended service "1865 at Appomattox, Va"; worked under Mr. Wilson; Master-Roland Turpin of Bedford County.

Madison County
Arrington, Angus-81/1924; Free Born; Infantry; "Body servant for General James L. Kemper"; served at the "request of Gen. Kemper"; began service in April/May 1861 until EOW; left service "after General Lee's surrender".
Jackson, Minor-81/1924; Blacksmith and Teamster; Quartermaster Department from 1863 to EOW leaving "upon the surrender of Lee"; Drive team from Gettysburg to EOW' Master-George N. Thrift.
Mallory, Littleton-79.1924; Teamster; Engineers on breastworks; in 1861 beginning service at Manassas until ordered home; Master-B.F.T. Conway.
Porter, Albert-76/1925; Cook and Hostler for Capt William Parras, Co. F, 13th Va Infantry; Master-Charles Graves; served from December 1861 to 1864; at Manassas; service terminated when Captain killed in action and he brought horse back for widow. Born at Somerset, Orange County.
Price, James-78/1924; Teamster; Quartermaster Department; 7th Va Inf, under Lt George N. Thrift, [Co. A] from 1863 in Hanover Junction and left service "upon the surrender of General Lee."
Roe, Montello-80/1926; Blacksmith; "shoeing horses for the Confederacy"; began service January 1, 1863 in Richmond serving until April 5, 1865 when discharged; Master-I.S. Ferguson.
Roe, Ben-79/1926; Blacksmith; "shoeing horses for the Confederacy"; began service January 1, 1863 in Richmond serving until April 5, 1865 when discharged; Master-Col James W. Ferguson. (Note: Appears to be brother of Montello).
Rowe, Daniel-79/1924; Teamster; QM Department "by request of Gen. Kemper".; Began service in June 1861 at Manassas and left in 1863 "on account of sickness".; Master Hiram Rogers.
Weaver, Frank-80/1924; Laborer on breastworks around Richmond; from January 1863 until ordered home; Master-Peter Close.

Mecklenburg County
Alexander, Allen-92/1924; Laborer on breastworks from 1861 near Richmond to 1865, EOW; Master-Mark Alexander.
Baskerville, Reuben-103/1928; Teamster; drove ammunition wagon from 1864 to 1865; "left at surrender"; in Mahone's Brigade; Master-B.K. Baskerville; witness James Valentine, recipient of servant's pension.
Boyd, William-81/1924; "Cook for Capt. W.G. Boyd and his messmates"; Cavalry; began service near Williamsburg in May 1862 and left service "when Lee surrendered".; Master-Alfred Boyd. [Capt was likely William T. Boyd, Co. A, Boydton Cavalry, aka Mecklenburg Dragoons, 3rd Va]
Boyd, Jim-80/1924; Laborer on artillery breastworks from summer 1864 to early fall of 1864; at Drewry's Bluff; Master-Boyd.
Broock, H.L.-75/1924; Cook for Capt Johnny Oliver (master), Infantry; began near New Market in 1862 and left "on account of my master being killed." [Capt John Oliver, Co. C, Oliver Greys, 21st Va Inf]
Brown, John-83/1924; Cook and servant to Capt Jonathan Farrar from 1861 to EOW; left

service "at the surrender"; Infantry.[Capt John P. Farrar, Co. F, 14th Va Inf, Chambliss Grays].
Farrar, Plummer-81/1924; Laborer on infantry breastworks from 14 November 1864 to Spring (March) of 1865; at Chaffin's Farm; "was sent home"; Master-Samuel Farrar.
Harris, William-85/1924; Free man; Teamster; drove wagons from 1862 to 1865.
Hutcheson, Henry-79/1924; Cook and laborer on breastworks; Infantry; cooked for Sgt. Peter Gayle and his messmates from 14 November 1864 to March 1865 when he was "ordered home". Master-Joseph C. Hutcheson.
Jones, Wiley-79/1924; Teamster; Commissary Dept/Drove wagons; began service in Clarksville January 1, 1864 and left "after surrender of Gen. Lee"; Boss-J. Snead; Master-William Jones.
Jones, Sam A.-79/1924; Laborer on infantry breastworks; from October 1, 1863 to 1864; around Richmond; Boss-J. Hardy; Master-Mrs. Mary Jones.
Moseley, Ben-81/1924; Laborer on breastworks near Richmond for 60 days then go sick and sent home; Master-A.G. Jeffreys; born in Charlotte County.
Taylor, Washington-98/1928; Laborer on breastworks and helped by moving the dead; began service in 1861 and continued for four years until EOW (1865); Master-Dr. C.D. Whittle; born in Lunenburg.
Taylor, Willie-88/1928; Teamster and Servant; from 1861 to 1863; Master-Capt John Taylor; served for him for 18 months until he was killed in action.
Taylor, Richard-81/1924; Laborer on breastworks and fortifications under master, Jonathan Taylor; began winter of 1863 at Drewry's Bluff and Clifton Farm when service terminated in 1863 "by order of Jno Taylor".
Valentine, Jim-80/1924; Free man; Servant and Cook to Capt Haskins, Infantry; from 1863 to EOW; service terminated "at surrender".
Watkins, Frank-84/1930; Body servant to James Terrell; "Waited on the Confederate soldiers in Company of Capt Ballard Bruce and Capt C. Overby"; Served from 1861 until "I came home with the body of my young master who was killed at Fredericksburg"; Master-John Terrell.

Montgomery County
Deaton, Caleb-87/1924; Teamster; "pressed into service by government"; began service in January 1864 near Christiansburg and continued until EOW; Master-Billy Davis.

Duncan, W.R.-65/1906; began service 01 May 1861 until discharged in April 1865; Under Capt J.J. Wade, Co. E, 54th Va Infantry, Trigg's Regt, J.E. Johnston.; served four years; with Johnston and Hood, discharged April 1865 in North Carolina.
Eggleston, John-83/1934; Teamster "hauling ammunition"; served from Summer in 1862 in Suffolk to 13 April 1865; left at "close of war"; Master-James Eggleston; born in Appomattox County.
Hambrick, J.C.-78/1931; Hostler/Teamster; under Capt Creed Taylor from 1861 to EOW; "worked as armorer assistant as soon as war started"; repaired swords.
Kyle, Calvin-86/1925; Laborer on breastworks; "Sapper and Miner"; "helped build breastworks in Richmond; worked for White Mine, in charge of men from Montgomery County"; began service in January 1862 to March 1862; Master-Dr. J.H. Otey, Walnut Springs, Montgomery County; born in Wythe County.
Rutherford, Neal-78/1924; "Teamster for General Lee's Army" from 1862 to EOW; under Capt Coker.
Tinsley, Clem-80/1925; Laborer on fortifications; 1864 at Drewry's Bluff.
Tucker, William-82/1925; Servant; Cook and Wash for Co. I, 3rd Va Cavalry; served from 1862 to 1865; "War over"; Master-Col Hart Tucker. Born in Brunswick.
Williams, Rowland-83/1924; Servant; from 1861 to 63/65?; Master-William Graham. Born in Campbell County.
Williams, Charles-80/1924; Laborer on breastworks; building fortifications and improving with piles; served two months to clear and deepen James River; served two months on breastworks around Richmond; from 1864 to EOW; Under Capt James Ryan.
Zink, W.H.-81/1929; Teamster; QM and Commissary Dept under Capt Hancock; "using father's team to haul forage" and hauling supplies to hospital in Bedford; age 16 at the time; served from September 1864 to EOW.

Nansemond County
Boone, Anthony-84/1924; Free Born; Laborer on breastworks under Captains Jones and Callahan then working in woods making railroad ties; Started service in 1862 in Gordonsville and continued to 1865.
Boone, Jason-91/1924; Free Born; Laborer/Infantry; ditching, grading and

constructing breastworks; under Mr. Robert Jones from 1862 to 1865.
Haley, Tom-83/__; Laborer on infantry fortifications in 1863 at Weldon, NC; "throwing up breastworks and mess tents"; Master-Holladay Haley.
Newby, John-82/1929; Teamster/Cook under Capt Connolly; Co. G, from Spring 1862 until regiment was mustered out.

Nelson County
Mitchell, W.J.-82/1926; Laborer on breastworks and in Hospital Division; Made coffins; served from 1863 until "after the surrender".
Taylor, Davy-81/1926; Laborer on breastworks around Richmond; under Capt Mason at Drewry's Bluff in 1864; served with 124 others pressed into service.
Wells, James-80/1925; Laborer on breastworks at Drewry's Bluff under Maj. Smith Stark; served from 1864 to 1865: Left service "at Gen. Lee's surrender"; Master-W.W. Harris
Carter, Lewis-77/1925; Water carrier and laborer from 1862 to 1864 when "Gen. Morgan let me come home"; Master-Nat Jones.

New Kent County
Davis, Reuben-80/1924; Cook for master, William Crump, Pamunky Artillery; served from 1862 along James River and at Camp Lee; Served to EOW.

Norfolk
Lee, William Mack (Rev)-86/1925; Cook; Co. G, 29th Va Infantry; Served under "Col Robert E. Lee" from January 12, 1861; "stayed through entire war".

Northumberland County
Cain, Charles-78/1924; Cook; from 1861 to 1865; at Appomattox;
Douglas, Randall-72/1902; Co. C, 40th Va Infantry under Capt. Edwin Batts.

Nottoway County
Epes, David-80/1926; Blackstone; Hostler and Body Servant to Dr. D.H. Hardaway; began service in 1862 at age 16; left service "at the close of the War Between the States"; Co E, 3rd Va Cavalry.
Ford, Fred-83/1927; Burkeville; Teamster beginning service near Richmond in 1863; Left service in 1865 "at the surrender at Appomattox C.H."; Master-Charles Oliver.

Lewis, Stephen-81/1925; Blackstone; Laborer on breastworks; Began service near Richmond in September 1863 and left three months later when term expired; drafted from Brunswick County; Master-W.H. Barrow.
Miller, Carter C.-76/1928; Burkeville; Body servant to Robert Dickenson, assistant to Burkeville Depot Quartermaster J.J. Waggoner; Entered service in October 1863 and left EOW. Master-Judge Asa Dickenson.

Orange County
Clay, Henry-78/1924; Servant to master George Pannill, Sr.; Later as nurse in hospital; served from July 1862 to EOW.
Comfort, Wilson-80/1924; Free Born; Cook; 13th Va Infantry from 1862 to April 1865.
Henderson, Ceasar-86/1924; Hostler; "looked after horses" of Master Perrin Graves, Conscript Officer, from 1862 to 1864.
Henderson, Jesse-78/1925; Laborer and Cook; Engineering Department; "building bridges and cooking"; "enlisted" in 1861 and served until Appomattox, 1865.; served under Lt. Herbert Harris; Master-Henry Harris.
Robinson, Solon-83/1925; Servant and Cook; Master-F.B. Davis; from 1863-1865.

Page County
Comer, James J,-82/1929; Armorer; "made grapeshot, cannon balls and bar iron for CS Army"; Worked in No. 2 furnace in Shenandoah under Henry Farrer, head of shops and forge. Under supervision of Major Wheat's Battalion and Capt Joseph Monger, from 1862-1865; Master-Farrer.
Dovel, Peter S.-85/1936; Blacksmith helper making harness irons; from 1864 to when job completed; Master-George Short, Jr., Shop Foreman at Stony Furnace.
Short, Isaac N.-83/1935; Confederate Servant; blacksmith helper making bridle bits, harnesses, etc. at Columbia Mills in Page County. From 1864-1865, EOW.
Short, John-80/1927; Blacksmith; making bridle bits, etc. for artillery; served from Spring 1863 to 1865; Master-M.A. McAlister.

Petersburg
Goodwyn, Thomas-95 to 100/1928; Servant and Hostler to Capt McGoodwyn; served from 1861 to EOW; "at Lee's surrender, Appomattox".
Sprigg, Lewis-86/1927; Servant from 1861-1865; Left service at "the surrender".

Pittsylvania County

Bolanz, G.M.-80/1932; Helper Mechanic from May 1864 to 1865; worked in father's blacksmith shop used by the Confederacy.

Connally, Green-101/1926; Laborer on infantry breastworks; started at Manassas Junction; served from 1864-65; Master-Franklin Connally.

Dickerson, Giles-86/1932; Teamster; Commissary Dept; hauled for saltpeter works under supervision of David Graves; served from 1864-65, EOW; Master-Crispin Dickerson.

Estes, Callie Hill-82/1925; Servant and Cook for Capt Benjamin Estes (master); 38th Va Infantry, Armistead's Bde; from 1861-65; service ended at "surrender at Appomattox CH."[Likely Capt Joseph H. Estes, Col K, Cascade Rifles]

Callie Hill Estes (Photo from the Museum of the Confederacy, Richmond, Va)

Finney, William-82/1933; Servant for Jackson Finney; aided in making salt petre; served in 1865.

Gilbert, Jackson-82/1924; Hostler for D. Freeman; July 1864 to EOW; Master-George Gilbert.

Hodnett, Dave-87/1932; Teamster; drove wagon to Lynchburg and Chatham and other places through war from government stables at Col. Joab Watson's Plantation. Master-Asa Hodnett.

Hubbard, Robert-98/1933; Teamster and laborer on breastworks from 1862 to EOW; Master-Allen Hubbard.

Ivy, Lewis Henry-85/1930-Laborer on breastworks from January 1864 until discharge at EOW; Master-Judge George Gilmer.

Lovelace, Sam-86/1933; Teamster; wagoner, Commissary Dept in Pittsylvania Co.; Master-Miss Polly Wooding; from 1864 to EOW; collected provisions for the army; service rendered at stable/horse bar at Chalk Level, Va.

Miller, Alex-83/1926; Hostler feeding and caring for cavalry horses; from 1864 to EOW; service ended "at surrender of General Lee". Supervisor-Capt Clay Harvey; Master-George Miles; born in Halifax.

Miller, Sam-77/1935; Hostler under Capt Clay Harvey and Lt. Davis; caring for horses used by Cavalry and artillery; from 1864 to EOW; rendered at Chalk Level, Va; Master-George Miller. [Possibly 19th Va Cavalry, Capt Lewis C. Harvey, Asst Surgeon and 1st Lt Punnels Davis, Co B]

Ramsey, Nat-82/1926; Laborer on breastworks; March to June 1864.

Saunders, James (Rev)-No further information.

Stone, Sam-84/1931; Hostler, drover and railroad laborer; drove cattle and collected supplies for Army Commissary Department; from 1864 to EOW at Danville under supervision of Mr. Jim Lovelace; Master-Miss Lizzie Stone.

Tarpley, Stephen-102/1933; Blacksmith at Swansonville; made instruments used in war; worked in same place all during the war from 1861 to 1865; Supervisor John and Jackson Hall; Master-Robert Tarpley.

Thompson, Charles-85/1935; Servant and Cook for Capt. Samuel Thompson; also helped with horses and "helped round up deserters with home guard".; from 1863 to EOW; "I stayed with him until surrender". (Note: may have been attached to Battery B, 10th Bn Va Arty].

Waller, Lewis Henry-79/1930; Water boy and drum carrier; about 12 or 13 years old at time of service; served six months then sent home; "My master was in [cavalry]"; Master-Willie Harnsberger; born in Prince William County.
Waller, Ferdnand-82/1924; Laborer on breastworks; Master-Hampton Waller; served two tours in Richmond and one in Danville from 1862.
Watson, John-87/1931; Teamster from 1861 to surrender (EOW); hauled weapons to Danville and Lynchburg. Master-Jacob Watson.
Wilson, William Anthony-85 to 90/1925; Laborer on breastworks, forts and stables at Greenfield; from 1863 to EOW; Master-Dr. John Wilson.

Powhatan County
Braxton, Henry-80/1924; Laborer on breastworks; two tours in 1862 and 1864 at Drewry's Bluff; "discharged at end of war"; Master-Capt. J. Dobson.
Brown, William-77/1924; Cook and Laborer building breastworks for artillery; Commander was Major Danse; served from March 1, 1864 to February 1865; Master-Judy Flournoy.
Drew, Tyler-85/1925; Body servant and laborer on breastworks under Phillip St. George Cocke (master); Remained until surrender; Affidavit by Giles B. Cooke, a member of St. George Cocke's Staff.
Fleming, George (Sr.)-94/1924; Free Man; Laborer on breastworks in Richmond from Spring 1861 to EOW; Under Capt. John Hay (Lay).
Jordan, Richard-86/1931; Laborer on breastworks near Petersburg; from 1863 to 1864 for one year under Lt. Bolling; Master-William J. Powers; born in Cumberland.
Pleasants, Ross-82/1926; Servant and Nurse; under Dr. Thomas McKenzie at Hugenot Springs Hospital; Master-Richard McKenzie. Served from 1864-65.
Trent, Carter-76/??; Servant; Master-Phillip St. George Cocke; "at Mt. Pleasants"; from 1862 to EOW.

Prince Edward County
Bell, William-88/1925; Laborer on breastworks under Capt. Carter; from 1864-EOW; Master-Tom Treadway.
Branch, Willis-79/1925; Hostler under A.T. Price; Master-A.B. West; served from 1863-1864.
Brightwell, Frank P.—78 to 80/1930; Conscripted by R.V. Davis to collect rations for the soldiers and deliver them to the government warehouse at Prospect; Issued rations every Friday to the soldier's families. Served from 1864 to 1865 under Major George Booker, QM Dept, CSA. Born about 1851.
Burke, Henry-89/1924; Laborer on breastworks in Prince George from May 1863 to EOW; Master Albert Borum. Born in Nottoway County.
Cheeley, Lewis-80/1924; Teamster and laborer on breastworks; served from 1863 to EOW; Master-Asa Dickinson. Born in Nottoway County.
Coles, Peyton-90/1934; Servant; "carried my master's baggage"; Master-Samuel L. Crute, CS soldier; served at High Bridge; served from January 1864 to "until Lee surrendered at Appomattox."
Dean, Ben-86/1931; Hostler and carried Confederate mail; served from 1861 to 1865; "When Col. Harrison was killed in battle (illegible) Turner and I were the ones who helped in carrying his body from the field."; Master-illegible.
Giles, Greeman-77/1925; Laborer on breastworks under Michael Carter; Master-Kit Crute; began service in Manchester in January 1864 and served to EOW.
Knight, James Reuben-89/1932; "errand boy at camp"; "General duties around camp"; reported for duty "when callup was made at Seafield's near Green Bay at camp"; Master-Dr. Reuben DeJarnette of Green Bay.
Lyle, Sam-80+/1925; Laborer on breastworks; sent home in regular course; served in 1864 at Richmond; Master-Jesse Michaux.
Martin, Thomas S.-85/1931; Servant to Captain Robert Martin (master); engaged in securing and transporting supplies and carried rations for the Confederate Army; served as teamster and provided rations to needy families of Confederate Army; (Note: Private, Co. D, 18th Va Inf, 17 Aug 63 to 24 Aug 64, disability)
Redd, Silas-80/1925; Laborer on breastworks and rifle pits; worked under Col. Carter in 1865 around Richmond; "surrendered and mustered out"; Master-Charley Redd.
Scott, Robert-87/1925; Laborer on breastworks near Richmond under Col. Carter; served in 1864 to 65; left service at "surrender of Gen. Lee"; Master-Tom Treadway.
Scott, James-76/1925; Teamster and Hostler "attending horses and cattle for army" under

Virginia's Black Confederates

A.F. Price; from 1862 to EOW; Master-Robert West.

Topp, Jack-80/1924; Laborer on breastworks around Richmond under Jim Michael Carter; Master-Branch Worsham.

Turner, Phil-84/1930; blacksmith and railroad track worker for two years; began service in 1861 at New River Bridge and ended service in 1865 "at Appomattox"; Master Archer Gills; Supervisor Buck Gills.

Prince George County

Berry, James-80/1929; Body servant to master, Henry Harrison, Prince George Cavalry [Co F, 5th Va Cav]; made POW at Fredericksburg and sent to Ft. Monroe and released.

Bowman, Henderson-79/1924; Servant; cavalry; from 1861 at Prince George CH to EOW; Master-Henry Teller Cocks.

Jones, Emmanual-Body servant to Willie Wilcox; no pension, mentioned in James Berry application; Prince George Cavalry.

"Moses"—Body Servant to Bob Bland; no pension, mentioned in James Berry application; Prince George Cavalry.

Stith, Cupid-87/1930; Teamster for the Confederate Army; from 1861 to EOW; Master-John T. Jamerson.

Prince William County

Lansdown, Charles-80/1924; Servant, Hostler and Teamster; Infantry; 1862 to EOW; at Appomattox after the surrender; Master-Cassius Foley.

Murray, Dallas-77/1924; Blacksmith; 4th Va Cavalry; 1862-1865; "I shod horses until the surrender"; Master-F. Holmes.

Pulaski County

Bell, Benjamin-85/1924; Laborer on breastworks and teamster; served from 1863-65; "I left after the surrender at Appomattox."; served under Major Fields; Master-William Cowherd; born in Albermarle County.

Holmes, Lewis W.-75/1924; Teamster and millworker for CSA Tanning Yard and Mill from 1863 to 1865; Master. C.A. Chrisaman.

Miller, James-78/1927; Laborer on breastworks; from 1864 in Richmond to EOW; served under Captain Davis and Capt Cole; Master-Henry D. Sayers.

Williams, Flemming-73/1924; Cook for cavalry; served from January 1, 1863 to Appomattox under Capt Henry Williams; Master-Nathaniel Williams.

Radford

Hundley, William Robert-82/1933; Factory worker at CSA armory; worked from 1863 to plant closure; helped in sword factory at Snowville, Va.

Richmond

Allen, James-81/1925; laborer on breastworks on Drewry's Bluff; from 1862 until term of enlistment expired; Master-Miss Mary Perkinson; born in Alabama but in Virginia since five years old.

Brown, Douglas-73/1924; Servant; 3rd Va Cavalry; 1861 to April 1865; servant to Dr. James Roane. [Likely Co D, Charles City Light Dragoons, Junious Roane, Assistant Surgeon]

Carrington, Linous-85/1925; Cook; First Va Corps Artillery until Brandy Station; served from 1861 to EOW; first master-Cushing Irwin, KIA at Brandy Station; 2nd master-William Quirk, Louisiana Tigers; surrendered at Greensboro, NC.

Coleman, John-72/1924; Servant to Capt. R.W. Talley, Commissary, 1st Va Infantry; served from summer 1864 to 10 April 1865; "Gen. Lee surrendered"; also served at Staunton River Bridge; Master-Capt. Talley.

Dabney, William-91/1930; Servant to Capt. Haynes; started at Yorktown in 1861 and continued to EOW in 1865; also at Manassas; born in King William County; Master-Dr. Elliott Hawes [Haynes?]

Fields, James Emmett-90/1935; Navy; Laborer at Navy Yard and Hospital at Petersburg; from 1864 to EOW "after the surrender"; Master-John Dodson.

Fund, Doctor-80/1925; Cook; 1861-1865; Artillery cook and orderly; under Lt. Jno M. Cunningham, late Captain of the Powhatan Artillery; Capt David ??; under Col. Hardaway; Master-Buck Meadow.

Gates, Thomas-76/1926; Stableman under Sgt. Bruce; served from 1861-1865; started service in Dinwiddie and was in Lynchburg at EOW; Master-Thomas Threat.

Graham, Richard R.-83/1924; Laborer on Army breastworks; 1862-1865 EOW; breastworks at Fulton near Richmond and Camp Winder; under Spencer Hancock; Master-Frenhorn (?); born in Winchester.

Henson, James-88/1934; Teamster in commissary department in North Carolina; Drove wagons between Rutherfordton, NC & Spartansburg, SC under Capt Tom Patton;

Virginia's Black Confederates

WIA in right arm, waist and thigh; Served to 1865; Master-Phillip Henson, Sr.
Jones, William-81/1930; Messenger for Gen. Robert E. Lee; 1862; ended service at "surrender at Appomattox, Va"; Master-Dr. Willis Robertson of Cumberland; Born in Cumberland.
Jones, Ben-83/1925; Teamster; Field's Division, QM Corps, Ordnance and handling ammunition wagon train under Capt Norton; Master-Dr. Isaac Rich, Charlotte CH, Va; served from October 1864 to April 12, 1865; "honorably discharged by QM"; born in Charlotte County.
Mayo, Edward-76/1924; Free; Cook for Capt. W.R. Weiseger and his officers; Manchester Artillery; from Jan. 1, 1862 at Sewall's Point to May 1, 1862.
Page, Jacob-83/1924; Teamster; Ambulance Team; "hauling wounded from Seven Pines to Richmond"; "Did not leave until war ended."; Master-Alexander Dudley, President of York River Railroad; born in King and Queen County.
Peters, Samuel-87/1924; Free Born; Hostler; Artillery from 1862 to EOW; Capt Dane from Lexington, Va; born in Henrico.
Scott, Zebedee-111/1933; Teamster; under Cap. W.B. Simes; ambulance driver; "picked up wounded soldiers and brought them to the hospital"; joined in 1861 in Clover, Va and left service "when Gen. Robert E. Lee surrendered."; served at Dutch Gap, Petersburg, Drewry's Bluff and Chaffin's Bluff.
Smith, Harrison-94/1925; also known as Harrison Chaffin; Laborer on breastworks in Richmond for six to eight months; served with master from from 1862 to EOW; with master through war and at surrender at Farmville; Master-William Chaffin of Charlotte County, Va; born in Charlotte County.
Wyatt, Johnson-77/1925; Servant, Co. B, 13th Va Cavalry; from 1861 to "when Genl Lee surrendered"; later transferred to ordnance; under Lt. John Kerr; Master-Dr. Robert Walker, half-brother of Kerr; born in Greensville County.
Mabrey, Frank-83/1934; Servant; from 1860 to EOW; Master-Embrey Gutredge; born in Greensville County.

Roanoke
Martin, Joe-85/1924; Laborer on breastworks in 1864 near Richmond; Master-B.T.Tinsley.
Preston, Alexander-89/1927; Servant and Laborer on breastworks at Petersburg; Master-Stephen Preston of Glade Hill, Franklin County.
Saunders, Radford-81/1925; Servant to Hibry Hatcher of Bedford County; slave of Rev. Hatcher; Infantry; from Spring 1863 to surrender in 1865.
Taylor, Samuel-82/1931; Teamster; from 1862 and "remained up to surrender"; hauling provisions; born in Franklin County.
Waller, Richard-76/1930; Hostler and servant; cavalry from 1861 to "surrender Appomattox, April 9, 1865"; Master-William Hanaberger; born in Prince William County.

Roanoke County
Arnold, Henry-96/1924; Laborer on breastworks in August and September when "sent home[2]; started at Chickahominy Swamp; Master-Wyatt Arnold; born in Campbell County.
Bolden, Clem Read-70/1925; Teamster in Col Poage's Battalion; drove a mule team; worked three months at Dutch Gap; began in Fall of 1863; and ended service at Appomattox; Wagon Sergeant named Burnett or Barnett; Master-David Read of Monterrey in Roanoke County.
Borzotra (Borsotra) William-74/1925; QM Branch; "drove a provision wagon during the whole war."; began service "when war started" and ended service "when war closed."; Master-Col Charles Dunmore(?).
Branch, Jim-Laborer on breastworks; Master-William Watts; no pension, referenced in James Hurt pension.
Carey, Ephraim-77/1924; Laborer on Army breastworks; served near Richmond from January 1863 to May 1863; Supervisor-Capt. Crawford; Master-Samuel Burks of Rockbridge; his older brother Tom Carey went in the draft near the end of war.
Day, John-104/1924; Free Born; Teamster; "drove teams, cooked, looked after horses and waited on officers"; began service in 1861 at Salem and left service "after Lee surrendered".; served under Capt Hupp, 1st Regt Va Artillery, Capt Hupp's Artillery.
Early, Ferdinand-79/1924; Laborer on breastworks; under command of Booker Law; began service below Richmond in 1863; "never left---stayed till surrender"; Master-William Childress.; affidavit of P.B. Reynolds; Born in Franklin County.
Huff, William Henry-99/1925; Hostler and Cook for officers from 1863 to EOW under

Capt J.B. Headon in western Virginia near the saltworks; master-Bird Huff.

Hurt, James-87/1924; Laborer on breastworks at Drewry's Bluff; from December 1864 "until driven away by Yankees"; Later replaced by Jim Branch; Master-William Watts.

Jones, Watt-90/1924; Laborer on breastworks; under Ben Tinsley (master) at Petersburg, Richmond and Chaffin's Bluff; began service in 1862 and ended service "after Gen. R.E. Lee surrendered."; born in Buckingham County.

Smith, Matt-76/1924; QM Branch; Servant of Alex McD. Smith (master); served from "start of war" to "whenever war was over—surrendered".

Tinsley, Flem-92/1925; Teamster; transferred provisions; hauled to Lynchburg everyday; served from 1863 to 1864 under Samuel Fishburne; sent home by Fishburne; Master-Hillis Tinsley.

Wester, Robert-77/1925; Cook; Infantry; served from April 1861 to 1863; began service near Richmond under Capt. DeWitt Booth; Master-Anthony Simmons; born in Franklin County. [Co. D, 58th Va].

Williams, James-76/1924; Laborer on breastworks; began service in 1864 below Richmond and sent home in winter of 1864 after working six months; Supervisor-Capt Burks; Master-George P. Tayloe.

Rockbridge County

Blair, Davy-101/1924; Teamster; Infantry; served under Jimmy Davis, "master and CS officer", from 1861 to "three or four weeks" before the surrender; "was sent home with team"; started service near Buffalo, Va. Born in Amherst County.

Dickerson, George W.-79/1924; Laborer on breastworks; began service nine miles below Richmond under supervision of Confederate Government in 1864 and "served the time for which drafted."; Master-John D. Garrett.

McMannaway, John A.-75/1925; Free; Teamster hauling supplies for the army between Lexington and Staunton, Va; "at the direction of my father. I do not know [who] he was acting for."; Began service in Lexington in December 1864 and ended service in March 1865; also worked on breastworks.

Nicholas, Cass Lewis-82/1924; Teamster; Infantry; drove team and worked in Blacksmith Shop; served from 1860 to 1865; Master-William Redd.

Richeson, Joseph-87/1932; Nurse waiting on sick soldiers; under Ruben Rhodes; from April 1864 to December 1864 at Allwood, Va; "patients got well"; born in Amherst; Master-Joe Lane.

Shields, Wash-80/1924; Laborer on breastworks near Richmond; served from three months under King and Boulder, officers in CS Army; service conducted in 1864; Master was Mrs. Nancy Glasgow but "young master" was Capt. Robert McCulloch; Nelson Jackson, "colored", also worked on breastworks.

Winston, Daniel-82/1931; Servant for officers under Samuel Richardson; "attended my master and other officers, carried mail and help to barricade roads."; Richards was a Captain, CSA,; Winston served "all during the war" and left service "at the end of the war"; born in Amherst County.

Rockingham County

Blakey, Abe-83/1926; Laborer on breastworks under Mr. Smith; performed service at Richmond, Chickahominy Swamp and Petersburg; served from July 1864 until "honorably discharged and sent home"; Master-P. Elliott of Martinsville; born in Martinsville.

Tompson, Robert W.-76/1924; Laborer; "helped to build pontoon bridges, bateaus, foot bridges for the troops of the Confederacy on the James River"; served from Spring 1863 to Fall 1863 near Richmond; under Capt. Breneman; Master-Robert Burrus; born in Albemarle County.

York, Wesley-79/1924; Laborer on breastworks; served at Drewry's Bluff and for two years from 1863, leaving service "at the close of war"; Supervisor-Jim Flanagan; Master-Thomas Garland; born in Albemarle.

Scott County

Davidson, Nathan-86/1924; Free; Cook; Infantry; began service in 1861 near Yorktown and served till EOW; born in Cumberland County, Va.

Quillen, S.M.-82/1933-White Man; body servant to father; gathering dirt to help make salt petre; served from 1862 to 1865; served by direction of "my father Ira R. Quillien"; father was in C.S. Army, Private, Co. G, 64th Va Infantry, Pound Gap Battalion and was "detailed to do this work"; under Major Sylvester McConnell.

Southampton County

Cypress, James-86/1930; Body servant in Surrey Cavalry [Co E, 5th Va Cav, later Co. G,

13th Va] from 1864 to EOW; Master-Dr. Jesse Holloway.
Turner, Henry-88/1930-Servant of Theo. Little who belonged to Co. A, 13th Va Cavalry; "This servant was with Mr. Little until he was captured and sent to Pt. Lookout and Turner was sent home with the horses.".
Williams, Joe Thomas-79/1930: Ambulance Driver; "helped to haul wounded soldiers to be operated on and looked after Dr. Hemming Dodson (master)"; began service in 1861 at Benn's Church and served until 1864; Dr. Dodson "sent me home one year before the war was over."; born in Nansemond County.

Spotsylvania County
Gallahan, Joe M.-78/1930; Free Man; Cook; began service in Stafford in 1864 and served until EOW; Served under Capt Allen of Co. E, 30th Va Infantry; Gallahan states he had three uncles with Capt Allen; "They insisted on me to join with them so I did and served from 1864 til the war ended 1865."

Staunton
Barnhart, Richard-81/1924; Hostler and body guard; Infantry; under Col Kenton Housifer; began service in 1862 and ended service in 1865; "left service when Lee surrendered"; born in Augusta County.

Surry County
Hardy, William-90/1924; Teamster and laborer on breastworks; "mother sent me to serve"; began service at Jamestown in September 1863 for three months "then drove wagon for Army"; Master-John Weldon.
Hill, William-84/1925; "Was Free"; Teamster and Cook under John Clayton from 1862 to 1865 "when Genl Lee surrendered".
James, John-90/1931; Free; Cook; Co. G, 13th Va Cavalry; under Capt. B.C. Drew and later Capt Francis; served from 1862 to 1864; "granted leave of absence and could not get back on account of Yankees destroying bridges"; began service at Days Neck; grandmother freed by Micajah Ellis.
Nelson, John-81/1931; Cook's Assistant and Mess Boy for Hospital; under Capt. Tucker and Bill Fretfull; Master-William R. Wilson; began service in Danville in 1862 and ended service in 1865 "after Lee surrendered"; served in Hospital No. 6 in Danville; His sister Hattie Nelson was a cook at the wagon yards in Danville and Corneilia Drew saw service in Petersburg; Nelson was one of five children, aged 10 to 15, taken by Kendall and Hobbs to serve government.
Roberts, Cope-80/1924; Free; Co. G, 13th Va Cavalry; servant for Capt. Ben Drew; also worked on breastworks; began service at Days Neck, Isle of Wight County, Va; left service "near close of war when Capt Drew [re]assigned."

Sussex County
Booth, Robert-78/1931; servant for Lt. Hadrian Neaves (master); acted as nurse and servant when Neaves was wounded; 13th Va Cavalry. [Lt Hadrian A. Neaves was assigned to Co I, 3rd Va Cav. Pensioner may have been confused or recorder was in error.]
Spratley, Sandy-78/1924; Servant to Lewis Hargrove; Cook and cared for horse; 13th Va Cavalry; from April 1862 to May 1865; left service due to the "surrender". [Sgt J.L. Hargrove was in Co G, 13th Va Cav]

Tazewell County
Hairston, James-83/1931; Horse attendant; Cavalry; Master-Sam Hairston; began service in 1861 serving in Roanoke and Manassas; left service "at the end of the war in 1865"; "I distinctly recall being at Manassas Junction for seven days and also being in the battle of Seven Pines"; Mr. Hairston reportedly sent "several young Negro slaves to serve Confederate forces".; born in Franklin County near Martinsville.
Martin, John-82/1928; Teamster, body servant and cook; 9th Kentucky Cavalry; from 1863 to 1864; Master-Vince Browning; born in Russell County, Va.
Reed, Henry Clay-106/1924; Hostler; began service 14 January 1864 at Portsmouth, Va; Took care of horses in stable year before surrender; served under Capt. Wicker; born in New London (Bedford County).
Thompson, John R.-83/1931; Hostler, Cook and body servant; Co. H, 8th Va Cavalry; under Capt. Henry Bowen; began service in 1862 at Liberty Hill until Fall of 1864 after Capt Bowen was captured and taken to Ft. Delaware; Master-Gen. Rees T. Bowen.

Warren County
Beedon, John-80/1924; Teamster and worked in munitions factory under Capt. John Tanner; Master-John Stinson; began service in Fall of 1862 near Richmond; Hauled ammunition from Richmond to Chickahominy Swamp; worked at Rolling Mill in Richmond, the CS Mill where ammunition and other implements of

war were made for the Confederate government.
Robinson, George-90/1924; Laborer; Infantry; 1862-1865.

Washington, D.C.
Wright, Morris-84/1932; Body servant and laborer; initially under Adjutant William Mosby, 43rd Bn Va Cavalry; Master-Alfred D. Mosby; served from 1862 under EOW; left service "after the surrender [and] Col. Clarkston disbanded the men employed under him at Wytheville, Va and ordered them to their masters."; Col. Clarkston commanded CS forces at Salt works.

Washington, County
Moss, Tobe-90/1930; Free Man; QM Branch; Cook, Hostler, Teamster and Minor of salt petre; under Capt. Valentine Rush; served from 1861 to EOW; "The war closed [and] Capt Rush notified us that we were no longer needed."; "My former master was William Spuryer who set my mother and her children free when I was about ten years old."
Pool, Simeon-84/1927; Teamster; Medical Corps; under Gen. W.E. Jones at Abingdon; began in Fall 1861; along with others in same company was detailed to salt petre works (six to seven months under Capt Watkins) then transferred to hospital at Emory and Henry College doing work for Assistant QM for 27 months to EOW.

Westmorland County
Ashton, John-98/1923; Free Man; Cook; served from 1863 to 1865 under Capt. Lucien [Richardson?], [James City Artillery?].
Montague, Porter-80/1924; Waiter and Cook under M.M. Walker; from 1862 to "later part of war"; Master-M.M. Walker.
Willis, John-78/1924;

Winchester
Boxwell, Aaron H.-69/17 April 1909; Teamster in artillery company of Capt Bayou Lovett and Lt. Thomas Carter; served about two years at Gainsborough; 1861-1862 until after First Manassas; sent to Capt. Hamilton's Battery, Georgia Troops.
Boxwell, Susanna (widow)-73/1917; husband was Aaron M. Boxwell; was in state militia and made a teamster when mustered into regular Confederate service; member of 34th Va Militia, Co. F, in December 1861; was at First Manassas; served until 26 January 1865; died 26 December 1916; comrade-Samuel K. McDonald.
Cook, George Edmund-81/1930; Servant of Dr. William Henry; 24th Va Cavalry; began service in 1861 near Hanover and left service in 1865 at close of war; Master-Frank Taylor.

Wise County
Lamar, Floyd-91/1934; began service March 25, 1862; carried master home when he was wounded in action; "I was offered my freedom but would not leave"; Master was M.B. Lamar, 4th Corporal, 6th Alabama Infantry Home Guard; later under Capt. John. M. Franklin, Co. C, 5th Alabama and Co. C, 56th Alabama.

Wythe County
Howard, George-81/1925; Laborer on breastworks at Walker's Mountain; Master-Melvin Moore.
Howard, David-78/1925; Teamster from 1864 to EOW; Master-Col. A.C. Moore.

York County
Bartlett, John [James] Archer-86/1924; Teamster with the artillery; under Capt. Robert N. Garrett; "driving baggage wagon and also worked on tent"; Master-I/J. Bowden; served from 1861 to EOW;.
Coy, William-86/1924; Born Free; Cook; Infantry; served from Yorktown to EOW; born in Cumberland County.

Virginia's Black Confederates

Identified in Confederate States Records And Other Sources

This list compiled from Record Group 109 sources, specifically, *Selected Records of the War Department Relating to Confederate Prisoners of War, 1861-1865* (M598); *Confederate Citizens File; Confederate Papers Relating to Citizens or Business Firms, 1861-1865. Papers received by Confederate War and Treasury Departments*; NARA Publication M346; *Uniflied Papers and Slips Belonging in Confederate Compiled Service Records* (M347), Virginia Adjutant General, Department of Military Affairs, Confederate Military Records, Virginians listed in Tennessee Confederate Pension Applications and memoir sources. This list only includes those Black Confederates from Virginia or individuals identified as participating in events or incidents in or off the coast of Virginia. This list is not complete.

A

Adams, May – Laborer, Jan-March 1864, Engineer Bureau.[247]

Adkins, William – Laborer, Abington, Va, April 1864, 'FMC' for Free Man of Color.[248]

Adkins, William – Teamster, Dublin Depot, 1 July1864 to Feb 1865; Muster Roll of Free Negro at Dublin Depot.[249]

Alexander, Hugh – "Free Negro Conscript", clothing receipt, 29 December 1864.[250]

Alexander, Tarleton – "a colored Confederate who served from alpha to omega of the rebellion and surrendered at Appomattox, was on the streets in the morning wearing numerous badges and souvenirs presented by the veteran confederates as decorations of honor"; was at the unveiling of the Lee Monument in Richmond.[251]

Allen, George – "Free Negro conscript"; receipt roll; witness, Thomas Stephens; 1 Jan 1865.[252]

Allen, Joe – Nurse, Sept 1863, "Colored"; Ambulance Train[253]

Allen, Joe – "Nurse (colored)" in Richmond, October 1863; nurse, Ambulance Train, July 1863; Ambulance Train, September 1863[254]

Allen, Mike - Free Negro Conscript"; clothing receipt, 1 Jan 1865.[255]

Allen, Samuel – Free Negro, Laborer, Field Depot, February 1865.[256]

Allen, Simon - Free Negro, conscript, 1 Jan 1865.[257]

Allen, Tom – Laborer, Danville, Va; August 1862, "Colored".[258]

Allen, William – "Free Negro Conscript", clothing receipt, 1 Jan 1865.[259]

Allen, William – 'Private", Jackson Hospital, 7 August 1865; "Pvt. Colored Negro"; register of Jackson Hospital, Richmond, Va; admitted 7 August 1865; turned over to Provost Marshal 12 August 1865; "Returned to duty". Note: this record was contained in Confederate Archives, Chapter 6, File #183, p14. The information is obviously after the April surrender suggesting a data entry error regarding August in lieu of April or 1861-4 in lieu of 1865.[260]

Allison, Elbert – Laborer, September 1864; Detachment, 3rd Regiment Engineer Troops; "Free Colored"[261]

Allison, Isaac – Laborer, September 1864; Detachment, 3rd Regiment Engineer Troops; "Free Colored".[262]

Alvah, Vinton – Teamster, Army of Northern Va; 1 April to 31 May 1864; "Colored man hired from R. Fairfax"; pay of $40 per month; served two months; name on receipt roll for Supply Train, Pickett's Division, dated 28 July 1864.[263]

---

[247] *Unified Papers and Slips Belonging in Confederate Compiled Service Records*, Record Group 109, (M347) hereafter M347.
[248] M347
[249] M347
[250] M347
[251] *The [Washington] Evening Star*, 'Richmond Aftermath', 31 May 1890, p12,
[252] M347
[253] M347
[254] CSR (Confederate Records, Miscellaneous)

[255] M347
[256] M347
[257] M347
[258] M347
[259] M347
[260] M347
[261] M347
[262] M347
[263] M347

Ambler, S. – Laborer, Jackson Hospital, April 1865; Colored Engineering Corps; register at Jackson Hospital, Richmond, 11 April 1865 and turned over to Provost Marshal on 21 April 1865. [Note: His surrender to the Provost Marshal suggests he was a prisoner of war not yet paroled.].[264]

Anderson, Albert – "Negro Servant". Botetourt Artillery.[265]

Anderson, Edward – Blacksmith, C.S. Ambulance Shops, Richmond, Va; 20 June 1864; Quartermaster Dept; 37 y/o; Citizen of Chesterfield, Va; "free negro"; on a "list of men detailed, employed and hired at C.S. Ambulance Shops, Richmond, Va in charge of R.C. MacMurdo, Capt & AQM".[266]

Anderson, Garnett – Porter, Richmond, Va; January 1865; free negro; Manuscript 5820.[267]

Archer, Maria – Colored; May 1863; Nurse in General Hospital No. 11 in Richmond; seven days service; $5.09[268]

Arkins, Benjamin - blockade runner captured 1 October 1862 at the mouth of Quantico Creek; POW.[269]

Armstead, Addison – of Luray; employed on the breastworks around Richmond.[270]

Ashton, Samuel – Blockade Runner, Point Lookout Prison, 16 Sept-19 June 1864; "Colored Citizen"; on roll of POWs at Point Lookout, Md"; captured at Blackstone Island, Md. Released 19 June 1865[271]

Askins, William - Free Man of Color; Abington, Va; Quartermaster Department, April 1864.[272]

Atkins, Allen - Free Man of Color; Richmond; laborer, September 1863; $4.[273]

Atkins, J. – Patient, C.S. Hospital, Petersburg, Va, 15 Oct 1864; Free Negro; admitted 15 October 1864; [returned to] duty on 17 October 1864

Austin, Beverly - Free Man of Color; paid in June 1864 for labour, specifically helping unload cars of commissary and QM stores at the Richmond railroad depot; 20 1/3 days service for $102.50[274]

B

Bailey, James – Teamster, 1 April 1864; Free; receipt roll.[275]

Bailey, Jason – Laborer, Nitre Beds, Richmond, Va; March 1864; "free".[276]

Bailey, Robert – Name appears on a power of attorney; October 1861.[277]

Bailey, Thomas - Free Negro, was employed as cook at General Hosp Lynchburg, Va pay roll 191.[278]

Bainwright, Jesse - Free Negro; Oct 1862; for services as brakeman; $26.25; September 1862, $26.25; November 1862, $18.75.[279]

Bainwright, John - Free Negro, August 1862, $38.75; Sept 1862, for services as a fireman, 27 days, $35.25; December 1862 wages $38.75.[280]

Baker, Abraham – Teamster, Camp Curtis, Land's End; October 1861; "free".[281]

Baker, Albert - Colored; 3 Nov 1863; on receipt for wagons impressed to move wounded soldiers to Richmond and Manchester hospitals; $19.[282]

Baker, W.J. – Teamster; 6 Nov 1863; "Free Negro", clothing receipt.[283]

Barker, Jordan – (1841-?) body servant from Virginia, in many of the major battles, who settled in Hopkinsville, Ky after the war. He married a Sarah Davis and returned to her home in Danville, Virginia. While in Hopkinsville, he drove the city's first fire engine.[284]

---

[264] M347
[265] VDCMR is the Va Adjutant General, Department of Military Affairs, Confederate Military Records compiled after the war. Vol 18, p33, Reel 9.
[266] M347
[267] M347
[268] M346
[269] OR Navy, Series I, Vol. 5, p105
[270] *Richmond Dispatch*, 4 October 1902, p1. 'Turned Old Negro Down: Said He Rendered Service in Army Around Richmond'.
[271] *Selected Records of the War Department Relating to Confederate Prisoners of War, 1861-1865,* Record Group 109 (M598) hereafter cited as M598.; see also CSR (Confederate Records, Miscellaneous)
[272] M346
[273] M346
[274] M346
[275] M347
[276] M347
[277] M347
[278] *Confederate Citizens File; Confederate Papers Relating to Citizens or Business Firms, 1861-1865. Papers received by Confederate War and Treasury Departments*; NARA Publication M346, Record Group 109, hereafter cited as M346. These persons were primarily free who contracted their services to the Confederacy (not unlike modern Defense Contractors).
[279] M346
[280] M346
[281] M347
[282] M346
[283] M347
[284] *Hopkinsville Kentuckian*, 25 March 1911, no page number, 'Worthy Colored Man: After

Barns, War-blockade runner on the Potomac.[285]

Balfour, J. – Laborer; "negro laborer".[286]

Ball, Albert- blockade runner; POW; captured 26 January 1863 at Clement's Bay (Maryland) intending to run blockade to Virginia. All negro crew.[287]

Ball, George – Patient, C.S. Hospital, Petersburg, Va; February 1865; Admitted to hospital 10 Feb 1865. Died 16 Feb 1865; "Man of Color"[288]

Bandy, Eli – of Mattox, Va; blockade runner; POW; captured 10 Sept 1862.[289]

Banks, James (Jim) - Colored; Sept 1862; for services rendered as laborer for five days; $3.33; paid at Mount Jackson.[290]

Banks, Solomon – Free Negro; mulatto; worked on fortification near Pig Point; captured near Bethel.[291]

Bannister, Frank - Free Man of Color; Boatman; Narrows, New River & Central Depot; Receipt roll for clothing, Dec 31, 1864; reported in 4th Quarter 1863; reported at Giles Court House, Va, Quarter ending 31 March 1863; on rolls of QMD employees at New River, Jan 1865, age 29 years.[292]

Bannister, Frank – Boatman, at Narrows on the New River, Va and Dublin Depot; March 1863-January 1865; "FMC" for Free Man of Color; stationed at Narrows, New River and Central Depot; also at Giles CH (March 1863); see also "F. Bannister", on a List of Employees in the Quartermaster Department at Narrows of the New River and at Central Depot, Va in the employ of Capt. V.G. de l'Isle, Assistant Quartermaster, January 1865; Listed as 29 years old, Boatman, conscripted 22 Oct 1864; Muster Roll of Free Negro at Dublin Depot; transferred to Capt E.P. Williams, AQM, 1 Sept 1864.[293] [Same man found in two different record sections.]

Bannister, Frank – Laborer, September 1864; Detachment, 3rd Regt Engineer Troops: "Free Coloured".[294]

Bannister, Isaac – Laborer, Lexington, Va; Oct-Dec 1864; Quartermaster Dept; "Negro employee (free)"[295]

Bannister, J. William – Carpenter, Dublin Depot; 1 Dec 1863 to February 1865; also listed under J.W. Bannister; Free Negro; "appears on a muster all of employees (Free Negroes" in the Quartermaster Dept at Dublin, Va"[296]

Barber, Josiah – "Private", Spotsylvania C.H.; 12 May 1864; Co. B, 5th NC Infantry.[297]

Barksdale, Henderson-b. Va. 12th Tenn Infantry.[298]

Barrett, Tim – "Free Negro Conscript"; clothing receipt, 29 Dec 1864.[299]

Bartlett, Henry - Free Colored; Cook at hospital; one and one-third month at $15 a month for $20 total, July 18, 1862.[300]

Bartlett, Jennie - Colored; washer at hospital for two months at $10 a month, Dec 19, 1861 to Feb 19,1 1862; total of $20.[301]

Bartlett, Martha – Free Colored; washer at hospital for two months at $10 a month, Dec 19, 1861 to Feb 19,1 1862; total of $20.[302]

Battle, John - Colored; paid $114 for horseshoes and nails; December 15, 1862.[303]

Batts, Gloster – Steward, Norfolk, Va native; captured on the Potomac; probable blockade runner.[304]

Baley, Layton – Free Man of Color; Teamster; appears on a receipt roll dated 31 Dec 1863 for services provide from 1 October to 31 Dec in support of General Early's Division; rate of pay $20 per month.[305]

Lifetime Spen in Hopkinsville Moves'; see also 6 May 1915, p5; in Peter Morgan article.

[285] OR Navy, Series I, Vol. 5, p5
[286] M347
[287] OR Navy, Series I, Vol. 5, p225
[288] M347
[289] OR Navy, Series I, Vol. 5, p83
[290] M346
[291] **Official Records of the War of Rebellion** (hereafter OR), Series II, Vol. II. *Memoranda of Various Political Arrests-From Reports of Confederate Commissioners*, #1; 115-1428.
[292] M346
[293] M347
[294] M347
[295] M347
[296] M347
[297] M347
[298] **Tennessee Pension Applications: The information was compiled by John V. Brogden and Willie Robinson using the Index to Tennessee Confederate Pension Applications [Nashville, TN; Sistler & Associates, 1994] and Tennessee Confederate Pension Applications [SL&A, Microfilm Publication, 114 Reels] and posted on the internet.**
[299] M347
[300] M346
[301] M346
[302] M346
[303] M346
[304] M598
[305] **CSR (Confederate Records, Miscellaneous)**

Bean, William – Company Cook,, 7th Va Cavalry. (post war record; not in CSR; assessed as man of color).[306]

Beckley, Mortimer - Free colored; Wages for services rendered for Hospital Dept for two months; Danville, Va; March-May 1862; $30.[307]

Beckworth, Alfred – Farmer, Fairfax Co, Va; 27 Dec 1863.[308]

Bell, A. –"Col'd"; Private, Co. B, 13th Mississippi Infantry; Appears on a Register of Chimborazo Hospital No. 1, Richmond, Virginia; convalescent; admitted 24 April 1862; left without permission.[309]

Bell, B. – Private, Co. C, 15th Georgia Infantry; "Colored"; Appears on register at Chimborazo Hospital, Richmond, Va; convalescent; admitted 17 April 1862; discharged 23 April 1862.[310]

Berryman, William – Age 57, Blockade Runner, Westmorland County, Va.; POW on 8 April 1865; Released 2 May 1865; Point Lookout POW Roster.[311]

Beverly, Andrew- Free, September 30, 1863 "For my services as labourer on public defences at and near Richmond in July, August and September 1864. 2 months & 10 days at $11 per month. $25.66.[312]

Beverly, Edward - Engineers Camp near Manassas, Dec 6, 1861. I certify that the bearer Edward Beverly a free Negro was called out by order of Genl Johnston for work on Fortifications and has made 62 days of service. $31 wages. Thomas A. Williamson, Lt Col, Chief, Engineers, Potomac Dept.[313]

Beverley, Sylvester – "Free Colored"; Detachment of 3rd Regiment Engineer Troops; September 1864.[314]

Beverley, Sylv – Free Man of Color Boatman; on duty at Narrows, New River & Central Depot; on receipt roll for clothing December 31, 1864; also worked 4th quarter of 1863. [note: could be same as Sylvester Beverley, 3rd Regt, Engineers.][315]

Beverley, W.P. – Free Man of Color, Boatman in service at Narrows, New River & Central Depot, va; on receipt roll for clothing, December 31, 1864; on duty in fourth quarter of 1863 at Narrows;

Beverley, William- "Free Coloured"; Detachment, 3rd Regiment Engineer Troops in September 1864.[316]

Bias, Wyatt- "Free boy", November 1864, paid "for one month services as Teamster for the month of November 1864 Clothing and Rations furnished by Government'; paid $25 by Capt WM Jones, AQM, CS Army, 26 Nov 1864; receipt for August 1864, services for two months as laborer and forage, $50; bailing and securing forage, Lynchburg, Va., September 1864, $25.[317]

Bird, Albert – Farmer; Westmorland County, Va; 14 Nov 1863-Feb 1864; "smuggling goods".[318]

Bird, William – "free negro"; appears on register of Confederate States Hospital, Petersburg, Va; admitted 18 October 1864; Remarks, 2 Nov 64, Richmond, Va."[319]

Biscoe, Jacob-blockade runner on the Potomac; POW; captured 19 October 1862 in a canoe at Herring Creek en route Virginia..[320]

Blackburn, Robert - Free Colored; was employed as laborer at Richmond Arsenal, Va.[321]

Blackford, Charles - Slave, Tredegar Iron Works; slave of Mrs. F.G. Skinner of Culpeper County.[322]

Black Hark, John – Cook on staff of Colonel Turner Ashby's Headquarters Mess.[323]

Blanmire, George – "Colored"; Musician, Co. A, 3rd Va Infantry.[324]

Bowyer, Bean M. – "Free Negro"; at Dublin Depot from January to February 1865.; likely Quartermaster Department[325]

Bradmar, John-blockade runner on the Potomac.[326]

Bragg, Martha - Free Colored; June 1864; for services as laundress at General Hospital at Bristol, TN and Breckenridge Hospital at Marion, Va from March 1st to June 30th, 1864. Four months at $11 per month for total of $44.[327]

Bragg, Major – Richmond native; about 100 years old in 1905; claims to have been in Mexican War as an artilleryman and supporting Confederate artillery

---

[306] Ibid, McDonald, Laurel Brigade, p409
[307] M346
[308] M598
[309] CSR (Confederate Records, Miscellaneous)
[310] CSR (Confederate Records, Miscellaneous)
[311] Point Lookout POW Roster
[312] M346
[313] M346
[314] CSR (Confederate Records, Miscellaneous)
[315] CSR (Confederate Records, Miscellaneous)
[316] CSR (Confederate Records, Miscellaneous)
[317] M346
[318] M598
[319] CSR (Confederate Records, Miscellaneous)
[320] OR Navy, Series 1, Vol. 5, p131
[321] M346
[322] *Richmond Dispatch*, 24 July 1861, p7 as cited by mdgorman.com
[323] McDonald, William N. A History of the Laurel Brigade, originally The Asby Cavalry of the Army of Northern Virginia, (s.p. Mrs. Kate S. McDonald) 1907; p41.
[324] VDCMR, V 1, p113, Reel 1
[325] CSR (Confederate Records, Miscellaneous)
[326] OR Navy, Series I, Vol. 5, p5
[327] M346

in Civil War. Was at 2nd Battle of Winchester, also at Drewry's Bluff.[328]

Brannon, William – Teamster; Ordnance Reserve Department, Army of Northern Virginia; Period of service from April 1, 1863 to May 31, 1863 (two months); paid $20 a month, on June 19, 1863;

Brayboy, James – "Free Negro Conscript"; clothing receipt; 1 Jan 1865.[329]

Brazelton, Caroline – slave of W. Brazelton; "Negro employee at hospital"; appears on a receipt roll for clothing at Breckinridge Hospital, Marion Va; 12 Nov 1864.[330]

Brazelton, Jane – slave of W. Brazelton; "negro employee at hospital; appears on a receipt roll for clothing at Breckinridge Hospital, Marion Va; 12 Nov 1864.[331]

Brooks, Abram – Laborer; Captured at Charles City C.H., Va; 27 July 1863; Released August 1863; probable slave.[332]

Brooks, Beverly - Coloured; 15 Oct 1863; for materials furnished and repairs of fireplace at Engineer Pay Office in Oct 1863; Richmond, Va; paid $10.[333]

Botts, Willam- free negro, for services as brakeman from 1 to 28 August 1862 both inclusive (28 days) at $1.25 per day. $35; paid $38.75 on Oct 31, 1862 for services as fireman; paid $34.50 on 30 Nov 62 for services as a fireman.[334]

Bowser, Henry - Free; Nurse[335]

Broadway, William – Free Man of Color; Richmond, Va; paid as Laborer; $40, December 1863; $40, November 1863; paid laborer September 1863, $40.[336]

Brock, Alexander – Free Man of Color; Wytheville, working in Nitre business; September 1862; paid $5.57[337]

Brooks, Albert - On 3 May 1863 receipt in Richmond for delivery of two horses for artillery service.[338]

Brown, Andrew – "colored laborer in quartermaster department"; Admitted to "F.F.H. 10 A.C." [field hospital] on 29 August 1864 for rheumatism; [Confederate] Army of the James near Petersburg, Va; sent to general hospital on 30 August.[339]

Brown, George W. - Winchester, Va; three days service as carpenter repairing warehouses and locks for government stores; later of West Va (Colored).[340]

Brown, Jane – "Colored Girl"; Cook; on hospital muster roll for hospital at Jordan's Spring, Va from 18 June to 23 July 1863; "has not been paid".[341]

Brown, James – "Nurse (colored)"; Richmond, Va; October 1863.[342]

Brown, Jesse - Free Colored; May 1863; two months service as a teamster at Petersburg, in Ordnance Department; $40 payment. Record shows he was issued a pair of pants, one jacket, one shirt and three pair of socks for a total of $28,25 earning a net of $11.75.[343]

Brown, Jesse - Free Man of Color; Teamster from December 1862 to January 1863; $23.83; Petersburg; laborer in Richmond in October 1863, $40.[344]

Brown, John – "Colored Servant" of Capt. Barnes; on register of Prisoners of War at Old Capitol Prison; captured 16 April 1865 at Fairfax, CH; committed 19 July 1865.

Brown, Mark – Farm Hand; Fauquier County; 11 Nov 1863-1865.[345]

Brown, Sam – Free colored; wages for services as a Nurse, $35; Dec 1861-February 1862.[346]

Brown, William - Free Colored; for services rendered in taking ambulances to Manassas, 19-24 October, 1861; $6.[347]

Bruce, William - Free Colored; services rendered at Petersburg;$30 for month of September 1863.[348]

Bryant, Loftin – "Colored Free", Co. I, 5th Regiment North Carolina; appears on a register of Chimborazo Hospital No. 2, Richmond, Va; Typhoid pneumonia; admitted 18 Oct 1861 and "returned to duty" 5 January 1862.[349]

Bundy, Eli – Westmorland County, Va; 14 Nov 1863; "Smuggling goods" with Albert Bird.[350]

Burnett, Bolen (Bolin) – "free negro"; blacksmith; June, 1863; serving in Danville.

---

[328] The [*Washington DC*] *Sunday Star*, p8, 'When Evening Shadows Fall'
[329] M347
[330] CSR (Confederate Records, Miscellaneous)
[331] CSR (Confederate Records, Miscellaneous)
[332] M598
[333] M346
[334] M346
[335] M346
[336] M346
[337] M346
[338] M346
[339] CSR (Confederate Records, Miscellaneous)
[340] M346
[341] CSR, (Confederate Records, Miscellaneous)
[342] CSR (Confederate Records, Miscellaneous)
[343] M346
[344] M346; the two Jesse Brown receipts may be for the same man.
[345] M598
[346] M346
[347] M346
[348] M346
[349] CSR (Confederate Records, Miscellaneous)
[350] M598

Burton, Aaron –Servant to Col. John S. Mosby during duration of the war.[351]

Burton, Carbury - Free Man of Color; Richmond; Nov 1862; $75 for furniture repairs.[352]

Butcher, Frank – "Free Negro"; name appears on a register of Confederate States Hospital in Petersburg, Va; date of admission was 26 October 1864; Remarks: Nov. 9, [18]64 Richmond, Va"[353]

Butler, Joseph-free man of color; Virginia citizen; blockade runner on the Potomac; POW; captured 1 Oct 1862 on the sloop *Ann Squires* at the head of Wicomico Bay with contraband goods intended for Richmond.[354]

Butler, William-steward and crew of Stern wheel steamer *Three Brothers*; POW; captured 21 October 1863 on Rappahannock River[355]

Burke, John – Teamster, Richmond, June 1864; Slave of Thomas J. Bagby.[356]

Burns, James – "Negro"; appears on a list of employees on duty in Emory Hospital, Emory, Va; not dated.[357]

Burwell, Carter – Cook, 2nd Co. H, 32nd Va Infantry. Enlisted 1 April 1864 at Chaffin's Farm. "Chief Cook for company with Regt [Regimental] wagons." Present through 31 Dec 1864[358]

Butler, John – Miller, Centreville, Va; 25 Sep 1864; [prisoner?] of Washington, DC; age 44.[359]

Butler, William – Seaman, Stonington, PA; 20 Oct 1863; Captured on the Rappahannock River; released 1 Nov 1863.[360]

Byers, Essex - Free negro; July 1862; For services as labourer in handling grain; $20 per month; $20.[361]

C

Carrell, Oscar – Chief Cook, 2nd Co. K, 32nd Va Infantry; Enlisted 15 March 1864 in Henrico. Present through 31 Dec 1864.[362]

Carter, Bob-b. Prince Edward County, Va; service in breastworks.[363]

Carter, Burwell – "Colored Cook", 2nd Co. H, 32nd Va Infantry.[364]

Carter, William – Free man, Colored Cook, Company and Headquarters Cook; enlisted 1 January 1863; last muster roll 28 Feb 1865; Co. C, 25th Battalion Va Infantry (Richmond City Battalion).[365]

Chavers, John – "Free Negro Conscript", receipt roll, 1 Jan 1865.[366]

Chavers, William – Free man of color, Teamster, Wagoner, originally from Greensboro, NC. Enlisted December 1863 and served in Quartermaster Department, Pickett's Division.[367]

Chavers, William – Laborer, Petersburg, Va; Jan-March 1864; "Name appears on a roll of non-commissioned officers and privates employed for extra duty at Petersburg, Va"[368]

Chavis, Thomas – Camp Holmes, 24 June 1864; Quartermaster and Commissary Dept; Conscript, "free negro"; on receipt roll.[369]

Chappell, Henry – Colored Cook and Servant. Co C, 3rd Va Cavalry.[370]

Cherry, Ralph – "Colored"; Musician, Co. A, 3rd Va Infantry.[371]

Chevus, Ervin – Private, 23 June 1864; Private, free, negro conscript; appears on a receipt roll for clothing; detailed.[372]

Chiles, Edward – Post-war Fairfax County resident; listed in obituary.[373]

Chisman, Oliver – Cook, 2nd Co. I, 32nd Va Inf; Enlisted 13 April 1864; "On duty at cook wagon. Slave owned by Lt. [William H.] Patrick. Payded from enlistment."[374]

Christian, William – "Negro Cook", Co. F, 25th Va (Richmond City) Battalion, Infantry; enlisted 1 Jan 1863; last muster roll February 1864.[375]

---

[351] **Mosby's Memoirs**
[352] **M346**
[353] **CSR (Confederate Records, Miscellaneous)**
[354] **OR Navy, Series I, Vol. 5, p113**
[355] **OR Navy, Vol. 5, p368**
[356] **M347**
[357] **CSR (Confederate Records, Miscellaneous)**
[358] **CSR, 32nd Va**
[359] **M598**
[360] **M598**
[361] **M346**
[362] **CSR 32nd Va**
[363] **Tennessee Pension Applications**
[364] **CSR**
[365] **CSR**
[366] **M347**
[367] **Confederate Compiled Service Records (CSR)**
[368] **M347**
[369] **M347**
[370] **VDCMR, V8, p247, Reel 4.**
[371] **VDCMR, Vol 1, p113, Reel 1.**
[372] **M347**
[373] **Manassas based author Jack Maples is the source of this information. He has a black Confederate section on his website www.calebstriump.com which has several good articles including one on George Lamb. He quotes Lamb's obituary as listing five other black Confederate veterans in Fairfax County. Chiles may be Edward Chives who received a pension.**
[374] **CSR 32nd Va**
[375] **CSR**

Chrisman, Oliver – Cook, 2nd Co. I, 32nd Va Infantry; slave.[376]

Cleapor, Charles -- "Col'd"; Naval Brigade.[377]

Cole, William--of Richmond, Free man; blacksmith; 3rd Va Cavalry.[378]

Cole, Elijah – Post-war Fairfax County resident.[379]

Cole, George Washington[380] – of King George, "a Confederate veteran, who served and fought the entire four years"; attended Confederate reunion in Fredericksburg; born about 1830; saw service in Virginia, Alabama and Arkansas;

Cook, Richard – of Ware District, Gloucestor, Va; regularly enlisted in the Confederate Navy. 6' 2" tall; When Captain Peter Smith "was ordered to another ship, he got Dick enlisted, in order to keep him as his servant. Dick says he was with Captain Smith when he blew up the gunboat on the James river. He also claims that he was on the steamer that took Vice-President A.H. Stephens and others down Hampton Roads, to meet President Lincoln. Dick also claims that on the trip Major Allen wore his (Dick's) shoes, as the Major's feet were so swollen with gout that he could not wear his own shoes…He surrendered at Appomattox."[381]

Cornish, Isaac-crew of Schooner *Vista;* POW; 28 Feb 1863[382]

Corum, John – Fauquier Co, Va; Nov 1863; Captured 6 Nov 1863 and held until 1865.[383]

Cousins, Henry-served under General William Mahone.[384]

Cousins, Jordan- Free Negro, Nottoway County; 11 July 1864; paid $52.50; "For my services as labourer on public defences at Richmond in February 1862 8 1/2 days at 50 cents per day -- $4.25; For my services as Carpenter on public defences at Fort Boykin in March '62. 25 3/4 days at $1 per day $25.75; for my services as above [carpenter] in April '62, 22 1/2 days at $1 per day $22.50; paid 11 July 1864 by J.B. Stanard, Captain, Engineers, PACS [Provisional Army of the Confederate States].[385]

Craig, Jasper – 29 Dec 1864; "Free Negro conscript"; receipt roll.[386]

D

Davis, James – "Colored", Cook, Co. C, 38th Va Infantry.[387]

Davis, John – Hospital Steward; surrendered at Appomattox; in service to Dr. John H. Claiborne, Surgeon.[388]

Davis, Lewis-blockade runner; member of crew; POW; captured 30 October 1862 "off Mathias Point, crossing the Potomac River clandestinely and violating the blockade."[389]

Davis, Samuel – status unknown, served in Confederate Navy. He indicated in October 1902 that he was "the only colored Confederate soldier or seaman admitted to registration in the district of Norfolk, Virginia"[390]

---

[376] CSR

[377] VDCMRV19, p253, Reel 9; see also p264-265, <u>Camp Fires of the Confederacy: A Volume of Humorous Anecdotes, Reminiscence</u>. Edited by Ben LaBree (Louisville, KY: Courier-Journal Job Printing) 1898. Captain John M Jolly says, "There were three negroes on the [CSS] Chicora, regularly enlisted. These Negroes were free before the war. One of these Negroes, whose name was Charley Cleapor, was the servant of Captain Hunter, our commander."

[378] *Carter Diary*. Diary of William R. Carter, Lt. Col. CSA, <u>Sabres, Saddles and Spurs</u>, edited by Walbrook D. Swank, Colonel, USAF, (Ret). Lt. Col. Carter's memoirs.. 3rd Va Cavalry.. Diary Entry for April 16, 1864 reads as follows: "Got Chas [Charles] Smith & Wm [William] Cole, free negroes conscribed in Richmond, assigned to the Regiment as blacksmiths, by order of Secretary of War."

[379] George Lamb obituary as quoted by Maples.

[380] *The Times Dispatch*, November 20, 1910, p2(?), 'A Colored Confederate Veteran'

[381] *Richmond Dispatch*, 4 October 1902; 'That Confederate Negro: Name is Richard Cook; Sailor Under Captain Peter Smith'.

[382] OR Navy, p239

[383] M598

[384] Congressional Serial Set (USG: GPO) 62nd Congress, 3rd Session, *House Documents*, Vol 122, 1914, p93. Mentioned in an article concerning burial of Congressman Charles Gordon of Tennessee.

[385] M346

[386] M347

[387] VDCMR, V4, p255, Reel 2.

[388] SHSP, Vol 28, p21.

[389] OR Navy, Series I, Vol. 5, p144

[390] *Richmond Dispatch*, 3 October 1902, page9, as cited by Terry Foenander, <u>U.S. Civil War Navies: A Collection of Articles, Muster Rolls and Images of the Union and Confederate Naval Services</u>, (http://www.tfoenander.com). This is an excellent site with a great amount of transcribed primary source information to include ship rosters. Foenander lists many black Confederates in the C.S. Navy including Ship's Pilot Billy Bugg, whose

Virginia's Black Confederates

Dickenson, Willis – Status unknown; employee at Tredegar Iron Works.[391]
Dims, William-slave of T.W. Gough; engaged in blockade running on the Potomac;[392]
Dix, Austin--Field and Staff (June 30, 1861); 18th Va Infantry; freed black; drummer; discharged from service August 31, 1863.[393]
Douglass, John-blockade runner on the Potomac; POW; captured at mouth of Quantico Creek.[394]
Downs, Ned-blockade runner on the Potomac.[395]

E
Elbert, Allison – 3rd Regt, Engineer Corps; "free colored"; Sept 1864.[396]
Epps, Daniel – Colored Cook and Servant; Co. C, 3rd Va Cavalry.[397]
Evans, Frank – deck hand on blockade runner on Schooner *Hampton;* POW; captured 12 January 1863 at Dividing Creek running the blockade with a general cargo from Baltimore.[398]
Evans, William – servant to Chaplain and Lt. Richard McIlwaine, 44th Va Infantry.[399]
Evans, William T. – (1816-1905) Body Servant and Guard for General Robert E. Lee. Was at Appomattox at time of surrender. Born a slave; freed at two years of age; free man during the war.[400]
Ezekiel – Cook and Teamster; Enlisted Co I and F, 32nd Va Infantry, June 4, 1864 and present through Nov/Dec 1864; "Free Negro with wagon".[401]

LEE'S BODY SERVANT DIES IN NORTHLAND

Was at Appomattox With the General and Drifted North When Latter Died.

(Special to The Times-Dispatch.)
ASBURY PARK, N. J., November 4.— William T. Evans, former body-servant and guard for Confederate General Robert E. Lee, lies dead in West Asbury Park. Evans's age is believed to have been about eighty-one. He was a slave. Evans was at Appomattox when Lee met Grant at the surrender. Evans witnessed also the hanging of John Brown. Evans's freedom was purchased when he was two years old.
After General Lee's death Evans drifted North, and he refused to mingle with the Northern "colored trash," as he called them. For a time he was a waiter, but didn't like the business. He did odd jobs for little pay and with the memory of his Southern luxury and distinction to cheer his old age.

F
Fentress, George – Private, Colored Cook, Co. C, 15th Va Cavalry.[402]
Freeman, John – Co. E, 25th Battalion (Richmond or City Battalion); "Free Colored Cook"; enlisted January 1, 1864; present through 29 September 1864 when listed as "deserted".[403]
Ford, Lindsay - Post-war Fairfax County resident.[404]
Ford, Tom - Free Negro of Powhatan County; one of sixteen signatures on a Letter of Appointment (1862) for an attorney to ensure pay for services rendered the Confederacy.[405]

---

status was akin a modern Warrant Officer, and Moses Dallas, killed in action on 3 June 1864 in Ossabaw Sound, Georgia, possibly the only Black Confederate Navy Pilot *"to give his life in service of the Confederacy."* He was killed during the capture of the *USS Water Witch*; see also *Richmond Dispatch,* 3 October 1902, 'A Colored Confederate?'. Davis used his military service to justify his registration following voter registration changes that came with the 1902 Virginia Constitution which required a literacy test except for Civil War veterans and their sons..

[391] *Richmond Dispatch*, 13 May 1862, as cited by mdgorman.com.
[392] OR Navy, Series I, Vol. 5, p5, Enclosure
[393] Compiled Service Records (CSR) as recorded by Dr. James I. (Bud) Robertson in Regimental History, <u>18th Va Infantry</u>. (Lynchburg: H.E. Howard, Inc., 1984).
[394] OR Navy, Series I, Vol. 5, p105
[395] OR Navy, Series I, Vol. 5, p5
[396] CSR
[397] VDCMR, V8, p247, Reel 4.
[398] OR Navy, Series I, Vol. 5, p210
[399] McIlwaine, Richard. <u>Memories of Three Score Years and Ten</u> (Washington, DC: The Neale Publishing Company) 1908; p193

[400] *The Times Dispatch*, 5 November 1905, p1, 'Lee's Body Servant Dies in Northland'
[401] M346 and CSR
[402] VDCMR, V10, p447, Reel 5.(two entries for this man.)
[403] CSR
[404] George Lamb obituary as quoted by Maples.
[405] M346

Foster, Jack – Servant to officers, 36th Va Inf, stationed at Princeton, Mercer County (now WV).[406]

Freeman, Augustus – deserter; unit not identified.[407]

G

Gaines, Lucian – "Colored soldier", Wagon Driver, Co. A, 7th Va Cavalry.[408]

Giles, Daniel - Free Negro of Powhatan County; one of sixteen signatures on a Letter of Appointment (1862) for an attorney to ensure pay for services rendered the Confederacy.[409]

Gilliam, Robert: b. Va. 1843/44[410]

Goffney, Robert M. - Post-war Fairfax County resident.[411]

Gordon, John-free man of color engaged in blockade running on the Potomac.[412]

Green, Ann –"Colored (free)"; Laundress at General Hospital at Mount Jackson, Va; 1 March to 26 March 1862.[413]

Green, Larkin – Farmer, Fauquier Co, Va; 14 Nov 1863; POW Roster; listed as contraband.[414]

H

Hairston, John-b. Va. organization unknown; application rejected.[415]

Hall, William - Free Negro of Powhatan County; one of sixteen signatures on a Letter of Appointment (1862) for an attorney to ensure pay for services rendered the Confederacy.[416]

Hall, Moses – blockade runner; crew; POW; captured 3 Sept 1864 in Potomac.[417]

Harden, Silas – Laborer, City Point, Va; 18 Oct 1864; 17 years old.

Hardman, William – Farmer, Westmorland Co, Va; 25 July 1863-September 1863; POW Roster; listed as contraband.

Harris, John G. - Passenger on Sloop James Landry; POW; captured 28 October 1864 off Alexandria, Va "for having cargo on board not mentioned on his manifest, also six passengers without passes and not mentioned on his manifest.[418]

Harris, John J. – Laborer, Washington, DC; 27 Oct 1864; 19 years old.[419]

Harris, Phillips - Free Negro of Powhatan County; one of sixteen signatures on a Letter of Appointment (1862) for an attorney to ensure pay for services rendered the Confederacy.[420]

Harris, Thomas – "Blockader"[421]

Harris, Tom – blockade runner; POW; captured in James River on sloop *J.C. McCabe* on 18 January 1863.[422]

Harris, William – 44th Battalion of Virginia Infantry; "colored ambulance driver"; appears on a receipt roll for clothing, dated December 1864.[423]

Harrison, P. – Blockade Runner; POW Roster; "Taken by a vessel of the Potomac Flotilla…violating blockade"; Released July 13, 1863; A side note appears to say 'mulatto' but is difficult to read.[424]

Hassell, Joe – 29 Dec 1864; "Free Negro Conscript"; clothing receipt.[425]

Heck, J. – "Col'd"; Naval Brigade.[426]

Henly, John - Free Negro of Powhatan County; one of sixteen signatures on a Letter of Appointment (1862) for an attorney to ensure pay for services rendered the Confederacy.[427]

Henry, Henry – Blockade Runner; POW Roster.[428]

Hineman, Spencer – Co. H, 25th Battalion Virginia Infantry (also known as Richmond City or City Battalion); Chief Cook; Enlisted 1 September 1864; present Nov/Dec 1864 roll and Jan/Feb 1865 rolls.[429]

Holland, Henry – Free Negro, died and was buried in 2nd Quarter of 1862. Buried with over 100 Confederate soldiers in Richmond by Binford and Porter, contracted by the Confederate government to bury deceased military personnel.[430]

Howell, David - Free Negro of Powhatan County; one of sixteen signatures on a Letter of Appointment (1862) for an attorney to ensure pay for services rendered the Confederacy.[431]

---

[406] Virginia Historical Society (VHS), *Tompkins Family Papers, 1800-1871*, Mss1T5996d, Sec. 11.
[407] OR Navy, Series I, Vol. 10, p111
[408] VDCMR, Vo9, p129, Reel 5. (There are two entries for this man.)
[409] M346
[410] Tennessee Pension Applications
[411] George Lamb obituary as quoted by Maples.
[412] OR Navy, Series I, Vol. 5, p5
[413] CSR (Confederate Records, Miscellaneous)
[414] M598
[415] Tennessee Pension Applications
[416] M346
[417] OR Navy, Vol. 5, p479
[418] OR Navy, Series I, Vol. 5, p491
[419] M347
[420] M346
[421] M598
[422] OR Navy, Series I, Vol. 5, p449
[423] CSR
[424] M598
[425] M347
[426] VDCMR, V19, p255, Reel 9
[427] M346
[428] M598
[429] CSR
[430] M346
[431] M346

Hughes, Henry - Free Negro of Powhatan County; one of sixteen signatures on a Letter of Appointment (1862) for an attorney to ensure pay for services rendered the Confederacy.[432]

Humbles, James – Bugler, Co C, 1st Va Cavalry, enlisted 18 April 1862 in Lexington, Va; present July/August 1861.[433]

Hurdman, William – blockade runner; POW; captured 30 Nov 1863.[434]

J

James, Cornelius - Free Negro of Powhatan County; one of sixteen signatures on a Letter of Appointment (1862) for an attorney to ensure pay for services rendered the Confederacy.[435]

James, Henry - Free Negro of Powhatan County; one of sixteen signatures on a Letter of Appointment (1862) for an attorney to ensure pay for services rendered the Confederacy.[436]

Jackson, Eli – b. 1835; slave of Capt. Forbes of Longstreet's staff; served as a courier during the war.[437]

Johnson, Frank – 31 Dec 1864; Engineer Dept; free negro; clothing receipt roll.[438]

Jones, James A. – "Col'd"; Co. K, 46th Va Infantry.[439]

Jones, William – Cook, 2nd Co. H, 32nd Va Infantry; slave; enlisted 10 April 1864 at Chaffin's Farm; paid through 30 June 1864; Present through 31 Dec 1864; "Present with Regt wagons.[440]

Johnson, Charles – of Hague, Va; blockade runner; POW; captured 10 September 1862.[441]

Johnson, George Floyd-b. Pulaski Co., Va, 1843; service in Wilcox Bde.[442]

Johnson, Joseph ---"Col'd";.Naval Brigade.[443]

Johnson, Richard-b. Va. 14th Mississippi Infantry.[444]

Jones, Jacob – (1st) Co. A (Salem Flying Artillery), 9th Virginia Infantry; Musician (Drummer); enlisted 14 May 1861 at Camp Hupp for 12 months; present July/Aug 1861, Sept/Oct, Nov/Dec 1861 rolls; "discharged by order of Col. Smith 18 December 1861".[445]

Jordan, Stephen - Passenger on Sloop James Landry; POW; captured 28 October 1864 off Alexandria, Va "for having cargo on board not mentioned on his manifest, also six passengers without passes and not mentioned on his manifest.[446]

K

Kean, Aleck – 2nd Co., Richmond Howitzers, at Sailor's Creek.[447]

Kelley, Thomas - FMC, Free Man of Color; paid February 1862 for two months service "cooking for Prisoners Yorktown"; $20[448]

Keys, Selden – blockade runner; POW; captured 30 November 1863.[449]

King, Lomax – Seaman; of DC, 2 June 1864; "Subject to Secretary of the Navy Order"; appears to be blockade runner; captured at Piney Point.[450]

Kune, Henry-crew of Schooner *Vista*; POW; captured 28 February 1863.[451]

L

Langford, Tom – Hostler; Co. B, 12th Va Cavalry, Baylor Light Horse.[452]

Lamb, George - Post-war Fairfax County resident.[453] Co. D, 17th Va Infantry. Born 1834, died 19 March 1926. He was buried at Jermantown Cemetery. He was a body servant to Capt. William H. Dulaney and after the war worked as a blacksmith in the Fairfax C.H. shop of Joseph Cooper. Obituary appeared in *Fairfax Herald* on March 26, 1934, page 3.

Laws, Edward – Farmer, Fauquier, Co, Va; 11 Nov 1863; POW Roster; listed as 'contraband'.[454]

Lee, William - Post-war Fairfax County resident.[455]

Lee, William – Passenger on Sloop James Landry; POW; captured 28 October 1864 off Alexandria, Va

---

[432] M346
[433] CSR, 1st Va Cavalry.
[434] OR Navy, Series I, Vol. 5, p376
[435] M346
[436] M346
[437] *The Evening Star*, Albuquerque, NM, 13 April 1918; p19
[438] M347
[439] VDCMR, V5, p188, Reel 3.
[440] CSR, 32nd Va
[441] OR Navy, Series I, Vol. 5, p83
[442] Tennessee Pension Applications
[443] VDCMR, V19, p255, Reel 9
[444] Tennessee Pension Applications
[445] CSR
[446] OR Navy, Series I, Vol. 5, p491
[447] Judge George L. Christian in *Confederate Veteran Magazine*, 20 [1912] cited by Barrow, p133.
[448] M346
[449] OR Navy, Series I, Vol. 5, p376
[450] M598
[451] OR Navy, p239
[452] SHSP, V31, p365
[453] George Lamb website (www.calebstriumph.com).
[454] M598
[455] George Lamb obituary as quoted by Maples.

"for having cargo on board not mentioned on his manifest, also six passengers without passes and not mentioned on his manifest"[456]

Lewis, Jim – Stonewall Jackson's body servant. Reportedly of Rockbridge County, Va. Died before 1875 and buried in an unmarked grave in Evergreen Cemetery, Lexington, Va.[457]

Lewis, John – Seaman; Alexandria, Va; 20 Oct 1863; POW Roster; Captured on Rappahannock River; probably blockade runner.[458]

Lewis, John – fireman and crew aboard Stern-wheel steamer Three Brothers; POW, captured 21 October 1863 on Rappahannock River. (May be same John Lewis above).[459]

Lewis, Preston - Free Negro of Powhatan County; one of sixteen signatures on a Letter of Appointment (1862) for an attorney to ensure pay for services rendered the Confederacy.[460]

Lightfoot, Jim – of Hanover County, Tredegar Iron Works.[461]

Lincoln, A. - blockade runner; POW; captured 26 January 1863 at Clement's Bay (Maryland) intending to run blockade to Virginia. All negro crew.[462]

Lucas, Phil-Blockade runner on the Potomac; POW; captured at Nanjemoy Creek running the blockade on 24 Oct 1862.[463]

Lucas, William- Blockade runner on the Potomac; POW; captured at Nanjemoy Creek running the blockade on 24 Oct 1862.[464]

Lynch, Robert - Free Negro of Powhatan County; one of sixteen signatures on a Letter of Appointment (1862) for an attorney to ensure pay for services rendered the Confederacy.[465]

M

Madison, Lewis – Teamster, Richmond, Va; June 1864; Slave of Thomas J. Bagby.[466]

Marshall, Addison-blockade runner, POW; captured 20 July 1863.[467]

Marshall, Thomas – "Colored" Cook, Co. H, 7th Va Cavalry, Laurel Brigade, ANV.[468]

Marshall, Thomas – "Colored", Private, Co. H, 12th Va Cavalry.[469]

Mayo, Henry – "Negro slave"; Private. Co. G, 56th Va Infantry.[470]

Mayo, Henry - Free Negro of Powhatan County; one of sixteen signatures on a Letter of Appointment (1862) for an attorney to ensure pay for services rendered the Confederacy.[471]

Mayo, Joe – or Richmond. "hostler, cook, washer and ironer, milkers and caterer" to Captain William W. Parker, Parker's Battery, Va Light Artillery. Later Sexton of Trinity Church in Richmond.[472]

Mayo, Robert – Colored Cook, Co. I, 16th Va Infantry.[473]

Mayo, Tom - Free Negro of Powhatan County; one of sixteen signatures on a Letter of Appointment (1862) for an attorney to ensure pay for services rendered the Confederacy.[474]

Mayo, William —"Negro Servant"; Botetourt Artillery.[475]

Milburn, Wesley – deck hand on blockade runner, Schooner *Hampton;* POW; captured running blockade with cargo from Baltimore on 13 January 1863.[476]

Miller, Levi[477] - Born in Rockbridge County and living in Winchester in 1912. His half-brother George lived in Lexington. Born 9 January 1836, was a slave of Robert McBride. According to a press report, "When the Civil War broke out Captain John McBride came from Texas and took Levi into the

---

[456] OR Navy, Series I, Vol. 5, p491
[457] See www.findagrave.com and search for 'Jim Lewis'. This man was referenced in Hunter McGuire's Address at the dedication of Jackson Memorial Hall at the Virginia Military Institute and repeated before the R.E. Lee Camp, No. 1, Confederate Veterans, Richmond, Va July 2, 1897. McGuire was Medical Director of Jackson's Corps. He presented a bound copy to the University Va Library. Other references to Jim have made their way into the many histories of Stonewall Jackson.
[458] M598
[459] OR Navy, Vol. 5, p.368
[460] M346
[461] *Richmond Dispatch*, 13 May 1862 as cited by mdgorman.com.
[462] OR Navy, Series I, Vol. 5, p225
[463] OR Navy, Series I, Vol. 5, p135
[464] OR Navy, Series I, Vol. 5, p135
[465] M346
[466] M347
[467] OR Navy, p308
[468] Ibid, McDonald, Laurel Brigade, p476
[469] VDCMR, V10, p185, Reel 5
[470] VDCMR, V6, p235, Reel 6
[471] M346
[472] Figg, Royall W. Where Men Only Dare Go! Or the Story of a Boy Company (Richmond, Va: Whttet & Shepperson) 1885;p248-255
[473] VDCMR, RG46. Note. No volume, page or reel number is provided for this entry.
[474] M346
[475] VDCMR, V18, p33, Reel 9
[476] OR Navy, Series I, Vol. 5, p210
[477] *The Lexington (Va) Gazette*, 6 March 1912, 'Colored Confederate Receives A Pension', p1.

army with him as his body servant. "Uncle Levi" has in his possession a letter written by Captain J. E. Anderson of Company C, 5th Texas Regiment, which gives his war record and of which he is very proud. The letter, in part, follows: 'In accordance with your request I have this day written Mr. B.C. Shull of Marlboro, Va., giving him a full account of your connection with our army. I told him of all the campaigns you were in, beginning with Yorktown, Fair Oaks and seven days in front of Richmond, Maryland, Fredericksburg, Suffolk, Pennsylvania, Chickamauga, East Tennessee, the Wilderness, and Spotsylvania Court House, where, in the morning of May 10, 1864, you ran across to us over an open field and the Yankee sharpshooters fired several shots at your before you could get into our trench. You brought me some rations and you had to stay all day before you could get out, and how on that day the Yankees made a rushing charge on us, and you stood by my side and fought as gallantly as any man in the company; an after we had driven the Yankees away, Jim Swindler made the motion that Levi Miller be enrolled a full member of Company C, Fifth Texas Regiment. I put the motion and it was carried by a unanimous vote. I immediately enrolled your name on the roll of the company, and I still have that same roll."[478]

Morgan, Peter [479] – Body servant to Captain A. F. Morgan of Belfonte. "Peter was with him at Manassas, Bull Run, Petersburg, and was in the advance to Frederick City, Md., within 13 miles of the Capital (sic). He was at Gettysburg and when Capt. Morgan, who took part in the magnificent charge of Picket's Division, was shot down, his faithful body servant sought him out and carried him off the battlefield in his arms. Capt. Morgan survived the war and lived to a good old age and died of apoplexy at his home at Belfonte, Va in 1908. Capt. Morgan was related to Gen. Robt. E. Lee and was attached to his personal staff a part of the time. Peter was the cook for a mess of four, Capt. Morgan and other officers, and was about the camp of Gen. Lee a great deal of the time. In 1867, armed with a personal letter of recommendation from Gen. Lee, Peter Morgan came to Kentucky...". He worked for 36 years at the Western Kentucky Lunatic Asylum in Hopkinsville, Ky. Later became sexton of "Cave Spring Colored Cemetery". In May 1915, he is said to be over 70 years of age and in good health, educated and respected. A member of the Methodist Church. "He has always been loyal to the Lost Cause and loves to attend the reunions of the old soldiers in gray."

Morris, Edward - Free Negro of Powhatan County; one of sixteen signatures on a Letter of Appointment (1862) for an attorney to ensure pay for services rendered the Confederacy.[480]

Morris, Paden-b. 1846; Va unit.[481]

Mosby, James – of Pulaski; "James Mosby, a colored Confederate veteran, who fought in the Southern army throughout the Civil War, died this week in Pulaski. The negro enlisted in the Confederate army in Lynchburg with a company in 1861, which was later attached to Floyd's Brigade. The negro was captured during the war, but later made his escape from a Northern prison and made his way back to the South, latter joining his command and served till the end of the struggle. Mosby was a free born negro and never saw slavery. At the time of his death he was seventy years old."

Moton, Booker – Body Servant to a Captain Womack of Cumberland. Booker Moton was the son of famed African-American educator Robert Russa Moton (1867-1940).[482]

Murray, Branch:-b. Petersburg; Co. K, 17th Texas Infantry.[483]

N

Nelson, W.B. – Cook, Co.C, 32nd Va Inf; enlisted 1 January 1864 at Chaffin; ppaid through 20 June 1864; slave of Capt Octavius. Coke.[484]

Nevitt, James - Passenger on Sloop James Landry; POW; captured 28 October 1864 off Alexandria, Va "for having cargo on board not mentioned on his manifest, also six passengers without passes and not mentioned on his manifest.[485]

Nevitt, Thomas - Passenger on Sloop James Landry; POW; captured 28 October 1864 off Alexandria, Va "for having cargo on board not mentioned on his manifest, also six passengers without passes and not mentioned on his manifest.[486]

---

[478] The [Richmond] *Times Dispatch*, 12 October 1912
[479] *Hopkinsville Kentuckian*, 6 May 1915, p5
[480] M346
[481] Tennessee Pension Applications
[482] Moton, Robert Russa. **Finding A Way Out: An Autobiography** (New York: Doubleday, Page & Co) 1921, p12-13.
[483] Tennessee Pension Applications
[484] CSR, 32nd Va Infantry
[485] OR Navy, Series I, Vol. t, p491
[486] OR Navy, Series I, Vol. 5, p491

O

Otey, Ephraiam-b. Va. Feb 1845; QM Department.[487]

Owens, Ned-blockade runner on the Potomac.[488]

P

Page, Charles – Colored Cook, Co E, 32nd Va Infantry. Enlisted 26 Sept 1864; on company muster roll through 31 Oct 1864.[489]

Paul, Armstead – Co. H, 22nd Virginia Infantry; Chief Cook; enlisted 8 May 1861 in Kanawha (Charleston), Va (now West Va); muster rolls show present through December 1863 when absent on furlough; returned to duty and on muster rolls through October 1864 roll (the last); on receipt roll for clothing, 4th quarter 1864; "appears on a Descriptive Roll of Confederate Prisoners fo War paroled by order of Col. John H. Oley, commanding 1st Separate Brigade, Dept. West Va, at Lewisburg, Va. Roll not dated. Paroled April 26, 1865. Occupation: Farmer, age 40 Eyes: Dark, Hair: Blk, Complexion: Blk; Height, 5'6". Name appears in column of signatures as 'A. Paul'". Name appears on two other lists of POWs with the rank of "Corporal" and "Private" respectively. Parole in file.[490];

Perry, Franklin – Captain of the Sloop James Landry; POW; captured 28 October 1864 off Alexandria, Va "for having cargo on board not mentioned on his manifest, also six passengers without passes and not mentioned on his manifest"[491]

Perry, Manson-Va Unit.[492]

Peters, Tom – Teamster, at Sailor's Creek.[493]

Peters, Samuel - Free Negro; request for pass for Mayo Bridge; employed on public defences.[494]

Poplar, Dick – POW[495]; Co. H, 13th Va Cavalry; captured on the retreat from Gettysburg and was POW for 20 months at Ft. Delaware (5 months) and remainder at Point Lookout; Returned to Petersburg home after release and worked as a cook at the Bollingsbrook Hotel. Maples quotes Petersburg Index-Appeal obituary states "he was buried with full Confederate honors as befitting a loyal Son of the South." His pallbearers were Confederate veterans to include Colonel Everard Mead Field, Commander, 12th Va Infantry; Capt Edward A. Goodwyn, Co E, 13th Va Cavalry; Capt John R. Patterson, Provost Guard, 12th Va Infantry; Captain Stith Bolling, Co G, 13th Va Cavalry; Private Jesse Miller Newcomb, Co. F, 13th Va Cavalry and Private Rufus M. Dobie, Co. H, 13th Va Cavalry.

Poole, William – mulatto, servant of Capt. William Chamberlayne, Artillery Staff, 2nd Corps, Army of Northern Virginia; present at Gettysburg; POW.[496]

Porter, William-blockade runner; POW; captured 3 Sept 1864 in Potomac.[497]

Q

Quall, Isaac- blockade runner; POW; captured at Plowdon's Wharf, 29 December 1863.[498]

R

Ransell, Jacob – of Vienna, Va; bodyguard to General JEB Stuart; born in slavery on a Fairfax County farm about 1827; "he was known on account of his faithful service to the famous Confederate leader throughout the war. 'Uncle Jake' never had ceased to mourn the tragic death of General 'Jeb' Stuart who died from a shot by a Federal trooper near the close of the conflict"; Wounded in action on two occasions, once in thigh and once in the ear; "He was with General Stuart during some of the fiercest battles of the war, including Gettysburg and Brandy's Station. It was the duty of 'Uncle Jake' to care for General Stuart's horse, tent, and to do personal services for him all the time." He did odd jobs after the war in Vienna and spent several months in the charity ward of Washington hospital before he died. He was "supported by his daughter, and by the charity of others include Mrs. Stuart Mosby Coleman, daughter of the Confederate chieftain [John S. Mosby]".; In an interview, he said, "I want to say General Stuart was the finest man that ever lived…I was his bodyguard and servant during all the war."[499]

---

[487] Tennessee Pension Applications
[488] OR Navy, Series I, Vol. 5, p5
[489] CSR, 32nd Va Infantry
[490] CSR
[491] OR Navy, Series I, Vol. 5, p491
[492] Tennessee Pension Applications
[493] Southern Historical Society Papers, Vol 38, p9.
[494] M346
[495] SHSHP, V.35, P1; see also Maples website (www.calebstriumph.com).
[496] Chamberlaine, William. **Memoirs of the Civil War Between the Northern andSouthern Sections of the United States of America 1861-1865** (Washington, DC: Press of Byron S. Adams) 1912; p52,73-74.
[497] OR Navy, Vol. 5, p479
[498] OR Navy, Vol. 5, p381
[499] The *Washington Times*, 29 February 1912, 'Old Uncle Jake Will Be Buried at Village of Vienna'; see also Ibid, 25 September 1911, p12., 'Stuart's Slave Is Dying In Tenement On Bed of Husks'; see also [Richmond] *Times Dispatch*, 13 October 1910, p5, 'Stuart's Old Body Servant' where *Times Dispatch* requested funds to help Ransell.

Reid, Alfred - colored, served as office's cook and steward aboard the *CSS SEA BIRD*; captured at Roanoke Island, NC in February 1862, paroled and sent to Norfolk, Va on 19 Feb 1862.[500]

Rice, Daniel – deckhand on blockade runner and Schooner *Hampton*; POW; captured running the blockade with a general cargo from Baltimore, at Dividing Creek, Va.[501]

Robinson, Carter – Mess Cook, Co. B, 12th Va Cavalry, Baylor Light Horse.[502]

Robinson, Edward-crew member on Schooner *Emily Murray*; POW; captured by U.S. Navy, 9 February 1863 for running blockade.[503]

Roe, Robert – Colored Cook and Servant., 3rd Va Cavalry.[504]

S

Saunders, William-blockade runner; POW; captured at mouth of Quantico Creek on 1 October 1862; POW.[505]

Schoolfield, Henry Mathis-b. Va 1842; Co. F, 24th Tennessee Cavalry[506]

Scott, Ben – Richmond; 15th Virginia Infantry; *"I vollentterley Firerd 3 Shots at the yankee at little Beathel [Bethel]"* the first battle of the war in Virginia; at First Manassas on the battlefield "all day"; born free and apprenticed as plasterer under Patrick Russell when war broke out; enlisted as a company cook when war started; stated in letter, *"I have often [wondered why] you Peppel (sic) for get the neggro he follerd you through the War as Cooks and Washers and Waters, and [stood by]you through the theckes of Battels have ben so far forgotten".*[507]

Scott, James-Laborer; slave of Benjamin Weaver of King George Court House; "employed helping to build batteries at Mathias Point".[508]

Scott, John – A member of Major Turner's Battalion of Confederate Colored Troops. Scott deserted taking several pairs of pants and jackets with him leading to a small article in the Richmond Sentinel. As no known roster of Turner's battalion exists, Scott may be the only member of Major Thomas P. Turner's battalion that has been identified.[509]

Servant, Frank – Laborer, Camp Lewis, Sept 1863; "Free Boy"; on the roll for 30 days service as laborer.[510]

Shelton, Humphrey – of Charlottesville. Servant to Major M. Green Peyton. Co. H, Albemarle Light Artillery, 1st Regiment of Virginia Artillery. "After the war, 'Uncle Humphrey' became a trusted servant to the University [of Virginia], where he served faithfully and efficiently for almost fifty years, and was pensioned by the Visitors during the last five years of his life."[511]

Shields, Jefferson- Of Lexington. In 1913 Shields identified himself as a cook for Stonewall Jackson and this was later documented as such in 1920 by Elihu S. Riley in his work Stonewall Jackson: A Thesaurus of Anecdotes of and Incidents in the Life of Lieutenant General Thomas Jonathan Jackson, C.S.A. Ann Dewitt reports new research by Richard Williams indicating Shields was the body servant of Col James Kerr Edmondson of Lexington, 27th Va Infantry and that Shields cooked for members of the Stonewall Brigade.[512]

Sinclair, Archie – Colored; Cook; Co. C, 49th Va Infantry, the Fauquier Guards under Capt Edward Murray. Fauquier County. Notation in register states, "Archie Sinclair, colored, Capt. B.M. Randolph's cook, as such he served throughout the war, was captured in 1864 near Fisher's Hill, Va by the enemy, made his escape and returned to the Regt." [513]

Slate, Dick--Field and Staff (June 30, 1861); Colored; served as drummer in 18th Va Infantry through April 1862.[514]

Slave, J. – 2 Nov 1862; 50th Georgia Infantry.[515]

Slave, J.J. – Seamstress, Sept 1863; QM Dept.

Smith – Servant to General Henry A. Wise.[516]

---

[500] *Daily Dispatch* (Richmond, Va), 19 February 1862, as cited by Foenander, U.S. Civil War Navies..
[501] OR Navy, Series I, Vol. 5, p210
[502] SHSP, V31, p365
[503] OR Navy, p229
[504] VDCMR, V8, p247, Reel 4.
[505] OR Navy, Series I, Vol. 5, p105
[506] Tennessee Pension Applications
[507] *Richmond Dispatch*, June 21, 1896.. p2, 'An Old Army Cook'.
[508] OR Navy, Series I, Vol. 4, p645, Report of Commander Craven, etc.
[509] *Richmond Sentinel*, 30 March 1862, page 2, Col. 7, as cited by mdgorman.com.
[510] M347
[511] Memorial History of the John Bowie Strange Camp, United Confederate Veterans (Charlottesville, Va: The Michie Company) 1920; p50-51. By F.P. Dunnington.
[512] See http://kevinmweeks.com/wordpress/?p=1627 is the source of this information.
[513] VDCMR, V5, p339, Reel 3.
[514] CSR, 18th Va Infantry.
[515] M347
[516] Henry Wise, Southern Historical Society Papers, Vol. 25, p. 16-18, *'The Career of Wise's Brigade'*; see also Barton Haxall Wise, The Life of Henry A. Wise of Virginia (New York: MacMillan

Smith, Billy – "Colored", cook in Co. H, 7th Va Cavalry, Laurel Brigade.[517]

Smith, Billy – "Colored"; Private, Co. H, 12th Va Cavalry.[518]

Smith, Charles--of Richmond; Free man; blacksmith; 3rd Va Cavalry.[519]

Smith, Charles – Cook, 2nd Co. I, 32nd Va Infantry; enlisted 1 June 1864; "on duty at Cook wagon. Slave owned by John Presson."; Present through Dec 1863.[520]

Smith, G.W. – Cook, Co. C, 32nd Va Infantry; enlisted 1 January 1864; "slave of J.H. Barlow"; Present through 31 Jan 1864; "discharged at expiration of service [1 Jan 1865]."; "Slave regularly enlisted for one year, discharged & paid at expiration of term of service Dec 31/64." Barlow paid $138.38 for Smith's services.[521]

Smith, Noah – "Colored", cook, Co. H. 7th Va Cavalry, Laurel Brigade.[522]

Smith, Noah – "Colored"; Private, Co. H, 12th Va Cavalry.[523]

Sorrell, John – Teamster; aka 'Uncle'; Co. B, 12th Va Cavalry, Baylor Light Horse.[524]

Stone, Fee-b. Richmond County, Va. 17 Sept 1843; Served on Island #10.[525]

Strother, Tom – served in Virginia, body servant to General Richard Taylor.[526]

T

Tabb, William –body servant of August Crenshaw of Richmond. POW at Point Lookout. Entry annotated "body servant" captured at High Bridge on April 6, 1865. [Augustus P. Crenshaw, Private, Co. D, 3rd Va Cavalry]..[527]

Tatem, Samuel – Enlisted Company D, 61st Va Infantry, Henrico County, 1 September 1862 for a period of three years or war; Records show he was present, issued clothing and paid through October 1864 when rolls no longer taken.[528]

Taylor, James – Co. E, 32nd Virginia Infantry; "free colored"; present on Nov/Dec 1864 payroll.

Temple, Edmund – Laborer for Wood Train; Richmond, Va; June 1863; Slave of Thomas J. Bagby.[529]

Terrell, George – servant to Charles T. O'Ferrall, Capti of Co. I, 12th Va Cav; later Colonel of 23rd Va Cavalry. O'Farrell became governor of Virginia.[530]

Thomas, Ben-b. Caroline Co., Va 1847; Co. A, 31st Alabama Infantry (rejected).[531]

Thomas, John - Passenger on Sloop James Landry; POW; captured 28 October 1864 off Alexandria, Va "for having cargo on board not mentioned on his manifest, also six passengers without passes and not mentioned on his manifest.[532]

Thompson, George – blockade runner; POW; captured 26 January 1863 at Clement's Bay (Maryland) intending to run blockade to Virginia. All negro crew.[533]

Thompson, William - blockade runner; POW; captured 26 January 1863 at Clement's Bay (Maryland) intending to run blockade to Virginia. All negro crew.[534]

Tucker, William – Colored Cook and Servant; Co. C, 3rd Va Cavalry.[535]

Tyler, George Jr. - Free Negro of Powhatan County; one of sixteen signatures on a Letter of Appointment

---

and Co, Ltd., 1899), p364; see also John Sergeant Wise, <u>The End of an Era</u> (New York: T. Yoselof, 1965), pp.318 and 433

[517] Ibid, McDonald, <u>Laurel Brigade</u>, p476
[518] VDCMR, V10, p185, Reel 5
[519] *Carter Diary*. Diary of William R. Carter, Lt. Col. CSA, <u>Sabres, Saddles and Spurs</u>, edited by Walbrook D. Swank, Colonel, USAF, (Ret). Lt. Col. Carter's memoirs.. 3rd Va Cavalry.. Diary Entry for April 16, 1864 reads as follows: "Got Chas [Charles] Smith & Wm [William] Cole, free negroes conscripted in Richmond, assigned to the Regiment as blacksmiths, by order of Secretary of War." (Neither man is listed in Thomas Pl. Nanzig's Third Va Cavalry, H.E. Howard, 1989, Lynchburg)
[520] CSR, 32nd Va
[521] CSR, 32nd Va
[522] Ibid, McDonald, <u>Laurel Brigade</u>, p476
[523] VDCMR, V10, p185, Reel 5
[524] SHSP, V31, p365
[525] Tennessee Pension Applications
[526] Taylor, Richard. <u>Destruction and Reconstruction: personal experiences of the late war</u> (p62-64;67;70; 81; 84; 197;228)

---

[527] National Archives, Record Group 109, Confederate States Records, *POW Rolls for Pt. Lookout, Md*. Boxes 283-285, Roll 8, Volume II. Paper copies of microfilm on file at Appomattox National Historic Park.
[528] CSR, 61st Virginia Infantry.
[529] M347
[530] O'Farrall, Charles T. <u>Forty Years of Active Service</u> (New York: The Neale Publishing Co.) 1904; p121-122
[531] Tennessee Pension Applications
[532] OR Navy, Series I, Vol. 5, p491
[533] OR Navy, Series I, Vol. 5, p225
[534] OR Navy, Series I, Vol. 5, p225
[535] VDCMR, Vol 8, p247, Reel 4.

(1862) for an attorney to ensure pay for services rendered the Confederacy.[536]

Tyler, Robert - Free Negro of Powhatan County; one of sixteen signatures on a Letter of Appointment (1862) for an attorney to ensure pay for services rendered the Confederacy.[537]

W

Walker, Chelse – Chief Cook, (2nd) Co. I, 32 Va Infantry; enlisted for one year at Chaffin's Farm on 13 April 1864; "on duty at Cook Wagon. Slave owned by Capt [William J.] Stores.".[538]

Walker, Fielding – of Loudon County, Va. Reported in 1918 as a servant of Robert E. Lee who was at Appomattox.[539]

Washington, George – Tredegar Iron Works employee.[540]

Walker, Frank — "Col'd". Company I, 46 Va Infantry.[541]

Wesley, Charles – of Lancaster County, Va; servant to Capt W.F. Dunaway, Co. I, 40th Va Inf; at Gettysburg.[542]

Weever, J. – crew of Schooner *A.W. Thompson*; POW; captured 28 Feb 1863.[543]

West, Richard – Colored Cook, Co A., 32nd Va Infantry, slave.; enlisted 25 Dec 1864 at Chesterfield,; "(Col'd Cook) Slave of [Corporal] Rich'd T. West".[544]

Williams, Phil – Hostler; ; Co. B, 12th Va Cavalry, Baylor Light Horse[545].

Wilson, Robert (Bob) –Co. H, 16th Va Infantry from 9 Oct 1862 to 31 May 1863 Died January 13, 1948 at Elgin State Veterans Hospital, Illinois..[546]

Winfield, Henry-b. Lynchburg, Va January 9, 1827; Claimed service as Jefferson Davis bodyguard.[547]

Y

Yerby, Joe – Colored Cook, Co. K, 9th Va Cavalry.[548]

Young, Henry-Laborer; slave of Dr. Young at Orange Court House, Va; "employed helping to build batteries at Mathias Point".[549]

No Last Names Provided

--, Abram – servant and teamster in 1864 to BG E. Porter Alexander.[550]

--, Abraham – in Virginia Hospital, 26 June 1863. Co. E, 4th Alabama Infantry; "Name appears on a register of officers and soldiers of the Army of the Confederate States who were killed in battle, or who died of wounds or disease"; Personal effects included "sundries" in charge of the Surgeon.[551]

--, Adam – Cook, Co. E, 32nd Va Infantry; slave.[552]

--, Addeline – Nurse, Jackson Hospital, July-Sept 1864, Slave of Thomas J. Bagby.[553]

--, Albert – servant to Chaplain and Lt. Richard McIlwaine, 44th Va Infantry.[554]

--, Albert – Blacksmith, Richmond, June 1864, Slave of Thomas J. Bagby[555]

--, Albert – 2nd Cook, Co. A, 25th Bn Va Inf; 1 Sept - 31 Dec 1864.[556]

--, Allen – slave, age 35, Tredegar Iron Works.[557]

--, Andrew – Cook, Co. G, 25th Bn Va Inf; enlisted 17 March 1862; through 31 Dec 1862 muster.[558]

--, Austen – Laborer, Slave of Selden Family of Charles City County; died while working at the Jamestown fortifications.[559]

--, Ben – Free man, servant to Confederate Officer Francis (Frank) Smith Robertson, [Co. I] 48th Va Infantry, Mahone's Brigade.[560]

--, Benjamin – Cook, Goochland Light Arty; enlisted 1 Nov 1864 through 31 Dec 1864 muster.[561]

---

[536] M346
[537] M346
[538] CSR, 32nd Va
[539] *The Evening Herald*, Albuquerque, NM, 13 April 1918, p19
[540] *Richmond Dispatch*, 13 May 1862 as cited by mdgorman.com.
[541] VDCMR, V5, p185, Reel 3
[542] Dunaway, W.F. (Rev), <u>Reminiscences of a Rebel</u> (New York: The Neales Publishing Company) 1923; p61-62
[543] OR Navy, p239
[544] CSR,
[545] SHSP, V31, p365
[546] Fold3.com, 'Confederate African-Americans – Civil War. http://www.fold3.com/page/1201_confederate_african_americanscivil_war/
[547] Tennessee Pension Applications

[548] VDCMR, V9, p439, Reel 5.
[549] OR Navy, Series I, Vol. 4, p645, Report of Commander Craven, etc.
[550] Ibid, Figg, <u>Where Men Only Dare</u>, p192
[551] M347
[552] CSR
[553] M347
[554] Ibid, McIlwaine, <u>Memories</u>, p209
[555] M347
[556] CSR
[557] *Richmond Dispatch*, 2 May 1862.
[558] CSR
[559] VHS, *Selden Family Papers, 1811-1868.* Mss1Se487a.
[560] Robertson, Francis (Frank) Smith. *Reminiscences*,p.48 VHS. Robertson was an officer in Mahone's Brigade at Sailor's Creek.

--, **Betsey** – Nurse, Jackson Hospital, July-Sept 1864; Slave of Thomas J. Bagby.[562]

--, **Bill** - Slave of Otho Hill, of Harrisonburg, at Liggon Hospital.[563]

--, **Billy** – servant to Colonel Thomas T. Munford; "a cook, hostler and manservant"; aged 16.[564]

--, **Bob** – Mulatto servant of JEB Stuart.[565]

--, **Bob** – Servant to General George Pickett.[566]

--, **Bob** -- Free man, servant, 48th Va Infantry at Sailor's Creek.[567]

--, **Bob** – Servant/Cook to Sergeant Joseph C. and Private Samuel B. Shannon (brothers), Co. D, 7th Va Infantry. "Bob was noted for his propensity for laughing, and when in a good glee he could be heard half a mile. He was very patriotic, and declared his purpose to go into battle with his young masters; that he could and would fight as well as we, and shoot as many Yankees."[568]--, **Burr** – Nurse, Jackson Hospital, June-Sept 1864; Slave of Thomas J. Bagby.[569]

--, **Cambridge** – Possible slave, employee of Tredegar Iron Works.[570]

--, --,**Charles** – "colored servant" to Gen. A.P. Hill.[571]

---, **Charles** – crew of Schooner *A.W. Thompson*; POW; captured 28 Feb 1863,[572]

--, **Charles** – Cook, Co. A, 25th Bn Va Inf; enlisted 1 July 1863; present through 28 Feb 1865 muster[573].

--, **Charles** – Quartermaster Department; slave hired out by Mary Emily Payne Gee of Culpeper.[574]

--,**Charley** – servant to E.P. Alexander at Sailor's Creek.[575]

--,**Cornelius** – Helper, Richmond; June 1864; Slave of Thomas J. Bagby.[576]

--, **David** – Cook, Goochland Light Artillery; aka 'Davey'; enlisted 6 Jan 1863 through 28 Feb 1865 muster. Paid $12 per month through 9 June then $19 per month thereafter.[577]

--, **David** – Laborer, of Mecklenburg County, impressed for 30 days service; owner was Edward Walker.[578]

--,**Edmund** –2nd Va Cavalry; slave; participated in charge and killed enemy leader; mentioned in dispatches by Gen. J.E.B. Stuart, Report of Cavalry Operations on First Maryland Campaign[579]

--, **Edmund** - Slave, age 32, mulatto, blacksmith, slave of William Robinson of Danville.[580]

--, **Edward** – servant to W.O. English, Co. K, 2nd Va Cavalry; "followed his master in the charge andshot one of the [Union Captain Samuel C.] Means party."[581]

--, **Elijah** – Laborer, Prince Edward County. Slave of James H. Evans. Died of disease while working on fortifications in Richmond.[582]

--, **Emily** – Nurse, Jackson Hospital; Slave of Thomas J. Bagby.[583]

--, **Essex** - servant to blockade runner Capt. John Wilkinson of Amelia County.[584]

---

[561] CSR
[562] M347
[563] *Richmond Dispatch*, 20 June 1862 as cited by mdgorman.com
[564] Peck, R.H. Reminiscences of a Confederate Soldier of Co. C, 2nd Va Cavalry (s.p. R.H. Peck) Fincastle, Va, 1913?
[565] Borcke, Heros Von. Memoirs of the Confederate War for Independence (Philadelphia: J.B. Lippincott & Co) 1867, p186, 282; see also McClellen, H.B. The Life and Campaigns of J.E.B. Stuart, Commander of the Confederate Cavalry Corps (Richmond, Va: J.W. Randolph and English) 1885; p161
[566] Pickett, George E. The Heart of A Soldier. (New York: Seth Moyle, Inc.) 1908. Letters of George Picket to his wife. His servants Bob and George are mentioned in his letters.
[567] Ibid, Robertson, *Reminiscences*,p.48.
[568] Johnston, David Emmons (1845-1917), The Story of a Confederate Boy in the Civil War (Electronic Edition). Academic Affairs Library, (UNC-Chapel Hill, 1998) p58.
[569] M347
[570] *Richmond Dispatch*, 13 May 1862 as cited by mdgorman.com.
[571] SHSP, V11, No. 12
[572] OR Navy, p239

[573] CSR
[574] VHS, *Payne Family Papers,1832-1892*, Mss1P2936c.
[575] Edward Porter Alexander, Fighting for the Confederacy., p522. Alexander was Longstreet's Chief of Artillery and on the retreat.
[576] M347
[577] CSR
[578] VHS, *Evans Tanner Papers, 1816-1887*. Mss2T1577b.
[579] SHSP, V13
[580] *Richmond Dispatch*, 2 September 1862 as cited by mdgorman.com
[581] McClellan, H.B. The Life and Campaigns of Major-General J.E.B. Stuart, Commander of the Cavlary of the Army of Northern Virginia (Richmond, Va: J.W. Randolph and English, 1885; p109.
[582] VHS, *James H. Evans Papers, 1856-1865*. Mss2Ev265a1.
[583] M347

--, **Ferry** – Laborer, slave of John Baylor of Caroline County., 26 Oct 1864.[585]

--, **Fleming** – Of Brook Turnpike, employee of Tredegar Iron Works.[586]

--, **Frank** – Cook, Goochland Light Artillery; Enlisted 13 Jan 1863 through 29 Feb 1865 muster; hospitalized for smallpox.[587]

--, **Frederick** – Cook, Goochland Light Artillery, enlisted 26 Feb 1863 through Feb 1865 muster.[588]

--, **George** – servant to Thomas Devereux, 2nd Corps, Army of Northern Virginia[589]

--, **George**. Servant to General George Pickett.[590]

--, **George**. – Cook, Co. F, 32nd Va Infantry; enlisted 25 August, 1864. "Slave with the wagons". Present through 31 Dec 1864.[591]

--. **George** – 2nd Cook; Co. A, 25th Bn Va Inf; Enlisted 29 Feb 1864 in Richmond; present through August 1864.[592]

--, **Gustin** – Cook, Co. F, 32nd Va Inf; enlisted 22 July 1864 at Chester; "Absent. Slave with wagons"; through 31 Dec 1864.[593]

--, **Hannah** – "company cook negro"; Co. B, 25th Bn, Va Inf; enlisted 1 Jan 1864 through 28 Feb 1865 muster.[594]

--, **Hays** – Nurse, Staunton, Va Hospital; Jan 1863; Slave of W.A. Abney.[595]

--, **Henry**, aka Harry. Servant to Heros Von Borcke, JEB Stuart's Cavalry staff.[596]

--, **Henry** – Cook, "free colored", Co. G, 25th Bn Va Inf; Enlisted 1 Jan 1864 through 1 March 1865 muster.[597]

--, **Howard** -- Hospital Steward; servant of J.H. Slater, in service to Dr. John H. Claiborne, Surgeon. Howard surrendered at Appomattox.[598]

--, **Ike** – Cook, Co. G, 25th Bn Va Inf; enlisted 1 May 1864, Chaffin's Bluff through last muster 1 March 1865.[599]

--, **James** - 3rd Cook, Co. A, 25th Bn Va Inf; Enlisted 1 Jan 1865 through 28 Feb 1865 muster.[600]

--, **James** – March 1863; hired out, possibly as carpenter-mechnic in Danville; slave of Hugh Blair Grigsby of Charlotte County, Va.[601]

--, **Jack** – Chief Cook, Capt. W.S. Reed's Co (President's Guard), Co. F, 25th Bn Va Inf; enlisted 15 March 1862.[602]

--, **Jim** – Servant to Gen. Stonewall Jackson.[603]

--, **Jim** -- "colored", age 14, related by Col. J.H. Averill, Trainmaster, Richmond & Danville Railroad; twin brother of Tom, age 14.[604]

---, **Joe** – Co. H, 13th Virginia Cavalry (formerly 16th Battalion Va Cavalry and 5th Va Cavalry); "Colored Teamster"; in CSA General Hospital in Charlottesville from January 7; 'Returned to duty' on 23, 1864 for pneumonia.[605]

--, **Joseph** – Colored, Chief Company Cook, Co. A, 49th Va Infantry; enlisted 15 Dec 1863 in Orange, Va.[606]

--, **Joseph** – (of Lawrence); Cook; Co. F, 61st Va Infantry; enlisted 21 May 1862 or 63 (record conflicts) at Fredericksburg; present through October 1864 muster.[607]

--, **Joshua** - One of two servants of General Henry Wise at Sailor's Creek.[608]

--, **Leahy** – Nurse, Jackson Hospital; July-Sept 1864; Slave of Thomas J. Bagby.[609]

--, **London** – Laborer, Richmond, Feb-Dec 1864; Slave of Thomas J. Bagby.[610]

--, **Lowden** – Laborer, at HQs; Richmond, Nov 1863-February 1864; Slave of Thomas J. Bagby.[611]

---

[584] Wilkinson, John. <u>Narrative of a Blockade Runner</u>, (New York: Sheldon & Company) 1877. p194-195

[585] VHS, *Caroline County, Va, enrolling office, certificate, 1864.* Mss4C22144a1.

[586] *Richmond Dispatch*, 13 May 1862 as cited by mdgorman.com.

[587] CSR

[588] CSR

[589] Devereux, Thomas. CV, *From Petersburg to Appomattox*, p257-261.

[590] Ibid, Pickett, <u>Heart of A Soldier</u>.

[591] CSR

[592] CSR

[593] CSR

[594] CSR

[595] M347

[596] Ibid, Borcke, p286, 395, 403, 424, 426.

[597] CSR

[598] SHSP, V28, p21

[599] CSR

[600] CSR

[601] VHS, *Hugh Blair Grigsby Papers, 1745-1944.* Mss1G8782b. Sec 74 and 82.

[602] CSR

[603] SHSP, Vol XLIII; possibly Jim Lewis.

[604] SHSP, V25, p267

[605] CSR

[606] CSR

[607] CSR

[608] Henry Wise, <u>Southern Historical Society Papers</u>, Vol. 25, p. 16-18, 'The Career of Wise's Brigade'; see also Barton Haxall Wise, <u>The Life of Henry A. Wise of Virginia</u> (New York: MacMillan and Co, Ltd., 1899), p364; see also John Sergeant Wise, <u>The End of an Era</u> (New York: T. Yoselof, 1965), pp.318 and 433.

[609] M347

[610] M347

Major – servant to Lt. Brown, Parker's Battery, Va Light Artillery[612]

--, **Martha** – Laundress, Jackson Hospital; July-Sept 1864; Slave of Thomas J. Bagby.[613]

--, **Martin** – servant to Colonel Thomas H. Carter, artillery, Army of Northern Virginia.[614].

--, **Maurice** – Musician, Co. B, Regiment of Cavalry, later Co B, 5th Va Cavalry. On July/August 1861 muster; "Name on roll. Did not appear afterwards."[615]

--, **Minnis** – 3rd Cook, Co. A, 25th Bn Va Inf; enlisted 29 Feb 1864 through 29 Feb 1865 muster.[616]

--, **Monroe** – Teamster, servant of Phebe Bailey of Halifax; hired out, 1865.[617]

--, **Morgan** – servant to Gen. Eppa Hunton; Sailor's Creek.[618]

--, **Morres** – Officer's Servant; 6 April 1865; "Col'd Boy"; Officer's Servant captured at Sailor's Creek, 6 April 1865; Transferred to Elmira [Prison], NY, May 11, 1865.[619]

--, **Mortimer** – Cook, Goochland Light Arty; enlisted for war 1 Oct 1865 through Feb 1865 muster.[620]

--, **Murry** – servant to Logan Household and Col. Eaton Coleman at Staunton River Bridge.[621]

--, **Ned** – servant to Thomas Watkins Leigh at Staunton River Bridge.[622]

--, **Ned** – Slave of Capt (Rev) George White of Brunswick. Aided in capture of Wilson-Kautz raiders, June 1864.[623]

--, **Nelson** - Slave; in Petersburg from November 1863 to Jan 1864; $128; owner Joseph Gates.[624]

--, **Newton**. – Mulatto servant of Alabama native John Pelham, Chief of JEB Stuart's Artillery.[625]

--, **Nottingham** – Servant; listed as 'Private'; 2nd Company K, 32nd Virginia Infantry.[626]

--, **Nutrum** – Patient, Chimborazo Hospital, Richmond, Va; 26 April 1862; Co. M, 5th NC Infantry Regt; Register Hospital No. 1, Richmond, Va; convalescent; "left without permission".[627]

--, **Oliver** - Teamster, Supply Wagon near Richmond, in December 1864; slave hired out by Hugh Blair Grigsby of Charlotte County, Va. Sent letter written for him by Thomas Black suggesting he was attached to Co. E, 41st Va Inf; alternative is Thomas G. Black, Davis-Chamberlayne's Battery, 13th Bn, Va Light Artillery.[628]

--, **Oscar** – servant to Capt. Benjamin Farinholt at Staunton River Bridge.[629]

--, **Ottoway** – 4th Cook, Co. A, 25th Bn Va Inf; enlisted 1 Sept 1863.[630]

--, **Overton** – Cook; slave of Timberlakes; Co. B, 12th Va Cavalry, Baylor Light Horse.[631]

---, **Pad** – Servant and Cook; Co. D, 40th Va Inf; enlisted 1 August 1864; present Nov/Dec 1864 roster; servant of Thomas Omohundro.[632]

--, **Paul** – Laborer, slave of John Baylor, Caroline County, 26 October 1864.[633]

--, **Patrick** – Laborer, Slaughterhouse, Richmond, June 1863; Slave of Thomas J. Bagby.[634]

--, **Patrick** – Cook, "slave colored"; Co. G, 25th Bn, Va Inf; Enlisted 1 Jan 1864 through 1 March 1865 muster.[635]

--, **Patrick** – Laborer, slave of Stone Family of Pittsylvania County, December 1864.[636]

---

[611] M347
[612] Ibid, Figg, Where Men Only Dare, p21
[613] M347
[614] Armstead Lindsay Long, Memoirs of Robert E. Lee, (London: Sampson Low, Marston, Searle, and Rivngton) 1886; p385-386
[615] CSR
[616] CSR
[617] VHS, Bailey Family Papers, 1824-1886. Mss1B1565a, Microfilm Reel C380.
[618] Papers of Eppa Hunton, Va Historical Society Collection, VHS Mss1H9267a, items 38-65, Sec. 12.
[619] M598
[620] CSR
[621] W. Carroll Headspeath, The Battle of the Staunton River Bridge (s.p) 30; Ibid, 27.
[622] Ibid
[623] Memoirs of Rev. George W. White, manuscript, U.Va. Special Collections, 34-35 as cited by Ervin L. Jordan, Jr., Black Confederates and Afro-Yankees (Charlottesville, Va: University Press of Virginia, 1995), 228.
[624] M346

[625] Ibid, Borcke, p320.
[626] Confederate Records, Virginia Index Cards
[627] M347
[628] VHS, Hugh Blair Grigsby Papers, 1745-1944. Mss1G8782b. Sec 74 and 82.
[629] Letter, Benjamin Farinholt to wife Lelia, dtd 28 July 1864, from his Headquarters, Staunton Bridge. Copy of letter on file at Staunton River Battlefield State Park. Farinholt returned Oscar to a cousin and notes in the letter the existence but not the names of two other men employed as body servant and cook, respectively.
[630] CSR
[631] SHSP, V31, p365
[632] CSR
[633] VHS, Caroline County, Va, enrolling office, certificate, 1864. Mss4C22144a1.
[634] M347
[635] CSR
[636] VHS, Edmund Fitzgerald Stone, letter, 7 December 1864. Mss2St714a1.

--, **Pete**- cook in Washington College Company of the Rockbridge Artillery.[637]

--, **Pembroke** – Colored; August 1863; paid $3 for repairing Provost Marshal's Office, furnishing lock and hinges.[638]

--, **Richard** – Laborer, Richmond, Va; Slave of Thomas J. Bagby.[639]

--, **Robert** – Cook, Co. G, 25th Bn Va Inf; on March through April 1863 muster; paid through 28 Feb.[640]

--, **Sam** – Helper, Richmond, Va; Slave of Thomas J. Bagby.[641]

--, **Samuel** – servant, 37th Virginia Cavalry.[642]

--, **Samuel** - Cook, Capt Jonathan Talley's Co, Goochland Light Artillery enlisted 26 Feb 1863 through August 1864 muster.[643]

--, **Sam**, slave of Confederate officer Francis (Frank) Smith Robertson, 48th Va Infantry, Mahone's Brigade.[644]

--, **Sarah**. – Laundress, Jackson Hospital; Slave of Thomas J. Bagby.[645]

--, **Scott** – 2nd Cook, Co. A, 25th Bn Va Inf; "Free Colored"; later in Co. G, 25th; Enlisted 1 July 63 through April 1864 muster.[646]

--, **Smith** – One of two servants of General Henry Wise at Sailor's Creek.[647]

--, **Squier** – Servant, Treasury Dept, Richmond, Va, 1 April 1862.[648]

--, **Tim** - Tredegar Iron Works, slave of Jas. Duvall, Caroline Co.; age 20/21.[649]

--, **Texas** – Cook, 2nd Co. I, 32nd Va Infantry; enlisted 21 May 1864 for one year at Chaffin's Farm; "on duty at Cook wagon. Slave owned by R.W. Davidson."[650]

--, **Thomas** – Cook, Co. F, 32nd Va Infantry; enlisted 1 Nov 1864 for one year, at Chester; "absent, slave with wagons"[651].

--, **Thomas** – Cook, Co G. 25th Bn Va Inf; Present Jan/Feb 1863; probably same as 'Tom' present March/April 1863.[652]

--, **Thorn** – Servant to Edgar B. Montague in 1862. [Possibly Col Edgar Montague.[653] 32nd Va Infantry].

--, **Thornton** – Cook, "negro"; Co. F, 25th Bn Va Inf; Enlisted November 1863 "for war"; present through Feb 1865 muster. "Slave Cook".[654]

--, **Tom** – "colored", age 14, related by Col. J.H. Averill, Trainmaster, Richmond & Danville Railroad; twin brother of Jim, age 14.[655]

Unnamed – Hospital steward, 16 y/o; servant of Dr. John H. Claiborne, Surgeon.[656]

--, **Unnamed** – Hospital Nurse, mother of 16 y/o; servant of Dr. John H. Claiborne, Surgeon.[657]

--, **Walker** – Laborer on Wood Train; Richmond, Va, June 1863; Slave of Thomas J. Bagby.[658]

--, **Watkins** – Laborer, of Halifax, hired out by Clement McPhail in 1865.[659]

--, **William** - Servant to Heros Von Borcke, JEB Stuart's Cavalry staff.[660]

--, **William** – "slave cook"; Co. F, 25th Bn Va Inf; enlisted 1 Sept 1864 through 28 Feb 1865 muster.[661]

--, **Willis** - Slave of Otho Hill, of Harrisonburg, at Liggon Hospital.[662]

--, **Wilson** – Cook, Co. G, 25th Bn Va Inf; Enlisted March 1862; present through April 1864 muster.[663]

Unknown
Unknown –"Sixteen white and nine colored men" were arrested 10 August 1862 in the Potomac for blockade running 203 bushels of wheat, 10 sacks of salt, 30,000 cigars, 28 ounces of quinine,, 12 ounces of morphine, four pounds of opium, etc.[664]

---

[637] Moore, E.A. **The Story of a Cannoneer Under Stonewall Jackson (Lynchburg, Va: J.P. Bell Company, Inc) 1910; p68**
[638] M346
[639] M347
[640] CSR
[641] M347
[642] Hagy, P.S. *The Laurel Hill Retreat in 1861*, CV v24 (1816) p170
[643] CSR
[644] Ibid, Robertson, *Reminiscences*, p48
[645] M347
[646] CSR
[647] Ibid, Henry Wise, etc.
[648] M347
[649] *Richmond Dispatch*, 2 August 1862 as cited by mdgorman.com.
[650] CSR

[651] CSR
[652] CSR
[653] VHS, *Harrison Family Papers, 1768-1908*, Mss1H2485b.
[654] CSR
[655] SHSP, V25, p267
[656] SHSP, V28, p21
[657] SHSP, V.28, p21
[658] M347
[659] VHS, *Carrington Family Papers, 1755-1839.* Mss1C2358f.
[660] Ibid, Borcke. p90, 259.
[661] CSR
[662] *Richmond Dispatch*, 20 June 1862, as cited by mdgorman.com.
[663] CSR
[664] OR Navy, Series I, Vol. 5, p58

U.S. National Park Service
Black Confederate Employees at Chimborazo Hospital 1861-1865

Editor's note: Richmond National Battlefield Park took a step in documenting the role of Virginia's black Confederates when Michael D. Gorman transcribed the list of employees at Chimborazo hospital. Gorman lists thousand employees including approximately 490 black Confederates, free and slave, who worked in the hospital. Gorman compiled the list from National Archives sources in 2002 specifically, National Archives Record Group (RG) 109, Chapter 6, and Volumes 85, 98, 301, 307, 316 and 317. Individuals seeking greater detail should consult Gorman's web link *Civil War Rich*mond at:
http://www.mdgorman.com/Hospitals/Chimborazo_Hospital_%20Employees.htm

Name	Position	Div	Date(s) employed/associated	Owner (if slave)	Remarks
[no name]	Nurse	2	7/?/1864 - 9/25/1864	Lea & Christian	$25/mo; dischd 9/25/1864
Abraham	Nurse	5	1/1/1863	Pearce, George	$200/yr
Adam	Cook	1	1/1/1864	Temple, B.	$300/yr
Albert	not stated	1	1/1/1865	Curtis, Mrs. E. B.	Employed in Dining Room in 1865
Albert	not stated	1	1/1/1863	Ferrell, E. T.	$25/mo
Albert	Nurse	5	1/1/1863	Moore, James	boy; $100/yr
Albert	Nurse	5	1/1/1864	Twisdale, Wm. H.	$300/yr
Alexander	Nurse	5	1/1/1863	Doswell, Thos. W.	$200/yr in 1863; $300/yr in 1864; owned by Miss T. W. Doswell in 1864
Alfred	Nurse	1	1/1/1864	Ferrell, E. T.	$300/yr; Employed in Ward 4 in 1865
Alfred	Nurse	3	1/1/1863	Ferell, E. T.	$240/yr; "Belonging to Wm. Clark"
Allen, Jim	Kitchen	1	1/1/1865	Mears, Gilbert	
Allen, Lewis	not stated	1	not stated	Allen, Maj. Wm.	
Allen, William	not stated	1	5/2/1864	Gilbert & Mears	$25/mo
Allen, Wm.	Kitchen	1	5/3/1864	Mears, Gilbert	$25/mo
Alonzo	Nurse	4	1/1/1863	Enders, John	$240/yr
Alsop, Addison	Nurse	1	1/1/1863	Alsop, Dr. G. E	$240/yr in 1863; $300/yr in 1864; employed in Ward 10 in 1865
Alsop, Jim	Nurse	1	1/1/1863	Alsop, Dr. G. E.	$240/yr; Division 1 closed 1/1/1864
Alsop, Moses	Nurse	1	1/1/1863	Alsop, Dr. G. E.	$240/yr; Division 1 closed 1/1/1864
Alsop, Ned	Nurse	1	1/1/1863	Alsop, Dr. G. E.	boy; $180/yr; Division 1

Virginia's Black Confederates

Name	Role		Dates	Employer	Notes
					closed 1/1/1864
Alsop, Tom	Nurse	1	1/1/1863 - 4/6/1863	Alsop, Dr. G. E	died 4/6/1863; $240/yr
Alsop, Willis	Nurse	1	1/1/1863	Alsop, Dr. G. E.	$240/yr in 1863; $300/yr in 1864
Alsop, Wm.	Nurse	1	1/1/1863	Alsop, Dr. G. E.	$240/yr; Division 1 closed 1/1/1864
Anderson, Chester	Nurse	3	1/1/1863	Boswell, W. A.	$120/yr
Anderson, James	Cook	2	1/1/1864	Clopton & Lyne	$300/yr
Anderson, Nelson	Nurse	4	1/1/1863	Enders, John	$240/yr
Andrew	Nurse	1	1/1/1863	Alsop, Dr. G. E.	$240/yr in 1863; $300/yr in 1864
Ann	not stated	1	1/1/1864	Browne, Dr. P. F.	$25/mo
Anthony, John	Nurse	2	2/1/1863 - 6/1/1863	Eppes, Dr.	$200/yr
Arthur	Nurse	3	5/1/1863	Durett, James T.	$240/yr
Austin	not stated	1	1/3/1864	Beals(?), Jas.	
Austin	Nurse	3	1/1/1864	Smith, Dr. E. H.	$400/yr
Babcock, Monroe	Nurse	3	1/1/1863	Babcock, Dr. W. H.	boy; $180/yr
Bagby, Wm.	Nurse	1	1/1/1863	Bagby, G. W.	$200/yr; Division 1 closed 1/1/1864; employed in Kitchen in 1865
Baker, Lewis	not stated	1	not stated	Clopton & Lyne	
Ball, Mark	Nurse	4	1/1/1863	Enders, John	$240/yr
Ball, Moses	not stated	1	not stated	Ball, Dandridge	
Banks, D.	Nurse	4	1/1/1864	Gwathmey, George	$300/yr
Banks, Robert	Nurse	1	1/1/1863	Cocke, B. W.	$240/yr; Division 1 closed 1/1/1864
Banks, Robt.	not stated	1	not stated	Hardgrove, T. & S.	
Barnes, Algenas	Nurse	2	1/1/1863	Moore, James	$200/yr; Division 2 closed 1/1/1864
Barrett, Gustavus	Nurse	4	1/1/1864	Barrett, Wm. T.	$400/yr
Batte, Bob(?)	Nurse	2	8/8/1864	Scott, T. W.	
Baylor, Charles	Nurse & Cook	2	4/23/1863	Baylor, Dr. Jno. C.	$400/yr; listed as cook in 1863 & 1865 list
Ben	not stated	1	1/1/1865	Powers, J.	Employed "matrons" in 1865
Ben	Nurse	1	1/1/1864	Warring, L. E.	$300/yr
Ben	not stated	1	1/1/1864	Williamson, Mrs.	$300/yr
Ben	Cook	2	3/1/1863	Tally, B. W.	$240/yr; Division 2 closed 1/1/1864
Ben	Nurse	4	1/1/1863	Eacho, E. D.	boy; $216/yr
Benjamin	Nurse	5	1/1/1864	Turpin & Yarbrough	$300/yr
Bennett, Thomas	Nurse	3	1/1/1863	Bennett, L.	$200/yr
Betsy	Cook	1	3/26/1863 - 8/1/1863	Pope, M	dischd 8/1/1863; $240/yr
Bill	not stated	1	5/10/1864	Cherry, Dr.	$25/mo
Billups, Gabe	Nurse	2	1/10/1863	Tabb, P. M. & Son	boy; $144/yr; Division 2 closed 1/1/1864
Billy	Nurse	1	1/1/1864	Browne, Dr. P. F.	$300/yr
Billy	Nurse	1	2/25/1863 - 3/23/1863	Slater, Seldon	dischd 3/23/1863; $240/yr

Civil War Sesquicentennial Edition

Virginia's Black Confederates

Binford, Wm.	Nurse	3	1/1/1863	Grant, James H.	$200/yr
Bingham, John	Nurse	4	1/1/1863	Dunn, J. L.	$200/yr in 1863; $400/yr in 1864
Bird, Ambrose	Cook	4	1/1/1863 - 5/1/1863	Free	$240/yr
Blair, Gustus	Nurse	4	1/1/1863	Barrett, Wm. T.	$216/yr
Blakey, George	Cook	1	1/1/1863	Grant, James H.	$200/yr; Division 1 closed 1/1/1864
Brokenbrough, J.	Nurse	2	3/25/1865	Haw, Jno.	
Brown, Marshall	Nurse	2	6/29/1864 - 9/15/1864	Lea & Christian	boy; $15/mo; dischd 9/15/1864
Brown, Ned	Nurse	3	1/1/1864	Kay, Joseph	$300/yr
Brown, Phil	Nurse	2	1/1/1863 - 2/1/1863	Clopton & Lyne	$240/yr; died 2/1/1863
Browne, Bill	Nurse	1	1/1/1863	Browne, Dr. P. F.	$240/yr; Division 1 closed 1/1/1864; Employed "matrons" in 1865
Browne, Frank	Nurse	1	1/1/1863	Browne, Dr. P. F.	$180/yr; Division 1 closed 1/1/1864; Employed in Kitchen in 1865
Browne, Wm.	Nurse	1	1/1/1863	Browne, Dr. P. F.	$240/yr; Division 1 closed 1/1/1864; Employed in Dining Room in 1865
Bufort, Robert	Nurse	4	1/1/1863	Barrett, Wm. T.	$216/yr
Bunell	Nurse	1	3/1/1863	Hanison, Dr. J. P.	$240/yr; Division 1 closed 1/1/1864
Candis	Cook & Nurse	2	5/1/1863 - 7/25/1864	Free	$240/yr & Cook in 1863; $400/yr & Nurse in 1864; Dischd. 7/25/1864
Carrington, Phil	Cook	3	1/1/1863	Grant, James H.	$200/yr in 1863; $300/yr in 1864
Carry, Beverly	Nurse	4	1/1/1864	Gwathmey, George	$300/yr
Carter	Nurse	2	12/1/1863	Cox, Ben	Division 2 closed 1/1/1864
Carter, Doctor	not stated	1	not stated	Allen, Maj. Wm.	
Carter, John	Cook	2	5/23/1864 - 7/31/1864	Allen, Wm.	Dischd. 7/31/1864
Carter, Robert	Nurse	2	1/1/1863	Royster, G. W.	boy; $180/yr; Division 2 closed 1/1/1864
Carter, Robert	Cook	4	1/1/1863	Kerr, John	$240/yr
Chamberlayne, Claiborne	Nurse & Cook	2	7/1/1864	Powers, Dr. Frederick	$25/mo & Cook in 1864; Nurse in 1865
Charles	Nurse	3	2/1/1863	Eacho, E. D.	$240/yr
Charles	Nurse	5	1/1/1863	Greanor, Wm.	$200/yr in 1863; $300/yr in 1864
Cherry, Thomas	Cook	5	1/1/1863	Cherry, Dr. J. J.	$200/yr in 1863; $300/yr in 1864; owned by Eugene Cherry in 1864
Cherry, Wm.	Nurse	5	3/1/1863	Cherry, Dr. J. J.	$200/yr
Christian, Albert	Nurse	2	5/27/1864 - 6/27/1864	Walker, J. H.	Dischd. 6/27/1864
Christian, Jim	Cook	2	1/1/1865	Powers, Dr. W. M.	
Christian, Jim	Nurse	2	1/13/1863	Woodard, Dr.	$240/yr; Division 2 closed 1/1/1864
Christian, L.	Nurse	3	1/1/1863	Grant, James H.	$200/yr
Christian, Thomas	Nurse	2	1/27/1865	Barney, Jas. I.	Dischd. 3/1/1865
Christian, Wm.	Nurse	4	1/1/1864	Pollard & Walker	$200/yr

Name	Role		Date	Employer	Remarks
Church, Henry	Nurse	1	1/1/1863	Patterson, Dr.	$240/yr in 1863; $300/yr in 1864; Employed in Ward 9 in 1865
Claiborne	Nurse	5	1/1/1864	Adcock, W. F.	$300/yr
Claiborne	Cook	5	1/1/1863	Frayser, Miss E.	$240/yr
Claibourne	Cook	1	1/1/1864	Turpin & Yarbrough	$300/yr
Clare, Warner	Nurse	2	6/29/1864	Lea & Christian	$25/mo
Clayton, Jno	Nurse	2	4/8/1864	Vaiden, H. D.	illegible remarks
Clements, Ben	not stated	1	5/18/1864	Turpin & Yarbrough	$25/mo
Cobb, Tom	Nurse	4	1/1/1864	Gwathmey, George	$300/yr
Colston, Charles	Nurse	4	1/1/1863	Greanor, Wm.	$200/yr
Cooper, George	Nurse	2	1/1/1863	Pointer, Jno.	boy; $150/yr; Division 2 closed 1/1/1864
Copeland, Ro.	Nurse	3	1/1/1863	Grant, James H.	$200/yr
Cornelius	Nurse	1	1/1/1863	Apperson, E. B. W.	$200/yr in 1863; $300/yr in 1864
Cosby, Henry	Nurse	3	1/1/1863	Cosby, B. F.	$240/yr
Cox, Daniel	Nurse	3	1/1/1863	Grant, James H.	$200/yr in 1863; $300/yr in 1864
Cox, Geo.	Nurse	2	1/1/1864	Free	$300/yr
Cox, George	Nurse	2	1/1/1863	Free	$240/yr; Division 2 closed 1/1/1864
Cox, Henry	Nurse	3	1/1/1863	Grant, James H.	$200/yr in 1863; $300/yr in 1864
Craddock, Dick	Nurse	3	1/1/1863	Enders, Jno.	$240/yr in 1863; $300/yr in 1864
Crawford, Griffin	Nurse	3	1/1/1863	Washington, Dr. L.	$240/yr in 1863; $400/yr in 1864
Curran, Jane	Cook	4	1/1/1863	Bates, G. M.	$216/yr
Curtis, Aleck	Nurse	2	1/1/1863	Tabb, P. M. & Son	boy; $144/yr; Division 2 closed 1/1/1864
Custis, Alec	Nurse	2	1/1/1864	Tompkins, S. L.	$240/yr
Dabbs, Scott	Carpenter	2	5/27/1864 - 8/1/1864	Pleasants, G. D.	Dischd. 8/1/1864
Dandridge, James	Nurse	2	6/15/1863	Atkinson, _ H.	$240/yr; Division 2 closed 1/1/1864
Daniel	Nurse	1	1/1/1864	Browne, Dr. P. F.	$180/yr
Daniel	not stated	1	1/1/1865	Carson, R. T.	
Daniel	not stated	1	1/1/1864	Stokes, Mrs.	$300/yr
Davenport, Melvin	Cook	4	1/1/1863	Free	$240/yr in 1863; $400/yr in 1864; boy
David	not stated	1	1/18/1864	Free	$25/mo
David	not stated	1	6/18/1864	Parrish, F. M.	$25/mo
David	Nurse	5	1/1/1863	Tabb, P. M. & Son	boy; $100/yr
Davis, Peter	Nurse	4	1/1/1864	Gwathmey, George	$300/yr
Davis, Thadeus	Nurse	2	1/13/1863	Powers, J.	boy; $240/yr; Division 2 closed 1/1/1864
Davis, Wm.	Nurse	1	1/1/1863	Grant, James H.	$200/yr; Division 1 closed 1/1/1864

Name	Role		Date	Employer	Notes
Dennis, Jim	Kitchen	1	1/1/1865	Mears, Gilbert	
Dickinson, Edwin	Nurse	2	1/1/1863	Dickinson, Rev. A. E.	boy; $150/yr in 1863; $200/yr in 1864
Dickson, Reuben	Nurse as Baker	3	1/1/1863	Tabb, P. M. & Son	$250/yr in 1863; $400/yr in 1864
Dixon, Jim	Cook	2	6/21/1864 - 8/31/1864	Oliver, R. W.	$25/mo; dischd 8/31/1864
Dudley, John	Cook	4	1/1/1863	Barrett, Wm. T.	$216/yr in 1863; $400/yr in 1864
Ealloe	not stated	1	4/26/1864	Enos	$25/mo
Edmund	Nurse	1	4/4/1863	Eacho, E. D.	$300/yr; Division 1 closed 1/1/1864
Edmund	Nurse	5	1/1/1863	Fox, Richd	$240/yr
Edwards, Abraham	Nurse	3	1/1/1863	Grant, James H.	$200/yr in 1863; $300/yr in 1864
Emaline	Nurse	5	1/1/1863	Woodard. Dr. W. M.	$200/yr in 1863; $300/yr in 1864
Emanuel	Nurse	3	1/1/1864	Snellings, Dr. Wm. Q.	$300/yr
Emily	Nurse	2	12/1/1863	Cox, Ben	Division 2 closed 1/1/1864
Enders, Lewis	Nurse	4	1/1/1863	Enders, John	$240/yr
Enders, Peter	Nurse	4	1/1/1863	Enders, John	$240/yr
Eppes, Wm.	Cook	2	1/12/1863 - 4/1/1863	Eppes, Dr.	$200/yr; died 4/1/1863
Esau	Cook	3	1/1/1863	Grant, James H.	$200/yr in 1863; $300/yr in 1864
Foster, Wyatt	Cook	2	5/23/1864	Wilkins, Richard	
Frank	Nurse	1	1/1/1864	Browne, Dr. P. F.	$180/yr
Frank	not stated	1	5/19/1864	Free	$25/mo
Frank	not stated	1	5/19/1864	Skinner, F. G.	$25/mo
Fulcher, Ezekiel	Nurse	2	1/1/1863	Tabb, P. M. & Son	$200/yr; Division 2 closed 1/1/1864
Fuzzle, John	Cook	1	1/1/1863	Eacho, E. D.	$200/yr; Employed in Dining Room in 1865
Garland	Nurse	5	1/1/1863	Doswell, Miss T. W.	$300/yr
Garthright. Peter	Nurse	2	7/1/1864	Garthright, J. O.	boy; $15/mo
Gates, Spencer	Cook	1	1/1/1863	Grant, James H.	$200/yr; Division 1 closed 1/1/1864
Gatewood	Nurse	5	1/1/1863	Kay, Joseph	$200/yr
Geddins, James	Nurse	2	1/1/1863	Jones, P.	boy; $180/yr; Division 2 closed 1/1/1864
George	Nurse	1	4/4/1863	Eacho, E. D.	$300/yr; Division 1 closed 1/1/1864
George	Nurse	2	1/1/1863	Halstead, J. D.	boy; $150/yr; Division 2 closed 1/1/1864
George	Nurse	2	1/1/1863 - 6/1/1863	Morecock, Wm. E.	boy; $192/yr; dischd 6/1/1863
George	Nurse as Carpenter	4	1/1/1863 - 11/15/1863	Eacho, E. D.	$240/yr
George	Nurse	4	3/1/1863	Tabb, P. M. & Son	$216/yr
George	Nurse	5	1/1/1863	Doswell, Thos. W.	$200/yr in 1863; $300/yr in 1864
George	Nurse	5	1/1/1863	Kay, Joseph	$200/yr

Name	Role	Div	Date	Owner/Employer	Notes
Goode, Jim	Cook & Nurse	2	1/1/1863	Goode, W. W.	$200/yr & Cook in 1863; $300/yr & Nurse in 1864; listed as cook in 1865 list
Goodwin, Allen	Nurse	2	1/1/1863	Jones, P.	boy; $150/yr; Division 2 closed 1/1/1864
Grant, Isaac	Nurse	4	1/1/1863	Grant, J. H.	$200/yr
Graves, John	Nurse	2	5/26/1864 - 8/3/1864	Oliver, R. W.	Dischd. 8/3/1864
Greanor, Eli	Nurse	4	1/1/1863	Greanor, Wm.	$200/yr
Grew, Peter	not stated	1	not stated	Clopton & Lyne	
Griffin	Nurse	1	1/1/1863	Taylor, W. F.	$192/yr; Division 1 closed 1/1/1864
Griffin	Nurse	1	1/1/1863	Wolfe, Mrs. Maria	$192/yr; Division 1 closed 1/1/1864
Griffin, Charles	Cook	4	1/1/1863	Barrett, Wm. T.	$216/yr in 1863; $400/yr in 1864
Hackett	Nurse as Carpenter	3	1/1/1863	Rollins, Miss S.	$480 listed over $300
Hackett, Frederick	Carpenter as Nurse	3	1/1/1864	Smith, Wm. K., Agt.	$500/yr
Hamberry, Wm.	Nurse	4	1/1/1863	Tabb, P. M. & Son	$168/yr
Hanes, Squire	Nurse	3	1/1/1863	Harris, Mrs. N. A.	$240/yr in 1863; $300/yr in 1864; 1864 owned by Smith, Wm. K Agt.
Hannibal	Nurse	3	1/1/1864	McCaw, Dr. J. B.	$300/yr
Hannibal	Nurse	3	1/1/1863	Yeatman, Chas.	$240/yr
Harold, Isham	Nurse	4	1/1/1863	Tabb, P. M. & Son	$200/yr
Harris, Ben	Nurse as Baker	3	1/1/1863	Harris, Mrs. N. A.	$240/yr in 1863; $300/yr in 1864; 1864 owned by Smith, Wm. K Agt.
Harris, Ed	Nurse	2	8/3/1864 - 9/15/1864	Fisher, John	$20/mo; dischd 9/15/1864
Harris, Henry	Nurse	3	1/1/1863	Free	$240/yr; possibly owned by Smith, Wm. K. in 1864
Harris, Henry	Nurse	3	1/1/1864	Smith, Wm. K., Agt.	$400/yr
Harris, Horatio	Scabinger	2	1/1/1865	Free	
Harris, Jefferson	Cook	4	1/1/1863	Barrett, Wm. T.	$216/yr
Harris, Oratio	Nurse	5	7/27/1863	Free	$200/yr in 1863; $300/yr in 1864; listed as "Ratio" in 1864
Harris, Thaddeus	Cook	2	1/1/1864	Porter, J. L.	$300/yr
Harrison, Carter	Nurse	2	1/1/1863	Phillips, W. S.	$200/yr; Division 2 closed 1/1/1864
Harrison, Ro.	Nurse	2	1/1/1863	Phillips, W. S.	$200/yr; Division 2 closed 1/1/1864
Harvey, Lewis	Nurse	4	1/1/1864	Trice, G. W.	$300/yr
Harwood, Lewis	Nurse	2	6/22/1864	Rady, C. P.	boy; $15/mo
Henderson, James	Nurse	4	1/1/1863	Greanor, Wm.	$200/yr
Henry	not stated	1	1/1/1865	Curtis, Mrs. E. B.	Employed in Dining Room in 1865
Henry	not stated	1	1/13/1864	Free	$25/mo
Henry	not stated	1	6/13/1864	Parrish, F. M.	$25/mo
Henry	Nurse	1	4/21/1863	Trice, G. W.	$204/yr; Division 1 closed 1/1/1864

Virginia's Black Confederates

Name	Role		Date	Owner/Employer	Notes
Henry	Nurse	2	5/21/1863	Hughes, J. W.	$138/yr; Division 2 closed 1/1/1864
Henry	Nurse	5	1/1/1863	Gathwright, Francis	$200/yr in 1863; $300/yr in 1864
Henry, Jas.	Nurse	1	1/1/1864	Turpin & Yarbrough	$300/yr
Henry, Wm.	Cook	1	1/1/1863	Holt, J. T.	$200/yr; Division 1 closed 1/1/1864
Henry, Wm.	Cook	2	1/1/1863	Halstead, J. D.	boy; $150/yr; Division 2 closed 1/1/1864
Henry, Wm.	Nurse	2	3/1/1863	Morecock, Wm. E.	$240/yr; Division 2 closed 1/1/1864
Henry, Wm.	Nurse	2	1/1/1864 - 4/1/1864	Taylor	$400/yr; Dischd. 4/1/1864
Henry, Wm.	Nurse	4	1/1/1863	Stratton, M. L.	$216/yr
Hill, Billy	Nurse	2	4/30/1864 - 9/1/1864	Alexander, W. F.	Dischd. 9/1/1864
Hill, Edward	not stated	1	5/13/1864	Hill, W. B.	$25/mo; Employed in Dining Room in 1865
Hill, John	not stated	1	5/13/1864	Hill, W. B.	$25/mo; Employed in Ward 12 in 1865
Hill, Richard	Scabinger	2	1/1/1865	Shepherd, Mrs. La.	
Hill, Roy	Nurse	3	1/1/1863	Grant, James H.	$200/yr
Hine, Jim	Nurse	2	7/13/1864 - 8/7/1864	Royall, John M.	boy; $20/mo; dischd 8/7/1864
Holt, Jacob	Nurse	1	1/1/1863	Holt, J. T.	$200/yr; Division 1 closed 1/1/1864
Hubbard, Ro.	Nurse as Baker	3	1/1/1863	Schmeltz, Mrs.	$300/yr
Hubbard, Wm.	Nurse	3	1/1/1863	Schmeltz, Mrs.	boy; $240/yr
Hughes, James	Nurse as Baker	3	1/1/1863	Causey, Wm	$240/yr
Hunter, Henry	Nurse	3	1/1/1863	Bowen, Dr. J. W.	$240/yr in 1863; $300/yr in 1864
Isaac	Nurse	1	2/28/1863 - 3/15/1863	Apperson, E. B. W.	dischd 3/15/1863; $240/yr
Isaiah	not stated	1	6/29/1864	Apperson, E. B. W.	$25/mo
Isham	not stated	1	1/1/1864	Minge, Dr. Jno.	$25/mo
Isham	Nurse	5	1/1/1863	Woodard. Dr. W. M.	$200/yr in 1863; $300/yr in 1864
Israel	Nurse	5	1/1/1863 - 9/1/1863	Frayser, Miss E.	$240/yr
Jack	Nurse	1	5/9/1863 - 10/1/1863	Wilkins, Maj.	dischd 10/1/1863; $240/yr; Empld in Dr. McCaw's Office
Jackson, Henry	Nurse	2	1/1/1864 - 12/1/1864	Grainor, Wm	$300/yr; Died 12/1/1864; owner scratched, then: J. W.
Jacob	Nurse	1	1/1/1863	Bagby, G. W.	$200/yr; Division 1 closed 1/1/1864
Jacob	Cook	5	1/1/1863	Kay, Joseph	$200/yr
Jacob	Nurse	5	1/1/1863	Moore, James	$200/yr
Jacob	Nurse	5	1/1/1864	Ray, Jos. W.	$300/yr
James	not stated	1	1/12/1864	Wheldon, Capt.	
James	Cook	2	1/21/1863 - 5/17/1863	Eacho, E. D.	$240/yr
James	Nurse	4	3/1/1863	Tabb, P. M. & Son	$216/yr
James	Nurse	5	1/1/1863	Frayser, Miss E.	$240/yr
James	Nurse	5	1/1/1863	Moore, James	boy; $130/yr

Virginia's Black Confederates

Name	Role		Date	Employer	Notes
James	Nurse	5	1/1/1863	Pearce, George	$200/yr
James, Daniel	Nurse	4	1/1/1864	Gwathmey, George	$300/yr
James, Ned	Nurse	3	1/1/1863	Grant, L. J.	$200/yr in 1863; $300/yr in 1864
Jamima	Cook	1	1/1/1863 - 4/18/1863	Walker, J. L.	dischd 4/18/1863; $200/yr;
Jamison, Wm.	Nurse	2	4/30/1864 - 2/1/1865	Free	Dischd. 2/1/1865
Janice	Nurse	2	12/1/1863	Tabb, P. M. & Son	Division 2 closed 1/1/1864
Jefferson, Wm.	Nurse	3	1/1/1863	Smith, Dr. E. H.	$240/yr
Jennings, Ro.	Nurse	3	1/1/1863	Grant, James H.	$200/yr
Jeper	Cook	2	1/1/1863 - 3/1/1863	Ruff, Chas.	$240/yr; dischd 3/1/1863
Jerry	Nurse	5	1/1/1863	Frayser, Miss E.	$240/yr
Jerry	Nurse	5	1/1/1863	Kay, Joseph	$200/yr
Jim	Nurse	1	1/1/1864	Alsop, Dr. G. E.	$300/yr; employed in Ward 5 in 1865
Jim	not stated	1	5/12/1864	Free	worked "for board"
Jim	Nurse	1	1/1/1864	Grant, James H.	$300/yr
Jim	not stated	1	5/19/1864	Skinner, F. G.	$25/mo
Jim	Nurse	1	2/13/1863	Trice, G. W.	$180/yr; Division 1 closed 1/1/1864
Joe	Cook	1	1/1/1863	Curtis, Robt.	boy; $180/yr; Division 1 closed 1/1/1864
Joe	Nurse	1	1/1/1864	Curtis, Robt.	$180/yr
Joe	Nurse	1	8/3/1863 - 12/1/1863	Parker, J. R.	dischd 12/1/1863; $240/yr
John	Nurse	1	1/1/1864	Eacho, E. D.	$300/yr
John	Boatman	2	1/17/1865	Lottier, Capt. L.	
John	Nurse	2	1/1/1863	Morecock, Wm. E.	boy; $192/yr; Division 2 closed 1/1/1864
John	Nurse	4	3/1/1863	Tabb, P. M. & Son	$100/yr
John	Nurse	5	1/1/1863	Pearce, George	$200/yr
John	Nurse	5	1/1/1863	Phillips, W. H.	boy; $75/yr
Johnson, Bernard	Nurse	2	1/12/1863	Royster, G. W.	boy; $180/yr; Division 2 closed 1/1/1864
Johnson, Harrison	Nurse	3	1/1/1863	Grant, James H.	$200/yr in 1863; $300/yr in 1864
Johnson, Henry	Cook	2	1/13/1863	Greanor, Wm.	$200/yr; Division 2 closed 1/1/1864
Johnson, Jno.	Nurse	2	1/1/1863	Pointer, Jno.	boy; $150/yr; Division 2 closed 1/1/1864
Johnson, Phillip	Nurse	3	1/1/1863	Moore, James	$200/yr
Johnson, Ro.	Nurse	2	1/12/1863	Royster, G. W.	boy; $180/yr; Division 2 closed 1/1/1864
Johnson, Sam	Nurse	2	1/1/1863	Pointer, J. A	$200/yr in 1863; $300/yr in 1864
Johnson, Sam	Nurse	3	1/1/1863	Grant, James H.	$200/yr
Johnson, Stephen	Nurse	2	5/1/1864	Alexander, W. F.	
Johnston, Jim	Cook	1	1/1/1863	Grant, James H.	$200/yr; Division 1 closed 1/1/1864
Johnston, Roy	Nurse	1	1/1/1863	Grant, James H.	$200/yr; Division 1 closed 1/1/1864
Jones, Tom	Nurse	2	3/25/1865	Clopton & Lyne	

Name	Role		Date	Employer	Notes
Joseph	Nurse	4	3/1/1863 - 8/1/1863	Dunn, J. L.	$216/yr
Julia	Cook	2	9/1/1864	Point, Mary G.	$25/mo
Kinney, Wm.	not stated	1	not stated	Hardgrove, T. & S.	
Kitt(?)	Nurse	5	1/1/1863	Moore, James	$200/yr
Lambert, Henry	Nurse	2	1/1/1863	Grant, James H.	$200/yr; Division 2 closed 1/1/1864
Lemuel	Nurse	5	1/1/1864	Miller, Miss	$150/yr
Levy	Nurse	1	2/26/1863 - 4/26/1863	Latimer, George	dischd 4/26/1863; $240/yr
Lewis	Nurse	1	2/13/1863	Trice, G. W.	$180/yr; Division 1 closed 1/1/1864
Lewis, John	Nurse	4	1/1/1863	Enders, John	$240/yr
Lewis, Wm.	Nurse	3	1/1/1863	Miller, Dr. H. J.	$200/yr
Lipscomb, Wm.	Cook	1	1/1/1863	Lipscomb, Wm.	$240/yr; Division 1 closed 1/1/1864
Lister, Daniel	Cook	3	1/1/1863	Grant, James H.	$200/yr
Lizzie	Nurse	2	5/16/1864 - 9/1/1864	Free	Dischd. 9/1/1864
Logan, Candace	Cook	2	1/1/1865	Free	
Logan, Henry	Nurse	3	4/1/1863	England, John L.	$240/yr
Lomax, Frank	Nurse	2	4/30/1864	Miller, D.	
Long, Henry	Nurse	2	1/1/1864	Phillips, W. S.	$300/yr
Lucy	Cook	4	1/1/1864	Ellett, Andrew	$300/yr
Lyne, James	Cook	2	1/23/1863	Lyne, Dr.	$240/yr; Division 2 closed 1/1/1864
Macon, Emanuel	Nurse	3	1/1/1863	Grant, James H.	$200/yr in 1863; $300/yr in 1864
Macon, Isham	Cook	3	1/1/1863	Grant, James H.	$200/yr
Macon, Jesse	Nurse	3	1/1/1863	Grant, James H.	$200/yr
Malberry, Beverly	Nurse	2	6/1/1864	Forrest, Jno. M.	
Malory, Alex	Nurse	3	1/1/1863	England, J. L.	$240/yr
Marcellus	Nurse	5	1/1/1863	Lewis, Mr(?). Wm.	boy; $135/yr
Marshall	Nurse	1	1/1/1863 - 2/9/1863	Smith, J. P. [Ro. B.?]	$240/yr; Division 1 closed 1/1/1864
Marsten, Stephen	Cook, Nurse, Scabinger	2	7/13/1863	Richardson, A. W.	$240/yr & Nurse in 1863; $300/yr & Cook in 1864; Scabinger in 1865
Martin	Nurse	1	1/1/1863 - 2/9/1863	Hinton, R. H.	dischd 2/9/1863; $240/yr
Martin	Nurse	2	3/24/1865	Phillips, W. S.	
Mary	Cook	3	1/1/1863	Smith, Dr. E. H.	$180/yr in 1863; $300/yr in 1864
Matthew	Nurse	4	1/1/1863	Greanor, Wm.	$200/yr
Mayo, Isaac	Cook	3	1/1/1863	Grant, James H.	$200/yr
Merrian, John	Nurse	1	1/1/1863	Grant, James H.	$200/yr; Division 1 closed 1/1/1864
Meunn(?), Jim	Nurse	2	6/29/1864 - 8/15/1864	Lea & Christian	boy; $15/mo; dischd 8/15/1864
Mills, John	Cook	2	1/1/1863	Grant, James H.	$200/yr; Division 2 closed 1/1/1864
Milton	Nurse	1	1/1/1863	Eacho, E. D.	$200/yr; Division 1 closed 1/1/1864
Mitchell, Wm.	Nurse	3	1/1/1863	Smith, Dr. E. H.	$240/yr in 1863; $400/yr in

					1864
Montague, Wm	Nurse	2	3/1/1865	Montague, S.	
Moore, Chas.	Nurse	2	1/1/1863	Moore, James	boy; $150/yr; Division 2 closed 1/1/1864
Mooter, Richard	Cook	1	1/1/1863	Pryor, P. B.	$240/yr; Division 1 closed 1/1/1864
Morris	Nurse	5	1/1/1863	Frayser, Miss E.	$240/yr
Moseley, Henry	Nurse	4	1/1/1864	Mosley, B.	$300/yr
Moses	Cook	1	1/1/1864	Warring, L. E.	$300/yr
Muse, Jeff	Cook	2	1/1/1863	Grant, James H.	$200/yr; Division 2 closed 1/1/1864
Ned	not stated	1	1/1/1865	Curtis, Mrs. E. B.	Employed in Office in 1865
Ned	Nurse	5	1/1/1863	Kay, Joseph	$200/yr
Ned	Nurse	5	8/10/1863	Thompson, Mary L.	$200/yr in 1863; $300/yr in 1864
Nelson, John	Cook	1	1/1/1863	Grant, James H.	$200/yr; Division 1 closed 1/1/1864
Nicholas, Spotswood	Nurse	3	1/1/1863	Whitlock, L. E.	$200/yr
Nick	not stated	1	4/27/1864	Inde, L. M.	$25/mo
Norwood, Henry	Nurse	3	1/1/1864	Norwood, Dr.	$300/yr
Oliver	Cook	5	1/1/1863	Woodard. Dr. W. M.	$200/yr in 1863; $300/yr in 1864
Pack, Charles O.	not stated	1	not stated	Christian & Lea	
Page, Irving (Jerry?)	Nurse	4	1/1/1864	Gwathmey, George	$300/yr
Palmer, Wm.	Nurse	3	1/1/1863	Grant, James H.	$200/yr
Pane, Jeff	Cook	2	1/1/1863	Grant, James H.	$200/yr; Division 2 closed 1/1/1864
Pankey, Thomas	Cook	3	1/1/1863	Bennett, L.	$200/yr in 1863; $300/yr in 1864; 1864 owner Q?. Bennett
Patsey	not stated	1	1/1/1864	Minge, Dr. Jno.	$25/mo
Patterson, Joseph	Cook	4	1/1/1863	Barrett, Wm. T.	$216/yr in 1863; $400/yr in 1864
Patterson, Ro.	Nurse & Cook	2	1/1/1863	Hughes, J. W.	Boy; $150/yr & Nurse in 1863; $200/yr & Cook in 1864; listed as nurse in 1865 list
Payne, Jeff	Nurse	2	1/1/1864	Grant, J. H.	$300/yr
Peter	Nurse	5	1/1/1863	Pearce, George	$200/yr
Peter, Elisha	Nurse	4	7/1/1863 - 7/1/1863	Free	$240/yr
Phil	Nurse	1	9/1/1863	Davis, W. A.	$240/yr; Division 1 closed 1/1/1864
Phil	Nurse	5	1/1/1863	Moore, James	$200/yr
Phillip	Nurse	1	1/1/1864	Davis. Geo.	$300/yr; Employed in "matrons" in 1865
Pleasants, James	Nurse	4	1/1/1863	Barrett, Wm. T.	$216/yr
Pleasants, Robert	Nurse	4	1/1/1863 - 8/1/1863	Free	$240/yr
Pleasants, Thos.	Nurse	3	1/1/1863	England, J. L.	$240/yr
Poindexter, Jesse	Nurse	3	1/1/1863	Grant, James H.	$200/yr
Poiner, Alfred	Nurse	3	1/1/1863	Poiner, Mrs. M. S.	$200/yr; Died 4/1/1863

Name	Role		Date	Owner/Employer	Notes
Polk, James	Nurse	3	1/1/1864	Snellings, Dr. Wm. Q.	$300/yr
Porter, Willis	Cook	2	1/1/1864	Porter, J. L.	$300/yr
Powell, Ro.	Nurse	3	1/1/1863	Grant, James H.	$200/yr
Price, Alex	Nurse -1863 Cook - 1864	2	1/1/1863	Clopton & Lyne	$240/yr in 1863; $300/yr in 1864
Price, Ben	Cook	2	5/23/1864 - 7/1/1864	Royster, Mrs.	Dischd. 7/1/1864
Prince	Nurse	3	1/1/1864	Washington, Dr. L.	$400/yr
Pryor, Tom (Prior?)	Nurse & Boatman	2	7/28/1864	Scott, T. W.	$300/yr & Nurse in 1864; Boatman in 1865
Quickley, Bascum	Nurse	2	1/1/1864	Williams, Mrs. M.	$300/yr; owner listed as M. A. Williamson in 1865 list
Randolph	Nurse	4	1/1/1863	Barrett, Wm. T.	boy; $192/yr
Reuben	Nurse	5	1/1/1863	Doswell, Miss T. W.	$300/yr
Richard	Nurse	4	1/1/1864	Ellett, Andrew	$60/yr; boy
Richard	Nurse	4	1/1/1863	Enders, John	$240/yr
Richard	Nurse	5	1/1/1863	Doswell, Miss T. W.	$300/yr
Richards, Ronnie(?)	Nurse	3	1/1/1863	Kay, Joseph	$200/yr in 1863; $300/yr in 1864
Richardson, James	Nurse	4	1/1/1863	Barrett, Wm. T.	$216/yr in 1863; $400/yr in 1864
Richardson, Julius	Cook	2	11/1/1864	Richmond, Turner	$25/mo
Riley, Wm.	Cook	4	1/1/1863 - 12/22/1863	Mayo, Mrs.	$216/yr
Robert	Nurse	1	1/1/1863	Alsop, Dr. G. E	boy; $180/yr; Division 1 closed 1/1/1864
Robert	not stated	1	1/1/1864	Minge, Dr. Jno.	$300/yr
Robert	Nurse	4	1/1/1863	Enders, John	$240/yr
Robert	Nurse	5	1/1/1863	Frayser, Miss E.	boy; $240/yr
Robert	Nurse	5	1/1/1863	Harwood, Mrs.	$240/yr
Robert	Nurse	5	1/1/1863	Moore, James	boy; $75/yr
Roberts, William	Nurse	3	1/1/1863	Grant, James H.	$200/yr
Robin	Nurse	3	1/1/1863	Smith, Dr. E. H.	$240/yr
Robinson, Milton	Cook	2	1/1/1863	Wilson, _	$240/yr; Division 2 closed 1/1/1864
Rones, Strother	Nurse	4	1/1/1864	Trice, G. W.	$125/yr; boy
Ruffin	Nurse	3	1/1/1863	Smith, Dr. E. H.	$240/yr in 1863; $400/yr in 1864
Ryland	Nurse	5	1/1/1864	Turpin & Yarbrough	$300/yr
Salsar	not stated	1	1/16/1863	Anderson, J. M.	$25/mo
Sam	not stated	1	1/1/1863	Browne, Dr. P. F.	$25/mo
Sam	Nurse	1	1/1/1863 - 9/1/1863	Mason, Major J. J.	dischd 9/1/1863; $240/yr; vol. 307 says commissary
Sam	not stated	1	1/1/1865	Nowland, Mrs.	Employed in Ward 2 in 1865
Sam	Nurse	1	4/1/1863	Thom, Dr.	$240/yr; Division 1 closed 1/1/1864
Sam	not stated	1	4/26/1864	Vaughan, George	$300/yr
Sam	Cook	2	1/1/1863 - 7/1/1863	Morris, B. P.	boy; $150/yr; dischd 7/1/1863

Name	Role		Date	Employer	Notes
Sam	Nurse	5	1/1/1864	Miller, Miss	$150/yr
Samuel	Cook	5	1/1/1863	Doswell, Thos. W.	$175/yr in 1863; $300/yr in 1864
Samuel	Nurse	5	1/1/1863	Moore, James	boy; $125/yr
Scott	Carpenter	1	1/1/1863	Pleasants, Mrs.	$300/yr; Division 1 closed 1/1/1864; vol 307 says owned by E. D. Eacho
Scott, Charles	Nurse	2	9/1/1864	Warner, Mary F.	boy; $15/mo
Scott, Charles	Nurse	3	1/1/1863	Bell, Mrs.	$240/yr
Scott, Jim	Nurse	2	1/1/1863	Grant, James H.	$200/yr; Division 2 closed 1/1/1864
Shadrick	Nurse	4	1/1/1863 - 11/3/1863	Bates, G. M.	$216/yr; dischd 11/3/1863
Shadrick	Nurse	5	1/1/1863	Frayser, Miss E.	boy; $240/yr
Sharp, Aaron	Nurse	4	1/1/1864	Gwathmey, George	$300/yr
Shephard, Wm.	Nurse	1	1/1/1863	Grant, James H.	$200/yr; Division 1 closed 1/1/1864
Shepheard, Ro.	Nurse	3	1/1/1863	Grant, James H.	$200/yr in 1863; $300/yr in 1864
Shepherd, Joseph	Nurse	3	1/1/1863	Grant, James H.	$200/yr
Sinton, Anderson	Nurse	2	1/1/1863	Grant, James H.	$200/yr; Division 2 closed 1/1/1864
Sinton, Geo.	Nurse	3	1/1/1863	Grant, James H.	$200/yr
Slaton, James	Nurse	4	1/1/1863	Barrett, Wm. T.	boy; $192/yr
Smith, ___	Nurse	2	4/26/1864	Phillips, W. S.	
Smith, Americus	Nurse	2	7/1/1864 - 8/3/1864	Oliver, R. W.	$25/mo; dischd 8/3/1864
Smith, Jack	Nurse	2	4/30/1864	Carter, M. L.	
Smith, Jack	Nurse	2	1/1/1865	Gates, L. L.	
Smith, Reuben	Nurse	2	2/27/1863 - 5/17/1863	Hughes, J. W.	$192/yr; dischd 5/17/1863
Snellings, Albert	Nurse	1	1/1/1863	Snellings, Dr. Wm. O.	$240/yr; Division 1 closed 1/1/1864
Snellings, Artimus	Nurse	3	1/1/1863	Snellings, Dr. Wm. Q.	boy; $240/yr in 1863; $300/yr in 1864
Snellings, Sam	Nurse	1	1/1/1863 - 2/17/1863	Snellings, Miss	$222/yr; Division 1 closed 1/1/1864
Snellings, Thomas	Nurse	3	1/1/1863	Snellings, Dr. Wm. Q.	$240/yr in 1863; $300/yr in 1864
Snelson, Allen	Nurse	4	1/1/1863	Barrett, Wm. T.	$216/yr in 1863; $400/yr in 1864
Southall, Edward	Nurse	2	1/12/1863	Royster, G. W.	boy; $180/yr; Division 2 closed 1/1/1864
Spatt, Albert	not stated	1	not stated	Snellings, Dr. Wm. O.	
Spencer	Nurse	2	2/26/1863	Clopton & Lyne	$240/yr; Division 2 closed 1/1/1864
Spencer, John	Nurse	2	5/26/1864	Dill & Myers	
Spencer, John	Cook	2	1/1/1865	Staples, W. T.	
Stephen	not stated	1	not stated	Hardgrove, T. & S.	
Street, George	Nurse	4	1/1/1863	Enders, John	$240/yr
Sweeney, Bob	Nurse	3	1/1/1864	Peake, J.	$60/mo
Syke	Nurse	3	1/1/1863	Grant, James H.	$200/yr

Virginia's Black Confederates

Name	Role		Date	Employer	Notes
Tabb, Isreal	Nurse	2	4/6/1863	Blakey, J. M.	$240/yr in 1863; $300/yr in 1864
Talley, Ben	Cook	2	1/1/1864	Clopton & Lyne	$300/yr
Taylor, Alfred	Nurse	4	1/1/1864	Gwathmey, George	$300/yr
Taylor, Billy	Cook	2	1/1/1863	Morris, B. P.	$200/yr in 1863; $300/yr in 1864
Taylor, Bradley	Cook & Nurse	2	2/1/1863	Eppes, Dr.	$200/yr & Cook in 1863; $400/yr & Nurse in 1864
Taylor, Griffin	Nurse	2	6/29/1864 - 8/20/1864	Lea & Christian	$25/mo; dischd 8/20/1864
Taylor, John	Nurse	3	1/1/1863	Smith, Dr. E. H.	$240/yr in 1863; $400/yr in 1864
Taylor, Osugill(?)	Nurse	2	5/25/1864 - 7/1/1864	Ford, James	Dischd. 7/1/1864
Tazwell, John	Nurse	4	1/1/1863	Greanor, Wm.	$200/yr
Temple	Nurse	5	1/1/1863	Gathwright, Francis	$200/yr; "With Hutson" (see Hutson, D. W., musician, above)
Temple, Adam	Nurse	1	1/1/1863	Temple, Benj.	$150/yr; Division 1 closed 1/1/1864
Temple, David	Nurse	1	1/1/1863	Temple, Benj.	$200/yr; Division 1 closed 1/1/1864
Temple, Frank	Nurse	1	1/1/1863	Temple, C. W.	$200/yr; Division 1 closed 1/1/1864
Temple, Isaac	Cook	1	1/1/1863	Temple, C. W.	$200/yr; Division 1 closed 1/1/1864
Temple, William	Nurse	1	1/1/1863	Temple, Benj.	$175/yr; Division 1 closed 1/1/1864
Thomas	not stated	1	5/19/1864	Skinner, F. G.	$25/mo
Thomas	Scabinger	2	1/1/1865	Kease(?), J. B.	
Thomas	Scabinger	2	1/17/1865	Tomblin, M. E.	
Thomas	Nurse	4	1/1/1863	Archer, Dr. J. L.	$216/yr
Thomas	Nurse	5	1/1/1863	Keesee, Jesse B.	$200/yr in 1863; $300/yr in 1864
Thomas, John	Nurse	4	1/1/1863	Barrett, Wm. T.	$216/yr
Thomas, Wm.	Cook	2	1/1/1863	Grant, James H.	$200/yr; Division 2 closed 1/1/1864
Thompson	not stated	1	5/3/1864	Westwood, W. J.	$25/mo; Employed in Ward 9 in 1865
Tinsley, Henry	Nurse	4	1/1/1864	Trice, G. W.	$300/yr
Tinsley, Jim	Nurse	4	1/1/1864	Trice, G. W.	$300/yr
Todd, Wm.	Nurse	4	1/1/1864	Wilson, Col. J. D.	$300/yr
Toddy, Ned	Nurse	4	1/1/1863	Barrett, Wm. T.	$216/yr
Tom	Nurse	1	2/20/1863	Ellett, T.	$240/yr; Division 1 closed 1/1/1864
Tomblin, Willis	Scabinger	2	1/1/1865	Turpin & Yarborough	
Tompkins, Alex	Nurse	2	1/1/1865	Tompkins, S. L.	probably the same as Alec Custis
Tompkins, Solomon	Nurse	2	1/1/1864	Tompkins, S. L.	$200/yr; misspelled last name in 1865 list
Triplett, Phillip	Nurse	2	4/26/1864	Phillips, W. S.	

Turner	Nurse	5	1/1/1864	Turpin & Yarbrough	$300/yr
Vaughan, Charlie	Nurse	4	1/1/1863	Vaughan, Miss Bettie	$96/yr in 1863; $180/yr in 1846; boy
Walker, George	Nurse	1	1/1/1863	Walker, J. L.	$240/yr; Division 1 closed 1/1/1864
Walker, Gilbert	Cook	3	1/1/1863	Grant, James H.	$200/yr
Walker, Isaac	Cook	1	1/1/1863	Walker, J. L.	$180/yr; Division 1 closed 1/1/1864
Walker, John	Nurse	4	1/1/1863	Barrett, Wm. T.	boy; $192/yr
Walker, Thompson	Nurse & Baker	3	1/1/1863 - 6/1/1863	Schmeltz, Mrs.	$300/yr; Died 6/1863
Warner	Nurse	1	1/1/1863	Grant, James H.	$200/yr in 1863; $300/yr in 1864
Washington, George	Nurse	3	1/1/1863	Smith, Dr. E. H.	$240/yr in 1863; $400/yr in 1864
Washington, James	Nurse	4	1/1/1864	Gwathmey, George	$300/yr
Washington, Jim	not stated	1	not stated	Hardgrove, T. & S.	
Washington, Jno.	Cook	2	1/1/1863	Hughes, J. W.	$200/yr in 1863; $300/yr in 1864
Watt	Nurse	2	3/24/1865	Phillips, W. S.	
West, Geo.	Nurse & Cook	2	1/1/1863	Hughes, J. W.	$200/yr & Nurse in 1863; $300/yr & Cook in 1864; listed as nurse in 1865 list
West, George	Cook	2	7/1/1864	Cansey, William	$25/mo
West, George	Nurse as Baker	3	1/1/1863	Causey, Wm	$300/yr in 1863; $60/mo in 1864
Wiley	Nurse	4	1/1/1863 - 6/1/1863	Dunn, T. R.	$216/yr
Wilkinson, Joe	Nurse	4	1/1/1864	Gwathmey, George	$300/yr
William	Nurse	1	1/1/1864	Alsop, Dr. G. E.	$300/yr
William	Cook	1	1/1/1864	Bagby, Geo. R.	$300/yr
William	Nurse	1	1/1/1864	Browne, Dr. P. F.	$300/yr
William	Nurse	1	2/24/1863 - 4/24/1863	Chewman, Mr.	dischd 4/24/1863; $240/yr
William	Nurse	1	1/1/1864	Grant, James H.	$300/yr
William	Nurse	1	1/1/1864	Lipscomb, C. B.	$400/yr; Employed in Dining Room in 1865
William	Nurse	1	5/1/1863 - 11/1/1863	Smith, E. A.	dischd 11/1/1863; $240/yr
William	not stated	1	4/27/1864	Watts, Mrs. Eliza	$25/mo
William	Nurse	2	12/1/1863	Tabb, P. M. & Son	Division 2 closed 1/1/1864
William	Cook	3	1/1/1864	Smith, Dr. E. H.	$300/yr
William	Nurse	4	1/1/1863	Greanor, Wm.	$200/yr
William	Nurse	5	1/1/1863	Bagby, T. J.	$100/yr
William	Nurse	5	1/1/1863	Starke, P. H.	$100/yr
Williams, Dandridge	Nurse	2	1/1/1863	Pointer, Jno.	$240/yr; Division 2 closed 1/1/1864
Williams, George	Nurse	4	1/1/1863	Barrett, Wm. T.	$216/yr
Willis	not stated	1	5/25/1864	Taylor, Robt.	$25/mo
Willis	Nurse	2	1/1/1863	Porter, J. L.	$240/yr; Division 2 closed 1/1/1864

Willis	Nurse	5	1/1/1863	Moore, James	$200/yr
Wilson, Isham	Nurse	3	1/1/1863	Grant, James H.	$200/yr
Winslow	not stated	1	not stated	Clopton & Lyne	
Winston	Nurse	5	1/1/1863	Tabb, P. M. & Son	$200/yr
Woodson	not stated	1	6/1/1864	Parrish, F. M.	$25/mo
Wright, Lee	Nurse	2	1/1/1863 - 9/15/1863	Nail, W. F.	$240/yr; returned to master 9/15/1863
Wright, Wm.	Scabinger	2	1/1/1865	Barrett, Wm.	
Wright, Wm.	Nurse	4	1/1/1863	Barrett, Wm. T.	$216/yr
Wyatt	Nurse	4	1/1/1863 - 12/6/1863	Dunn, T. R.	$216/yr
Young, Francis	Nurse	2	1/21/1865	Free	Dischd. 3/25/1865

Chimborazo Hospital (Library of Congress)

The Museum of the Confederacy Needs Help to Preserve Confederate History!

The Museum of the Confederacy's Eleanor Brockenbrough Archives holds hundreds of Muster Rolls, which were never abstracted into the Compiled Military Service Records contained at the National Archives. Among these are muster rolls from the Confederate Quartermaster's Department and Engineer Department which contain the names of black Southerners who worked for the Confederate War effort.

Archivist Teresa Roane says, "Conservation efforts are underway but financial help is needed to ensure conservation and preservation." She says the Mylar protectors used to help preserve the documents cost between $75 and $185 per document, depending on its size.

In order to make the collection accessible, work must begin on the monumental task of description and arrangement while placing documents in the protective Mylar.

Roane says, "The goal is to provide historians, researchers and staff with a synopsis of the document, its location within the collection, and some context for the individuals mentioned therein. This skilled, technical labor entails not only a knowledge of the war and antebellum Southern society but also, extensive experience and coursework in the practices of the Society of American Archivists."

The amount of labor for this portion is contingent upon several variables for each document. These might include the legibility of the author's handwriting; the effects of the passage of time on the ink and paper itself; and the amount of

HELP PRESERVE HISTORY - Museum of the Confederacy Archivist Teresa Roane (right) and Intern and Assistant Archivist Eric Richardson are leading the Museum's research activities on black Confederates. Roane explains there are hundreds of source materials in the pages of Quartermaster and Engineer

research necessary to contextualize the people mentioned in the documents.

Over 500 muster rolls are among papers that include items from all the major Confederate Departments. The Museum receives no monies from Federal, State or local governments. If the collection is going to survive and continue to provide new, exciting discoveries of our Nation's rich history, it needs financial support. Roane says, "We are stewards of the people's words which must be preserved for future generations. "

Civic organizations and individuals interested in helping preserve Confederate history can write checks to The Museum of the Confederacy, annotating "Archives Preservation Fund (QMD)". Mail checks to The Museum of the Confederacy, 1201 East Clay Street, Richmond, Va 23219

Photographs of Black Confederates Needed

Individuals wishing to share their photographs and information on family members who were black Confederates for the next edition of Virginia's Black Confederates may contact the The Eanes Group, LLC at 105 Guy Ave, Crewe, Va 23930.

Editor's Note: As this work was going to press, it was learned that Teresa Roane had accepted the position of Archivist for the United Daughters of the Confederacy which is headquartered in Richmond, Virginia.

The Museum of the Confederacy announced in January 2013 a partnership with the American Civil War Center at Tredegar Iron Works in Richmond. Together they will establish in 2016 the new American Civil War Museum on the Tredegar grounds.

Virginia's Black Confederates

INDEX

[Adams?], Juniper
    Mosby's Command, 36
[Hutchinson], Ben
    Cabell Teamster List. *See* 7th Regiment South Carolina
        Volunteers
[Notman], Edward
    Cabell Teamster List, *95*
[Stout], Michael
    Cabell Teamster List, *95*
2nd Va Cavalry
    Co. K, 163
5th North Carolina Cavalry
    Dove, William H., 40
    Dove, Willis, 40
    Farrington, Joe (Co. E), 40
    Lynch, William, 40
    Rudd, William, 40
Abram
    servant to Porter Alexander, 13
Abram (servant to Porter Alexander, 162
Adam
    32nd Virginia Infantry, 10
Africanus, Scipio
    Co. B, 18th Georgia Inf Battalion, 54
Albemarle County, 122
Albermarle, 121
Albert
    servant in 44th Va Infantry, 13
Albert servant in 44th Va Infantry, 162
Aldridge, Bill
    Cabell Teamster List. *See* 5th North Carolina Infantry
Alec, George
    Cabell Teamster List. *See* Seymour's Brigade
Alexander, E. Porter (General), 13, 93
Alexander, Tarleton
    at Appomattox, 27
Allen, Wilson
    Cabell Teamster List. *See* Jones' Brigade
Amelia, 121
Amelia County, 122
Amherst County, 123
Appomattox
    "lines of surrender", George Wyatt, 131
    Alexander, Tarleton, 147
    appears to have been at or near surrender, Tillman
        Majors, 134
    appears to have been at surrender, Jesse Henderson,
        139
    appears to have left at surrender, John Eggleston, 138
    at or near surrender, Richard Stewart, 131
    at surrender, 124
    at surrender, Callie Hill Estes, 140
    at surrender, Andrew Miller, 126
    at surrender, Ben Fuller Skipwith, 128
    at surrender, Benjamin Bell, 142
    at surrender, Burroughs Whitfield Johnson, 127
    at surrender, Charles Cain, 139
    at surrender, Charles Lansdown, 142
    at surrender, Charles Willis, 134
    at surrender, Clem Read Bolden, 143
    at surrender, Drew Tyler, 141
    at surrender, Edmund Johnson, 125
    at surrender, Emanuel Pollard, 134
    at surrender, Flemming Williams, 142
    at surrender, Frank Edmonds, 126
    at surrender, Frank Lee, 132
    at surrender, Fred Ford, 139
    at surrender, George Epps, 135
    at surrender, George W. Sheffield, 136
    at surrender, George Washinton Robinson, 127
    at surrender, Henry Jackson, 129
    at surrender, Henry Turpin, 137
    at surrender, Howard, Hospital Steward in service to
        Dr. John H. Claiborne, 164
    at surrender, Isaac Edmundson, 134
    at surrender, Isaac Jones, 126
    at surrender, John Anderson, 132
    at surrender, John Clark, 127
    at surrender, John Coleman, 142
    at surrender, John Moore, 127
    at surrender, John servant of Dr. John H. Claiborne, 153
    at surrender, John Williams, 132
    at surrender, Joseph Hackley, 132
    at surrender, Louis Jones, 123
    at surrender, Moses Jones, 126
    at surrender, Patrick Goode, 124
    at surrender, Peyton Coles, 141
    at surrender, Phil Turner, 142
    at surrender, Pompey Tucker, 131
    at surrender, Richard Waller, 143
    at surrender, Rufus Hawthorne, 137
    at surrender, Sam Tweedy, 127
    at surrender, Simon Jones, 126
    at surrender, Thomas Goodwyn, 139
    at surrender, William Jones, 143
    at surrender, Willliam Henry Boyd, 131
    at surrender, Wilson D. Ellis, 126
    at surrender, Wyatt Creasy, 127
    Evans, William T. (Robert E. Lee's Servant), 154
    James Price left "upon the surrender of General Lee",
        137
    left service "on account of surrender", James Willis, 134
    other black Confederates present, 63
    paroled black Confederates, 62
    possibly at surrender, George T. Glascoe, 129
    possibly at surrender, Jordan Coleman, 135
    possibly at surrender, Sam Brown, 126
    possibly at surrender, Tom Sears, 126
    possibly at surrender, Tom Shields, 126
    possibly at surrender, Walker Morgan, 127
    possibly at surrender, William Tucker (3rd Va Cav), 131
Appomattox County, 124
Armstead, Addision (laborer on breastworks)
    Denied vote, 30

Virginia's Black Confederates

Arnett, Charles
    Cabell Teamster List. *See* 1st Regiment of Georgia Regulars
Artillery, 131, 133, 134, 143, 146
    13th Battalion, Light Artillery (Davis-Chamberlayne Battery), *165*
    20th Battalion Heavy Arty, Co. A, 124, 127
    20th Battalion, Va Heavy Arty, Co. A, 124
    2nd Corps Staff, ANV, 159
    Albemarle Light Artillery, 160
    Alleghany Rough Battery, 10
    Army of Northern Virginia, 165
    Bayou's Battery, 146
    Chaffin's Bluff, 125
    1st Virginia Light Artillery, 160
    Dinwiddie Artillery, 131
    Donaldsonville Artillery, at High Bridge, 55
    E. Porter Alexander's Staff, 162
    First Corps Artillery, 142
    Goochland Light Artillery, Crutchfield's Brigade, 55
    Goochland Light Arty, 162, 163, 164, 165
    Goochland Light Arty, Talley's Co., 166
    Hamilton's Battery, Georgia Troops, 146
    Hampton's Legion, 96
    Hanover Artillery, 135
    Hupp's Battery, 143
    James City Artillery, 146
    Longstreet's Corps, 127
    Manchester Artillery, 143
    Pamunkey Artillery, 139
    Parker's Battery, 157, 165
    Powhatan Artillery, 142
    Reserve Ordnance Train, 52
    Rockbridge Artillery, 10, 135, 166
    Staunton Hill Artillery, 128
    Surry Light Artillery, 8
    Third Corps, Ordnance Train, 51
    Walker's Battery, 133
Ashby, George
    Cabell Teamster List, *97*
Ashby, Turner
    (Colonel), 150
Ashby, Turner (Colonel), 10
At Staunton River Bridge
    Murry, 40
    Ned, 40
    Oscar (Farinholt's servant), 40
    unnamed laborers, 40
At Staunton River Bridge (US)
    Farnsworth, Abram, 41
    Laurey, Samuel, 41
    Lee, George Washington (servant to General Kautz), 41
    Washington, Henry, 41
Augusta County, 124
Averall, Henry
    Cabell Teamster List. *See* 15th Georgia Regiment
Bacchus, Frank (free man)
    at High Bridge, 58

Baily, Andy (servant)
    7th Georgia Infantry, 15
Banks, Solomon, 149
Barney, Addison
    Cabell Teamster List. *See* Simm's Brigade
Battle
    Big Bethel, 160
    Big Bethel, 73, 74
    Brandy Station, 10, *159*
    Bull Run, 134
    Deatonsville, 56
    Drewry's Bluff, 125
    First Manassas, 10, 17, 74, 77, 94, 129
    Fredericksburg, 132
    Gaines' Mill, 74
    Gettysburg, 13, 14, 15, 21, 128, 136, 137, 158, *159*
    Hunter's Raid, 125
    Leesburg, 15
    Manassas, 122, 124, 158
    Mt. [Cedar?] Hill, 127
    Nottoway Court House (also known as 'the Grove'), 41
    Petersburg, 13, 158
    Ream's Station, 46
    Sailor's Creek, black experiences, 49
    Seven Pines, 145
    Spotsylvania (Levi Miller), *158*
    Staunton River Bridge, 40
    Valley Campaign, 17
    Wilson's Creek, 18
Bean, William (cook)
    7th Va Cavalry, 150
Beauregard, P.G.T. (General), 94
Bedford County, 121, 124
Ben
    Cabell Teamster List. *See* 1st Mississippi Regiment
    Free man, servant to F.S. Robertson, 52
Beverly, Rubin
    Cabell Teamster List, *98*
Billy
    servant to Gen. Thomas T. Munford, 10
Billy
    servant to Gen. Thomas T. Munford, 163
Black Confederate
    a definition, v, 2
    as defense contractors, 31
    as substitutes in Confederate units, 57
    pay for certain jobs, 9, 11
    pay if conscripted by 1864 Act, 11
    recognition as veterans, 24
    reunion of black Confederate veterans, 26
    servant responsibilities in the company, 12
Black Confederate Units
    black teamsters defend river crossing, Gettysburg Campaign, 93
    Confederate States Colored Troops, 61
    infantry company at Capitol Square, 74
    Jackson Hospital Battalion, 55
    Major Chambliss' Negro Battalion, 55

Virginia's Black Confederates

Pegram-Turner Negro Brigade, 56
Black Confederates in battle
    Dick Slate at First Manassas, 77
Black Confederates in Battle
    see individual index entries for Killed, Wounded in Action, and Prisoner of War and by battle name, 77
Black Hawk, John (servant)
    Servant to Colonel Turner Ashby, 150
Blaine, Nick (black soldier)
    at UCV Reunion, 26
Bland County, 125
Bloke, Joe (servant)
    7th Georgia Infantry, 15
Blum, H.
    Donaldsonville Artillery, 55
Bob
    Cabell Teamster List, *95*, See 7th Regiment South Carolina Volunteers
    Free man, servant to F.S. Robertson, 52
    slave of Tom Campbell, 43
Booker, Branch, 52
Booker, Henry, 52
Boutetourt County, 125
Breastworks, 122, 126, 127, 130, 132, 133, 136, 152
    around Richmond, 136, 137
    Artillery, 122, 124, 125, 126, 127, 141
    Artillery, near Richmond, 133
    Artillery, Petersburg, 127
    undetermined, 122
    Blandford, 131
    Chaffin's Bluff, 125, 126
    Chaffin's Bluff, Richmond, Peterburg,, 144
    Chaffin's Farm, 138
    Chapin Farm, 135
    Chesterfield County, 128
    Chickahominy Swamp, 126, 127, 133, 143
    Chickahominy Swamp and Mattoax, 122
    Chickahominy Swamp, Richmond and Petersburg, 144
    Chula and Mattoax, 123
    Craney Island, 79
    Days Neck, Isle of Wight County, 145
    Dinwiddie, 124
    Drewry's Bluff, 123, 125, 126, 127, 128, 133, 134, 135, 137, 138, 141, 142, 144
    Drewry's Bluff, around Richmond, 139
    Drewry's Bluff, Clifton Farm, 138
    Drewry's Bluff, Petersburg, Richmond, 128
    Fulton, Camp Winder, 142
    Gordonsville, 138
    Greenfield, 141
    Hanover Junction, 126
    Henrico County, 122
    High Bridge, 124
    High Bridge and Chula, 122
    Infantry, 138
    James River, around Richmond, 138
    Jamestown, 145, 162
    Lynchburg, 126
    Manassas, 123, 124, 137
    Manassas Gap, Drewy's Bluff, 137
    Manassas Junction, 140
    Manchester, Richmond, 132
    Mattoax, 123
    Mechanicsville Turnpike, 135
    Mulberry Island, 123, 127, 134
    near Richmond, 137, 139
    Petersburg, 124, 133, 141, 143
    Prince Edward County, 133
    Prince George, 141
    Richmond, 123, 124, 125, 126, 129, 130, 132, 133, 135, 138, 141, 143, 144
    Richmond,, 143
    Richmond, Danville, 141
    Richmond, Petersburg, 137
    Richmond, Petersburg and Lynchburg, 123
    Staunton River Bridge, 128, 134
    undetermined, 122, 123
    Walker's Mountain, 146
    Weldon, NC, 139
    Williamsburg and Mechanicsville, 123
    Yorktown, 122
Breckinridge Hospital (Marion, Va), 151
Brent, Richard
    Cabell Teamster List, *97*
Brogden, George (free man)
    at High Bridge, *59*
Brook, Henry
    Cabell Teamster List. *See* Simm's Brigade
Brooks, Ned
    Cabell Teamster List. *See* Longstreet's Brigade
Brown, Joe
    Cabell Teamster List. *See* Longstreet's Brigade
Brown, Ludwell, 78
Brunswick County, 125
Buchanan County, 126
Buckingham County, 126
Burks, Hubbert (frre man)
    at High Bridge, 58
Burton, Aaron
    Mosby's Command, 33
Burwell, Carter (aka Burrell)
    32nd Virginia Infantry, 10
Burying dead, 124
Butler, Billy
    Cabell Teamster List. *See* Longstreet's Brigade
Butler, Harrison
    Cabell Teamster List. *See* 5th North Carolina Infantry
Butler, Wm [William]
    Longstreet's Brigade, *98*
Cabell Teamster list, 97
Cabell Teamster List, 95, 96, 97, 98, 99
Cabell, William L. (Major)
    Quartermaster for CS Army of the Potomac, 94
Camp Lee, 121
Campbell County, 126
Capps, Moses

Virginia's Black Confederates

Craney Island List, *82*
Capps, William
    Craney Island List, *82*
Carney, John
    Craney Island List, *82*
Carney, Willis
    Craney Island List, *82*
Caroline County, 127, 164, 165
Caroll County, 121
Carroll County, 121
Carter, French
    Cabell Teamster List, *98*
Carter, Thomas
    Cabell Teamster List. See 15th Georgia Regiment
Carter, Wash
    Cabell Teamster List. See 5th north Carolina Infantry
Carter, Welan
    Cabell Teamster List. See
Cavalry, 123, 126, 127, 128, 129, 130, 131, 132, 133, 135, 136, 140, 141, 142, 143, 145
    10th Va, Co. E (2nd), 123
    12th Va, Co. B, Baylor Light Horse, 156, 160, 161, 162, 165
    12th Va, Co. H, 157, 161
    12th Va, Co. I. *See*
    12th Virginia, Co. B, 10
    13th Va, 145
    13th Va, Co. A, Southampton Cavalry, 145
    13th Va, Co. B, Petersburg Cavalry, 143
    13th Va, Co. G, Surry Cavalry, 145
    13th Va, Co. G, Surry Cavalry, 145
    13th Va, Co. H, Sussex Light Dragoons, 159
    13th Virginia, Co. H, 164
    15th Va, Co. C (formerly Co C, 14th Battalion Va Cav, Princess Anne Cavalry), 154
    19th Va, Co. B, 140
    1st Tennessee, Co. A, Forrest's Cavalry Division, 28
    1st Va, Co. C, Rockbridge Dragoons, 156
    1st Va, Co. G, Amelia Light Dragoons, 123
    23rd Texas, Co. K, 19
    23rd Va, staff. *See*
    24th Tennessee, Co. F, 160
    24th Va, 146
    2nd Va, 125, 163
    2nd Va, Co. I, Campbell Rangers, 126
    37th Virginia, 166
    3rd Va, 131, 137, 153, 160, 161
    3rd Va, Co H, Catawba Troop, 131, 134
    3rd Va, Co K, Prince Edward Dragoons, 122
    3rd Va, Co. A, Boydton Cavalry, 137
    3rd Va, Co. C, Black Walnut Dragoons (Halifax Co), 128, 134, 152, 154, 161
    3rd Va, Co. D, Charles City Light Dragoons, 142, 161
    3rd Va, Co. E, Nottoway Troop, 139
    3rd Va, Co. I, 131, 138, 145
    43rd Battalion (Mosby's Partisan Rangers), 146
    4th Va, 142
    4th Va, Co D, Little Fork Rangers, 129
    4th Va, Co. B, Prince William Cavalry, 127
    4th Va, Co. G, Randolph Cavalry, 135
    4th Va, Co. G, Randolph Cavalry, 135
    4th Va, Co. H, Black Horse Troop, 134
    5th North Carolina (Barringer's Brigade), 39
    5th Va, Co. A, Princess Anne Cavalry, 134
    5th Va, Co. B, 165
    5th Va, Co. E, King and Queen Cavalry, 136
    5th Va, Co. E, Surry Cavalry, 144
    5th Va, Co. F, Prince George Cavalry, 142
    6th Va, 134
    6th Va, Co. K, 124
    7th Va, 150
    7th Va, Co. A, Mountain Rangers (Fauquier Co), 155
    7th Va, Co. H, 10, 157, 161
    8th Va, Co. H, Tazewell Troop, 145
    9th Kentucky, 145
    9th Va, 15, 134, 136
    9th Va, Co B, Caroline Light Dragoons, 127
    9th Va, Co. D, Lancaster Cavalry, 136
    9th Va, Co. F, Essex Light Dragoons, 132, 135
    9th Va, Co. K, Richmond County Cavalry, 162
    Gen James Dearing's Provost Guard, 123
    Hampton's Legion, 96
    Laurel Brigade, 9
    Thomas T. Munford's staff, 163
Cavalry (JEB Stuart's staff), 164, 166
Champ, Alfred
    Cabell Teamster List. See Longstreet's Brigade, See 15th Georgia Regiment
Champ, Burchase
    Cabell Teamster List. See Longstreet's Brigade
Charles
    Cabell Teamster List, *95*
Charles City County, 127, 162
Charlotte County, 121, 127, 164, 165
Chesterfield County, 128
Chimborazo Hospital, 150
Chimborazo Hospital No. 2, 151
Chrisman, Oliver
    32nd Virginia Infantry, 10
Chulle, William
    Craney Island List, *82*
Clayton, Edward
    Craney Island Roster, *82*
<u>Cleapor, Charles</u>
    <u>Confederate Navy</u>, 54
Cleaveland, Adam
    Cabell Teamster List. See 15th Georgia Regiment
Cole, George Washington ("Confederate veteran")
    at UCV Reunion, 26
Cole, Jim
    Cabell Teamster List. See Jones' Brigade
Coleman, Dw T.
    Craney Island List, *82*
Coles, Peyton (servant)
    at high Bridge, *60*
Colson, Jacob

Virginia's Black Confederates

Cabell Teamster List. *See* Simm's Brigade
Commissary Department, 121, 152
    Laborer, unloading railroad cars, 148
    Servant, 129
    Servant to Capt R.W. Talley, 1st Va Inf, 142
    Teamster, 125, 127, 138, 142
    Teamster (collected provisions for army), 140
    Teamster (collecting cattle), 132
    Teamster (collecting provisions, hauling supplies), 131
    Teamster (drove cattle, collected supplies), 140
    Teamster (haul forage and supplies), 138
    Teamster (hauled rations to the field), 136
    Teamster (hauled saltpeter), 140
    Teamster (hauling lumber), 130
Commissary wagon
    7th Va Infantry, 130
Confederate Certificates of Service
    honorable discharge certificates, 113
Confederate Navy, 55, 153
    Ashton, Samuel (blockade runner), 148
    Batts, Gloster (blocakde runner), 149
    Berryman, William (blockade runner), 104, 150
    Cleapor, Charles, 54
    Cook, Richard, 29
    Craney Island, 79
    CSS Virginia, 79, 81
    Davis, Samuel, 29, 153
    Fields, James Emmett (Pensioner), 142
    Gosport Navy Yard, 79
    Harris, Thomas (blockade runner), 155
    Harrison, P. (blockade runner), 155
    Heck, J., 55
    Henry, Henry (blockade runner), 155
    Johnston, Joseph, 54
    King, Lomax (blockade runner), 156
    Lewis, John (probable blockade runner), 157
    Terry, C.P., 55
Cook, Richard
    Confederate Navy, 29
Cooper, John
    Craney Island List, *82*
Cousins, Henry
    Mahone's Brigade, 153
Cousins, Jordan (free man)
    Contract laborers and carpenter, 56
Craney Island
    black experience at, 79
Craney Island List, 82, 83
Crocker, William
    Craney Island List, *82*
Crowley, Charley, 50
Culpeper County, 129
Cumberland County, 130, 144
Daniel
    Cabell Teamster List, *95*
Danville, 131, 148, 164
Davenport, Alexander (free man)
    at High Bridge and Staunton River, *60*

Davis, R.(free man)
    at High Bridge, *58*
Davis, Samuel
    Confederate Navy, 29
Deans, Henry
    Craney Island List, *82*
Deans, Jesse
    Craney Island List, *82*
Deans, John
    Craney Island List, *82*
Deans, Moses
    Craney Island List, *82*
Deans, Phillip
    Craney Island List, *82*
Deans, Shafer (or Shafir)
    Craney Island List, *82*
Denied Pension
    Bundie (Bundy), Rybune L., 121
    Canaday, Wilmore, 121
    Cubbage, David, 121
    Davis, George W., 121
    Goff, James, 121
    Gordon, Jack, 121
    Hackney, Joseph, 121
    Jenkins, J.E., 121
    Madesis, Charles H., 121
    Madison, Charles H., 121
    Marshall, James Leonard, 121
    Marshall, Levi, 121
    Pullen, Thomas, 121
    Slaughter, Charles, 121
    Talbert, W.H., 121
    Washington, Richard, 121
    Webster, Robert, 121
Dennis, Jas (James)
    Craney Island List, *82*
Denny, Wash
    Cabell Teamster List. *See* Longstreet's Brigade
Desmul, S. (free man)
    at High Bridge, *58*
Dinwiddie, 131
Discharge Papers
    Price, George (Free Man), Fifer, 18th Va Infantry, 116
    Smith, G.W., Slave, Cook, Company C, 32nd Va Infantry, 117
Dispatch Rider
    Broady, 123
Douglass, Frederick, 5
Drakes Branch, 121
Dublin, 125
Dublin Depot, 150
Dublin, Va, 121
Duke, William
    Craney Island List, *82*
Dunaway, Wayland Fuller (Captain)
    40th Va Infantry, Co. I, 7
Edward
    Cabell Teamster List. *See* 5th Alabama Regiment

Virginia's Black Confederates

Edward (servant)
   2nd Virginia Cavalry, 163
   in Leesburg Cavalry engagement, 15
Eli
   Cabell Teamster List. *See* 1st Georgia Regiment
Elizabeth City, 131
Elkton, Va, 121
Elliott, Alex
   Craney Island List, *82*
Elliott, Zacky [Zachary]
   Craney Island List, *82*
Emory Hospital, 152
Engineer Corps
   1st Regiment, 51
   3rd Regiment, 147, 150, 154
   Artillery battery construction, 125
   laborers at High Bridge,, 57
Engineer Department, 125
Engineers Corps
   Col. T.M.R Talcott, 79
Essex, 121
Essex County, 132
Estes, Callie Hill (Photo), 140
Evans, Willaim (servant), 13
Evans, William (servant)
   44th Va Infantry, 154
Ezekiel (free man)
   32nd Virginia Infantry, 10
Fairfax County, 132, *159*
Farmville Hospital, 122
Farmville, Va, 122
Field Hospital (Sailor's Creek Battlefield), 123
Field, Charles
   Cabell Teamster List, *98*
Figg, Royall W. (Parker Artillery)
   Unit Historian, 6
Floyd County, 132
Fluvanna County, 132
Ford, Carter
   Mosby's Command, 38
Fort Monroe, 128
Frank
   Cabell Teamster List. *See* 1st Mississippi Regiment
Franklin County, 121, 133
Frederick County, 133
Fredericksburg, 133
Free man
   Peters, Samuel, 143
Free Man
   Adkins, William, 147
   Alexander, Hugh, 147
   Allen, George, 147
   Allen, Mike, 147
   Allen, Samuel, 147
   Allen, Simon, 147
   Allen, William, 147
   Allison, Elbert, 147
   Allison, Isaac, 147

Alvah, Vinton, 147
Anderson, Edward, 148
Anderson, Garnett, 148
Anderson, Peter W., 122
Arrington, Angus, 137
Ashton, John, 146
Askins, William, 148
Atkins, Allen, 148
Atkins, J., 148
Austin, Beverly, 148
Bailey, James, 148
Bailey, Jason, 148
Bailey, Thomas, 148
Bainwright, Jesse, 148
Bainwright, John, 148
Baker, Abraham, 148
Baker, W.J., 148
Baley, Layton, 149
Ball, George, 149
Banks, Solomon, 149
Bannister, Frank, 149
Bannister, Isaac, 149
Bannister, J. William, 149
Barrett, Tim, 149
Bartlett, Henry, 149
Beckley, Mortimer, 150
Ben, 52
Ben (last name unknown), 162
Beverley, Sylv., 150
Beverley, W.P., 150
Beverley, William, 150
Beverly, Andrew, 150
Beverly, Edward, 150
Bias, Wyatt, 150
Bird, Ambrose, 167
Blackburn, Robert, 150
Bob, 52
Bob (last name unknown), 163
Bock, Alexander, 151
Boone, Anthony, 138
Boone, Jason, 139
Botts, William, 151
Bowser, Henry, 151
Bowyer, Bean M., 150
Brayboy, James, 151
Broadway, William, 151
Brogden, George, 59
Brooks, Albert, 103
Brown, Jesse, 151
Brown, S.T., 127
Brown, Sam, 151
Brown, William, 151
Bruce, William, 151
Bundie, Rybune L, 121
Burnett, Bolen (Bolin), 151
Burton, Carbury, 152
Byers, Essex, 152
Carter, William, 152

Chavers, John, 152
Chavers, William, 107, 152
Chavis, Thomas, 152
Chevus, Ervin, 152
Clayton, Edward, 82
Cole, William, 153
Comfort, Wilson, 139
Cousins, Jordan, 56, 153
Cox, George, 167
Coy, William, 146
Craig, Jasper, 153
Creasy, first name unknown, father of Wyatt Creasy, 126
Crump, George, 130
Davenport, Alex, 60
Davenport, Alexander D., 134
Davenport, Melvin, 167
David (last name uknown), 167
Davidson, Nathan, 144
Day, John, 143
Deans, Shafer, 82
Delaney, McDowel, 130
Dix, Austin, 111, 154
Elbert, Allison, 154
Elliott, Alex, 82
Evans, William T. (Robert E. Lee's Servant), 154
Ezekial, 10
Ezekiel, 109, 154
Fleming, George, 141
Ford, Tom, 154
Frank (last name unknown), 167
Gallahan, Joe M., 145
Garison, Caleb, 82
Giles, Daniel, 155
Godfrey, J.W., 132
Hall, William, 155
Harris, Edward, 136
Harris, Henry, 167
Harris, Horatio, 167
Harris, Oratio, 167
Harris, Phillips, 155
Harris, William, 138
Harrison, 95
Hassell, Joe, 155
Henly, John, 155
Henry, 167
Henry (last name unknown), 164
Hill, William, 145
Holland, Caleb, 82
Holland, Henry, 155
Howell, David, 155
Howell, Richard, 128
Hughes, Henry, 156
Humble, James, 107
Jack, 96
James, Corneilius, 156
James, Henry, 156
James, John, 145
Jamison, William, 167
Jim (last name unknown), 167
Johnson, Edmund, 125
Johnson, Frank, 156
Jones, Arnise, 82
Kelley, Thomas, 156
Langley, William, 82
Lewis, Preston, 157
Lipscomb, William, 130
Lynch, Robert, 157
Martin, Silas, 123
Mayo, Edward, 143
Mayo, Henry (of Powhatan County), 157
Mayo, Tom, 157
McMannaway, John A., 144
Meade, John, 125
Morris, Edward, 158
Mosby, James, *158*
Moss, Tobe, 146
Norris, Joseph Preston, 65
Owens, William, 82
Page, Samuel, 124
Perkins, John, 82
Peter, Elisha, 167
Peters, Paul, 123
Peters, Samuel, 159
Pleasants, Robert, 167
Price, George, 111
Rains, Burwell, 96
Rivers, Freeman, 125
Roberts, Cope, 145
Scott (last name unknown), 166
Scott, Benjamin, 73, 160
Scruggs, William T., 123
see 18th Virginia Roster, 111
see Craney Island list, 82
see High Bridge List, 58
see Power of Attorney (Powhatan County), 101
Servant, Frank, 160
Slate, Dick, 77, 111
Smith, Charles, 161
Smith, John, 82
Stewart, Richard, 64, 131
Taylor, James, 161
Tucker, William, 131
Tyler, George, Jr., 161
Tyler, Robert, 162
Valentine, Jim, 138
Ward, Charles, 97
Williams, George, 99
Young, Francis, 167
Free Woman
Bartlett, Martha, 149
Bragg, Martha, 150
Candis (last name unknown), 167
Green, Ann, 155
Lizzie (last name unknown), 167
Logan, Candace, 167

Fremantle, Arthur (British Colonel), 14
Fuller, William
   Craney Island List, *82*
Gardeen, Louis
   Co. C, 18th Georgia Inf Battalion, 54
Garrison, Caleb
   Craney Island List, *82*
George
   32nd Virginia Infantry, 10
George (servant)
   2nd Corps, ANV, 164
Gibson, George
   Cabell Teamster List, *98*
Gloucestor County, 134
Gloucestor, Va
   Ware District, 153
Godman, James, 48
Goins, Ben (free man)
   at High Bridge, *58*
Goochland County, 134
Gordon, Jim
   Craney Island List, *82*
Gordonsville, Va, 122
Gowin, Thomas
   Cabell Teamster List, *98*
Graves, Lewis
   Craney Island List, *82*
Gray, Elas (free man)
   at High Bridge, *58*
Gray, John
   Cabell Teamster List, *97*
Green, Charles
   Cabell Teamster List. *See* Early's Brigade
Green, Silas, 78
Greene County, 134
Griffin
   slave of Tom Campbell, 43
Grimes, Godfrey
   Craney Island List, *82*
Grimes, John
   Craney Island List, *82*
Guard, 124
Gustin
   32nd Virginia Infantry, 10
Halifax, 166
Halifax County, 134
Ham, Lewis
   Craney Island List, *82*
Ham, Luke
   Craney Island List, *83*
Hampton Roads Peace Conference, 153
Hannah
   at Appomattox, *62*
Hanover County, 135
Harris, John W. (servant)
   at High Bridge, *59*
Harrison
   Cabell Teamster List. *See* 7th Regiment South Carolina Volunteers
Harrison, George F.
   Mosby's Command, 37
Harrison, James
   Cabell Teamster List. *See* Ewell's Brigade
Harry
   Cabell Teamster List. *See* 2nd North Carolina Regiment
Haywood (servant)
   23rd Texas Cavalry, Co. K, 19
Heck, J.
   Confederate Navy, 55
Henderson, Forest
   Cabell Teamster List. *See* Jones' Brigade
Henrico County, 135
Henry
   Mosby's Command, 36
Henry County, 135
High Bridge
   black Confederate experience, 57
   Black Confederate Guards, 57
High Bridge, Va, 121
Hill, Booker (free man)
   at High Bridge, *58*
Hill, Lewis
   Cabell Teamster List. *See* Early's Brigade
Hillary, John
   Craney Island List, *83*
Hillsville, Va, 121
Hinton, Izreal
   Cabell Teamster List. *See* 4th North Carolina Infantry Regiment
Hoi, Ed
   Cabell Teamster List. *See* 5th North Carolina Infantry
Holland, Caleb
   Craney Island List, *82*
Holliday, Theodore W.
   Craney Island List, *83*
Homes, E. (free man)
   at High Bridge, *58*
Hostler, 139
Howard, Jake
   Cabell Teamster List. *See* 15th Georgia Regiment
Huger, Benjamin (General), 80
Hunt, Gabe, 78
Imboden, John D. (General), 93
Infantry, 123, 124, 126, 128, 130, 132, 137, 138, 143, 144, 145, 146
   "under Beauregard", 127
   10th Alabama, 5
   10th Va, Capt Rippoto's Company, 121
   10th Va, Co. L, Jeff Davis Guards, 130
   11th Va, Co. C, Clifton Greys, 127
   12th Battalion [Regt], Co. D, 127
   12th Georgia Infantry, Doles-Cook Brigade, 52, 53
   12th Georgia, Co. G, Doles-Cook Brigade, 52
   12th Mississippi Brigade, 97
   12th Tennessee, 149

12th Va, Co. I, 131
13th Mississippi Infantry, Co. B, 150
13th NC, 99
13th Va, 139
13th Va, Co. D, Louisa Blues, 136
13th Va, Co. F, Barboursville Guards, 137
14th Mississippi, 156
14th Va, Co. F, Chambliss Grays, 138
15th Georgia, 97
15th Georgia Infantry, Co. C, 150
15th Va, Co. C, Patrick Henry Rifles, 135
15th Va, Co. H, 73
15th Virginia, *160*
16th Mississippi, 124
16th Va, Co. I, Manchester Artillery, 157
16th Virginia Co. H, 162
17th Texas, Co. K, 158
17th Va, Co. D, Fairfax Riflemen, 156
18th Georgia, 54
18th Va, 77, 95, 111, 154, 160
1st Battalion Va Reserves, Co. G, Capt Abram L. Stiff's Company, 125
1st Georgia, 97, 99
1st Mississippi, 99
1st NC, 97
1st Va Reserves, 57
1st Va Reserves, Co. H (Amelia Reserves), 57, 60, 122
1st Va Reserves, Co. I (Powhatan Reserves), 57
1st Va, Commissary, 142
1st Virginia Reserves, Co. F (Nottoway Reserves), 57
20th Va Infantry, Co. F, Jeff Davis Guard (Powhatan County), 126
21st Va, Co. C, Oliver Greys, 137
22nd Va Bn, Co. H, 132
22nd Virginia Infantry, Co. H, 72
22nd Virginia, Co. H, 159
24th Va, 99
25th Battalion (Richmond or City Bn), Co. H, 155
25th Battalion Va Inf (Richmond or City Battalion), Co. E, 154
25th Bb, Co. A, 162
25th Bn, Co F (President's Guard), 164
25th Bn, Co. A, 163, 164, 165, 166
25th Bn, Co. B, 164
25th Bn, Co. F, 166
25th Bn, Co. G, 164, 166
25th Bn, Co. G, Richmond City Battalion, 164
25th Va (Richmond City) Battalion, 152
25th Va (Richmond City) Battalion, Co. C, 152
25th Va Bn, Co. G, 162
26th Va, Co. B (2), Gloucestor Grays, 134
27th Va, 160
29th Va, Co. G, 139
2nd NC, 96, 97
30th Infantry, Co. E, Caroline Grays, 145
30th Va, 132
31st Alabama, Co. A, 161
32nd Va, 7, 166

32nd Va Infantry, 2nd Co. I, 153
32nd Va, 2nd Co. K, 165
32nd Va, 2nd Company H, 152
32nd Va, Co. A, Wythe Rifles, 162
32nd Va, Co. C, 158, 161
32nd Va, Co. E, Hampton Greys, 159, 162
32nd Va, Co. F, 164, 166
32nd Va, Co. H, 152
32nd Va, Co. H(2), 156
32nd Va, Co. I, 161
32nd Va, Co. I (2nd), 152, 162
32nd Va, Co. I and K, 154
32nd Va, Co. K(2), 152
32nd Virginia, Co. E, 161
32nd, Co. I (2nd), 166
36th Va, 155
37th Va Inf, Co. A, Goodson Rifles, 133
38th Va, 132
38th Va, Co. C, Laurel Grove Riflemen, 153
38th Va, Co. K, Cascade Rifles, 140
3rd Georgia Battalion, 98
3rd Va Reserves, Co. I Appomattox Reserves, 60
3rd Va Reserves, Co. I, Appomattox Reserves, 124
3rd Va, Co. A, Dismal Swamp Rangers, 150, 152
40th Va, 136
40th Va, Co. C, Heathsville Guards, 139
40th Va, Co. D, 165
40th Va, Co. G, Northumberland Rifles, 134
40th Va, Co. I, 7, 162
41st Va, Co. B, Confederate Grays, 131
41st Va, Co. E, 165
42nd Va, Co. F, 127
44th Battalion, 155
44th Va, 13, 154, 162
44th Va, Co. A, Appomattox Invincibles, 124
44th Va, Co. I, Mossingford Rifles, 128
46th Va, Co. I, 162
46th Va, Co. K, 156
47th Va, 136
47th Va, Co. A, 133
48th Va, 163, 166
48th Va, Co. I, Mountain Marksmen, 162
48th Va, Mahone's Brigade, 52
49th Va, Co. A, Ewell Guards, 132, 164
49th Va, Co. C, Fauquier Guards, 160
4th Alabama, Co. E, 162
4th North Carolina, 97
50th Georgia, 160
53rd North Carolina, Grime's Brigade, 52
53rd Va, Co. A, Halifax Light Infantry, 134
53rd Va, Co. C, Old Dominion Riflemen, 121
53rd Va, Co. K, Charles City Southern Guards, 127
54th Va, Co G, 121
54th Va, Co. E, 138
54th Va, Co. H, 126
55th Va, Co. D, Essex Davis Rifles, 132
56th Alabama, Co. C, 146
56th Va, Co. G, Charlotte Defenders, 157

57th Va, Co. A, Jeff Davis Guard, 126
58th Va, Co. D, 121, 144
5th Alabama, 95
5th Alabama, Co. C, 146
5th Bn, Co A, Brunswick Guard, 125
5th North Carolina, 96, 97
5th North Carolina, Co. B, 149
5th North Carolina, Co. I, 151
5th North Carolina, Co. M, 165
5th Texas Infantry, Co. C, 32, 133
5th Texas, Company C, *158*
61st Va, Co. D, Jackson Light Infantry, 161
61st Va, Co. F, 164
6th Alabama, 96
6th Alabama, Home Guard, 146
6th South Carolina, Bratton's Brigade, 53
7th Georgia, 15
7th South Carolina Vols, 95
7th Va, 122
7th Va (commissary), 130
7th Va Infantry, staff, 137
7th Va, Co. A, Richardson Guards, 132, 137
7th Va, Co. D, Giles Volunteers, 163
9th Infantry, (1st) Co. A (Salem Flying Artillery), 156
9th Va, Co. I, 131
Bushrod Johnson's Division, Wise's Brigade, 50
Co. G, 25th Bn, 165
Drewry's Bluff, 131
Early's Brigade, 96
Early's Division, 149
Emaus Home Guard, Capt David M. Newsom, 124
Ewell's Brigade, 96, 97
Field's Division, Anderson's Brigade (CSA), 50
Floyd's Brigade, *158*
Gen. A.P Hill's Staff, 129
Hackney, Joseph, 121
Hampton's Legion, 96
Jones' Brigade, 96
Longstreet's Brigade, 97, 98
Longstreet's Staff, 50
Louisiana Brigade, 51
Ordnance Reserve Department, Army of Northern Virginia, 151
Pickett's Division, Hunton's Brigade, 50
Quartermaster Dept, 133
Seymour's Brigade, 97
Simm's Brigade, 97
Special Louisiana Battalion (1861), 74
Teamster, 124, 133, 142
Texas Battalion, 99
Va. Local Defense Troops, 2nd Quartermaster Battalion, 132
Va. Local Defense Troops, Richmond City Battalion, Co. B, 126
Washington, Richard, 121
Webster, Robert, 121
Injuries
   broken leg, 121

frostbite, 126
Jack
   Cabell Teamster List. See Simm's Brigade
Jackson, Lewis
   Cabell Teamster List, *98*
Jackson, Madison
   Cabell Teamster List. See Early's Brigade
Jackson, Sam
   Cabell Teamster List. See 15th Georgia Regiment
Jackson, Wm [William]
   Cabell Teamster List. See Simm's Brigade
James City County, 121, 136
James, George
   Craney Island List, *83*
Jerdon, Earl (servant)
   Nathan Bedford Forrest's Command, 14
Jerry
   Cabell Teamster List. See 17th Regiment Mississippi Volunteers
Jesse
   Cabell Teamster List, *95*
Jetersville, Va, 122, 123
Jim
   Cabell Teamster list. See 6th Alabama Regiment
   Cabell Teamster List, *95*, See 5th Alabama Regiment
Joe
   Cabell Teamster List. See 1st Missippi Regiment
John
   Cabell Teamster List. See 1st Mississippi Regiment, See 1st Georgia Regiment
John (Black Hawk)
   Turner Ashby's HQs cook, 10
John, W. (free man)
   at High Bridge, *58*
John, W.V. (free man)
   at High Bridge, *58*
Johnson, Gary
   Cabell Teamster List, *98*
Johnson, Henry
   Cabell Teamster List. See 15th Georgia Regiment
Johnson, Joseph (free man)
   at High Bridge, *58*
Johnson, Lewis
   Craney Island List, *83*
Johnson, Manuel
   Cabell Teamster List. See Jones' Brigade
Johnson, Sam
   Cabell Teamster List. See Longstreet's Brigade
Johnson, Sandy
   Cabell Teamster List. See Longstreet's Brigade
Johnson, Theo [Theodore]
   Craney Island List, *83*
Johnston, Joseph
   Confederate Navy, 54
Johnston, Joseph E. (General), 122
Jones, Albert (free man)
   at High Bridge, *58*
Jones, Anthony

Virginia's Black Confederates

    Cabell Teamster List, *97*
Jones, Arnise
    Craney Island List, *82*
Jones, Daniel
    Cabell Teamster List. *See* Jones' Brigade
Jones, Henry
    Cabell Teamster List, *97*
Jones, William
    32nd Virginia Infantry, 10
Jordan's Furnace, 121
Jordan's Spring Hospital, Va., 151
Joshua
    Servant to General Henry Wise, 50
Kean, Aleck
    2nd Company Richmond Howitzers, 51
Kemper, James Lawson (General), 137
Kian, Hillory
    Cabell Teamster List. *See* Hampton's Legion
Killed or Died of Disease or Injury
    Abraham, 162
    Alsop, Tom, 167
    Austen, 162
    Ball, George, 149
    Brown, Phil, 167
    Dallas, Moses, 18
    Elijah, 163
    Eppes, William, 167
    Godman, James (Teamster), 48
    Haywood (23rd Texas Cavalry), 19
    Holland, Henry (Free Negro), 155
    Jackson, Henry, 167
    Poiner, Alfred, 167
    Walker, Thompson, 167
    Walter (23rd Texas Cavalry), 19
King George County, 136, *153*
King William County, 136
Kingman, Chris
    Craney Island List, *83*
Kingman, Daniel
    Craney Island List, *83*
Kingman, Phillip
    Craney Island List, *83*
Lancaster County, 136
Langley, William
    Craney Island List, *82*
Lee
    Robert E., 1
Lee County, 136
Lee, Ab
    Servant, 12th Georgia Infantry, 52
Lee, Ford
    Cabell Teamster List. *See* Hampton's Legion
Lee, Robert E. (servants of)
    Evans, William T., 154
    Lee, William Mack (Reverend), 69, 139
    Norris, Joseph Preston, 65
    Riley, Anthony (Andy), 71
    Walker, Fielding, 76, 162

Lee, Tom (servant)
    at High Bridge, *60*
Leigh, Jack
    Craney Island List, *83*
Leport, L.
    Donaldsonville Artillery, 55
Leroy, John
    Co. A, 18th Georgia Inf Battalion, 54
Lewis
    Cabell Teamster List. *See* 18th Virginia Infantry (Withers)
Lewis, Alfred
    Cabell Teamster List. *See* Simm's Brigade
Lewis, Willis
    Craney Island List, *83*
Logan, S. (free man)
    at High Bridge, *58*
Logan, William (free man)
    at High Bridge, *58*
Longstreet's staff, 156
Louisa County, 136
Lucas, Charles
    Cabell Teamster List. *See* 12th Mississippi Brigade
Lucus, Flaveus
    Cabell Teamster List. *See* 5th North Carolina Infantry
Lumber mill, 126
Lunenburg County, 136
Luray Valley, Va, 123
Luray, Va, 148
Lynchburg, 137
Lynchburg, Va, *158*
MacGruder, John Bankhead (General), 127
Mackey, William
    Craney Island List, *83*
Madison County, 137
Magruder, John Bankhead (General), 122
mail carrier, 124
Major
    Cabell Teamster List. *See* 5th Alabama Regiment
Major (servant)
    Parker's Battery, Va Light Artillery, 165
Majors, Howard
    Cabell Teamster List. *See* Longstreet's Brigade
Manassas Gap, 128
Mannboro, Va, 123
Marcus, George
    Cabell Teamster List. *See* Texas Battalion
Marshall, Thomas (cook)
    Co. H, 7th Va Cavalry, 157
Mastrom, John
    Cabell Teamster List. *See* 5th North Carolina Infantry
Mattoax, Va, 122
Mayo, Joe (servant), 6, 12, 15
    Parker's Battery, Va Light Artillery, 157
McCall, Joseph
    Craney Island List, *83*
McCausland, John (General)
    life saved by servant (Maryland Campaign), 38

McClesky, Henry
    18th Georgia Infantry, Co. B, 54
McDonald, George (black enlisted soldier)
    of Florida, 18
McKagen
    Cabell Teamster List. *See* 6th Alabama Regiment
McManaway, John A. (pensioner), 23
Mecklenburg County, 137
Mempley, Jonathan
    Donaldsonville Artillery, 55
Mexican War
    Pringle, Stewart, 13
Mexican War veteran
    Bragg, Major, 150
    Dick Slate, 77
    Price, George, 111
Migar, Harry
    Craney Island List, *83*
Miller, Levi, 32
Misc Sources
    Abraham, 162
    Adam, 162
    Adams, May, 147
    Addeline, 162
    Adkins, William, 147
    Albert, 162
    Alexander, Hugh, 147
    Alexander, Tarleton, 147
    Allen, 162
    Allen, George, 147
    Allen, Joe, 147
    Allen, Mike, 147
    Allen, Samuel, 147
    Allen, Simon, 147
    Allen, Tom, 147
    Allen, William, 147
    Allison, Elbert, 147
    Allison, Isaac, 147
    Alvah, Vinton, 147
    Ambler, S., 148
    Anderson, Albert, 148
    Anderson, Edward, 148
    Anderson, Garnett, 148
    Andrew, 162
    Archer, Maria, 148
    Arkins, Benjamin, 148
    Armstead, Addison, 148
    Armstead, Paul, 159
    Ashton, Samuel, 148
    Askins, William, 148
    Atkins, Allen, 148
    Atkins, J., 148
    Austen, 162
    Austin, Beverly, 148
    Bailey, James, 148
    Bailey, Jason, 148
    Bailey, Robert, 148
    Bailey, Thomas, 148
    Bainwright, Jesse, 148
    Bainwright, John, 148
    Baker, Abraham, 148
    Baker, Albert, 148
    Baker, W.J., 148
    Baley, Layton, 149
    Balfour, J., 149
    Ball, Albert, 21, 149
    Ball, George, 149
    Bandy, Eli, 149
    Banks, James (Jim), 149
    Bannister, Frank, 149
    Bannister, Isaac, 149
    Barber, Josiah, 149
    Barker, Jordan, 148
    Barksdale, Henderson, 149
    Barnes, War, 149
    Barrett, Tim, 149
    Bartlett, Henry, 149
    Bartlett, Jennie, 149
    Bartlett, Martha, 149
    Battle, John, 149
    Batts, Gloster, 149
    Bean, William, 10
    Beckley, Mortimer, 150
    Beckworth, Alfred, 150
    Bell, A., 150
    Bell, B., 150
    Ben, 162
    Benjamin, 162
    Berryman, William, 150
    Betsey, 163
    Beverley, Sylvester, 150
    Beverley, W.P., 150
    Beverley, William, 150
    Beverly, Andrew, 150
    Beverly, Edward, 150
    Bias, Wyatt, 150
    Bill, 163
    Bird, Albert, 150
    Bird, William, 150
    Biscoe, Jacob, 20, 150
    Blackburn, Robert, 150
    Blackford, Charles, 150
    Blanmire, George, 150
    Bob, 163
    Bob (free man) 48th Va Inf, 163
    Bob (servant to Gen. George Pickett)--,, 163
    Bob (servant to JEB Stuart), 163
    Botts, William, 151
    Bowser, Henry, 151
    Bowyer, Bean M., 150
    Bradmar, John, 150
    Bragg, Martha, 150
    Brannon, William, 151
    Brayboy, James, 151
    Brazelton, Caroline, 151
    Brazelton, Jane, 151

Bright, James, 8
Broadway, William, 151
Brock, Alexander, 151
Brooks, Abram, 151
Brooks, Albert, 151
Brooks, Beverly, 151
Brown, Andrew, 151
Brown, George W., 151
Brown, James, 151
Brown, Jane, 151
Brown, Jesse, 151
Brown, John, 151
Brown, Mark, 151
Brown, Sam, 151
Brown, William, 151
Bruce, William, 151
Bryant, Loftin, 151
Bundy, Eli, 151
Burke, John, 152
Burnett, Bolen (Bolin), 151
Burns, James, 152
Burr, 163
Burton, Aaron (servant to Col John S. Mosby), 152
Burton, Carbury, 152
Butcher, Frank, 152
Butler, John, 152
Butler, Jospeh, 152
Butler, William, 152
Byers, Essex, 152
Cambridge, 163
Carrell, Oscar, 152
Carter, Bob, 152
Carter, Burwell, 152
Carter, William, 152
Chappell, Henry, 152
Charles, 163
Charles (blockade runner), 163
Charles (Co. A, 25th Bn Va Inf), 163
Charles (servant in 30th Va Cavalry), 17
Charles (servant to Gen. A.P. Hill), 163
Charley (servant to Gen. E.Porter Alexander), 163
Chavers, John, 152
Chavers, William, 152
Chavis, Thomas, 152
Cherry, Ralph, 152
Chevus, Ervin, 152
Chiles, Edward, 152
Chrisman, Oliver, 152, 153
Christian, William, 152
Cleapor, Charles, 153
Cole, Elijah, 153
Cole, George Washington, *153*
Cole, William, 153
Cook, Richard, 153
Cornelius, 163
Cornish, Isaac, 153
Corum, John, 153
Cousins, Jordan, 153

Craig, Jasper, 153
David (aka Davey), 163
Davis, James, 153
Davis, John, 153
Davis, Lewis, 20, 153
Davis, Samuel, 153
Dickenson, Willis, 154
Dims, William, 154
Dix, Austin, 154
Douglass, John, 154
Downs, Ned, 154
Edmund (blacksmith), 163
Edmund, 2nd Va Cavalry, 163
Elbert, Allison, 154
Elijah, 163
Emily, 163
Epps, Daniel, 154
Essex, 163
Evans, Frank, 21, 154
Evans, William T. (Robert E. Lee's Servant), 154
Ezekiel, 154
Fentress, George, 154
Ferry, 164
Fleming, 164
Ford, Lindsay, 154
Ford, Tom, 154
Foster, Jack, 155
Frank, 164
Frederick, 164
Freeman, Augustus, 155
Freeman, John, 154
Gaines, Lucian, 155
George, 164
George (Co A, 25th Bn Va Inf), 164
Geroge (32nd Va Inf, Co F), 164
Giles, Daniel, 155
Gilliam, Robert, 155
Goffney, Robert M., 155
Gordon, John, 155
Graves, John, 8
Green, Ann, 155
Green, Larkin, 155
Hairston, John, 155
Hall, Moses, 155
Hall, William, 155
Hannah (25th Bn Va Inf), 164
Harden, Silas, 155
Hardman, William, 155
Harris, John G., 155
Harris, John J., 155
Harris, Phillips, 155
Harris, Thomas, 155
Harris, Tom, 155
Harris, William, 155
Harrison, P., 155
Hassell, Joe, 155
Hays, 164
Heck, J., 155

Virginia's Black Confederates

Henley, John, 155
Henry, 164
Henry (Co. G, 25th Bn Va Inf), 164
Henry, Henry, 155
Hineman, Spencer, 155
Holland, Henry, 155
Howard, 164
Howell, David, 155
Hughes, Henry, 156
Humbles, James, 156
Hurdman, William, 156
Ike, 164
Jack, 164
Jackson, Eli (courier), 156
James, 164
James, Cornelius, 156
James, Henry, 156
Jim (Richmond and Danville RR), 164
Joe, 164
Johnson, Charles, 156
Johnson, Frank, 156
Johnson, George Floyd, 156
Johnson, Joseph, 156
Johnson, Richard, 156
Jones, Jacob, 156
Jones, James A., 156
Jones, William, 156
Jordan, Stephen, 156
Joseph, 164
Joshua (servant to Gen. Henry Wise), 164
Kean, Aleck, 156
Kelley, Thomas, 156
Keys, Selden, 156
King, Lomax, 156
Kune, Henry, 156
Lamb, George, 156
Langford, Tom, 10, 156
Laws, Edward, 156
Leahy, 164
Lee, William, 156
Lewis, Jim, 157
Lewis, John, 157
Lewis, Preston, 157
Lightfoot, Jim, 157
Jim (servant to Gen. Stonewall Jackson, 164
Lincoln, A., 21, 157
London, 164
Lowden, 164
Lucas, Phil, 157
Lucas, William, 20, 157
Lynch, Robert, 157
Madison, Lewis, 157
Marshall, Addison, 157
Marshall, Thomas, 10, 157
Martha, 165
Martin, 165
Maurice, 165
Mayo, Henry (free), of Powhatan, 157

Mayo, Henry, of Charlotte, 157
Mayo, Robert, 157
Mayo, Tom, 157
Mayo, William, 157
Milburn, Wesley, 21, 157
Miller, Levi, 157
Minnis, 165
Monroe, 165
Morgan (servant to Gen. Eppa Hunton), 165
Morgan, Peter, 158
Morres, 165
Morris, Edward, 158
Morris, Paden, 158
Mortimer, 165
Mosby, James (free man of color), *158*
Moton, Booker, 158
Murray, Branch, 158
Murry, 165
Ned (at Staunton River Bridge), 165
Ned (slave of Capt George White), 165
Nelson, 165
Nelson, W.B., 158
Nevitt, James, 158
Nevitt, Thomas, 158
Newton, 165
Nottingham (servant), 165
Nutrum, 165
Oliver, 165
Oscar, 165
Otey, Ephraiam, 159
Ottoway, 165
Overton, 165
Owens, Ned, 159
Pad, 165
Page, Charles, 159
Patrick, 165
Paul, 165
Pembroke, 166
Perry, Franklin, 159
Perry, Manson, 159
Peters, Samuel, 159
Peters, Tom, 159
Poplar, Dick, 159
Porter, William, 159
Quall, Isaac, 159
Ransell, Jacob, 159
Reid, Alfred, 160
Rice, Daniel, 21, 160
Richard, 166
Robert, 166
Robinson, Carter, 10, 160
Robinson, Edward, 160
Roe, Robert, 160
Rose, William, 8
Sam (slave of Thomas J. Bagby), 166
Sam, 48th Va Inf, 166
Samuel, 166
Sarah, 166

Saunders, William, 160
Schoolfield, Henry Mathis, 160
Scott, 166
Scott, Benjamin, 160
Scott, John, 160
Servant, Frank, 160
Shields, Jefferson, 160
Sinclair, Archie, 160
Slate, Dick, 160
Slave, J., 160
Slave, J.J., 160
Smith, 160
Smith (servant of Gen. Henry Wise), 166
Smith, Billy, 10, 161
Smith, Charles, 161
Smith, G.W., 161
Smith, Noah, 10, 161
Sorrell, John, 10, 161
Squier, 166
Stone, Fee, 161
Strother, Tom, 161
Tabb, William, 161
Tatum, Samuel, 161
Taylor, James, 161
Temple, Edmund, 161
Texas, 166
Thomas, 166
Thomas (Co. G, 25th Bn Va Inf), 166
Thomas, Ben, 161
Thomas, John, 161
Thompson, George, 21, 161
Thompson, William, 21, 161
Thorn, 166
Thornton, 166
Tim, 166
Tom, 166
Tucker, William, 161
Tyler, George Jr., 161
Tyler, Robert, 162
Unknown - nine colored men running the blockade, no names given, 10 Aug 1862, 166
Unnamed Hospital Nurse (servant to Dr. Claiborne), 166
Unnamed Hospital Steward (servant to Dr. Claiborne), 166
Walker, 166
Walker, Chelse, 162
Walker, Fielding (Robert E. Lee's servant), 162
Walker, Frank, 162
Washinton, George, 162
Watkins, 166
Weever, J., 162
West, Richard, 162
William, 166
William (Co F, 25th Bn Va Inf), 166
Williams, Phil, 10, 162
Williamson, James, 8
Willis, 166
Wilson, 166
Winfield, Henry, 162
Yerby, Joe, 162
Moneta, Va, 121
Monroe, George
    Cabell Teamster List. *See* 5th North Carolina Infantry
Monroe, Nathan
    Cabell Teamster List. *See*
Montgomery County, 138
Morgan
    Servant to General Eppa Hunton, 50
Morris, John
    Craney Island List, *83*
Morven, Va, 123
Mosby, James (free man)
    POW, 19
Mosby, John S. (Colonel), *159*
Mosby, John S., (Colonel), 132
Mosby's Command, 146, 152
    Adams?, Juniper (Chaplain's servant), 36
    Burton, Aaron (Mosby's servant), 33
    Ford, Carter, 38
    Harrison, George F., 37
    Henry (Surgeon's servant), 36
    Withers, John B., 37, 130
    Wright, Morris, 38
Moses
    identified in James Berry Pension, 142
Moton, Booker
    Servant, 13
Moton, Robert Russa
    describing fatheras Confederate servant, 13
Munford, Thomas T. (General), 10
Musician
    Austin Dix (drummer), 154
    Dick Slate (drummer), 160
    George Blanmire, 150
    Henry Lewis Waller (drum carrier), 141
    Humbles, James (Bugler), 156
    Ralph Cherry, 152
Nace
    Cabell Teamster List. *See* 5th Alabama Regiment
Nailer, Ben
    Cabell Teamster List. *See* 5th North Carolina Infantry
Nansemond County, 138
Naval Brigade
    Commodore Tucker's, Custis Lee's Division, 54
Neal, Levi
    Cabell Teamster List. *See* 15th Georgia Regiment
Ned
    Cabell Teamster List. *See* 18th Viriginia Infantry (Withers)
    helped capture Union cavalrymen, 43
Negro, John
    Cabell Teamster List. *See* 1st Georgia Regiment
Nelson County, 139
Nelson, W.B.
    32nd Virginia Infantry, 10

Virginia's Black Confederates

New Kent County, 139
Newman, Frank
   Cabell Teamster List, *97*
Newman, Henry
   Cabell Teamster List, *97*
Nichols, Hubbard
   Cabell Teamster List. *See* 1st and 2nd North Carolina
      Infantry Regiment
Norfolk, 139
Norris, Isaac
   Cabell Teamster List. *See* Hampton's Legion
Norris, Joseph Preston
   Robert E. Lee's servant, 65
Northumberland County, 139
Nottoway, 135
Nottoway County, 131, 135, 139, 153
   Blackstone, 131, 139
   Burkeville, 139
Oates, Reuben
   Cabell Teamster List. *See* Longstreet's Brigade
Oden, John
   Craney Island List, *83*
Oliver
   Cabell Teamster List. *See* 17th Regiment Mississippi
      Volunteers
Orange County, 139
Owens, William
   Craney Island List, *82*
Page County, 139
Page, Charles
   32nd Virginia Infantry, 10
Pamplin, Va, 121
Parker, Anthony
   Cabell Teamster List. *See* Early's Brigade
Parker, Dav [David]
   Cabell Teamster List. *See* Longstreet's Brigade
Parker, Tom
   Cabell Teamster List, *98*
Parker, William (Captain), 6
Parkman, Joe
   Co. A, 18th Georgia Inf Battalion, 54
Parrott, Bill
   Cabell Teamster List. *See* Jones' Brigade
Paul, Armstead
   Discharge Paper, 72
Payne, David
   Cabell Teamster List. *See* Jones' Brigade
Payne, Presley
   Cabell Teamster List. *See* Hampton's Legion
Pearson, Newton
   Cabell Teamster List. *See* 3rd Georgia Battalion
Pensioner
   Abbitt, Archer, 124
   Adams, Powhatan, 134
   Alexander, Allen, 137
   Allen, James, 142
   Allen, Samuel, 135
   Anderson, David Lewis, 135

Anderson, John, 132
Anderson, John G., 132
Anderson, John Thomas, 123
Anderson, Peter W., 122
Anderson, Robert, 122
Archer, George W., 134
Armstead, Moses, 130
Arnold, Henry, 143
Arrington, Angus, 137
Ashton, John, 146
Austin, Edward, 124
Ball, Penny, 132
Banks, Jasper, 126
Banks, John. L. Sr., 129
Barnhart, Richard, 145
Bartlett, John [James] Archer, 146
Baskerville, Reuben, 137
Beard, Yancey, 134
Beedon, John, 145
Bell, Benjamin, 142
Bell, William, 141
Bell, Wyatt, 128
Berry, James, 142
Berry, John, 123
Blair, Davy, 144
Blakey, Abe, 144
Bolanz, G.M., 140
Bolden, Clem Read, 143
Booker, Cornelius, 126
Booker, Henry, 122
Booker, J. Churchill, 122
Boone, Anthony, 138
Boone, Jason, 138
Booth, Robert, 145
Borzotra (Borsota), William, 143
Bowman, Henderson, 142
Boxwell, Aaron H., 146
Boxwell, Susanna (widow), 146
Boyd, Isaac, 126
Boyd, Jim, 137
Boyd, William, 137
Boyd, William Henry, 131
Bradley, Edmund, 127
Branch, Jim, 143
Branch, Willis, 141
Braxton, Henry, 141
Brightwell, Frank P., 141
Broady, William H., 123
Brogden, George, 127
Broock, H.L., 137
Brooks, William, 122
Brown, Dick, 136
Brown, Douglas, 142
Brown, Gabriel, 127, 128
Brown, John, 137
Brown, Kit, 128
Brown, Randol, 130
Brown, Robert Lewis, 135

Virginia's Black Confederates

Brown, S.T., 127
Brown, Sam, 126
Brown, William, 141
Brugh, R.M., 125
Bundy, Nat, 127
Bundy, Ryburn L., 132
Burke, Henry, 141
Burks, Pharoah, 126
Burnett, Joe, 135
Butts, Irwin, 125
Byrd, James Henry, 134
Cabell, William, 126
Cain, Charles, 139
Carey, Ephraim, 143
Carrington, Henry, 134
Carrington, Linous, 142
Carter, Gabrel, 134
Carter, Henry, 123
Carter, Lewis, 139
Carter, Sr., Anderson, 123
Cary, Tom, 126
Chandler, George, 133
Cheatham, Albert, 136
Cheeley, Lewis, 141
Chives, Edmund, 132
Chivis, Jabe, 129
Clark, Adam, 126
Clark, John, 127
Clay, Henry, 139
Clore, Champ, 129
Cole, John, 131
Coleman, James, 137
Coleman, John, 142
Coleman, Jordan, 135
Coles, Peyton, 141
Comer, James J., 139
Comfort, Wilson, 139
Conaway, Hyram, 136
Connally, Green, 140
Conway, Harry, 136
Cook, George Edmund, 146
Cores, John, 135
Coy, William, 146
Crawley, Silas, 128
Creasy, Wyatt, 126
Cross, Richard, 131
Crump, George, 130
Cypress, Eldridge, 128
Cypress, James, 144
Dabney, William, 142
Davenport, Alexander D., 134
Davidson, Nathan, 144
Davis, Davie, 125
Davis, Reuben, 139
Day, John, 143
Dean, Ben, 141
Deaton, Caleb, 138
Delaney, McDowel, 130

Dickerson, George W., 144
Dickerson, Giles, 140
Douglas, Randall, 139
Dovel, Peter S., 139
Drew, Tyler, 141
Duncan, W.R., 138
Early, Ferdinand, 143
Edmonds, Frank, 126
Edmondson, Isaac, 134
Eggleston, John, 138
Ellis, Charles, 123
Ellis, Wilson D., 126
Epes, David, 139
Epps, George, 135
Epps, Milton M., 122
Estes, Callie Hill, 140
Evans, Aaron, 128, 134
Evans, Marshall, 129
Farrar, Plummer, 138
Fauntleroy, Lewis W., 136
Fauntleroy, Thomas, 136
Ferguson, Walker, 134
Fields, James Emmett, 142
Finney, William, 140
Fleming, George, Sr., 141
Fleming, Isaac, 135
Ford, Carter, 132
Ford, Fred, 139
Fralin, Jim, 133
Fry, Albert, 132
Fund, Doctor, 142
Gallahan, Joe M., 145
Gaskins, Beverly, 136
Gates, Thomas, 142
George, Duke, 129
Gilbert, Jackson, 140
Giles, Greeman, 141
Glascoe, George T., 129
Godfrey, J.W., 132
Goode, Patrick, 124
Goodwyn, Thomas, 139
Graham, John, 135
Graham, Richard R., 142
Grayson, William, 132
Green, Claiborne, 125
Green, Frank, 124
Green, Louis, 129
Green, Silas, 137
Hackley, Josephy, 132
Hairston, D.W., 135
Hairston, James, 145
Haley, Tom, 139
Hall, Austin, 124
Hall, Leroy, 127
Hambrick, J.C., 138
Hardy, Jim, 124
Hardy, William, 145
Harris, Edward, 136

Virginia's Black Confederates

Harris, John W., 122
Harris, William, 138
Harrison, George F., 132
Haskins, Miles, 122
Haskins, Sib, 134
Hawthorne, Rufus, 136
Hays, William, 132
Henderson, Archie, 122
Henderson, Ceasar, 139
Henderson, Jesse, 139
Henderson, Thomas, 125
Henderson, William, 125
Henson, James, 142
Hill, Steven E., 130
Hill, William, 145
Hobson, Isaac, 130
Hodnett, Dave, 140
Holland, Claiborne, 133
Holland, Cornelius, 133
Holland, Creed, 133
Holley, Austin, 125
Hollins, Archie, 123
Holman, Harrison, 132
Holmes, John, 125
Holmes, Lewis W., 142
Howard, David, 146
Howard, George, 146
Howell, Richard, 128
Hubbard, Robert, 140
Huff, William Henry, 143
Hughes, Richard, 132
Hundley, William, 122
Hundley, William Robert, 142
Hunt, Gabe, 127
Hunter, Phillip, 137
Hurt, James, 144
Hutcheson, Henry, 138
Ingram, Anderson, 137
Ivy, Lewis Henry, 140
Jackson, Henry, 129
Jackson, Lewis, 136
Jackson, Minor, 137
Jackson, Taylor, 129
Jackson, Thomas, 135
James, Charles, 133
James, John, 145
Jasper, Carry, 122
Jennings, Joseph, 132
Johns, Preston, 123
Johnson, Andrew, 131
Johnson, Burroughs Whitfield, 127
Johnson, Edmund, 125
Johnson, Henry, 125
Johnson, Jacob, 124, 136
Johnson, Melvin, 123
Johnson, Nathan, 129
Johnson, Stillman, 130
Johnson, Watt, 130

Jones, Albert, 126
Jones, Ben, 143
Jones, Emmanual, 142
Jones, George R;, 123
Jones, Henry, 123
Jones, Isaac, 126
Jones, Louis, 123
Jones, Moses, 126
Jones, Sam A., 138
Jones, Sidney, 131
Jones, Simon, 126
Jones, Watt, 144
Jones, Wiley, 138
Jones, William, 143
Jordan, Charles, 123
Jordan, Richard, 141
Kasey, Steven (Stephen), 133
Kelly, John W., 125
Knight, James Reuben, 141
Kyle, Calvin, 138
Lacy, Horace, 128
Lamar, Floyd, 146
Lanier, Heartwell, 131
Lansdown, Charles, 142
Law, Jack, 133
Lawson, Abner, 131
Lee, Frank, 132
Lee, George, 123
Lee, Thomas, 126
Lee, Tom, 124
Lee, William Mack (Rev), 139
Leigh, Samuel, 134
Lemons, John, 133
Lewis, Stephen, 139
Lightfoot, Addison, 129
Lightfoot, Henry Clay, 129
Linthicum, Carter, 127
Lipscomb, William E., 130
Lovelace, Sam, 140
Lucas, Cornelius, 133
Lumpkins, Ned, 133
Lyle, Sam, 141
Mabrey, Frank, 143
Majors, Tillman, 134
Mallory, Littleton, 137
Manns, George, 136
Mansfield, George, 136
Marks, Robert, 122
Martin, Joe, 143
Martin, John, 145
Martin, John Wesley, 125
Martin, Scott, 127
Martin, Silas, 123
Martin, Thomas S., 141
Mathews, Brice, 133
Mayo, Edward, 143
McKinney, Pink, 124
McMannaway, John A., 144

Virginia's Black Confederates

Meade, John, 125
Menefee, J.H., 133
Michens, Roderick, 136
Miles, Mitchell, 128
Miller, Alex, 140
Miller, Andrew, 126
Miller, Carter C., 139
Miller, James, 142
Miller, Levi, 133
Miller, Sam, 140
Mitchell, George, 131
Mitchell, Jackson, 136
Mitchell, W.J., 139
Montague, Porter, 146
Moody, Peter, 134
Moody, Phillip, 134
Moore, Henderson D., 125
Moore, Jesse, 130
Moore, John, 127
Moore, Richard, 122
Morgan, Sam, 131
Morgan, Walker, 127
Mosby, Walsh, 136
Moseley, Ben, 138
Moseley, Cambridge, 126
Moss, Tobe, 146
Murray, Dallas, 142
Nelson, John, 145
Newly, John, 139
Nicholas, Cass Lewis, 144
Oliver, Kitt, 134
Oulds, Henry, 127
Overby, Ned, 137
Page, Jacob, 143
Page, Samuel, 124
Palmer, Thaddeus, 132
Parrish, Edmond, 134
Patillo, Jack, 124
Pegram, Arthur, 123
Pegram, Paul, 131
Peters, Paul, 123
Peters, Samuel, 143
Petty, B.S., 135
Pitts, Robert, 132
Pleasants, Ross, 141
Pollard, Emanuel, 134
Pools, Simeon, 146
Porter, Albert, 137
Porterfield, Jacob, 124
Preston, Alexander, 143
Preston, Isaac Lewis, 137
Price, Alexander, 135
Price, George, 133
Price, James, 137
Price, Jordan, 123
Prichard, John, 133
Quillen, S.M., 144
Ramsey, Nat, 140
Randall, William, 129
Randolph, Alfred Thompson, 130
Randolph, Samuel, 130
Redd, Silas, 141
Reed, Henry Clay, 145
Reed, John, 127
Reeves, Armstead, 133
Richeson, James D., 124
Richeson, Joseph, 144
Rivers, Freeman, 125
Roane, General, 135
Roberts, Cope, 145
Robertson [Robinson], Warner, 135
Robertson, Richard, 133
Robinson, George, 146
Robinson, George Washington, 127
Robinson, James Henry, 130
Robinson, Parker, 128
Robinson, Solon, 139
Roe, Ben, 137
Roe, Montello, 137
Rogers, James, 128
Rose, Given, 124
Rowe, Daniel, 137
Russell, William, 131
Rutherford, Neal, 138
Sadler, Henry, 126
Saunders, James (Rev), 140
Saunders, Radford, 143
Saunderson, Carter, 130
Scott, James, 141
Scott, Morris, 130
Scott, Robert, 141
Scott, Wise, 137
Scott, Zebedee, 143
Sears, Tom, 126
Seay, William, 133
Sheffield, George W., 136
Shields, Tom, 126
Shields, Wash, 144
Short, Isaac N., 139
Short, John, 139
Simms, Lewis, 130
Skaggs, Henry, 136
Skipwith, Ben Fuller, 128
Slaughter, William H., 130
Smith, Abram, 135
Smith, Daniel, 133
Smith, Harrison, 143
Smith, John, 128
Smith, Matt, 144
Smith, William, 133
Spinner, Henry, 125
Spratley, Sandy, 145
Sprigg, Lewis, 139
Stewart, Osborne, 136
Stewart, Richard, 131
Stith, Cupid, 142

Stone, Sam, 140
Stuart, Mary, 130
Tarpley, Stephen, 140
Taylor, Davy, 139
Taylor, John, 131
Taylor, Richard, 138
Taylor, Samuel, 143
Taylor, Thornton, 132
Taylor, Washington, 138
Taylor, Willie, 138
Terry, James, 127
Thomas, George Lee, 135
Thompson, Charles, 140
Thompson, Jerry, 136
Thompson, John R., 145
Thornhill, William, 128
Thornton, Joe May, 136
Tinsley, Clem, 138
Tinsley, Flem, 144
Tompson, Robert W., 144
Topp, Jack, 142
Trent, Carter, 141
Tucker, Pompey, 131
Tucker, William, 131, 138
Turner, Arthur, 133
Turner, Charles, 132
Turner, Henry, 145
Turner, Phil, 142
Turpin, Henry, 137
Tweedy, Sam, 127
Tyree, Henry D., Sr., 122
Valentine, Jim, 138
Waddell, Thomas, 123
Walker, Samuel, 133
Walker, William, 131
Wallace, Henry, 130
Waller, Ferdnand, 141
Waller, Lewis Henry, 141
Waller, Richard, 143
Warner, William, 124
Washington, Lewis, 132
Watkins, Frank, 138
Watkins, William, 128
Watson, John, 141
Weaver, Frank, 137
Webb, William, 127
Webster, Daniel, 123
Wells, James, 139
Wester, Robert, 144
Whitaker, R.D., 124
White, Henry, 133
White, Richard, 135
Wilkerson, James, 135
Williams, Charles, 138
Williams, Flemming, 142
Williams, Isham, 130
Williams, James, 144
Williams, John, 132

Williams, Rowland, 138
Williams, Simon, 132
Williams, Steptoe, 136
Willis, Charles, 134
Willis, James, 134
Willis, John, 146
Wilson, William Anthony, 141
Wimbush, Henry, 135
Winfield, Isham, 131
Winfree, Alpheus, 123
Winfree, Augustus, 131
Winslow, Edmund, 130
Winston, Daniel, 144
Withers, John B., 130
Wood, Charles H., 131
Wooden, Lewis, 125
Woodson, George, 131
Woody, Peters, 133
Wooldridge, William, 131
Wright, Morris, 146
Wyatt, George, 131
Wyatt, Johnson, 143
Wynne, Ben, 136
York, Wesley, 144
Yowell, John L.[Y], 130
Zink, W.H., 138
Perkins, George (free man)
    at High Bridge, *58*
Perkins, John
    Craney Island List, *82*
Pete
    cook to Rockbridge Artillery's Washington College company, 10
Pete (cook)
    Rockbridge Artillery, 166
Peters, Joe
    Cabell Teamster List. *See* 15th Georgia Regiment
Peters, Paul, 123
Peters, Tom
    Teamster, 51
Petersburg, 139
Peyton (servant)
    11th Mississippi Infantry, Co. K, 16
    Espionage activities, 16
Peyton, George
    Cabell Teamster List. *See* 5th North Carolina Infantry
Phenix, Va, 121
Pickett's Division, 121, 122
Pittsylvania, 140
Pittsylvania County, 165
Polk
    Cabell Teamster List. *See* 1st Mississippi Regiment
Polk, James
    Co. B, 18th Georgia Inf Battalion, 54
Poole, William (servant), 13
    Artillery Staff, 2nd Corps, ANV, 159
Powell, Adolphus
    Cabell Teamster List. *See* Hampton's Legion

Virginia's Black Confederates

Powhatan County, 141
Price, George (Free Man), 116
Prince Edward County, 121, 122, 141, 163
Prince George County, 142
Prince William County, 142
Princeton, Va (now WV), 155
Pringle, Stewart, 17
Pringle, Stewart (servant), 13
Prisoner of War
    15 black teamsters, 93
    35 to 40 black Confederates at Gettysburg, 21
    Arkins, Benjamin, 148
    Ashton, Samuel (blockade runner), 148
    Ball, Albert, *21*, 149
    Bandy, Eli, 149
    Batts, Gloster, 149
    Batts, Gloster (blockade runner), 149
    Berryman, William, 104, 150
    Berryman, William (blockade runner), 150
    Biscoe, Jacob, 20, 150
    Brooks, Abram, 151
    Brown, John, 151
    Butler, Joseph (Captain), 152
    Butler, William (Seaman), 152
    C.P. Terry, 21
    Poole, William, 159
    Tabb, William, 55
    Barber, Josiah; Co. B, 5th NC Inf, 103
    Banks, Solomon, 149
    Butler, John, 103
    Charles (no last name), 163
    Conaway, Hyram, 136
    Confederate Negro battalion at Deatonsville, 56
    Corum, John, 153
    Crenshaw, August, 161
    Davis, Lewis, 153
    Douglass, John, 154
    Evans, Frank, *21*, 154
    Bob; JEB Stuart's servant, 15
    Goodgame, Abe, 20
    Green, Larkin, 155
    Hall, Moses, 155
    Hardman, William, 155
    Harris, Tom, 155
    Harrison, P., 155
    Harrison, P. (blockade runner), 155
    Haywood, 19
    Henry, Henry (blockade runner), 155
    Hurdman, William, 156
    James Berry, 142
    James Mosby, 19
    John Butler, 152
    Johnson, Charles, 156
    Keys, Seldon, 156
    King, Lomax, 156
    King, Lomax (blockade runner), 156
    Laws, Edward, 156
    Lewis, Davis, 20
    Lewis, John (Seaman), 157
    Lincoln, A., *21*, 157
    Lucas, Phil, 157
    Lucas, William, 20, 157
    Marshall, Addison, 157
    McCleskey, Henry (Sailor's Creek), 54
    Milburn, Wesley, 21, 157
    Moore, Henderson D., 125
    Morres, 165
    Poplar, Dick, 159
    Porter, William, 159
    Quall, Isaac, 159
    Reed, John, 127
    Reid, Alfred (Seaman), 160
    Rice, Daniel, *21*, 160
    Robinson, Edward, 160
    S. Ambler, 148
    Terry, C.P, 55
    Saunders, William, 160
    Sinclair, Archie, 112
    Sinclair, Archie (made successful escape), 160
    Tabb, William, 161
    Thompson, George, *21*, 161
    Thompson, William, *21*, 161
    Unknown, nine men, 166
    Walter, 19
    Webb, William, 127
    Willaim Tabb, 21
Private
    (rank), 121, 125, 137, 147, 149, 152, 154, 157, 161
Puckett, Henry
    Cabell Teamster list. *See* Longstreet's Brigade
Puckett, Simon
    Cabell's Teamster List. *See* Simm's Brigade
Pulaski County, 142
Pulaski, Va, *158*
Quartermaster Department, 121, 123, 151, 152, 163
    Abington, 148
    Ambulance Shops, blacksmith, 148
    Blacksmith, 137
    Cook, 131, 133
    Dublin, 149
    Narrows, 149
    Pickett's Division, Teamster, 152
    Servant to Capt J.J. Waggoner, 139
    Teamster, 125, 137
    Teamster ("supply service"), 125
Radford, 142
Rains, Burwell
    Cabell Teamster Llist, *96*
Rains, Wm [William]
    Cabell Teamster List. *See* Hampton's Legion
Randall, Red, 41
Ransell, Jacob (servant)
    servant to JEB Stuart, 18
Read, William
    Co. C, 18th Georgia Inf Battalion, 54
Redman, Lewis

  Cabell Teamster list. *See* Texas Battalion
Redman, Saul
  Cabell Teamster List. *See* Texas Battalion
Reuben
  Cabell Teamster List, *95*
Reunion of Black Confederates, 26
Richard
  Cabell Teamster List, *95*
Richards, Daniel
  Cabell Teamster List. *See* 4th North Carolina Infantry Regiment
Richmond, 142, 165
Richmond Howitzers
  Second Company, 51
Riddicke, Jas [James]
  Craney Island List, *83*
Riddicke, Joe
  Craney Island List, *83*
Rix, Corneilus
  Craney Island List. *See*
Rix, Gus
  Craney Island List, *83*
Roanoke, 121, 143
Roanoke County, 143
Roberson, John
  Cabell Teamster List. *See* Longstreet's Brigade
Robert E. Lee, servants of
  Jones, William (messenger), 143
Roberts, Preston (Pete)
  Forrest's Cavalry Division, 28
Robertson, Jonathan
  Craney Island List, *83*
Rockbridge County, 121, 144, 157
Rockingham County, 144
Romax, Henry
  Cabell Teamster List. *See* Simm's Brigade
Royal, Alfred, 41
Royster, Reubin
  Cabell Teamster List. *See* Texas Battalion
Sam
  Cabell Teamster List, *95*
  Servant and slave of F.S. Robertson, 52
Samuel (servant)
  37th Va Cavalry, 166
Sanford, Dav [David]
  Cabell Teamster List. *See* Longstreet's Brigade
Scott County, 144
Scott, Benjamin (fee man)
  later Captain, Va Militia and in Confederate Infantry Company, 73
Scruggs, First Name Unknown (brother to William T. Scruggs), 123
Semple, Jonathan
  Donaldsonville Artillery, 55
Servant, 121, 125
  carry water to hospital patients, 126
  in combat, 15
Servants of Robert E. Lee

Walker, Fielding, 76
Shelton, Humphrey (servant)
  Co. H, Albemarle Light Artillery, 1st Regt Va Light Artillery, 160
Shephard, Miles
  Craney Island List, *83*
Shropshire, Ben
  5th Texas Cavalry, 18
Simm, Lee
  Cabell Teamster List. *See* Hampton's Legion
Simm, Lewis
  Cabell Teamster List. *See* Early's Brigade
Simmons, Allen
  Craney Island List, *83*
Slate, Dick (free man)
  18th Va Infantry musician, 77
Slaughter, Charles
  at High Bridge (servant, 59
Smith
  Servant to General Henry Wise, 50
Smith, Beverley
  Cabell Teamster List, *97*
Smith, Billy (cook)
  7th Va Cavalry, Co. H, 161
Smith, Charles
  32nd Virginia Infantry, 10
  Cabell Teamster List. *See* Longstreet's Brigade
Smith, G.W., 7
  32nd Virginia Infantry, 10
Smith, G.W. (slave), 117
Smith, John
  Craney Island List, *82*
Smith, Noah (cook)
  7th Va Cav, Co. H, 161
Smith, Peter
  Captain, C.S. Navy, 153
Soldier, 122
Solomon
  Cabell Teamster List, *96*
Southampton County, 144
Spotsylvania County, 145
Stableman, 124
Staunton, 145
Stauntton, John (free man)
  at High Bridge, 58
Stephens, John
  Craney Island List, *83*
Stratford, Hampton
  6th South Carolina Infantry (at Sailor's Creek, Va), 53
Stuantton, J.T. (free man), *58*
Stuart, J.E.B. (General), *159*
Stuart, John
  Cabell Teamster List. *See* 4th North Carolina Infantry Regiment
Surrender, 123
Surry County, 145
Sussex County, 145
Swann, Jas [James]

Cabell Teamster List. *See* Jones' Brigade
Sweeny, Peter
    Cabell Teamster List, *98*
Sylvatus, 121
Tabb, William
    Servant, POW at Sailor's Creek, 55
Tait, William
    Cabell Teamster List. *See* 4th North Carolina Infantry Regiment
Tart, Abraham
    Craney Island List, *83*
Tart, George
    Craney Island List, *83*
Tart, Simon
    Craney Island List, *83*
Taylor, Alex
    Craney Island List, *83*
Taylor, Beverly
    Craney Island List, *83*
Taylor, Elie
    Cabell Teamster List. *See* Texas Battalion
Taylor, George
    Craney Island List, *83*
Taylor, Moses
    Craney Island List, *83*
Tazewell County, 145
Teamster, 121, 122, 123, 124, 125, 126, 127, 128, 129, 130, 139
    Cloverdale Furnace, 125
    Fincastle Barracks, 125
    Ordnance wagon, 30
    Supply Wagon, 165
Teamsters
    black experience as, 91
Terrell, George
    12th and later 23rd Va Cavalry, 161
Terry, C.P.
    Confederate Navy, 55
Texas
    32nd Virginia Infantry, 10
Thomas, Beverly
    Cabell Teamster List, *98*
Thomas, Morris
    Servant, Co. G, 12th Georgia Infantry, 53
Thomas, Plate
    Craney Island List, *83*
Thomas, W.H.
    at High Bridge, *58*
Thomas, William (free man)
    at High Bridge, *58*
Thomas, Wyat
    Cabell Teamster List, *98*
Thornhill, W. (free man)
    at High Bridge, *58*
Thornton
    Cabell Teamster list. *See* 18th Virginia Infantry (Withers)
Thornton, Dangerfield

Cabell Teamster List. *See* 1st and 2nd North Carolina Regiment
Thoroughgood, Peter
    Craney Island List, *83*
Turner, Perry
    Cabell Teamster List. *See* Longstreet's Brigade
Tyler, Jack
    Cabell Teamster List, *96*
United Daughters of the Confederacy (UDC)
    award Southern Cross of Honor to black veteran, 28
Ustace, George [poss mispelled Eustis]
    Craney Island List, *83*
Vessy, Tilman
    Cabell Teamster List, *98*
Vienna, Va, 159
Virginia's 1902 Constitution
    ex-Confederate exemptions, 29
Volunteer
    Evans, Marshall, 129
    Jerdon, Earl, 15
    Kelly, John, 125
    Slaughter, William H. "I asked to go", 130
    Wesley, Charles, 7
Waddell, George
    Co. A, 18th Georgia Inf Battalion, 54
Walker, Carter
    Cabell Teamster List. *See* Jones' Brigade
Walker, Fielding (photo)
    Robert E. Lee servant, 76
Wallace, George
    Servant, Co. G, 12th Ga Infantry, 52
Walter (servant)
    23rd Texas Cavalry, Co. K, 19
Ward, Charles
    Cabell Teamster List. *See* 5th North Carolina Infantry
Ward, Eli
    Cabell Teamster List. *See* Ewell's Brigade
Warren County, 145
Washington
    Cabell Teamster List. *See* 1st Mississippi Regiment
Washington County, 146
Washington, Booker T., 5, 27
Washington, Booker T. (note on social complexity of the period), 1
Washinton, Booker T., 4
Washinton, D.C., 146
Waters, Henry
    Cabell Teamster List. *See* 5th North Carolina Infantry
Watson, Robert
    Cabell Teamster List. *See* Jones' Brigade
Webster, Gustry
    Cabell teamster List, *98*
Wesley, Charles (servant), 7
    40th Va Infantry, Co. I, 162
West, Richard
    32nd Virginia Infantry, 10
Westmorland County, 146
Wilinson, Austin

Cabell Teamster List. *See* Ewell's Brigade
William
    Cabell Teamster List. *See* 7th Regiment South Carolina Volunteers
Williams, George
    Cabell Teamster List. *See* 13th North Carolina Infantry Regiment
Williams, George Washington, 4, 12
Williams, Henry
    Co. B, 18th Georgia Inf Battalion, 54
Williams, Henson (Confederae soldier)
    shot to death, 29
Williams, Joe Thomas, 145
Williams, Samuel W.
    Attorney General, 30
Wilson, Robert
    Craney Island List, *83*
Wilson, William
    Cabell Teamster List. *See* 24th Virginia Infantry Regiment
Wilson-Kautz Raid
    the black experience in, 39
Winchester, 146, *157*
Wise County, 146
Wise, Frank
    Craney Island List, *83*
Wise, Westly
    Craney Island List, *83*
Withers, John B.
    Mosby's Command, 37
Woodchopper, 123
Woodson, Carter G., 4
Wounded in Action
    Brooks, William, 122
    Henson, James, 143
    Jacob Ransell, servant to JEB Stuart, 18
    Lee, William Mack (Rev), 69
    McDonald, George, 18
    Abraham, 162
    Hannah, 62
    Ransell, Jacob, *159*
    Scott, Morris, 130
    Shropshire, Ben (5th Texas Cavalry), 18
Wouser, Aaron
    Cabell Teamster List, *98*
Woylus? [poss Willis]
    Cabell Teamster List. *See* Texas Battalion
Wright, Morris
    Mosby's Command, 38
Wythe County, 146
Wytheville
    salt works, 146
Yerby, Joseph (servant)
    9th Va Cavalry, 15
York County, 146
York, Alvin C., Sgt, 6
Yorktown, 131, 144

Made in the USA
Columbia, SC
07 September 2020